THE
ENDS
OF
THEORY

THE
ENDS
OF
THEORY

EDITED BY

Jerry Herron, Dorothy Huson,
Ross Pudaloff, AND Robert Strozier

WITH AN INTRODUCTION BY
Wallace Martin

Wayne State University Press   Detroit

Library of Congress Cataloging-in-Publication Data

The ends of theory / edited by Jerry Herron . . . [et al] ; with an introduction by
Wallace Martin.
    p.   cm.
Includes bibliographical references and index.
ISBN 0-8143-2520-3 (pbk. : alk. paper)
   1. Criticism.   I. Herron, Jerry, 1949-   .
PN81.E44   1996
801'.95—dc20   95-470

Designer: Elizabeth Pilon

to George Tysh
for his help in organizing
the Ends of Theory conference

Nous ne faisons que nous entregloser.
—Montaigne

Contents

Contributors

RONALD BOGUE is Professor and Head of Comparative Literature at the University of Georgia. His publications include *Deleuze and Guattari* (Routledge, 1989), *Mimesis in Contemporary Theory: An Interdisciplinary Approach. Vol. 2: Mimesis, Semiosis and Power* (editor) (John Benjamins, 1991), *The Play of the Self* (co-editor, with Mihai Spariosu) (SUNY, 1994) *and Violence and Meditation in Contemporary Culture* (co-editor, with Marcel Cornis-Pope) (SUNY, forthcoming).

PAUL BOVÉ teaches English at the University of Pittsburgh.

STEVEN COLE teaches English at Temple University.

CHRISTOPH COX studied philosophy, semiotics, and cultural theory at Brown University and the University of California, Santa Cruz. He currently teaches philosophy at Hamilton College and is writing a book on Nietzsche's epistemology and ontology.

ARTHUR C. DANTO is Johnsonian Professor Emeritus of Philosophy, and, since 1984, the art critic for *The Nation*. His books, until 1981, were primarily in analytical philosophy, but since then, beginning with *The Transfiguration of the Commonplace*, he has mainly written on the philosophy of art.

STEVEN GOLDSMITH is an Associate Professor of English at the University of California, Berkeley. He is the author of *Unbuilding Jerusalem: Apocalypse and Romantic Representation* (Cornell, 1993).

JERRY HERRON teaches English at Wayne State University, where he is also Director of American Studies. His most recent book is *After-Culture: Detroit and the Humiliation of History*. He is currently completing a book entitled *Homer Simpson's Eyes and the Culture of Late Nostalgia*.

DOROTHY HUSON is a faculty member at Wayne State University. She writes about the production and interpretation of ancient and early modern texts, especially texts read as religious or didactic. Her current work concerns the relation between visual and verbal elements in those texts.

JOSHUA KATES is an Assistant Professor at St. John's College in Santa Fe. His work on the early Derrida (Derrida on Husserl, Foucault, and others) has led him to a strong interpretation of the role of history in contemporary criticism. His current project concerns the notion of constitution as it relates to contemporary feminist theory.

DONALD KUNZE received his Ph.D. in geography from Penn State in 1983. He now teaches integrative arts and architecture at Penn State, where he is developing "electronic" courses in arts criticism and architecture theory. He has lectured and published on the relation of architecture to drawing, death, toys, food, narrative, and critical philosophy. He is the author of a book on Giambattista Vico. He is currently applying ideas about virtual space in art to the artifacts of travel and tourism.

CATHERINE GIMELLI MARTIN is an Associate Professor of English at Memphis State University. She is the author of articles on theory and on seventeenth-century literature. She has a book forthcoming on *Paradise Lost*.

WALLACE MARTIN teaches English at the University of Toledo. His latest book is *Recent Theories of Narrative*.

STEVE MCCAFFERY is a poet, theorist, and author of over twenty books, most recent of which are *Theory of Sediment*, 1991, and *Rational Geomancy* (with the late bp Nichol). An anthology, *Imagining Language*, co-edited with Jed Rasula, is forthcoming from MIT Press. McCaffery currently teaches in the English Department, Queen's University, Kingston, Canada.

BOB PERELMAN has published 10 books of poetry, most recently *Virtual Reality* (New York: Roof Press, 1993), *Captive Audience* (Great Barrington: The Figures Press, 1988), and *Face Value* (New York: Roof Press, 1988). He has written two books of criticism, *The Trouble with Genius: Reading Pound, Joyce, Stein, and Zukofsky* (Berkeley: University of California Press, 1994) and *The Marginalization of Po-*

etry: Language Writing and Literary History (Princeton: Princeton University Press, 1995). He is Assistant Professor of English at the University of Pennsylvania.

Ross J. Pudaloff teaches English at Wayne State University and has written on a variety of subjects (including religion, witchcraft, movies, sexuality, and textuality) in American literature and culture. He is currently finishing a book about captivity and imprisonment as preconditions for the emergence of the "American identity" in the early nineteenth century.

Robert Strozier teaches English at Wayne State University. His latest book is *Saussure and Derrida*.

Barrett Watten is the author of *Total Syntax*, essays on modern and contemporary poetics, as well as of essays in *Postmodern Culture*, *Poetics Today*, and *Cultural Studies*. He co-edits *Poetics Journal* with Lyn Hejinian and through 1994 was associate editor of *Representations*. Sun & Moon Press will publish his collected poems, *Frame: 1970–1990*, in 1995. He teaches modernism and cultural studies at Wayne State University.

Sharon Willis is Associate Professor of French and visual and cultural studies at the University of Rochester, where she also teaches film and women's studies. With Constance Penley, she co-edited *Male Trouble* (Minnesota, 1993). She is currently completing a book entitled *High Contrast: Race and Gender in Contemporary Film*.

Introduction

The one duty we owe to history is to rewrite it.
                                        —Wilde

The Ends of Theory

Wallace Martin

The conference on "The Ends of Theory" at Wayne State University in 1990 occurred at a time when, by many accounts, the epoch of theory was over. During the 1970s, theory's opponents had been literary historians, new critics, reactionaries, political activists, and distinguished journals of popular opinion such as the *New York Times Book Review* and the *New York Review*. In "Against Theory" (1983), Steven Knapp and Walter Benn Michaels initiated a new phase in the assault on pointless speculation about literature, arguing that "the whole enterprise of critical theory is misguided and should be abandoned." "There will come a time," wrote Stanley Fish in his contribution to the volume *Against Theory* (ed. Mitchell, 1985), "when the calling of still another conference on the function of theory in our time will elicit only a groan. That time may have come: theory's day is dying; the hour is late" (pp. 12, 128).

From 1985 to 1990, the prophesied decline of theory proceeded at an accelerating rate. There were collections exploring *The States of "Theory"* and *The Limits of Theory*, as well as books on *The End of Literary Theory* by Stein Haugom Olsen, *After Theory* by Thomas Docherty, and *In the Wake of Theory* by Paul Bové. But the story of theory's birth (1960s), maturity (1970s), and decline (1980s) has not forestalled speculation about *The Future of Literary Theory* and *Literary Theory's Future(s)* (both published in 1989). Perhaps Barbara Johnson is right in suggesting that the speculators have no sense of the market, that it's time "to stop investing in theory futures" (*Consequences of Theory*, p. viii). On the other hand, a few years ago it was considered the height of folly to hold on to czarist bonds. Like aliens in a video game, theories keep popping into view, no matter how often we shoot them down.

Lacking a disciplinary counterpart of the Chicago Board of Trade, critics cannot agree on the price, much less the value, of theoretical issues. Paul Bové is one of many who hold that theory, as we knew it before 1980, has been overshadowed by the social and political interests evident in such ascendant movements as cultural studies and the new historicism. Ralph Cohen, the editor of *The Future of Literary Theory*, sees this change as a metamorphosis rather than a displacement: the chrysalis of theory, in his view, has been reborn in a study of textual traditions rediscovered through our interest in race, gender, and ideology. Like Cohen, Martin Kreiswirth and Mark Cheetham, in their introduction to *Theory between the Disciplines*, hold that theory has begun to extend its imperium across the humanities and social sciences. In support of this conclusion, they cite J. Hillis Miller's assertion, in 1986, that theory has "triumphed" (p. 1). But the (nominally) same Miller, in his contribution to Cohen's collection, reflects gloomily on the "massive shift" away from theory in the old sense to an emphasis on the " 'extrinsic' relations of literature," including a "return to old-fashioned biographical, thematic, and literary historical methods" (p. 102).

About a shift in the topics most often discussed by critics there is little disagreement. Conflicting assessments concern the issue of whether theory has been fulfilled, forgotten, or compromised by this change. Joseph Natoli's penetrating introduction to *Literary Theory's Future(s)* envisages "a future for a literary theory transformed into a cultural critique without losing its identity as a *literary* critique" (p. 3), but he acknowledges that cultural criticism harbors suspicions and hostilities that forestall this accommodation. Although Bakhtin's dialogics and heterology afford us a benign view of such conflicts, Natoli recognizes that the mere proliferation of competing voices is no solution. He would associate cultural critique with "ontological interrogation" (p. 26). Yet it is precisely the lack of such interrogation that Bové sees as characteristic of regnant historicisms in cultural criticism (*In the Wake of Theory*). His assertion that our recent critical "progress" has been achieved through a forgetting of Heideggerian and poststructuralist analyses of historiography (pp. 20–24) echoes the conclusions of Carolyn Porter and Jean-Luc Nancy in *The States of "Theory"* (ed. David Carroll).

Genetic history, which theorists dismantled and pronounced defunct, has proven as resilient as its antagonists. Its rhetoric of growth and decay, health and disease, crisis, death, and birth, now announces the emergence of postmodernism. Fish's "there will come a time" is a prophecy with a pedigree (Virgil's *veniet aetas*, Seneca's *venient annis*, Milton's "time may come"). Yet theorists resorted to the same rhetoric when they announced the death of man and the end of the book in the late 1960s. "The (End of the) End of History," as Christoph Cox reminds us in one of the following essays, is the oldest of annunciations, one that we have inherited from

Hegel and he inherited from Christianity. Peter Collier and Helga Geyer-Ryan, the editors of *Literary Theory Today*, note in their introduction, subtitled "Beyond Postmodernism," that the contributors "all acknowledge the crisis in literary and cultural theory" (p. 2). Does it differ from the one that Paul de Man identified in "The Crisis of Contemporary Criticism" (1967) and the one that Harry Levin discussed in "Criticism in Crisis" (1954), or are all three simply variants of "Philosophy and the Crisis of European Humanity and Philosophy" that Husserl described in 1935?

In pathology, a crisis results from a disease. In criticism, it is a sign of health, both words growing from the same root: *kri(nein)*, to separate, sift, judge; to dispute or fight; to examine, accuse, arraign. "The calling of still another conference" at Wayne State elicited not "a groan" but an interesting collection of participants and papers, as the following pages attest. Despite occasional disputes, few declared themselves for or against theory. Working with examples from the verbal and visual arts, as well as with ideas that are the tools of the critical trade, they showed that theory itself may be a form of practice. If that conjecture is plausible, it would explain why, after theory has ended, we find it all around us.

2

Before describing the practices that I find exemplified in these essays, it may be useful to sort out the varied meanings attached to *theory* in recent debates. To associate it with the beginning or end of an epoch (modernism; the Enlightenment; philosophy since Plato) may prove too grandiose, just as attempts to depict it as an aberration of the past few years are unwarranted.

For those with practical and political interests, theory is any abstraction from experience or action. So conceived, it is a useless if not pernicious distraction from the pleasures of art and the urgencies of social change. When Lennard Davis and M. Bella Mirabella sought comments on their introduction to *Left Politics and the Literary Profession*, they found themselves being "attacked on both sides —for being anti-intellectual, by our colleagues who did theory, and as justifying 'Lacan-speak,' by our comrades who centered their work on activism and radical pedagogy" (p. 7). Such dissentions don't occur on the political right, where literary theory is universally anathematized. Rising above politics, the most influential literary journals have joined forces with novelists and men and women of letters to defend the lay reader from foreign jargon. The threat is so serious as to justify recourse to patriotism. In America, the source of the plague is said to be Europe; John Gross says it came from Americans and Continentals, who "confer authority on their British disciples" ("The Men of Letters," p. 15). (In an essay that appears in *Theory between the Disciples*, Bill Readings explores the question "Why Is Theory Foreign?") Plato describes this popular and perdurable opposition of theory and practice in the *Theaetetus* (173c), and Goethe enshrined it in *Faust*: "Gray, dear friend, is all theory; / And green the golden bough of life."

Less polemically, a theory is a group of rules "abstracted from a multitude of conditions. . . . To the intellectual concept that contains the rule, an act of judgment must be added whereby the practitioner distinguishes whether or not something is an instance of the rule." That is how Kant defines it in "On the Old Saw: That May Be Right in Theory but It Won't Work in Practice." The definition, of course, antedates Kant and survives today: theories (hypothetical, unlike laws) organize and produce knowledge, providing a way to move from rough groupings of experience and rules of thumb to refutable conjectures about systematic relationships. So conceived, they have never played much part in literary study. In the first half of the century, practical criticism was opposed not to theory but to "principles of criticism," and some (Gerald Graff, for one) still use the word *theory* to mean the conditions of possibility, necessary presuppositions, or general questions implied by critical discourse. For dissemination of the term in Anglo-American criticism, we are largely indebted to René Wellek and *Theory of Literature* (1942), a work in which *theory* is defined as "the principles of literature"— everything that philology, historical scholarship, and value judgments are not.

Conceived as a way of producing reliable knowledge, theory belongs to science, not art, and that is why its importation into the humanities is especially dangerous. In this century, humanists troubled by the encroachments of scientific methods into the social sphere launched a counterattack, indicting theory as such. Gadamer's *Truth and Method* is one instance: "Modern theory is a tool of construction, by means of which we gather experiences together" (what could be wrong with that?) "in a unified way" (look out!) "and make it possible to dominate them." Theory, then, is a means of dominating not just nature, as Bacon said, but minorities, social classes, whole societies. Even when the disinterested scientist has "no particular practical purposes" in mind, Gadamer says, "theoretical knowledge is itself conceived in terms of the will to dominate what exists" and hence is hegemonic apart from anyone's intentions (p. 412).

This thesis, convincingly presented in Horkheimer and Adorno's *Dialectic of Enlightenment* and in Foucault's works, is not a plank in one or another party platform; it is the voice of humanity itself, struggling to escape conditions imposed not just by its enemies but by bureaucracies with the best of intentions. Theory turns things into "objects" and substitutes, for the persons and relations it touches, falsifying concepts. Looking on theory as an impartial tool, the theorist escapes from awareness of the contingencies that self and circumstance introduce into understanding. Thus, theory not only facilitates domination, but it blinds its users, enabling them to avoid knowing what they are doing.

In Foucault and in Horkheimer and Adorno, however, *theory* is not a code word for these developments (the latter two say that they are presenting a "theory" of history). The real danger is Enlightenment thought, or social rationalization, political technologies of the body, state apparatuses, or modernity itself. Nevertheless, the tendency to discover a single souce of everything deplorable since the *Odyssey* is almost irresistible, and the quest ends up as a warlock-hunt in which theory is redefined to be indictable as the culprit.

For Kant, as for science, the application of rules to cases entails an act of judgment. For Gadamer, this act—the intervention of the human—is a manifestation of the will to power or the desire to dominate. For other demonizers of theory, the danger is precisely the opposite: theory is an application of rules that eliminates the human element. According to Fish, "the model for the 'true' rule and, therefore, for theory is mathematics," which is "formal, abstract, general, and invariant," always yielding the same result, regardless of the interests of its users (*Against Theory*, p. 108). Rorty conceives it differently: "in its unobjectionable sense, 'theory' just means 'philosophy'" (*Against Theory*, p. 136). No, counters Derrida, what is called *theory* in literature departments is not mathematics, not philosophy, and certainly not what goes by that name in science ("Some Statements," pp. 80–82).

This array of conflicting definitions helps explain why theory survives its antagonists: like Proteus, it takes many forms, changing its meaning as soon as someone claims to have pinned it down. What is shown, in arguing that understanding emerges from contingency, interest, and purpose, rather than being based on timeless abstractions, is that every use of *theory* is likewise contingent. To think otherwise—to represent it as an implacable Turing machine, a tool of sinister technologists or of mindless bureaucrats—is to imagine that theory itself has a timeless essence. To argue that it is invariably harmful (or helpful) is quite clearly to have a theory about it, based on one's situation and purpose. Because of its contingency, we can understand critical theory only by looking at its history, which reveals why it could appear to be useful to critics in the 1960s and 1970s but less relevant to today's concerns. History is no less protean than theory.

After the scholarly and critical squabbles of the 1950s, literary study in the United States entered the 1960s with an ecumenical tolerance of different "approaches" to literature, sanctioned by pluralism and the house of many mansions erected by Northrop Frye. Theories provided different ways to do things to texts. In France and Germany, where higher education was financed and politically controlled by the government, within systems of certification and employment that entrenched uniform curricula and methods of study, different "approaches" to literature were the province of journalism. As many have observed, American tolerance of diverse perspectives in literary study brings with it the implicit assumption that such differences don't really matter much. On the Continent, the stakes were higher. Theory, often dismissed as irrelevant to political change and humanistic understanding, in some contexts can have not just political but revolutionary implications.

The fortunes of two theoretical developments in the 1960s—the structuralism of Barthes and the reception theory of Jauss—show that more than an ocean separates American and Continental literary study. Barthes, who lacked the *agrégation* necessary for normal academic appointment, eventually (in 1960) obtained a position in the outsider's university, the Ecole pratique des Hautes Etudes, the degrees of which were not officially recognized in the French educational system until 1974 (Thody, pp. 54–55). If his references to *"la critique universitaire"* angered the professors at the Sorbonne, especially because he implied that their professed objectivity was just another ideology, his own styles of structural analysis could hardly endear him to traditional Marxists. Neither the left nor the right needed quasi-scientific juxtapositions of linguistics and semiotics, or of popular culture and high literature, to forward its cause. Those intent on changing the world have little interest in changing their minds.

When, in the wake of May 1968, the National Assembly passed the Loi d'orientation de l'enseignement superiéur that November, its three main tenets—multidisciplinary study, autonomy for the universities, and participation of students in governance—were endorsed by all parties (Halls, pp. 208–14; Archer, pp. 166–69). The departments of General Literature at Vincennes and of the Science of Texts at Paris VII were among the consequences of that law. Cynics looking back on those events say that nothing changed. But pessimistic conservatives are more perceptive in arguing that something had changed: the very terms and conditions of the debate.

Although he taught at one of the new German universities, Jauss, unlike Barthes, was an academic insider—a professor *ordinarius*, at the top of the academic hierarchy. In comparison with the dazzling variety of Barthes's critical interventions, Jauss's reception theory has seemed tame to most American readers. Yet the shift of orientation that he and his Constance colleagues effected—from a literary history based on the masterpieces of a national tradition to a generative conception of literary production and reception—had unsettling implications for German literary study. As Wlad Godzich points out, "Jauss's ideas presented superficial analogies with the calls for educational and social transformation emanating from far more radical quarters. Or rather, Jauss was perceived by conservatives within the university and without, as not only legitimizing the oppositional forces of the S.D.S. and the A.P.O. . . . but as serving as their Trojan horse. . . . But the excoriation from the Right differed in no manner of degree from the denunciations of the Left, which readily recognized that Jauss's project was reformist and not revolutionary" (p. xiii). If the projects of Barthes and Jauss provide today's engaged critics with examples of the deficiencies of *theory*, they also show that theorists led the way in examining the social, political, and educational foundations of the "timeless truths" that theorists are accused of supporting.

There was good reason for both left and right to be suspicious of theory in the 1960s. As Paul de Man said, "it upsets rooted ideologies by revealing the mechanics of their workings; it goes against a powerful philosophical tradition of which aesthetics is a prominent part; it upsets the established canon of literary works and blurs the borderline between literary and nonliterary discourse" (*The Resistance to Theory*, p.11). But theory has these effects only when it is timely. A change in intellectual or political circumstance can turn today's intervention into an irrelevance or even a conservative force tomorrow. We have been witnessing this process at least since the Enlightenment. In challenging established powers (ecclesiastical, aristocratic, commercial, or even educational), those who are not sanctioned by custom, or backed by constituencies, appeal to reason. Late generations will condemn them because of their belief in universals, their philosophical idealism, their dissociation of science, morality, and art, or their faith in the power of theory to demystify practice. The universalism that yesterday helped create equality can today be an instrument of subjugation. On a smaller scale, the same is true of literary theory.

"The advent of theory," according to de Man, "the break that is now so often being deplored and that sets it aside from literary history and literary criticism, occurs with the introduction of linguistic terminology in the metalanguage about literature. By linguistic terminology is meant a terminology . . . that considers reference as a function of language and not necessarily an intuition" (p. 8). Thus viewed, theory in our time begins in French structuralism. Allying itself with the prestige of modern linguistics, structuralism envisaged a semiotic discipline of literary study that would dispel the spiritualizing fog of aesthetics and at the same time rescue literature from the positivistic reductionisms of psychology, sociology, politics, and history. In an attempt to reverse the trend of the preceding hundred years, literary study laid claim to a central place within the scientific enterprise of knowledge production. Having served its purpose in the 1960s (in France) and in the early 1970s (in the United States), structuralism yielded to other currents, Barthes and Genette being among those who recognized its inadequacies.

Because of its allegiances with philosophy and theory in the scientific sense, structuralism can serve as the paradigm of everything we are now against. But being against theory can mean many things. As in the case of the elections in Nicaragua, the fact that the majority was against the Sandinistas did not mean that they had anything else in common. For convenience, subjugating theory to my practical purposes, I distinguish three groups of anti-theorists. The first has been with us since the Enlightenment. To whatever it is they opposed—empiricism, positivism, system, rationalism, formalism, technology, universal grammar, experimental method, logical calculus—some anti-theorists offer an alternative: tradition, practice, life-world, community, history, belief, contextual specificity, lived experience, hermeneutics, errancy, or empathy. When opponents of theory resort to such terms, we can see in their work a repetition of earlier attempts to forestall the encroachments of science and technology—those of Dilthey, Windelband, Rickert, and Bergson, among others. Second in my arbitrary order and grouping are those who work within the analytic and pragmatic traditions of Anglo-American philosophy. Accepting the criteria of explanation proposed by their predecessors, philosophers in this tradition have shown that they simply don't work. Finally, there are those philosophers and critics who set themselves a higher goal. They try to pinpoint the generative sources of error, domination, and violence embedded in traditional theory, science, and philosophy, and/or to provide a liberating alternative. In this last group are Derrida, de Man, Foucault, Lyotard, and Deleuze.

For those concerned with intellectual history, the preceding classification is too crude to be useful. For polemicists, it may be too detailed. If you regard Wittgenstein, Heidegger, Kuhn, Quine, and Derrida from Richard Rorty's point of view, as they are situated on the landscape of Western thought just after sunset, they all look very much like John Dewey. (And Rorty himself can appear to provide a learned justification of two slogans recently popularized on television: "Why ask why?" and "Just do it!") In any case, Rorty's attempt to show what the varied strains of current thought have in common helps us recognize something that has been obscured by polemics: most of those who bear the stigma of being theorists are themselves against *theory*. They differ primarily in their conceptions of the range of activities included in that domain and the strategies they use to dismantle such theoretical activities as seem to them threatening.

3

Most of the essays in this collection were originally presented at the Wayne State conference on "The Ends of Theory"; a few others have been taken from the journal *Criticism*. The first group treats the theoretical impetus that descended from deconstruction to cultural criticism, and the second group concerns the imbrications of theory and practice one finds in such writers as Deleuze and the second generation of American theorists. Finally, there is a group of essays that might be called post-theoretical, or post-generic, or simply contemporary. If James Gleick's book *Chaos* is the scientific counterpart of postmodernism in literary theory (as some have suggested), the post-theoretical essays that conclude this collection might best be compared to the *Complexity* discussed in two recent books on the philosophy of science (by M. Mitchell Waldrop and Roger Lewin). This section includes essays on the visual arts and shows that indigenous trends deserve recognition alongside the prestigious theorizing that we borrow from the Continent. Theory (as Auden said of Yeats) is now "scattered among a hundred cities / And wholly given over to unfamiliar affections." Our distribution of the essays highlights some continuities at the expense of others; needless to say, we assume that readers will create their own itineraries of reading, despite the following attempt to persuade them that our serial ordering is the best one.

The first group of essays explores the old-fashioned ways of being anti-theoretical and the dilemmas that they generate. As Steven Cole and Paul Bové show in their discussions of Paul de Man, his writings in the 1960s, which today are often read as examples of theory, can also be understood as "historical, tactical, and purposive" responses to the disciplinary and institutional circumstances of that decade (Bové). It was a time when critical authority —the professors at the most prestigious universities, their students, and critical journals—associated the autonomous value of literature with its capacity to unify experience and consciousness in form, or the symbol. To oppose that view by insisting on the social and political relevance of literature—and there were some who did so— was simply not to participate in the discourse of academic criticism. De Man knew that discourse inside out and was sympathetic to its aims, as Cole shows. That is why, by mobilizing his knowledge of literary history and pushing the logic of that discourse beyond its limits, he was able to pry it apart from the inside.

In arguing that language could never secure a reconciliation of consciousness and experience (the anti-theoretical thrust of his early essays), de Man tacitly endorsed the view that consciousness gained this negative knowledge and could express it through the figurations of literary language. Cole shows that de Man's later writings, which are sometimes understood as marking a turn in his thought, are in fact a fulfillment of its inexorable logic. If language cannot adequately represent experience, how can it possibly represent, or be merged with, consciousness? Once we recognize that the unity of the self is a figure of language, rather than a fact of consciousness, we can no longer even claim negative knowledge of our circumstance. Language—seen as a combination of a mechanical grammar or logic, and uncontrollable tropology of reference, and a performative act of arbitrarily positing or gently persuading—provides de Man with a "universal theory of the impossibility of theory."

The reception of critical theories is no less contingent than their production. Bové reconstructs the situation in which "The Rhetoric of Temporality" (1969) was a challenge to the professors and their discourses. De Man's appeal at the time depended in part on this cast of his thought. Cole and Bové both discuss the reception and propagation of de Man's views by his students and admirers who subtly extend his insights while protecting his reputation and perforce repeating his critical moves. Set loose in critical history, de Man's thought has still other consequences, as it confronts challenges he could not anticipate. Subversiveness may be a useful tactic when one is trying to undermine disciplinary bulwarks, but, as Cole says, it is not in itself a sufficient end for criticism. Once the bulwarks have fallen, an uncontrollable negative critique can destroy all efforts to create a credible basis of community. For that task, Cole and Bové conclude, we need other kinds of thought and practice.

From de Man and Derrida, we learn how language functions to disarticulate any fixed relation between theory or language and reality. Foucault and Said, on the other hand, make it evident that despite the aporias of literary and philosophical language, disciplinary discourses mobilized by regimes and races function quite well, despite any disparities between the theories used and the situations to which they are applied. Nowhere is this process more clearly described than in Said's *Orientalism*, in which, as Catherine Gimelli Martin says, we see how the oppositions of Occident to Orient and of self to other "establish a dominant discourse for describing, teaching, and ruling the Orient, in fact *producing* the Orient politically, socially, and imaginatively."

Appearing nearly a decade after de Man's "Rhetoric of Temporality," at a time when deconstruction was well on its way to becoming a new orthodoxy, *Orientalism* (1978) pointed the way to a more productive relation between theory and practice. Yet, as Martin argues in "Orientalism and the Ethnographer," that book and Said's more recent writings are not without problems of their own. In assuming, with Foucault, an inescapable complicity of knowledge with power, and in showing how they chart the world through binary oppositions (Occident/Orient, self/other, civilized/barbaric), Said not only proves his point—one confirmed by the media every day—but leaves us trapped in an ideological structure from which understanding offers no hope of escape. The imperialistic Occident proves to be the mirror image of the Orient: totalized, stereotyped, its humanists blindly producing false knowledge that abets exploitation and subjugation.

Rather than rejecting Said's negative critique, Martin uses it to develop a more complex model of the relation between self and other. We must construe an enigmatic otherness in *some* terms, and the only ones available for mapping it are inversions of those that apply to the self. Elaboration of these differences constructs the self as well as the other. Recognizing that this process is ideological and hegemonic, we can distinguish it from the subjugation exercised in its name. The epistemic "violence of the relation to the other" is, as Derrida says, "at the same time nonviolence, since it opens the relation to the other." Drawing on François Hartog and Bourdieu, Martin argues that the system of distortions produced by cultural interactions can be recognized—that knowledge and power are in principle distinguishable—and that translation, rather than the effacement of difference, is the only viable model for the "severance and stitching together of cultures." Her conclusions (apart from the details of her analysis) are supported by Sara Suleri's *The Rhetoric of English India* (1992).

Difference, having been indicted as the source of domination and violence in the 1970s, became in the 1980s the basis of critical agendas that would either celebrate an egalitarian acceptance of variety (postmodernism) or empower those whom difference subjugates (feminism, Marxism, ethnic studies, cultural criticism). Because theory (as anti-theory) had discredited all varieties of essentialism, history and current social formations could be seen with new eyes. Nature, the self, transcendentals, and interiority having disappeared, society and culture revealed themselves as the producers of "personal identity." "In the Name of Theory," by Sharon Willis, points out that this shift of perspective, one in which gender is seen as a social construction, remains troubled by an interiority—a psychoanalytic identification of being and biological sex —that it can avoid only through repression.

Willis trenchantly surveys the dilemmas that issue from this state of affairs. Feminism challenges the ways in which men and the ideologies that they sustain lead to the subjugation of women. But in doing so, it seems to make sex/gender a pivotal difference, others being added on in a "familiar litany of political correctness" (race, class, ethnicity, sexual preference). Thus, feminism inadvertently plays into the hands of a dominant ideology that would make biological sex essential, isolate it from other areas of subjugation, and contain them all within "competitive arenas," economically and institutionally, so that they will perceive themselves as competing with one another for limited resources. If, on the other hand, all such differences are seen as equal, analogous to one another, in a "totalizing theory of difference," there is no possibility of understanding how these registers interact, and (dare one say it?) no basis for attributing "to white heterosexual males alone the 'bad representations' that we deconstruct." Willis suggests that rather than repressing phantasmic identifications by confining them to an imaginary "inside" limited to sex, we should explore the ways in which race, for example, shapes psychic development, in networks of overdetermination that are not based on binary oppositions and inside/outside dichotomies. Her line of thought meshes with Catherine Gimelli Martin's, and both point to the continuing relevance of Lacanian thought. Walter Benn Michaels's radical critique of cultural pluralism in "Race into Culture" is not incompatible with the projects Martin and Willis propose.

My reading of these essays is shaped by my view that the shift in criticism from theory (1970s) to practice (1980s) was less a product of theorizing than a reaction against it, a turn to practice after speculation led to inconsequence—an unmediated reversal, rather than a displaced succession. One thing that returned, after deconstruction and poststructuralism, was the Hegelian historicism that these movements opposed. Christoph Cox describes its return on the political right, via Alla Bloom and Fukuyama, in his essay "The (End of the) End of History." My own essay treats the more nuanced persistence of Hegelian strains in leftist thought. Although none of the essays in the first part of this collection provides solutions for the problems it identifies, the essays do show that our understanding of theory cannot be separated from the history and practices in which it is embedded.

4

Clear-cut oppositions of theory to practice and of humanistic historicism to varieties of deconstruction are signs that we have not yet assimilated the philosophical registers that cannot be encompassed in such categories. The critique of essentialism was able to account for everything except its own strategies of explanation. On the one hand, it was a Promethean effort to bring the transcendentals, ideas, and concepts of the gods back to mankind, showing that they are nothing but words; on the other hand, it showed that interiority, subjectivity, and experience were likewise verbal artifacts rather than real presences. In defeating idealism, anti-essentialists ran the risk of sacrificing reference and reality as well (a path followed by some postmodernists), or, alternatively, of abandoning theory altogether in the name of practice. Escape from these alternatives requires a more nuanced reading of the poststructuralist heritage.

Foucault, Deleuze, and Lyotard certainly participated in the semiotic, hermeneutic, and phenomenological revolutions that characterize what we loosely call poststructuralism. But our tardy reception of Lyotard and Deleuze, as well as continuing controversies about Fucault, are signs that their thought has important affiliations elsewhere—specifically (I would hazard) in European conceptions of science, in aspects of Nietzsche not important for deconstruction, in Bergson and nonphenomenological philosophic traditions. These writers harbor fusions of energy and expression that escape both referentiality and its vocabularies.

In "Gilles Deleuze: Postmodern Philosopher?" Ronald Bogue calls attention to Deleuze's affinities with Foucault and shows how both evade the categories we would use to characterize them. To simplify their views: societies consist of representations (Foucault's statements, Deleuze's consciousness and ideology) and the motor forces of the "unthought" (Foucault's power, Deleuze's desire and production). The relation between the two is not one of interiority to external manifestation or of energy to matter. There is no hidden truth to be discovered through ideological or psychoanalytic interpretation. As Bogue says, power and desire are "immanent within heterogeneous assemblages of bodies, institutions, discourses, and objects," operating not through classical laws of cause and effect but as *"dispositifs"* (gadgets, apparatuses) or *"agencements machiniques."* An analogy to this view can be found in connectionist models of language acquisition, in which it is multiple paths frayed through a network, rather than hierarchic applications of rules, that produce well-formed sentences.

Why do theorists so obsessively seek "codes" in the social text? One stimulus of their activity is the endless flood of new practices generated by an ever-changing society. But capitalism is not a coding system that sustains conventions and creates apparatuses to nip opposition in the bud. It "undermines traditional social codes . . . and releases uncoded fluxes of heterogeneous matter, ideas, affects and fantasies, but unlike schizophrenia, it constantly recodes fluxes and flows within new forms of social organization" (Bogue). Theorists try to organize the flotsam tossed up by capitalism in order to create communities of resistance, but their reactive procedures are always too late, and their recodings provide marginal stablity for a mobile system that is always one jump ahead of them. Rather than trying to slow down this runaway machine, one might try to spot its nodes of disintegration and the ideological workshops where repairs are made, and then accelerate its dispersive momentum. For Deleuze, "the function of art in our age is to exacerbate the play of cultural simulacra and extract from them the generative force of difference."

Those who have not read Deleuze may already be acquainted with many of his key terms. Jameson's renowned "Postmodernism, or the Cultural Logic of Late Capitalism," as Bogue says, "reads like a checklist of Deleuzian themes and practices." Does this imply that Deleuze himself is a postmodernist? By discussing three Deleuzian themes that have been appropriated by postmodernism—simulation, intensities, and schizophrenia—Bogue shows why this conclusion is probably inaccurate. Use of the term to designate an epochal change, marked by the emergence of a new art and a new sensibility, repeats a gesture that has been recycled endlessly by our successive modernisms, from the Neander ("new man") of Dryden's modernity to Virginia Woolf's assertion that "human nature changed" in 1910 (W. Martin). There is a danger, evident in the twenty-odd books on postmodernism published last year, of sliding back into the historicism and binarism that Deleuze and others try to avoid.

Postmodernism is the subject of seveal essays in the last part
of the collection, which concludes with essays that explore alternative ways of construing reading and representation. My account of
the critical shift from theory to practice during the past two decades
has emphasized major figures, catchwords, and notorious controversies—such are the simplifications from which we make history.
Most critical activity, and probably the most important part of it,
goes on outside the critical limelight, in the reading and writing
about texts where theory and practice mix. Essays exemplifying this
trend appear in the second part of this collection.

In Joshua Kates's "Tossings and Turnings," we see how one
critic brings disparate trends of recent criticism into productive interaction. An interest in literary language need not be set in opposition to something called reference. As Kates says, the linguistic turn
of poststructuralism was from its beginnings marked by thematic
concerns. The themes were teased out of the text itself through
analysis of "the workings of language," apart from referential entail-
ments. In Naomi Schor's early work, Kates finds that she pushes
immanent analysis beyond the confines of particular texts to recover
a linguistic history in which the concepts of aesthetic detail, gender,
and modernity are linked together. Such connections lend themselves to immediate referential application, confirming what we already know or suspect about a patriarchal culture.

But Schor is too scrupulous a historian, and too sensitive an
analyst of language, to avail herself of that easy conclusion. Language and practice don't always operate in tandem. A pervasive assumption may not appear in theoretical texts, and, contrariwise,
what such texts proclaim may contradict the practices that they purportedly describe. Faced with such disparities between practice and
representation, how can we comprehend either the past or the present? Only by *producing* them. Here reading is itself the mode of
production, a working through of the materials present to attention,
engendering a language that fits the facts thus made salient. In such
a project, the reconstituted present is not just a site where we happen to be sitting. At the end of his essay, Kates suggests that we can
see, in Schor's work and the new historicism, the emergence of "a
plurality of presents" that "render history irreducibly multiple, actively discontinuous."

In one sense, this conclusion brings us full circle, back to the
beginnings of the turn to theory. "Historical facts," Lévi-Strauss
wrote in 1962, "are no more *given* than any other. It is the historian,
or the agent of history, who constitutes them. . . . History is never
history, but history-for. It is partial in the sense of being biased even
when it claims not to be" (*The Savage Mind*, pp. 257–58). What has

changed, in the past three decades, is the way we construe this state of affairs. For Lévi-Strauss, it meant that because history was always an untrue representation, it should be discarded—in the name of truth. For the old left and the old and new right, on the other hand, there is (or we must believe there is) a true, totalizing story, one in which the real past is transparently represented. Fights about the contents of school textbooks are possible only on the assumption that there could be a single book that told the true story. Society may fall apart, we are told, if we don't get the story right. Some of those incredulous of metanarratives think that the only alternative is to give up storytelling. The residual animus against representation that we find in Foucault, Deleuze, and even Rorty stems from the age-old linkage of representation with truth and untruth; perhaps all three must go.

In "The Textual Logic of Democracy," Steven Goldsmith argues that the conflicting interpretations, histories, and representations sanctioned by poststructuralism, far from being an unprecedented threat to the social fabric, are simply a renewed expression of ideas that have been with us since the American and French revolutions. Unmediated truth is unavailable to us, save through revelation or apocalypse. To insist that the basis of authority and power be codified, and that surrogates be allowed to speak for groups within the populace, is to insist on linguistic and political representation as the ground of government. Goldsmith's association of aesthetic, epistemological, and political representation is not mere wordplay; the historical connections between these varied meanings of the word have long been recognized, as older editions of the *Encyclopaedia Britannica* attest. By insisting that claims to authority be put in a text, and that all be permitted to textualize their political claims, one makes power visible, deprives it of its ontological sanction, and pluralizes representation, leaving no hope of totalizing recuperation. "The collapsing of power into language marked the invention of modern politics."

Is it possible that, as Goldsmith claims, there is a symbiotic relationship "between contemporary critical theory and democratic politics"? I found this claim illuminating in 1990, when I heard Goldsmith's paper, because of the startling statements that renowned theorists were making as communism collapsed. Endorsements of democracy and market economy from the left (notably from Habermas) were then as unexpected as the imperturbability of my friends who didn't think that this momentous change had anything to do with their projects in cultural criticism. For a fuller understanding of Goldsmith's argument, one can turn to his recently published *Unbuilding Jerusalem: Apocalypse and Romantic Represen-*

tation (Cornell, 1993). If we are now situated in a post-theoretical, postmodernist moment, one in which partialities of representation provide the only basis we have for understanding and action, then theory will have not disappeared but rather changed its form once again: merged with practice, it will be embedded in representations (partial, fallible, contested, occluded).

5

One of the unheralded American precursors of our current outlook is Arthur C. Danto, whose *Analytical Philosophy of History* and *Nietzsche as Philosopher* (both published in 1965) touched on lines of thought that were then emerging in French philosophy. In "The Art World Revisited," which opens the final part of this collection, Danto recalls the circumstances that in 1964 led him to answer the question "What is art?" in a way that has proven influential. While literary criticism was warming up for the battle between essentialists and social constructionists, philosophers and art critics were, in their own sphere, settling it. Despite the importance of their philosophic differences, most agreed that the aesthetic was a socially constructed category. As Danto indicates, artists themselves have led the way, for more than a century, in putting pressure on the conventions that distinguish art from non-art. In doing so, they force us not just to "take a position on the past" but also to construct a history and marshal reasons for construing something as art and interpreting it as we do. Here, what Kates and Goldsmith suggest concerning the production of history and the plurality of representation reach their apex. Danto implies that meaning is a necessary condition for calling anything a work of art. What then of nonobjective art? From what Danto says, I infer that such works are "about" the history and the theory that we are forced to produce in order to construe them as part of the story of art.

While providing a brilliant example of how this process works, Barrett Watten's "Nonnarrative and the Construction of History" shows that our stories of art are impoverished if they are not embedded in social contexts, and in addition that historical narratives may now occlude both past and present. Critical theory long ago recognized the ways in which aesthetic innovations lend themselves to commodification. The realization that narrative is an ideological as well as an aesthetic tool is of more recent origin.

To clear a breathing space amid the ideological saturation of the narratives constructed daily by the media, Watten proposes a jumbling or displacement of registers that intercalate events; a manipulation of codes that frees memorials from the forgetting they induce; a history of the present that reinscribes random signs from the past. His description of how the visual image, in its passage from the sensible to the intelligible, reveals a meaning while hiding an event bears comparison with Derrida's treatment of this process in "The *Retrait* of Metaphor." But Watten goes further in suggesting the possibility, in art, of a reversed passage from a sign to its "nonexistent endpoint at the center of . . . awareness," one that escapes the ironic mode that is, for Hayden White, the only alternative to totalizing historicism.

In "Rubble and Narrative: The New Sentence," Bob Perelman notes that narrative fragmentation and parataxis already have been reappropriated for commercial use. As participants in the "new sentence" movement, to which they add their own inflections, Watten and Perelman know that no technique is in itself, apart from the materials that inform it, hegemonic or contestatory. Their work, like most significant "creative writing" since Wordsworth, is already a product of strategic and tactical reflection. Explanations of the new sentence sometimes bear an uncanny resemblance to Lyotard's contemporaneous discussions of the sentence and the phrase in *Just Gaming* (1979) and *The Differend* (1983). As a result, there has been a tendency to assimilate the new sentence to Lyotard's postmodernism. Swept away by that movement's fragmentation, pastiche, schizophrenia, and surface intensities, readers can overlook too easily the insights and wry humor available to those who seek something more than zany heterogeneity in texts.

By attending to what writers say about their texts, we may learn something and help release them from their subjugation to theorists that, as Steve McCaffery says, began with Socrates's assertion that poets don't really know what they're doing. He finds in Michel de Certeau a useful distinction between strategic and tactical reading: the latter, forsaking the theoretical impulse to produce a totality, is an "improvisation upon constraints, the insinuation of errant itineraries" resulting from the varied conjunctions of text and reader.The result may well be a rewriting, as in the examples he discusses, which preserve the materiality of the text's signs while reconstituting their meaning (bricolage, found poems, and "translitics" also fall within this category). The products of McCaffery's "nondiscursive practice of reading" range from "passive voyeurism" to "unfettered, idiosyncratic usage."

Do such practices achieve a level of emancipation that could not be envisaged through theory? Not quite. Beyond voyeurism and idiosyncrasy lies idiocy—"The Idiot as Artist / The Idiot as Critic," in the subtitle of Donald Kunze's essay in Part III. Idiosyncrasy, as idiocy, separates each subject from communal understanding, and the price exacted for voyeurism is the fate of Acteon, torn to pieces by the hounds of desire (cf. Klossowsk's *Le Bain de Diane*; on Lacan's use of the myth, see Borch-Jakobsen). Kunze's paper juxtaposes "anecedotal evidence" and "neuropsychology, semiology, and philosophy." "In keeping with the theme of idiocy, I have not made any attempt to connect these two kinds of evidence," he says, "in hopes that the poetic dimension of the problem will prevail." Here, *theory* takes on the meaning that Derrida concludes it has in our academic settings: "the opening of space, the emergence of an element in which a certain number of phenomena usually associated with literature will call for trans-, inter-, and above all ultra-disciplinary approaches, which, up to now, met nowhere, in no department, in no area of any discipline." Thus construed, theory is "a form of questioning and of writing . . . which destabilized . . . even the new categories in the history of ideas (such as episteme or paradigm) that allowed one to think this new configuration in the mode of self-consciousness" (pp. 82-83).

In his reference to Foucault's epistemes and Kuhn's paradigms, Derrida reminds us of how such preeminently *theoretical* concepts undermined *theory* in the old sense, and of how, since their appearance in the 1960s, these concepts have themselves generated further displacements. In every case, the changes emerged from specific institutional and political circumstances, some of which I discussed above. But among the factors that provide a potential for change, at each juncture, we must number the disciplinary formations which, though they usually remain insulated within their own spheres, may at any time be grafted onto another disciplinary matrix. Although such interactions often produce local clarifications, and occasionally issue in new totalizing hypotheses, their net effect is disruptive.

As theoretical matrices multiply and compete, fear of totalizing systems seems less and less plausible. Equally odd is the fear of a lack of cohesion that purportedly existed at some point in the past. The latter leads to preposterous claims about the unity of culture and universal reason, and prompts in response a resistance to reason in any form.

What I would coax the essays in this volume into implying is that the ends of theory are scarcely distinguishable from the ends of practice; that neither can secure much traction without the other; that by setting them in opposition and tying them to the whole range of binarisms that have in the past decade proved so convenient for our polemical stances, we may have delayed the emergence of more efficacious ways of achieving whatever ends we have in mind. While particular essays may oppose these conclusions, they must perforce contend with one another for our attention, and the productive relations among them obviate any terminus of theory and practice.

Works Cited

Archer, Margaret S. "Education." In *France Today*, ed. J. E. Flower. London: Methuen, 1983.

Borch-Jakobsen, Mikkel. *Lacan: The Absolute Master*. Stanford: Stanford University Press, 1991.

Bové, Paul. *In the Wake of Theory*. Hanover: Wesleyan University Press, 1992.

Carroll, David, ed. *The States of "Theory": History, Art, and Critical Discourse*. New York: Columbia University Press, 1990.

Cohen, Ralph, ed. *The Future of Literary Theory*. New York: Routledge, 1989.

Collier, Peter, and Helga Geyer-Ryan, eds. *Literary Theory Today*. Ithaca: Cornell University Press, 1990.

Davis, Lennard J., and M. Bella Mirabella, eds. *Left Politics and the Literary Profession*. New York: Columbia University Press, 1990.

————. "Criticism and Crisis." In *Blindness and Insight: Essays in the Rhetoric of Contemporary Criticism*. New York: Oxford University Press, 1971.

Derrida, Jacques. "Some Statements and Truisms about Neo-logisms, Newisms, Postisms, Parasitisms, and Other Small Seismisms." In *The States of "Theory,"* ed. David Carroll. New York: Columbia University Press, 1990.

Docherty, Thomas. *After Theory*. London: Routledge, 1990.

Gadamer, Hans-Georg. *Truth and Method*. New York: Crossroad, 1975.

Gleick, James. *Chaos: Making a New Science*. New York: Viking, 1987.

Godzich, Wlad. "Introduction." In *Aesthetic Experience and Literary Hermeneutics*, by Hans Robet Jauss. Minneapolis: University of Minnesota Press, 1982.

Gross, John. "The Man of Letters in a Closed Shop." *Times Literary Supplement*, Nov. 15, 1991.

Halls, W. D. *Education, Culture and Politics in Modern France*. Oxford: Pergamon, 1976.

Husserl, Edmund. "Philosophy and the Crisis of European Man." In *Phenomenology and the Crisis of Philosophy*. New York: Harper and Row, 1965.

Johnson, Barbara, and Jonathan Arac, edds. *Consequences of Theory*. Baltimore: Johns Hopkins University Press, 1991.

Kavanaugh, Thomas M., ed. *The Limits of Theory*. Stanford: Stanford University Press, 1989.

Knapp, Steven, and Walter Benn Michaels. "Against Theory." In *Against Theory: Literary Studies and the New Pragmatism*, ed. W. J. T. Mitchell. Chicago: University of Chicago Press, 1985.

Kreiswirth, Martin, and Mark A. Cheetham, eds. *Theory between the Disciplines: Authority/Vision/Politics*. Ann Arbor: University of Michigan Press, 1990.

Levin, Harry. "Criticism in Crisis." In *Contexts of Criticism*. Cambridge, Mass.: Harvard University Press, 1957.

Lévi-Strauss, Claude. *The Savage Mind*. Chicago: University of Chicago Press, 1966.

Lewin, Roger. *Complexity: Life at the Edge of Chaos*. New York: Macmillan, 1992.

de Man, Paul. *The Resistance to Theory*. Minneapolis: University of Minnesota Press, 1986.

Michaels, Walter Benn. "Race into Culture: A Critical Genealogy of Cultural Identity." *Critical Inquiry* 18 (1992): 655–85.

Mitchell, W. J. T., ed. *Against Theory*. Chicago: University of Chicago Press, 1985.

Nancy, Jean-Luc, "Finite History," in *The States of "Theory*," ed. David Carroll.

Natoli, Joseph, ed. *Literary Theory's Future(s)*. Chicago: University of Illinois Press, 1989.

Olsen, Stein Haugom. *The End of Literary Theory*. Cambridge: Cambridge University Press, 1987.

Porter, Carolyn. "Are We Being Historical Yet?" In *The States of "Theory*," ed. David Carroll.

Readings, Bill. "Why Is Theory Foreign?" In *Theory between the Disciplines*, ed. Martin Kreiswirth (Ann Arbor: University of Michigan Press, 1990).

Thody, Philip. *Roland Barthes: A Conservative Estimate*. London: Macmillan, 1977.

Waldrop, M. Mitchell. *Complexity: The Emerging Science at the Edge of Order and Chaos*. New York: Simon and Schuster, 1992.

Wellek, René, and Austin Warren. *Theory of Literature*. New York: Harcourt, Brace, 1942.

Part I
Critics and Criticism

We live amid surfaces.
—Emerson

Paul de Man: Some Notes on the Critic's Search for Authority against Consensus

Paul A. Bové

Paul de Man published "the Rhetoric of Temporality" in 1969.[1] (One likes to think of him writing it in 1968.) It is one of his most highly regarded essays. In the "Introduction" to his edition of de Man's *Critical Writings, 1953–1978*, entitled "Paul de Man: Life and Works" (1989), Lindsay Waters says that "'The Rhetoric of Temporality' is rightly (I think) felt to be his most fully achieved essay."[2] Daniel O'Hara, in "Paul de Man: Nietzsche's Teacher" (1985), lets "The Rhetoric of Temporality" occupy the center of his own meditation on the erotics of de Man's writing.[3] In *Critical Genealogies*, Jonathan Arac twice notes the importance of this essay, once as a moment in contemporary criticism's rewriting the history of Romanticism and once as an instance of Benjamin's importance for contemporary criticism.[4] "The Rhetoric of Temporality" is also important in Donald Pease's revision of Matthiessen's construction of the "American Renaissance." Pease's accomplishment depends in large measure on his reading of Poe as the allegorist of Hawthorne's loss of cultural memory, a reading that draws on "The Rhetoric of Temporality" to help establish its own conclusions.[5] One could, of course, name other critics who have dealt with this essay—some more and some less sympathetic to de Man and deconstruction.

Lindsay Waters makes clear that he feels this essay deserves its high reputation because, in "The Rhetoric of Temporality," de Man "had the tools he needed to achieve what he knew was impossible before."[6] Like Arac and others, Waters takes note that in this essay, de Man has occasion to make use of his readings in Benja-

Reprinted from *Criticism*, Spring 1990, Vol. 32, no. 2, pp. 149–61.
Copyright © 1990 Wayne State University Press, Detroit, Michigan 48201.

min's book, *The Origin of German Tragic Drama*.[7] For Waters, Benjamin allows de Man "to reapproach the question of history that had always been central to his work" and get beyond the Heideggerian discourse on temporality. He puts "the language of rhetoric in the place of that of temporality."[8] And with this displacement, as Waters reads it, de Man takes on Benjamin's project: "In the end he rejected the notions of interiority and inwardness as tools of analysis and he also rejected the inner/outer dichotomy that he had derived from the tradition of German idealism."[9] The Benjaminian turn in "The Rhetoric of Temporality," in Walters's opinion, lets de Man attend to the materiality of literature as a ruin that "bears the imprint of the progression of history inscribed within it."[10] Of course, de Man's essay so troubles the very possibility of history under the sign of "anteriority" that to accept Waters's reading, we would first need to deconstruct his own dualistic rhetoric of inside/outside. Pointing out this small slip in Waters's writing about de Man's movement away from these dualisms does not single out Waters for having made an "error" in reading. As de Man himself would no doubt have it, Waters could not write of these matters without reinscribing what we might call, in the context of "The Rhetoric of Temporality," a symbolist rhetoric and position, a language of identity, of commensurability between language and a nonlinguistic "history" "inscribed" "within it."

"The Rhetoric of Temporality" is a remarkably complex essay; it is de Man at his performing best. The two parts of the essay on allegory and irony, respectively, bring preliminary historicizing into contact with theoretical writing that subverts its needed historicism, and they do so in such a way as to enact a "truth" or "understanding" that could not appear in the concept alone. This last sentence is a dense (hopefully not simply unclear) and abstract statement about some important aspects of de Man's essay. As we recall, the essay's first part seems to recount historically how Romanticism's production of a symbolist aesthetic in a rhetoric of subjectivity parallels or is accompanied by the development of a new rhetorical mode that de Man, after Benjamin, calls allegory. De Man goes on to tell us that the nineteenth century forgot "allegory" in its valorization of a subjectivist, symbolist aesthetic and that, in part, his essay aims to recover the lost rhetorical form and, in the process, rewrite the history of Romanticism. Along the way of this history, de Man encapsulates understandings of the Germans, particularly Goethe, Schiller, and Schlegel; of the English, especially Coleridge; and of the French, especially Rousseau. He also makes a number of what we would call theoretical remarks about the nature of language, allegory, and the symbol, emphasizing their relation to time, history, the self, and difference.

The second part of the essay is in a disjunctive but complementary relation to the first. The second section is on irony and is insistently non- or even antihistorical; it insists that irony has history as its enemy and can never be historicized; indeed, as a trope, irony can account for the production of selves, some of which, we might say, are narrativized in allegorical duration. But the structure of de Man's essay does not result in a simple "inversion of hierarchies" or "subversion" of itself. De Man's insight is always of such a kind that only on the level of his own performance can one begin to see (or could he begin to make visible) the "truth" of his own "understanding." Were we to read the essay very closely—and there is not space to do so here—we would be able to write many things about the interwoven structures of truth/error, blindness/insight, etc., that are all caught up in what we now call the materiality of the sign.[11]

It would be extremely interesting and important to rewrite de Man's writing here, to follow his own "purpose," as it were, in working out the impersonal, often "inhuman" nature of language at the level of the conditions for the production of meaning and value. One can justifiably defer this project in part because Carol Jacobs has already done a powerful rewriting of de Man's essay and done so in such a way that it lets others begin to talk about not only de Man's concern for but his actual authority within the profession.

Jacobs opens her rewriting of de Man with the sort of paragraph many of those who take de Man seriously must write whenever trying to write about him:

> There is no way to say adequately what the significance of de Man might be. It could not be otherwise, for he himself linked death to the impossibility of defining man as presence and with man's perpetual transgression of his own sense of self as totalized. And, given that the transgression is perpetual, it took no literal death to both upset and set the task, that of reading the man, which is to say, writing about him.[12]

Just what are the expectations fulfilled by this remarkable paragraph? One wants to begin by saying that the pargraph is allegorical in that it is allusively figural as de Man describes Julie's garden to be—that is, as Rousseau's language alludes to and derives from *The Romance of the Rose* and *Robinson Crusoe*, Jacobs's language is itself formulaic, borrowed almost "whole cloth," as a *doublure*, we might say, from the texts that carry de Man's signature. Of course, we immediately notice the characteristic joke, the pun on "reading the man," the sort of move that marks the "grim rigor" of de Man's own work. Also, there are many familiar de Manian ideas here; Jacobs finds she cannot begin to write "about" de Man, as it were, except from within his own problematic, from within what *Yale French Studies* has taught us to call "The Lesson of Paul de Man."[13] What we note, too, is a characteristic dialectic of the sort that Said once called "authority" and "molestation."[14] In other words, we see how de Man has enabled Jacobs's own essay: without de Man's writing of the link between death (and rhetoric) and the transgression against the totalized self, Jacobs, we might say, could have mistakenly written about the dead de Man in some way other than "reading the man"—an authorization that itself guides her through a powerful rewriting of one of the most complex and insightful essays of the past twenty years. So de Man saves Jacobs from mistakes whenever she writes; at least, he saves her from the conventional and never-banished forms of mystification, if only by raising her struggle with and against them to a higher plane where the fatality of theory provides understanding, even if no alternative to the entrapments it reveals, reworks, and reinscribes.

Yet de Man's authority is also a "molestation" because Jacobs cannot begin her writing on de Man—given the rigor of her own reading—but from within de Man's lesson. To be enabled and constrained by consequences: this is a difficult thing to understand or to say. Said would have it that molestation is simply "a consciousness of one's duplicity, one's confinement to a fictive, scriptive realm."[15] Perhaps de Man has helped us more than Said to understand this "confinement" as a state of language; from a point of view like de Man's, Said's formulation is naive because it speaks of a consciousness that senses its own confinement to a fictive realm on the basis of its sense of a difference from "reality," a difference that, in Said's view, leads the molested author to feel herself to be confined to a realm of illusion. De Man, of course, is always more precise when he speaks of such things, so, in "The Rhetoric of Temporality," he writes of "a disjunction between the way in which the world appears in reality and the way it appears in language" (p. 191). What Said calls molestation is, then, only a weak interpretation of the incommensurability of language and human experience and is, as such, a historicization of an ahistorical, indeed inhuman, structure that in part underlies the production of history, of narrative.

To put the matter another way, we might say that the dialectic of Jacobs's relation to the lesson of the master is caught by the figure of allegory itself. With Nietzsche, we might call it the dialectic of belatedness or of the structural relation between priority and anteriority. Jacobs, after all, is in a consequent position, for, as Michael Hays is wont to remind us, de Man is dead.[16] To be as true to the

lesson of de Man, then, as Jacobs would have herself be, this consequent relation can only be, as de Man says in writing of allegory, "a
relationship between signs in which the reference to their respective
meanings has become of secondary importance." It becomes, to use
a shorthand, an act of reading. De Man's teaching and his death become signs postulated as being "in the past" or even "at the origin"
in Jacobs's, of course, self-conscious allegory. The never-present,
transgressed, and now dead de Man has become a repetition of a
sort de Man himself has theorized:

> But this relationship between signs necessarily contains a con-
> stitutive temporal element; it remains necessary, if there is to
> be allegory, that the alleogorical sign refer to another sign that
> precedes it. The meaning constituted by the allegorical sign
> can then consist only in the *repetition* (in the Kierkegaardian
> sense of the term) of a previous sign with which it can never
> coincide, since it is of the essence of this previous sign to be
> pure anteriority. The secularized allegory of the early roman-
> tics thus necessarily contains the negative moment which in
> Rousseau is that of renunciation, in Wordsworth that of the
> loss of self in death or in error. (p. 207)

In a performance like Jacobs's, then, the relation between master and apprentice can only be repetition; and so wherever there is
or has been a strong teacher, the student can only be an allegorist:
allegory, the story of ruin, can be the ephebe's only form.[17] Jacobs
knows this, of course, and in a full repetition of de Man's most brilliant performance, "ends" her essay by ironizing her ironic play
with de Man's dialectics:

> After this long digression [into the performative aspects of
> "The Rhetoric of Temporality"] which was, of necessity, both a
> definition and transgression of de Man's text, we might return
> to the original crises, that of saying not only what de Man
> means but also what we mean when we say de Man. No
> doubt this essay, I confess, in de Man's words, produces "a
> darkness more redoubtable than [any] error . . . it might dis-
> pel." To be sure, this is no excuse. But, whatever I have done
> in reading his text, if the reader will forgive the rhetorical
> question, would it not still be possible to assert that it is "Ah!
> encore de Man"?[18]

Rewriting de Man means turning to the master for the authority to write, to use certain figures, without reverting to an unproblematic—or pre-de Manian—sense of language and its nonrelation

to death, history, experience, and so on. Jacobs, we should say, writes without losing sight of de Man's lesson; she writes—and can write—only by virtue of positioning herself in relation to a pure anteriority that de Man has become in the allegory of his students. Jacobs's first reminder to her own readers is that the self is always transgressed by death; in this allegory, however, death is the pure anteriority that defines the ephebe's authorized position, or, to put it another way, "the man" is death, the transgression of the self. (Can we say this is an allegory of the ephebes' "murder" of the master?)

This is the sort of reading of de Man that many object to. Some of de Man's students—those who are merely ephebes[19]—object because it is a reading that lacks rigor and—dare one say it?—sympathy and understanding. It is also the sort of reading that makes many of deconstruction's right- and left-wing critics politically, ethically, and professionally unhappy with de Man and his influence: the ephebes—if not the master—seem to be paralyzed, spinning their wheels within a repetition that has become old news, that has no effective politics, that has hardly transformed even the profession except, for the cynical, by too easily making some too quickly distinguished careers.

Rather than attempt to propose an entirely different way of approaching de Man—as others are now trying to do—I want to draw attention to a few aspects of "The Rhetoric of Temporality" that, as far as I know, have received little attention. Other commentators have made much of irony, allegory, anteriority, symbolism, rhetoric, and other key terms of de Man's developing rhetorical criticism in this essay. Of course, any serious commentary on the essay must do so. But were one to read the essay with slightly different emphases, were one to see it in a slightly different tradition, perhaps the importance of these terms would take on a slightly different sense, a tactical sense.

I want to propose a look at this essay that begins with a recollection and a repetition of my own. De Man tells us that the relation of the present to the past in allegory is repetition in a Kierkegaardian sense. Kierkegaard, we should remember, insisted that repetition is recollection forward, that it is a structure that ensures futurity as anteriority, a futurity marked by difference, that is, distance from equally figurative pasts and presents. Of course, such a notion lets us argue that the ephebes' allegory of their own derivative and perhaps murderous authority can be just such a futurity. There are at least two things interesting about this allegorical moment: that the profession allows or allowed it to be institutionalized, and that de Man's work so clearly—as Jacobs's brilliantly troubling immanental readings show—enables and authorizes that allegory of professional authorization. Ezra Pound's *Cantos* give us one language to say this: the ephebes enter the enchanted realm of authority, the space where one can come to be known.[20]

Ought one not consider if de Man's text offers other "futurities," as it were, and if it might be, in a way, a most clever—and he was nothing if not clever—analysis of the professional and ideological realities that form this powerful nexus of authority, professional privilege, and death? "The Rhetoric of Temporality" came to me (or I came to it) in graduate school of the 1970s from the tradition of Nietzsche (a claim that I suppose shocks no one) and from the tradition of Marx (a claim that others will, perhaps, find somewhat more surprising or even foolish).[21] But coming on the essay, and on de Man generally in these ways, lets me say, if you will, that there are certain oppositional and even historical movements in the essay that some other readers choose not to discuss.

R. P. Blackmur once wrote of how a good critic, like a good poet, will always produce a "cumulus" of meaning in a "conjury" of words, a cumulus that, like a symbol as Blackmur understood it, always had social implications and emerged from social realities.[22] Looking at part of de Man's essay in light of Blackmur's thought suggests different emphases from those common to many of de Man's students' readings of his work.

Most obviously, de Man is criticizing what he sees as the ideological, intellectual, and academic dominance of the discourse of the symbol. The critique is part and parcel of his ongoing struggle with Hegel and the institutionalization of his thought, his philosophy, his figures; de Man makes clear some of what is at stake in this critique as he discusses the symbol:

> [T]he valorization of [the] symbol at the expense of allegory coincide[s] with the growth of an aesthetics that refuses to distinguish between experience and the representation of this experience. The poetic language of genius is capable of transcending this distinction and can thus transform all individual experience directly into language; the world is then no longer seen as a configuration of entities that designate a plurality of distinct and isolated meanings, but as a configuration of symbols ultimately leading to a total, single, and universal meaning. This appeal to the infinity of a totality constitutes the main attraction of the symbol as opposed to allegory, a sign that refers to one specific meaning and thus exhausts its suggestive potentialities once it has been deciphered. (p. 188)

"The Rhetoric of Temporality" is as much concerned with the discursive and institutional establishment of the symbol as it is with the linguistic or, if you will, "inhuman" structures that betray themselves in, and betray us into, the abysmal dialectics of allegory and irony. De Man's critique, in his discussion of allegory and irony, is a critique of the totality, as it is in his early essays on Nietzsche, perhaps most explicitly in "Genesis and Genealogy in Nietzsche's *Birth of Tragedy*."[23] It is above all a critique of the nineteenth century's forgetting of the tense relation between symbol and allegory in Goethe, Coleridge, and others. It is, if you will, as much a critique of the Professors as it is a critique of an inhuman linguistic structure. For example, to read Hölderlin symbolically is not only a mistake; it is an act that displaces Hölderlin's metaphors by the synecdoche of the organic symbol; and it is an act the burdens of which de Man tries to make explicit and to deconstruct.

The targets of de Man's weapons are equally the University Professors and their discourse—in this case, Abrams and Wasserman and the discourse on Romanticism. De Man draws attention to the academic consensus that is the institutional counterpart, the empowered figuration, of the ideology of the organic symbol—the desire for "totality." When he writes of the Professors, he says such things as "The main interpretative [sic] effort of English and American historians of romanticism has focused on . . ." as well as "recent articles by . . . Abrams and . . . Wasserman . . . make use of very similar, at times even identical material. The two interpreters agree on many issues, to the point of overlapping" (pp. 193, 194). Indeed, although de Man the polemicist finds evidence of the valorization of the symbol in Coleridge, it is the Professors who forgot Coleridge's ambiguities—the "allegory" of his texts—and reimagine him as someone who succumbs to the temptations of the symbolic aesthetic: "This strategy [of borrowing nature's stability for the self] is certainly present in Coleridge. And it is present, though perhaps not consciously, in critics such as Abrams and Wasserman, who see Coleridge as the great synthesizer and who take his dialectic of subject and object to be the authentic pattern of romantic imagery" (p. 197). De Man goes on to point out the same consensus-formation in the study of French and German as in that of English Romanticism. It is that discursive, ideological, and intellectual solidification—that orthodoxy, that consensus building—against which de Man directs the efforts of this essay. He repeatedly tells us that it is the "priority," the "superiority," the empowerment, if you will, of this set of intellectual judgments, this set of values, that must be displaced—presumably by driving it or them into abysmal oscillations, the insane vertigoes that he tries so hard to authorize as their replacement in the Professors' talk. Of course, the project is mad and failed. But ought we not see it as directed, historical, tactical, and the purposive act of an agent? Ought we not see it as, above all, an act that warns its beholders of its worst dangers—madness, death, and repetition?

But why must this orthodoxy be displaced? The Professors' commitment to the "symbol's" priority involves an inseparable commitment to totalization, to forms of history writing penetrated by the drive to totalize. Of course, given what has come to light about de Man's wartime involvements with fascism, we understand in a newly personal way why he would have been so sensitive to the equation between discourses that totalize and totalizing practices and totalitarian politics. It would be an exaggeration to say that the Professors are "totalitarians," but not to insist that both their discursive and ideological commitments to the symbolist aesthetic and its historical narratives, on the one hand, and their institutional consensus forming, their willful amnesiac "misreadings," on the other hand, exist as one cultural manifestation of an arrangement of "knowledge" and "language forms" that incontrovertibly exists in a continual relation with the politics of totalitarianism. Nothing less than this argument emerges in "Genesis and Genealogy."[24]

In that essay, de Man shows that organic models of literary history are analogous to Hegelian discourses of circular totality, of closure that marks an inescapable identity between "beginning" and "end": "*Das Resultat*," de Man quotes Hegel from the Introduction to *The Phenomenology of Spirit*, "*ist nur darum dasselbe, was der Anfang, weil der Anfang Zweck ist.*"[25] As de Man shows in "The Rhetoric of Temporality," the Professors of Romanticism tend to repeat the structures of Romanticism in the very act of writing its history. For de Man, one way to consider evading this duplication would be to imagine a nonorganic history of Romanticism. There is, however, one problem that must be dealt with prior to the effort to make this move: the fact that most historians of Romanticism are themselves still "pre-Hegelian," that is, "caught in a non-dialectical notion of a subject-object dichotomy."[26] There would be real reason, then, to carry out a study that would trace the organic model in Romanticism and its history. Of course, that model finds its latest literary-critical articulations in the Professors' works mentioned in "The Rhetoric of Temporality." Without following de Man through his readings of Nietzsche, it is nonetheless apparent what is "wrong," as it were, with the practice of these Professors, even in their Hegelian duplications of Romanticism. Like those much greater dialecticians, Auerbach and Benjamin, the Professors emulate Hegel in "bypass[ing] . . . the contemporary moment entirely."[27] Indeed, even deconstruction does not guarantee that organic totalizing history can be avoided; genetic history would merely redeploy itself. Deconstruction disrupts linear sequences so that "no sequence of actual events or no particular subject could ever acquire, by itself, full historical meaning." These events and subjects remain, however, "moments" within a process: since the movement consists of their totalization, they can still be said to share in the experience of this movement."[28]

De Man's general point is clear; equally important, however, are the implications of this theoretical insight for the institutionalized practices and discourses of the Professors: for the most part, their work is "pre-Hegelian," simply "Hegelian," or, even when "deconstructed," stubbornly "Hegelian." It totalizes by virtue of sharing the organic, genetic model of the "idea," "Romanticism," of which it claims to write the history. De Man's challenge to the Professors' history takes the form of a question: what if "the Romantics came closer than we do to undermining the absolute authority of this system"? "The ultimate test or 'proof' of the fact that Romanticism puts the genetic pattern of history in question would then be the impossibility of writing a history of Romanticism."[29]

De Man's criticism of the Professors and their institutions takes the form of delegitimizing the forms of historical discourse that ground their knowledge production. De Man's readings clearly show that he aims not just to reveal the "abyss" over which all language "hovers"; rather, he clearly aims to undermine authority, claims to originality or to knowledge, and institutional legitimacy. This constellation of contentions is clearest perhaps at the very end of "Genesis and Genealogy." There he shows, first, that he is interested in "consequences"; second, that the Professors do not know how to read; third, that they rest unaffected by the fact that such texts as Nietzsche's, when taken seriously, should indeed have consequences for the ways in which one thinks and works; and, fourth, that in this "resting" the Professors are, like all of us, the products of the "absolute authority" of systems, of "exemplary models."[30]

Returning to "The Rhetoric of Temporality," we can see that de Man's effort—to displace his predecessor Professors and their politically dangerous, naively inherited discourses—requires Benjamin's theory of allegory: the Romantic allegorizers and the Professors are all pure anteriority for a discourse that needs them to be such, to have no meaning of their own so they can be most effectively displaced. It is a move, however, that authorizes, indeed demands of his students a similar dialectical allegory of murderous reverence—but against whom should it be directed? There is a danger in this demand, though, for that way lies not only new authority and its questioning but necessarily death, madness, and redundant repetition: "absolute irony is a consciousness of madness, itself the end of all consciousness; it is a consciousness of a non-conscious-ness, a reflection on madness from the inside of madness itself." Absolute irony is a double movement; stabilizing itself in a linguis-tic self, a masked production, a doubling for which one can—the ironist, whoever he or she might be, hopes—come to see the writ-ing's madness. But this double reflection is not good enough; it could be mistaken for a real form of life, for sympathy and care. The absolute ironist must observe, disinterestedly, the temptation to care: this de Man sometimes calls theory. But theory is a moment of redundancy, redundancy of the very worst sort, knowing now what we know about collaboration and resistance:

> Technically correct rhetorical readings may be boring, monot-onous, predictable, and unpleasant, but they are irrefutable. They are also totalizing (and potentially totalitarian) for since the structures and functions they expose do not lead to the knowledge of an entity (such as language) but are an unrelia-ble process of knowledge production that prevents all entities, including linguistic entities, from coming into discourse as such. . . . They are, always in theory, the most elastic theoreti-cal and dialectical model to end all models and they can rightly claim to contain within their own defective selves all the other defective models of reading-avoidance, referential, semiological, grammatical, performative, logical, or whatever. They are theory and not theory at the same time, the universal theory of the impossibility of theory. . . . Nothing can over-come the resistance to theory since theory *is* this resistance. The loftier the aims and the better the methods of literary theory, the less possible it becomes.[31]

The New Critics, with their understanding of absolute irony, felt irony's great value to lie precisely in its making the authority of its speaker, its writer, invulnerable to irony, to all accusations of being incomplete, of inadequate complexity and knowledge, of hav-ing produced only a partial simulacrum of the universe.[32] De Man's warning about irony is that it always is tempted to collaborate, most especially at those moments when it is most dominant, most imper-vious to the humanity of other weaker, partial, less satisfacory posi-tions and perspectives. Irony and theory can resist this Professorial temptation to consensus, but their unique specularity ties them to a fatal repetition of their enemies' errors—albeit on a higher, more powerful level. Theory and irony—these are valued only as the sites of struggle, not as sites of victory: indeed, their victories end as collaborations no matter how they begin as resistance. Allegory and irony: the one leaves us with ruins, while the other "recapture[s] some of the factiousness of human experience" (226).

In his essay "The Tiger on the Paper Mat," which functions as a foreword to *The Resistance to Theory*, Wlad Godzich recovers something of the social origins of *theoria*, not as pure anteriority but as a sign of theory's social existence as an authorized "bearing-witness-to" which alone gives evidence, which alone allows entities to enter into discourse as existing and "true." With some irony of his own, Godzich leaves us with the reminder become obligation that de Man has left us with the problem of praxis.[33]

Notes

1. I shall cite this essay, parenthetically, from the following: Paul de Man, "The Rhetoric of Temporality," in *Blindness and Insight*, 2nd. ed., Introduction by Wlad Godzich (Minneapolis: University of Minnesota Press, 1983), pp. 187–228.

2. (Minneapolis: University of Minnesota Press, 1989), p. lvi.

3. In *The Romance of Interpretation: Visionary Criticism from Pater to de Man* (New York: Columbia University Press, 1985), p. 220.

4. *Critical Genealogies: Historical Situations for Postmodern Literary Studies* (New York: Columbia University Press, 1987), pp. 24, 196.

5. *Visionary Compacts: American Renaissance Writings in Cultural Context* (Madison: University of Wisconsin Press, 1987), p. 168.

6. "Introduction," p. lvi.

7. *Ursprung des deutschen Trauerspiels* (Frankfurt am Main: Suhrkampf, 1963); trans. John Osborne, introduction by George Steiner (London: New Left Books, 1977).

8. "Introduction," p. lvi.

9. Ibid., p. lvii.

10. Ibid., p. lvi.

11. For some further sense of how one might carry out this reading, see de Man's "Semiology and Rhetoric," *Allegories of Reading* (New Haven: Yale University Press, 1979), pp. 3–20.

12. "Allegories of Reading Paul de Man," in *Reading de Man Reading*, ed. Lindsay Waters and Wlad Godzich (Minneapolis: University of Minnesota Press, 1989), p. 105.

13. "The Lesson of Paul de Man," *Yale French Studies* 69 (1985).

14. Edward W. Said, *Beginnings: Intention and Method* (New York: Basic Books, 1975), esp. pp. 83–84.

15. Ibid., p. 84.

16. Michael Hays, "As If Spellbound by Magical Curves," paper given at Dartmouth College, spring 1989.

17. See my discussion of this problem in Ezra Pound's *Cantos* in *Intellectuals in Power* (New York: Columbia University Press, 1986), pp. 3–9.

18. "Allegories of Reading Paul de Man," p. 119; the quotation from de Man occurs in *Allegories of Reading*. On the use of the word *excuse*, Jacobs advises we see de Man's final chapter in *Allegories of Reading*, "Excuses." On the use of the "rhetorical question," Jacobs advises we see de Man's opening chapter, "Semiology and Rheto-

ric." The necessity to allegorize her own irony seems, despite her brilliant self-consciousness, to indicate some nostalgia for symbolism in the master's student.

19. One need not mention the names of specific critics to be understood here. The recent debates and exchanges of letters in the columns of journals and reviews make clear the differences between the students who learn and go on and the ephebes who can only echo and track the master.

20. See *Intellectuals in Power*, pp. 3–9, esp. on Canto XIII.

21. I have elsewhere written about the confluence of these two traditions, and so I won't repeat myself on that level here. See "The Metaphysics of Textuality: Marx's *Eighteenth Brumaire* and Nietzsche's *Use and Abuse of History*," *Dalhousie Review* 64 (Summer 1984): 401–22.

22. See *Language as Gesture: Essays in Poetry* (1952; rpt. New York: Columbia University Press, 1981), pp. 13ff.

23. *Diacritics* 2:4 (Winter 1972): 44–53; reprinted in *Allegories of Reading*, pp. 79–102; I shall quote from this reprinted edition.

24. Ibid., pp. 79–102.

25. Ibid., p. 80.

26. Ibid.

27. Ibid., p. 81.

28. Ibid.

29. Ibid., p. 82.

30. See Ibid., pp. 101–2.

31. Paul de Man, "The Resistance to Theory," in *The Resistance to Theory*, foreword by Wlad Godzich (Minneapolis: University of Minnesota Press, 1986), p. 19.

32. See Paul A. Bové, *Destructive Poetics* (New York: Columbia University Press, 1980), pp. 92–130.

33. *The Resistance to Theory*, p. xviii.

De Man's End

Steven E. Cole

Perhaps the most unsettling consequence of the controversy over Paul de Man's wartime journalism was the ease with which the harsh rigor of deconstruction was replaced by a kind of naive historicism in which both criticisms and defenses of de Man based their argument on whether continuity could be discovered between the early journalism and the later work.[1] Thus, defenders of de Man argued that the deconstructive denial of determinate meaning was simply incompatible with fascist and anti-Semitic rhetoric, while those who attacked de Man countered that both fascism and anti-Semitism depend on precisely the sort of refusal of ethical limitation that deconstruction itself advocates.[2] What was unsettling about this debate was not the rigidity of the positions, or even the unargued unassumption that de Man's later work was sufficiently understood to provide the basis for generalizations about how that work differed from the earlier journalism. Rather, what was unsettling was how irrelevant de Man's own arguments were to both his defenders and his attackers. Where de Man had struggled to establish that our most firmly held political and ethical intuitions cannot stand outside a rigorous scrutiny of our schemes of sense-making, now instead the political and the ethical seemed to function as a self-evident origin for any analysis of intellectual argument, and the historicist dispute about whether continuity could be discovered between the early and the late work seemed the only plausible means for discovering how de Man's work might be seen in relation to the politically and ethically self-evident demand that literary theory be uncontaminated by fascist ideology.

It would be wrong, however, to claim that such separating of de Man's own arguments from analysis of his work began with the debate over his wartime journalism. Rather, a constant feature of

An earlier version of this essay appeared as "The Dead End of Deconstruction: Paul de Man and the Fate of Poetic Language," *Criticism* 30 (1988): 91–112.

discussions of de Man has been the refusal to take seriously the arguments he offers, either by dismissing their relevance to actual experience or by insisting that their resistance to comprehension pre-
cludes any rational or logical assessment. Before the revelations
about de Man's wartime journalism, it was the latter response that
was most common, and much of the current glib dismissal of de
Man's work comes, I think, from the refusal of his admirers to offer
anything like serious commentary on the theoretical bases for the
deconstructive claim that both social and personal identity are illusory. Indeed, instead of serious theoretical analysis, what one finds
in the flood of commentary that has appeared since de Man's death
(and this is true even of Jacques Derrida's remarkable *Memoires*),[3] is
a kind of mimetic homage in which the acolyte gestures mysteriously at texts whose profundity is ensured by their resistance to
comprehension. Thus, in a memorial volume of essays, we are told
that de Man "will also teach us, once again, in his own voice, how
to read in new and unexpected ways, how to contend with the impossibility of reading,"[4] and warned that the attempt to find a value
system in de Man's deconstruction must confront "a mystery about
which no moral imperative to leap from textuality to subjectivity of
history can tell us more than de Man's stubborn labyrinths of rigor,
resistance, and profoundly meaningful unreliability."[5] In such proc-
lamations (and they are virtual commonplaces of de Man commentary), de Man's work stands as sacred writ, immune from the
searching historical and skeptical suspicion it embodies.

What explains this extraordinary protectiveness toward de
Man's work? In large part, it seems to stem from an uneasiness
about the actual content of what de Man has to say, a largely un-
spoken awareness that for all its logical brilliance and subtlety, de
Man's writing is profoundly unsettling and depressing. Certainly
this would explain the nervous, almost embarrassed generosity of
the memorial tributes that have been published: the recurrent
theme is an apology for the experience of loss occasioned by de
Man's death yet seemingly made impossible by his work.[6] Yet it
would be wrong to seize upon such an apparent discrepancy between work and world as evidence that de Man has in some way
been refuted. For, as we shall see, the significance of de Man's work
is not its denial of the ontology of experience; it is rather its insistence that such an ontology, while inescapable, must also remain in-
tractably inexplicable, and, more important, that such inexplicabil-
ity exposes the emptiness of political or social praxis.

Unfortunately, there is continuing reluctance to take de Man
at face value—a refusal to accept that positions that deny absolutely
the possibility of either affirmable meaning or value really mean

what they say. The reason for this seems obvious—for some time de Man's work has been seen as central to a more general project that would argue that the indeterminacy of linguistic meaning is subversive of politically or psychologically objectionable structures whose power inheres in their pretension to determinism.[7] But there is a terminological difficulty here: *subversion* is a notoriously slippery term, particularly in the absence of any shared agreement about that which is being subverted. Thus, while Paul Bové argues that "the deconstructive reversal of the New Critical project . . . authorizes the redeployment of critical energies into a new alignment of forces which preserves the integrity of the institution while providing original and praeter-naturally subtle insight into both the operations of textuality and the primordiality of writing,"[8] de Man himself wryly accepts what he calls the "supreme insult" that his work is "just more New Criticism. I can live with that very easily, because I think that only what is, in a sense, classically didactic, can be really and effectively subversive" (RT, p. 117). The dilemma here is fundamental to any effort at situating de Man's work: the attempt at locating a realm of thematic significance, whether this be ethical, political, or historical, seems frustrated by de Man's own anticipation of, and dismissal of, that attempt. Small wonder that Wallace Martin argues that it is simply wrong to believe that in de Man "the theory being advanced is some form of idealism, skepticism, or negative theology."[9] This is wrong, according to Martin, because "de Man is aware of this danger, is increasingly vigilant in attempting to avoid it, and presumably resigned in advance to being misunderstood, since his theory is designed to explain why such misunderstandings are inevitable" (p. xxxii).

What is missing here is, of course, any sense of what de Man's "vigilance" is designed to protect: the critical orthodoxy that has made de Man's work seem immune from the supposed banalities of ethical or political criticisms is remarkably silent about what a de Manian response to those criticisms might be. As we can see in Bové and Martin, the standard response to criticisms of de Man is to claim that de Man has a subversive relationship to some tradition that the critic is struggling to defend, the implication being that subversiveness is in and of itself a sufficient end for criticism. There is, however, an enormous difficulty with this position, which, following Whitehead, we might characterize as a fallacy of misplaced concreteness. If there is indeed a relationship between criticism and the politically objectionable, then that relationship can be addressed only by showing how criticism might help to subvert political institutions that are, presumably, external to criticism itself: the reification of subversion as an intrinsic good mistakenly transforms the dialectic of oppression and liberation from a characteristic possessed by real social institutions into a structural framework governing the analysis of any intellectual position. The point is a simple one: no argument can be seen as either oppressive or subversive without a specification of its real political consequences. And it is here that the claim that de Man's work is somehow "subversive" becomes extraordinarily curious. For while the rhetoric of subversion may tempt one to believe that the overcoming of any dominant tradition is necessarily politically liberating, in de Man's "subverting" of New Criticism, precisely the opposite conclusion is reached.

As we shall see, de Man never dissents from the New Critical belief that a coherent description of value requires the specification of a realm of experience ontologically autonomous from empirical determination. In this very abstract sense, value might be seen as subversive of empirical institutions. But what de Man's developing analysis of the ontology of autonomy insists is that experience itself is ultimately a delusion. The inexorable necessity of language as that which both defines the conditions and possibility of experience and equally makes the terms governing experience ontologically meaningless leads de Man to a belief that the very relational structures (structures embodying the relations of individuals to each other and to their material conditions) that determine political existence are necessary delusions, at best an inescapable burden. Far from providing the basis for a radical critique of existing social institutions, de Man's final insistence on linguistic indeterminacy cedes to existing institutions an inevitability from which there is no escape. The conclusion that de Man unflinchingly accepts (although this is largely ignored by his defenders) is that if meaning is indeed indeterminant, then the positive arguments required by the project of political amelioration are as condemned to error as any other discourse. By seeing the derivation of de Man's insistence that all meaning is a delusion (and nothing in de Man's position allows the bracketing of political meaning as somehow exempt from this claim) from his earlier, New Critical, hope that poetic language offers the possibility of existential and ontological reconciliation, we can begin to understand the enormous problems involved in claiming, as deconstruction wants to, that indeterminant usages of language are politically liberating.[10] My argument thus will be that de Man's project is finally (although unintentionally) therapeutic: by exposing the aporias that mark the ideology of linguistic autonomy, which is the unacknowledged premise of most contemporary literary theory, de Man's work demonstrates the necessity of a radical rethinking of both the origins and the aims of literary studies.

2

In trying to situate de Man's early work, it is important to keep in mind an essential premise of all the New Critics: statements about values are different fundamentally from statements about facts—different both in how they are expressed and in how they are justified.[11] New Criticism further argued that the difference between facts and values requires that values themselves be conceived in three related ways: first, they are immune from the determinations of the empirical world; second, they emerge from a private realm of experience; and third, their expression requires a nonreferential use of language.[12] At no point in his work does Paul de Man ever question either the distinction between facts and values or the conception of value upon which New Criticism relies; indeed, he assumes throughout his work that the New Critical description of value is the necessary presumption for any claim that value statements can articulate successfully the powers customarily claimed for them. Rather, his work is designed to show the impossibility of construing a realm of value that is empirically undetermined, privately produced, and linguistically articulated. He does this, however, not to propose a more adequate formulation of shared value but rather to deny its possibility.

We can see the beginnings of this position in an early essay on the New Critics, where de Man argues that the formalist method is governed by an ontological contradiction: it presumes an adequacy of language to experience (his example of this is I. A. Richards) that must ignore the constitutive role language plays with regard to experience. From this perspective, he argues that "the problem of criticism is no longer to discover to what experience the form refers, but how it can constitute a world, a totality of beings without which there would be no experience.[13] But it would be a mistake to assume that the emphasis must accordingly be on the social construction of the world, for de Man argues that "the problem of separation inheres in Being, which means that social forms of separation derive from ontological and metaphysical attitudes" (BI2, p. 240). De Man's critique of New Criticism is thus from the beginning less a challenge of its premises than an insistence that those premises must be explored more finely. His quarrel with Richards is not against the general claim that there exists a uniquely poetic realm of language but rather against the conclusion from that claim that poetic language can be seen to exhibit "an adequation of the object itself with the language that names it" (BI2, p. 244). Further, in his very formulation of the issue of representation as the relationship of linguistic construction to Being, we can see de Man's acceptance of the New Critical belief that the unity of experience is the telos of literary analysis, the value that literary analysis is to disclose. Thus, he argues that "the foremost characteristic of contemporary criticism is the tendency to expect a reconciliation from poetry; to see in it a possibility of filling the gap that cleaves Being" (BI2, p. 245). What is mistaken about this criticism in not the aim but its confidence about the ease with which that aim might be achieved: de Man criticizes Jean Pierre Richards's phenomenological optimism for its deluded belief that consciousness can reveal ontological substance, but he characterizes the project of reconciliation as the "supreme wager" to which is opposed only "the sorrowful time of patience, i.e., history" (BI2, p. 243). As we shall see, de Man's subsequent work is a nuanced exploration of the reasons for the loss of this wager and the consequent necessity of submitting to the aimless movement of history.

In a later essay, apparently written in the mid-1960s, de Man examines more closely the relationship of intentionality to formalist analysis. He argues once more that New Criticism was mistaken in believing that literary analysis might reveal an adequation between representation and Being, focusing now on the *intentionality* of the representation, and drawing a contrast to the status of natural objects: "The intentional object requires a reference to a specific act as constitutive of its mode of being."[14] What is interesting here is that de Man seems to accept the possibility that some usages of language can refer transparently to a natural world. He distinguishes between entities, such as a stone, "the full meaning of which can be said to be equal to the totality of their sensory appearances" and a chair: "the most rigorous description of the perceptions of the object 'chair' would remain meaningless if one does not organize them in function of the potential act that defines the object" (BI, pp. 23–24). This distinction seems to bracket intentionality as relevant only to a class of perceptions whose origin is not natural, but in drawing this distinction de Man assumes a class of natural entities whose perception, and finally whose meaning, is relatively unproblematic. Further, the claims de Man now wants to make about the nature of poetry require this distinction: he is able to single out a class of intentional objects that raise unique ontological dilemmas only if he is able to contrast that class with a realm of objects possessing a fundamentally different ontology. (The ontological dilemma of intentional objects is defined by their difference from natural objects.)

Needless to say, at this stage of the analysis, de Man's position is indistinguishable from Richards's; where in the earlier essay he had seemed to differ from Richards in denying any possible adequacy of representation to the objects being represented, he now, like Richards, would seem to grant representational adequacy to descriptions of natural objects. There is, however, a genuine difference between the two positions. De Man's critique of Richards stems from a disagreement about the range of objects that de Man would describe as intentional and that Richards would describe as having affective components. While Richards is willing to accept with tranquility the existence of natural objects whose being will never be reconciled with consciousness, de Man assumes throughout his work that the fundamental dilemma of existence is precisely such reconciliation. Thus, in a passage we examined above, he insists that even social separation is ontological in origin, and this belief is perhaps the source of what seems a shocking early judgment: "the central moment of *Ulysses*, the carefully prepared encounter between Bloom and Steven Dedalus . . . indicates, surely, the total impossibility of any contact, of any human communication, even in the most disinterested love."[15] Far from rejecting New Critical assumptions about poetic unity, de Man changes (and in some way raises) the stakes of what would count as reconciliation, and in doing so heightens also the thematic consequences, the *value*, of such reconciliation.

Indeed, what is at stake in both essays on the New Criticism is precisely a thematic question about what sort of knowledge, what sense of value, is offered by the conception of literary language that de Man finally wants to advance. De Man argues that, far from his understanding of intentionality comprising a threat to the New Critical project, it is instead its completion: "the intentionality of the act [of the work of literature], far from threatening the unity of the poetic entity, more definitely establishes this unity" (BI, p. 25). While descriptions of natural objects (insofar as they are descriptions) defy unity because they necessitate a distinction between the describer and the described, an act that is intentional "reflects back upon itself and remains circumscribed within the range of its own intent" (BI, p. 26). For this reason, such an act is both unified and "constitutes a perfectly closed and autonomous structure" (BI, p. 26). Thus, it would be a mistake to argue that the unity of a poem can have an organic model, since "the structural power of the poetic imagination is not founded on an analogy with nature, but . . . is intentional" (BI, p. 28). In this sense, de Man does seem to disagree with New Criticism. But the rejection of the metaphor of organicity is designed not to reject New Criticism but rather to prepare the ground for a sweeping endorsement of its most fundamental premise:

> True understanding always implies a certain degree of totality;
> without it, no contact could be established with a free knowl-
> edge that it can never reach, but of which it can be more or
> less lucidly aware. The fact that poetic language, unlike ordi-
> nary language, possesses what we call "form" indicates that it
> has reached this point. In interpreting poetic language, and
> especially in revealing its "form," the critic is therefore dealing
> with a privileged language: a language engaged in its highest
> intent and tending toward the fullest possible self-under-
> standing. The critical interpretation is oriented toward a con-
> sciousness which is itself engaged in an act of total interpreta-
> tion. The relationship between author and critic does not
> designate a difference in the type of activity involved, since no
> fundamental discontinuity exists between two acts that both
> aim at full understanding; the difference is primarily temporal
> in kind. Poetry is the foreknowledge of criticism. Far from
> changing or distorting it, criticism merely discloses poetry for
> what it is. (BI, p. 32)

Thus, the value of poetic language (the value the critic reveals in his
analysis of poetry) is that it exhibits a reconciliation, a totalization,
of consciousness and the (intentional) objects of its experience. Further, and perhaps more important, as we have seen, de Man wants
to stake the possibility of ameliorating social separation precisely on
the possibility of such totalization; the failure of the project he describes would leave us condemned to "the sorrowful time of
patience" where "any contact" or "human communication" would
indeed be impossible. And de Man himself, at the close of his essay,
seems certain that the project will fail: he praises Benjamin's definition of allegory "as a void 'that signifies precisely the non-being of
what it represents'" and argues that "the temporal labyrinth
of interpretation" leads to the "negative totalization" which
"constitutes the real depth of literary insight" (BI, p. 35). What is
perhaps too obvious to need mentioning is that this failure (which is
for de Man in fact a triumph) demands an initial acceptance of the
ontological premise that "the problem of separation inheres in
Being"—given this, the conclusions, both about language and about
totalization, follow inevitably, but in the absence of the premise, the
conclusions are incoherent.

3

The discussion so far has been intended to block one easy approach
to de Man's obvious reliance on New Critical assumptions about
poetic unity in his early criticism. This approach would argue that

de Man is relying only on a technique of exegesis and not on the thematic defense of that technique, and would thus make de Man an early instance of the general naturalization of New Critical technique in American theory. But such an approach would be not only overly easy but wrong. For, as we have seen, de Man's early dissent from New Criticism is not a denial of the ontological imperative of reconciliation but rather an insistence that the terms of the reconciliation need to be rethought. In particular, de Man's apparent acceptance, by the late 1950s, that an argument about reconciliation requires a distinction between referential and nonreferential language leads to an insistence that the representational status of nonreferential language must be explored much more carefully if conclusions about reconciliation are to be sustained.

In his doctoral dissertation, de Man draws a distinction between emblem and image in Yeats's poetry, arguing that the two imply distinct ontological commitments. The image, as de Man defines it, involves the use of "mimetic nouns referring to natural objects"[16] conjoined with human predicates in an attempt "to cross the gap between subject and object without apparent effort, and to unite them within the single unity of the natural image" (RR, p. 153). But, for de Man, this project is doomed to failure: while it relies on "the conception of fundamental unity of mind and matter" (RR, p. 153), it must blind itself to the fact that the terms of that unity are strictly a product of consciousness, that the movement from substance to predication involves an inevitable movement from a natural to a human world. Thus, while de Man grants that language itself has a referential component, he insists that referentiality be limited to the designation of natural objects, to the objects of perception, and he argues that it is a delusion to believe that language can go further in bridging the gap between consciousness and perception than simply identifying the objects that are perceived. In a close analysis of an attempt by Yeats to establish a unity between consciousness and nature by endowing the natural object with human predicates—his example is "a trumpet-twisted shell . . . Dreaming of her own melting hues" (RR, p. 153)—he shows that the paradoxical result is to establish even more firmly the very alienation the image was intended to overcome:

> The movement of the image, which started in perception, then fused the perceived object and the perceiving consciousness into one by means of a verbal transfer, now returns to the original perception, making the object itself into the perceiver. From purely perceptual, then metaphorical (or symbolic), the image has become one of self-reflection, using the material

> properties of the object (the colors) as a means to allow a self-reflective consciousness to originate. In the process, the center of interest, which first resided in the colors as the qualities by which the object was perceived, has shifted: the idea of a shell endowed with the highest form of human consciousness (self-reflection) is in itself so striking that the colors have lost most of their prominence; what arrests the mind, no doubt, are no longer the "melting hues" but the shell dreaming of its own beauty. The structure of the image has become that of self-reflection. The poet is no longer contemplating a thing in nature, but the workings of his own mind; the outside world is used as a pretext and a mirror, and it loses all its substance. Imagery by "correspondences" ends up in self-reflection, and the dominant mood of Yeats's earliest poetry is one of narcissistic self-contemplation. (RR, p. 154)

De Man's analysis here rests on an assumption that images in poetry confront an ontological dualism which it is both their aim to overcome and their nature to reaffirm: the origination of the image in consciousness ensures that perceptual reference is delusory and thus that the real function of the image is to mirror precisely the workings of consciousness which it had been designed to transcend. What is significant here is de Man's privileging of consciousness itself as the ultimate referent of poetic language. Trapped by its initial assumption that reference is itself the aspect of language that fixes its meaning, de Man's theory is thus driven to locate in consciousness a source for the meaning that his analysis of the structure of imagery has shown cannot be found in nature.

But the narcissism with which the present analysis has concluded is not adequate to the demands of consciousness, and thus de Man identifies the "emblem" as a further development in the project of adequation, of reconciling the demands of consciousness to the objects of its experience. For the victory consciousness achieves in discovering that the objects of its perception are in fact the mirror of its own self-reflection is now challenged by a further aspect of poetic language: its historicity. The self-reflection revealed by an analysis of reference must now confront the historically mediated aspect of the very images that were claimed to neutrally mirror self-reflection, since self-reflection itself would be impossible if the content of the reflection were itself irrevocably external. Thus, de Man identifies a movement in Yeats's poetry away from the attempt at mimetic reference and toward the usage of images that have "given up all pretense at being natural objects and have become something else. They are taken from the literary tradition and receive their meaning from traditional or personal, but not from natural associations" (RR, p. 165). De Man argues that such "emblems" (he derives the term from Yeats), precisely because their meaning has a historical or literary rather than natural derivation, can thus be seen as "determined, not by analogy with nature, but by the decrees of an independent will" (RR, p. 165). In examining this distinction between natural and literary reference, de Man goes on to argue that "the former leads to a (problematic) vision of unity that transcends the opposition between object and subject, while the latter finds unity preserved in language as the carrier of a devised, and therefore permanently repeated, pattern of experience; it postulates as an act of faith that the divine is immediately and audibly present to human consciousness in the very entity—language—that is the distinctive attribute of this consciousness" (RR, p. 172).

As one might suspect, de Man is highly suspicious that such divine presence can be sustained. In examining the conclusion of "Among School Children" ("How can we know the dancer from the dance?"), he argues that "the ways of the image and of the emblem are distinct and opposed; the final line is not a rhetorical statement of reconciliation but an anguished question; it is our perilous fate not to know if the glimpses of unity which we perceive at times can be made more permanent by natural ways or by the ascesis of renunciation, by images or by emblem" (RR, p. 202). The "ascesis of renunciation" for de Man is the abandonment of the delusion that reconciliation can involve an adequation of consciousness and nature; thus, while de Man here seems to grant an equivalence between natural and emblematic modes of fixing reconciliation (of making reconciliation permanent), his argument as a whole clearly insists that the latter is an advance on the former by acknowledging more fully the literariness of *expressions* of reconciliation. (Notice that for de Man, what is at stake is how an experience might best be represented.) What is important here is that de Man's analysis of the movement from image to emblem relies on an assumption that a literary usage of language necessarily makes reference to nature impossible and, further, that the aim of literary language is to achieve "the decree of an independent will" (RR, p. 165). While de Man is suspicious of any attempt at using language to make permanent the will's glimpses of unity, the failure of the emblem is a higher achievement because it responds more fully to what de Man assumes is an unbridgeable division between literary and referential usages of language. This is clear in the conclusion to the essay:

> The failure of the emblem amounts to total nihilism. Yeats has burned his bridges, and there is no return out of his exploded paradise of emblems back to a wasted earth. Those who look

to Yeats for reassurance from the anxieties of our own post-romantic predicament, or for relief from the paralysis of nihilism, will not find it in his conception of the emblem. He cautions instead against the danger of unwarranted hopeful solutions, and thus accomplishes all that the highest forms of language can for the moment accomplish. (RR, p. 238)

For de Man, the emblem must fail because its attempt at locating consciousness's glimpses of reconciliation in the historicity of poetic language cannot adequately account for the imperatives of the will. Poetic language is thus both the "highest form" that can be given to the relationship of consciousness and experience (it transcends the delusion that consciousness can ever experience a world of natural objects) and equally the defeat of the hope that consciousness and experience might be reconciled. For de Man, what is thus at stake in an analysis of poetic language is the capacity of such language to represent adequately the dream of reconciliation that he feels is the ultimate (though necessarily rejected) end of experience. While de Man feels that this project must fail, that it must produce a nihilistic denial that consciousness can be reconciled with anything external, he nonetheless finds a triumph in this failure, and that triumph will be the theme of his most important essays in the following ten years. But what is crucial is that throughout this period, de Man never questions (indeed he relies on) the New Critical privileging of the autonomy of poetic language and the need to use such language to express the reconciliation of discordant aspects of experience; his sole dissent is from the conclusions that might be drawn from a close analysis of these concepts.

This is clearest in his seminal essays of the 1960s, "The Intentional Structure of the Romantic Image" and "The Rhetoric of Temporality," where de Man interrogates more finely than he had earlier the claim that poetic language should be read as a reconciliation of tensions, arguing that this reconciliation can be conceived either as the delusory unity positioned by symbolic constructions or as a wiser and more authentic allegorical acceptance of the *negative* relationship between consciousness and nature. In the later instance, the reconciliation produced by poetic language is an acknowledgment of its own fictionality, an acceptance of its failure to endow nature with human meaning. But this wisdom, as de Man calls it, is importantly an act of value, an insight into the (negative) truth of existential Being, and it is his continued reliance in these essays on tacit assumptions about how poetic language can be seen to produce value and meaning that separates this work from the deconstructive essays of the 1970s.

In "The Intentional Structure of the Romantic Image," de Man challenges the attempt to construe poetic language as having an origination analogous to nature: "the natural object, safe in its immediate beginning, seems to have no beginning and no end," while "entities engendered by consciousness"—such as a poem—have "a beginning (which) implies a negation of permanence, the discontinuity of a death" (RR, p. 4). Further, while "in everyday use words are exchanged and put to a variety of tasks" and thus "are not supposed to originate anew" ("they are used as established signs to confirm that something is recognized as being the same as before"), "in poetic language words are not used as signs, not even as names, but in order to *name*" (RR, p. 3). Having defined a realm of poetic language that is distinct both from the natural world and from normal uses of language, de Man concludes that poetic language offers "a possibility for consciousness to exist entirely by and for itself, independently of all relationship with the outside world, without being moved by an intent aimed at a part of this world," and he argues that this "leaves the poetry of today under a steady threat of extinction, although, on the other hand, it remains the depository of hopes that no other activity of the mind seems able to offer" (RR, pp. 16–17). Similarly, in "The Rhetoric of Temporality," de Man argues that both allegory and irony involve a demystification of the attempt by symbolic poetic language to establish what he terms a "pseudo dialectic between subject and object" (BI2, p. 206): "Both modes are fully demystified when they remain within the realm of their respective language but are totally vulnerable to renewed blindness as soon as they leave it for the empirical world. Both are determined by an authentic experience of temporality which, seen from the point of view of the self engaged in the world, is a negative one" (BI2, p. 207).

In both of these essays, de Man assumes the possibility that poetic language, precisely because its rhetoric disrupts external referentiality, can adequately represent the *negative* relationship of consciousness to externality. Further, it is the representational adequacy of poetic language that allows de Man to conclude that his analyses reveal a "depository of hopes" of "an authentic experience of temporality"—de Man is able to discover in poetry a reconciliation of consciousness to its own delusions about the external world precisely because consciousness is not deluded about the adequacy of poetic language to represent that reconciliation. But while de Man is squarely within the New Critical tradition in assuming that the representational adequacy of poetic language is fixed by its difference from referential language (poetic language can represent consciousness because its meanings are determined by consciousness rather than the external objects that determine referential meaning), his assumption that reconciliation must itself involve a demystified severing of the relationship of consciousness to an external world (as opposed to the New Critical dream of reconciliation as the adequation of consciousness and externality) contains a propleptic anticipation of his later argument that poetic language is itself an external entity with no relationship to consciousness. For by pushing the ontological dualism he inherited as much from New Criticism as from phenomenology to its logical conclusion that the terms of the duality have no genuine interaction, de Man ensures that any analysis aimed at a recuperation of meaning is doomed to failure.

De Man's shift in emphasis from the relationship of consciousness to poetic language, to the impossibility of representation in poetic language itself, indicates clearly his refusal to settle for conclusions unwarranted by the terms of his analysis. Just as the definition of poetic language as nonreferential blocked any claim that poetic language offered a reconciliation of consciousness and *external* experience, so now the developing critique of representation itself leads to an increasing recognition that the very arguments used to deny a reference to externality in poetic language apply equally to the claim that poetic language refers to consciousness. In retrospect, the argument seems fairly obvious. If predication involves an unwarranted imposition of nonnatural qualities onto natural objects, then only an analysis of consciousness that was able to show that consciousness is itself nonnatural could ensure that predicates attached to the experience of consciousness were not as unwarranted as those attached to nature. But the unresolvable dilemma is that the attempt at offering the necessary analysis of consciousness involves a usage of language that it had been the aim of the analysis to defend. By using as part of its analysis the very terms it had been designed to analyze, the defense of consciousness as nonnatural (and thus as representable) finds itself caught in a vicious circle that finally requires the abandonment of consciousness itself. The *naming* of consciousness is as delusory as the naming of nature.

The approach I am taking to de Man here differs sharply from deconstructive accounts that seek to defend de Man by focusing primarily on the project of reading which he developed during the 1970s rather than the theoretical considerations that produced the project.[17] But the analysis of reading itself can be understood only if it is situated in the thematic context it is designed to support; the failure to consider such a context (and de Man is himself frequently guilty of this) changes the strategy of reading from a logical outgrowth of a philosophical analysis into a technique justified by its adequacy to the object it analyzes. We can see more sharply the need to consider the relationship between de Man's changing conception of literary language and the thematic defense of that conception by contrasting the reading of "Among School Children" in *Allegories of Reading* with the analysis in his dissertation at which we have already looked. In both cases, de Man insists that the concluding question be seen not as a satisfied acceptance of the impossibility of telling dancer from dance but rather as a literal question, as a demand to know. But this apparent similarity obscures the striking difference in the conclusions de Man now wants to derive from his reading. For where de Man earlier wanted to see an "ascesis of renunciation" of the hope that consciousness and externality might be reconciled, he now insists that the "rhetorical" meaning of the question (an insistence on "the potential unity of form and experience") is in fundamental conflict with its "literal meaning": "It is equally possible, however, to read the last line literally rather than figuratively, as asking with some urgency the question . . . *not* that sign and referent are so exquisitely fitted to each other that all difference beween them is at times blotted out, but, rather, since the two essentially different elements, sign and meaning, are so intricately intertwined in the imagined 'presence' that the poem addresses, how can we possibly make the distinctions that would shelter us from the error of identifying what cannot be identified?"[18] Thus, despite the apparent similarity in the two interpretations, de Man's later position would be forced to argue that the earlier hope for an "ascesis of renunciation" itself depended on an overly easy distinction between literal and rhetorical (one can say that the hopes of the rhetorical have been renounced only if the rhetorical itself can be properly delimited) which he no longer finds tenable. Now de Man wants to argue that analysis shows the distinction itself to be impossible:

> [T]wo entirely coherent but entirely incompatible readings can be made to hinge on one line, whose grammatical structure is devoid of ambiguity, but whose rhetorical mode turns the mood as well as the mode of the entire poem upside down. Neither can we say, as was already the case in the first example, that the poem simply has two meanings that exist side by side. The two readings have to engage each other in direct confrontation, for the one reading is precisely the error denounced by the other and has to be undone by it. Nor can we in any way make a valid decision as to which of the readings can be given priority over the other; none can exist in the other's absence. There can be no dance without a dancer, no sign without a referent. On the other hand, the authority of the

> meaning engendered by the grammatical structure is fully ob-
> scured by the duplicity of a figure that cries out for the differ-
> entiation that it conceals. (AR, p. 12)

As we have seen, de Man's earlier criticism had held out the hope
that figural language might adequately represent the need of consciousness to exist independently of external determinations. But
this hope that such a realm of autonomy might adequately be fixed
by figural language now collapses in de Man's realization that the
very terms by which one might describe a realm of figural language
are determined by a grammatical realism that it had been the aim of
figural language to deny. The consequence is that the representation
of an authentically autonomous self is now seen as a delusory
dream; the analysis of figural language confirms only the impossibility of representation itself.

This insistence on the interpretive aporia that results from a
distinction between literal and figural meaning provides the unifying focus of the essays collected in *Allegories of Reading*. In discussing *Julie*, de Man argues that "any reading always involves a choice
between signification and symbolization, and this choice can be
made only if one postulates the possibility of distinguishing the literal from the figural" (AR, p. 201). But this choice is contaminated
by the necessity of relying, in making the distinction, on the very
realms a naive reading would have assumed are already distinct:
the literal defines the figural, and the figural defines the literal. As
de Man argues, "the situation implies that figural discourse is always understood in contradistinction to a form of discourse that
would not be figural" (AR, p. 201). In an analysis of Nietzsche, de
Man is clear about the consequences of this dilemma for any attempt at delimiting a realm of language that might adequately represent the self: "the idea of individuation, of the human subject as a
privileged viewpoint, is a mere metaphor by means of which man
protects himself from his insignificance by forcing his own interpretation of the world upon the entire universe. . . . The attributes of
centrality and of selfhood are being exchanged in the medium of
the language. Making the language that denies the self into a center
rescues the self linguistically at the same time that it asserts its insignificance, its emptiness as a mere figure of speech. It can only
persist as self if it is displaced into the text that denies it" (AR, pp.
11–12). The paradox to which de Man points is that the nature of
figural language denies the very hope its initial identification as an
autonomous realm has been designed to secure.

There is thus a decided shift in de Man's work in the 1970s
from his earlier analysis of the phenomenology of being to an em-

phasis on the contradictions that emerge from an analysis of the realm of language—the figural—that had been earlier assumed to unmediatedly represent that being. But it would be a mistake to conclude that de Man's concerns have changed in any fundamental way, that he has moved from the attempt to find in a certain kind of language the confirmation of a phenomenological project to a focus on the nature of language itself. Rather, de Man's shifting view of language is necessitated by the very failure of the phenomenological project itself: the increasing attention to language in itself comes about not because of an arbitrary shift in commitment but rather because of an increasing recognition of the impossibility of identifying a specialized realm of language that might secure for consciousness its dream of autonomy. Thus, de Man's insistence on the mutually contradictory realms of the rhetorical and the literal can be understood finally only by examining the phenomenological consequences of this insistence. De Man's position changes not because of a greater understanding of language in itself but rather because he realizes that figural language cannot confirm the phenomenological project of an autonomous consciousness that he had assumed throughout his work is the telos of literary analysis. More important, because de Man never abandons his belief that figural language offers the best chance for representing an authentically autonomous consciousness, his realization that the hopes he had rested in figural language are delusory inevitably produces the phenomenological conclusions we will look at now.

In the essay on *The Triumph of Life* which he contributed to *Deconstruction and Criticism*, de Man offers perhaps his most direct statement of the phenomenological consequences of the deconstructive analysis of language. There, he focuses on Shelley's attempt at finding in Rousseau a confirmation of the power of language to posit an ontologically adequate realm of temporal experience. De Man argues that the arbitrariness and intrusivenes of language make such adequation impossible: "The positing power of language is both entirely arbitrary, in having a strength that cannot be reduced to necessity, and entirely inexorable, in that there is no alternative to it" (RR, p. 116). Here, de Man moves decisively beyond the phenomenological hope, best exemplified by Heidegger's reading of Nietzsche, that a recognition of the intrusive nature of human consciousness, a self-conscious overcoming of consciousness, might allow a reconciled acceptance of being-in-itself.[19] Instead, de Man's argument is that our very awareness of nature, and finally of our own existence, is contaminated in an absolute way by the very language that makes possible that awareness. Our representations of experience are "punctured by acts that cannot be made a part of it" (RR, p. 117). But this arbitrariness of language is both inescapable and inexorably understood: in representing, for example, the relationship of the stars and the sun, we are made aware both that the appearance of the sun is only retrospectively understood as part of a temporal sequence of events, as a part of "a dialectical relationship between day and night, or between two transcendental orders of being" (RR, p. 117), and equally that the inevitability of such retrospection must blind us to a more ontologically frightening knowledge which we also cannot escape: "the sun does not appear in conjunction with or in reaction to the night and the stars, but of its own unrelated power" (RR, p. 117). What de Man wants to show here is that language grips us in the power of a necessity of representation which is both inescapable and yet which we know to be false: language serves here as a purely arbitrary intrusion between consciousness and world, and thus the realms of value and facticity, far from emerging unscathed from their putative origins, are in fact rendered meaningless through their mediation in language. The "unrelated power" that de Man here ascribes to the sun might seem to contradict this general assertion of indeterminacy, but de Man's argument would surely be that "power" is itself a trope produced by the representational inevitability of language, and as such is reducible neither to an empirical world that might anchor its status as a fact nor to a consciousness that might proclaim its value. The knowledge produced by our analysis of language is purely negative: it is a knowledge of the impossibility of knowing.

The obvious question is how such knowledge is possible, and for de Man the answer is found in our attempts to come to terms with death or, more precisely, in our awareness of the inadequacy of our attempts to represent death. Thus, in analyzing Shelley's attempt at finding in the dead Rousseau a monument to life, de Man identifies a threat to representation that culminates in a crisis of reading: "to read is to understand, to question, to know, to forget, to erase, to deface, to repeat—that is to say, the endless prosopoeia by which the dead are made to have a face and a voice which tells the allegory of their demise and allows us to apostrophize them in our turn" (RR, p. 122). Our very awareness of death requires a recognition of the arbitrariness of representation, since the very terms by which we represent death are contaminated by their denial of death, by their construal of the dead as somehow alive. Further, de Man cautions explicitly against the Heideggerian hope (which had been his own hope in his earlier work) that this negative insight might somehow provide a sustaining knowledge: "No degree of knowledge can ever stop this madness, for it is the madness of words. What *would* be naive is to believe that this strategy, which is not *our* strategy as subjects, since we are its product rather than its agent, can be a source of value and has to be celebrated or denounced accordingly" (RR, p. 122). Instead, for de Man, the analysis of death culminates in pure nihilism: "nothing, whether deed, word, thought, or text, ever happens in relation, positive or negative, to anything that precedes, follows, or exists elsewhere, but only as a random event whose power, like the power of death, is due to the randomness of its occurrence" (RR, p. 122).[20]

The difficulty of knowing how to respond to a claim such as this is exhibited by an oddly defensive discussion of Jonathan Culler. According to Culler, de Man's concern with "truth and knowledge" here protect him (and, by implication, deconstruction) from the attack that deconstruction relies on an easy denial of truth, and later Culler ridicules what he calls the "rumors" that deconstruction "eliminates meaning and referentiality."[21] But the clear thrust of de Man's argument *is* to eliminate meaning, and for reasons that are precise and coherent. Perhaps Culler was misled by de Man's own denial that his position is nihilistic (RR, p. 122), for what Culler assumes is that a "commitment to the truth of the text when exhaustively read" (p. 280) protects deconstruction from the charge of a nihilistic denial of meaning. But de Man's position is more subtle, and more unnerving, than this. Having assumed from the beginning of his career that truth must itself be autonomous, and having accepted further that it is the self that must serve as the ground of the autonomy of truth, de Man culminates in a recognition that it is solely by virtue of its death that the autonomy of the self can be preserved. Further, the nihilistic denial of any relation is logically congruent with the insistence on autonomy as the necessary ground of truth: if death confirms the possibility of autonomy, and thus reveals truth, then its random denial of relation makes it impossible to sustain any description of meaning or truth predicated upon relation. Finally, because language is itself ontologically implicated in a plurality of determinations, in an endlessly proliferating web of relations, it must prove inadequate to the randomness and solitariness of death, and it is further such inadequacy that will expose the ultimate failure of language. It is only in death that de Man discovers both the ultimate fate and the triumph of autonomy, for it is only in death that we can be said to exist autonomously.

In an essay he apparently wrote near the end of his own life, de Man returns to the issue (which he had first raised in his analysis of formalist criticism) of how history relates to literary language, setting the discussion in an eerily appropriate context of mourning. For what de Man never ceases to realize is that his analysis of the ultimate privacy of experience requires some acknowledgment of those aspects of experience that are not private. He contrasts a deluded form of mourning which desires a "consciousness of eternity and of temporal harmony" with more genuine mourning which can "allow for non-comprehension and enumerate non-anthropomorphic, non-elegiac, non-celebratory, non-lyrical, non-poetic, that is to say prosaic, or, better, *historical* modes of language power" (RR, p. 262). What our experience of history should teach us, de Man seems to be saying, is a mournful refusal to impose on our experience those assertions of the self—the anthropomorphic and so on—which must involve a denial of relation that cannot be sustained. A clearer sense of the *prosaic* quality of history, its insistence on treating us as referentially related rather than lyrically autonomous (lyric autonomy is, of course, for de Man now itself exposed as relational), can be found in de Man's claim that Rousseau's hopes for political amelioration are less significant than his analysis of political identity itself:

> What the *Discourse on Inequality* tells us, and what the classical interpretation of Rousseau has stubbornly refused to hear, is that the political destiny of man is structured like and derived from a linguistic model that exists independently of nature and independently of the subject: it coincides with the blind metaphorization called "passion," and this metaphorization is not an intentional act. . . . If society and government derive from a tension between man and his language, then they are not natural (depending on a relationship among men), nor theological, since language is not conceived as a transcendental principle but as the possibility of contingent error. The political thus becomes a burden for man rather than an opportunity. (RR, pp. 156–57)

It is important to note here that this "burden" is the result not of contingent aspects of particular political institutions but rather of "political destiny" itself. Further, although de Man refers to an ethical realm treating the "relationship among men" as distinct from the political, his understanding of the political itself refers not merely to the positive institutions by which the state maintains its power but more generally to the complex relational structures that constitute any community. Given the constraints his own analysis of the illusion of relation would place on him, it's difficult to imagine how de Man could describe an ethical realm that differs from his description of the political. Indeed, de Man states quite explicitly that his focus is "the considerable ambivalence that burdens a theoretical discourse dealing with man's relation to man" (RR, p. 157).

If we add to the present discussion de Man's earlier claim that from the perspective of death, relations are themselves delusions that must be abandoned, we are now in a position to see the ultimate conclusions to which de Man's position leads. Having identified language as the repository of the hope for experiential reconciliation, while insisting at the same time that the nature of language makes such hope a delusion, de Man is forced to conclude that those aspects of experience that are "structured like and derived from a linguistic model" (and death is the sole aspect of experience for which this cannot be said) must be accepted as a burden. Uncompromisingly committed to the principle of autonomy, de Man ends in a mournful acceptance of the burden of community and an ascetic insistence that truth is to be found only in death.

4

In books that have little else in common, Jonathan Culler and Eugene Goodheart have each argued that the signal quality of contemporary literary theory is its skeptical denial of the authority of rules, of the possibility of finding a determinant ground for our actions.[22] Culler attacks Charles Altieri's Wittgensteinian attempt at showing that rules are embedded in the very actions that are their manifestation, arguing that while it is true that "we have experience of determining and grasping meanings," it is mistaken "to treat this experience as if it were a ground for the philosophical refutation of scepticism." The reason such an argument is mistaken is because a "redescription will alter rules or place an utterance in a different language game," and thus the attempt at seeing rules as immanent in practices cannot account for the proliferating and indeterminant nature of practices themselves (p. 140). The implication is that the sole possible response to skepticism is to establish determinant rules that cannot be challenged by the practices they constitute. Goodheart accepts that this is the skeptical challenge and tries to meet it by arguing that proliferating contingencies are themselves an aspect of determinant meaning: "Uncertainty or skepticism need not be the perspective from which we view all the seasons of our lives or the texts that occupy our lives. What is missing from the radically skeptical view of privilege is a historical sense of the conditions under which certain views emerge and are felt to have authority, including the skeptical view" (p. 178). While they disagree about the success of the skeptical critique, Culler and Goodheart are united in their belief that a successful challenge to skepticism involves a demonstration that skepticism is itself logically impossible.

This argument may seem initially to parallel the positions we have been examining. As we have seen, de Man's work proceeds out of an assumption that the success of our criteria for explaining our shared construal of the external world (the success of the empiricist account of referential language) requires the articulation of equally successful criteria if we are to explain our shared construal of experience. But in trying to ground such criteria in the assumption that experience must be conceived as autonomous, he ends in the skeptical conclusion that criteria for construing experience must fail. He argues that the best we can do is mournfully accept the prosaic determinations of our experience while insisting as well on the ultimate failure of those determinations, on the essential privacy of experience. It is this skeptical acceptance of the very criteria whose truth has been denied by the analysis of experience that is missing in both Goodheart's and Culler's descriptions of skepticism. De Man refuses to deny that our experience of the world is importantly marked by assumptions about shared experience; rather, his argument is that an examination of the best case he believes can be made for why shared experience is possible (the argument that shared experience is possible because it emerges out of a realm of experiential autonomy which is the defining characteristic of being human) must fail to account for the essential privacy and nonrelatedness of experience in itself.

The point here is that de Man's skepticism does not challenge the existence of what Wittgenstein called shared forms of life, but rather the adequacy of our attempts to explain *why* we participate in these forms. As Sal Kripke has argued, the most unsettling aspect of Wittgenstein's critique of the appeal to criteria as the ground of our knowledge is the perfectly plausible possibility that what we agree to account as shared knowledge has been arrived at through innumerably different and contradictory explanatory criteria.[23] While Kripke's focus is narrow—he wants to show that our agreement about the simplest mathematical operations masks the logical possibility that we have arrived at that agreement through radically different and incommensurable rules—his insistence that rules or criteria are themselves ultimately private (they cannot be derived from public practices) is precisely the claim that de Man wants to make about experience. Thus, when Kripke argues that agreement about as simple a mathematical function as $2 + 2 = 4$ cannot account for the possibility that in arriving at the correct answer you were relying on a standard "plus function," while I was relying on a nonstandard "quus function," he is close to de Man's belief that the terms of the relation are themselves described by the relation. To use Kripke's terms, de Man's position is that analysis of as simple a relational statement as "I love you" would reveal the possibility that the two agents denoted by the statement are, in their very agreement about the meaning of the statement, engaged in logically contradictory activities—that one is "plusing" while the other is "quusing." Kripke's point (and it is one that de Man would agree with) is that nothing about private experience (intention, say, or emotional attitudes) can either be deduced *from* the contexts or rules determining shared activities or be used to help explain such activities.

In insisting that shared experience is an inescapable fact of human existence, and is equally at best irrelevant to and at worst destructive of the private contingencies of individual experience, de Man is curiously close to Hobbes's insistence that political union is the necessary public shield against private brutality. Like de Man, Hobbes sees in language the vehicle of a shared perception that is both the defining characteristic of human community and the defense of such community against the capriciousness of private perception. Here, for example, is Hobbes's attempt to derive from the origin of language the foundation of human community: "But the most noble and profitable invention of all other, was that of SPEECH, consisting of *names* or *appellations*, and their connexion; whereby men register their thoughts, recall them when they are past, and also declare them to one another for mutual utility and conversation."[24] But this apparent tranquility about the power of language to give a publicly shared order, an enduring relational coherence, to experience is challenged by Hobbes's later insistence that individual experience poses a continual threat to public order: "I put for a general inclination of all mankind, a perpetual and restless desire of power after power, that ceaseth only in Death" (p. 161). Here we can see that the community Hobbes finds confirmed in the relational possibilities of language gains its authority because of its negative relationship to individual experience: the private drive for power that determines individual experience is defeated by publicly shared institutions that perpetuate community at the expense of individual need. Like de Man, Hobbes sees political institutions as an inescapable but necessary burden.

What this linkage of de Man and Hobbes allows us to see is that the focus of a genuine skeptical critique is not on the logical failure of criteria but rather on the *representational* failure of public institutions that those criteria are designed to explain. De Man's denial of public experience is thus a denial that the available models of such experience can be said to represent adequately the dimensions of private experience to which they are claimed to be related. We can contrast the resulting belief that public experience is a burden to be endured with Hegel's belief that public modes of ordering experience entail an obligation of adherence precisely because they embody the moral content of the individual.[25] As Sabina Lovibond puts it, "such obligation emanates from an 'ethical order with a stable content independently necessary and subsistent in exaltation above subjective opinion and caprice'—an order whose 'moments are the ethical powers which regulate the life of individuals.'"[26] This relationship of the individual to the ethical community gains its authority because the individual both perpetuates the community and discovers itself within the community, by maintaining an obligation to active participation. What de Man wants to argue is that this relationship to community must inevitably fail because of the representational inadequacy of the available terms for self-discovery.

In *The Claim of Reason*, Stanley Cavell argues that the consequence of what he calls the "skeptical recital" of the impossibility of having certainty about the experience of others is tragedy: "both skepticism and tragedy conclude with the condition of human separation, with a discovering that I am I; and the fact that the alternative to my acknowledgment of the other is not my ignorance of him but my avoidance of him, call it my denial of him."[27] But while the traditional approach to tragedy focuses on the role that the failure of moral agency plays in producing separation, Cavell instead shifts the focus to how separation is produced by the failure of what should be structures of social inclusion: "suppose that there is a mode of tragedy in which what we witness is the subjection of the human being to states of violation, a perception that not merely human law but nature itself can be abrogated. The outcast is a figure of pity and horror; different from ourselves, and not different" (p. 419). What the skeptical critique insists is that the inclusionary failure of public structures is an abrogation of, a denial of, our construal of the human. It is thus simply too easy to claim either that skepticism is itself merely a denial of the authority of rules or that an adequate response to skepticism is to show the impossibility of denying the very rules that are being denied. The skeptic is denying (tragically) the pull of objectivity, the claim of any externality on his existence, and he is doing so because he cannot *see* himself in any of the available external models. Further, in denying that such seeing is possible, the skeptical retreat into privacy robs us of our certainty that we are in turn being allowed to see, and it is here that Cavell understands tragedy as turning in on itself, as moving from the triumph of exclusion to the failure of inclusion.[28] One version of such a failure is produced by de Man's exposure of the aporias that mark the attempt to find in autonomous experience as stable an ontological foundation for human community as that which external reality is presumed to offer for empirical knowledge; beginning in the attempt to find in autonomous experience the *reality* of human existence, de Man's project ends in a denial that reality allows any confidence that the relational structures necessary for construing the human can be sustained. With regard to the tradition he is deconstructing, de Man is finally quite literally correct: *in reality*, there is no relation. The only response possible to his skepticism is to show that somewhere else, there is.

Notes

1. In an unpublished essay, "Reading de Manians Reading de Man," Reed Way Dasenbrock has demonstrated how those who seek to separate de Man's later work from the wartime journalism rely on notions of periodization which de Man himself would have rejected.

2. For defenses of de Man, see the essays collected in Lindsay Waters and Wlad Godzich, eds., *Reading de Man Reading* (Minneapolis: University of Minnesota Press, 1989); and Werner Hamacher, Neil Hertz, and Thomas Keenan, eds., *Responses: On Paul de Man's Wartime Journalism* (Lincoln: University of Nebraska Press, 1989). Although largely ignored or dismissed by literary theorists, David Lehman's *Signs of the Times: Deconstruction and the Fall of Paul de Man* (New York: Poseidon Press, 1991) is the most carefully researched and cogently argued attack on de Man's work that has yet appeared.

3. In a deliberate echo of de Man, Derrida asks, "Is it possible when one is in memory of the other, in bereaved memory of a friend, is it desirable to think of and to pass beyond this hallucination, beyond a prosopopeia of prosopopeia?" *Memoires for Paul de Man*, trans. Cecile Lindsay, Jonathan Culler, and Eduardo Cadava (New York: Columbia University Press, 1986), p. 28.

4. Shoshana Felman, "Postal Survival, or the Question of the Navel," *Yale French Studies* 69 (1985): 50.

5. Barbara Johnson, "Rigorous Unreliability," *Yale French Studies* 69 (1985): 80.

6. See especially the tributes of J. Hillis Miller, Geoffrey Hartman, and A. Bartlett Giamatti in "In Memoriam," *Yale French Studies* 69 (1985): 3–21.

7. The debate about the political implications of deconstruction is enormous, and largely amorphous. Within this debate, defenses of de Man have taken two forms: either it is asserted that critics of de Man simply do not understand what he is saying, or it is asserted that the implications of his thought are more subversive than has generally been recognized. For an example of the first defense, see Daniel T. O'Hara, *The Romance of Interpretation: Visionary Criticism from Pater to de Man* (New York: Columbia University Press, 1985), pp. 205–35. For examples of the second defense, see Dominick La Capra, *History and Criticism* (Ithaca: Cornell University Press, 1985), pp. 104–5; and Samuel Weber, *Institution and Interpretation* (Minneapolis: University of Minnesota Press, 1987), pp. 150–51. Wlad Godzich has combined the two approaches in his Afterword to *Institution and Criticism*, p. 155, and in "Foreword: The Tiger on the Paper Mat," in Paul de Man, *The Resistance to Theory* (Minneapolis: University of Minnesota Press, 1986), pp. ix–xviii (hereafter cited as RT). While there have been numerous criticisms of de Man's politics, there has been little or no attempt at showing the derivation of his political positions from his assumptions about language. For example, Jonathan Arac in his recent book, *Critical Genealogies: Historical Studies for Postmodern Literary Studies* (New York: Columbia University Press, 1987), criticizes de Man for ignoring "human relationships," argu-

ing that "these are the elements, no less than the figures, from which to construct a history of the contingencies that have put us in the odd place that we are" (p. 253). But Arac seems unwilling to criticize the premises about language and indeterminacy that have produced the conclusions from which he dissents. Other criticisms of de Man include Gerald Graff, *Literature Against Itself* (Chicago: University of Chicago Press, 1979); Edward Said, *The World, the Text, and the Critic* (Cambridge: Harvard University Press, 1983); and Frank Lentricchia, *Criticism and Social Change* (Chicago: University of Chicago Press, 1983). There is an excellent overview of the general dispute about poststructuralism and politics in Jonathan Arac's Introduction to *Postmodernism and Politics*, ed. Jonathan Arac (Minneapolis: University of Minnesota Press, 1986), pp. ix–xliii.

8. Paul Bové, "Variations on Authority," in *The Yale Critics: Deconstruction in America*, ed. Jonathan Arac, Wlad Godzich, and Wallace Martin (Minneapolis: University of Minnesota Press, 1983), pp. 16–17.

9. Wallace Martin, Introduction, in *The Yale Critics*, p. xxxii.

10. As Rudolf Gasché has argued, it is important to distinguish between deconstruction as a literary project and deconstruction as a philosophical project. In what follows, my focus is clearly on the literary uses that have been made of deconstruction, although *contra* Gasche, I would want to argue that a similar political critique could be made of deconstruction in its purely philosophical modes. See Rudolf Gasché, *The Tain of the Mirror: Derrida and the Philosophy of Reflection* (New York: Cambridge University Press, 1986), ff. 255–70; and "Deconstruction as Criticism," *Glyph* 9 (1979): 177–215.

11. See John Crowe Ransom, *The New Criticism* (Norfolk, Conn.: New Directions, 1941), pp. 281–91.

12. See Cleanth Brooks, *Modern Poetry and the Tradition* (Chapel Hill: University of North Carolina Press, 1939), p. 175; and *The Well Wrought Urn* (New York: Reynal and Hitchcock, 1947), p. 232.

13. Paul de Man, "The Dead-end of Formalist Criticism," in *Blindness and Insight: Essays in the Rhetoric of Contemporary Criticism*, 2nd ed., ed. Wlad Godzich (Minneapolis: University of Minnesota Press, 1983), p. 232 (hereafter cited as BI2).

14. Paul de Man, *Blindness and Insight: Essays in the Rhetoric of Contemporary Criticism* (New York: Oxford University Press, 1971), p. 24 (hereafter cited as BI).

15. Quoted in *Yale Critics*, p. 106.

16. Paul de Man, *The Rhetoric of Romanticism* (New York: Columbia University Press, 1984), p. 164 (hereafter cited as RR).

17. See, for example, Stanley Corngold, "Error in Paul de Man," in *The Yale Critics*, pp. 90–108.

18. Paul de Man, *Allegories of Reading: Figural Reading in Rousseau, Nietzsche, Rilke, and Proust* (New Haven: Yale University Press, 1979), p. 11 (hereafter cited as AR).

19. See, for example, Martin Heidegger, *Nietzsche*, 4 vols., *The Will to Power as Art*, vol. 1, trans. David Farrell Krell (San Francisco: Harper and Row, 1979), pp. 34–53.

20. These passages have become something of a crux for commentary on de Man. The best available discussion is Jonathan Arac, to Regress from the Rigor of Shelley: Figures of History in American Deconstructive Criticism," *Boundary 2* (Spring 1980): 280.

21. Jonathan Culler, *On Deconstruction: Theory and Criticism after Structuralism* (Ithaca: Cornell University Press, 1982), p. 280.

22. See Culler, *On Deconstruction*; and Eugene Goodhart, *The Skeptic Disposition in Contemporary Criticism* (Princeton: Princeton University Press, 1984).

23. See Saul Kripke, *Wittgenstein on Rules and Private Language* (Cambridge: Harvard University Press, 1982). A similar argument is made by Norman Bryson, *Vision and Painting: The Logic of the Gaze* (New Haven: Yale Univesitiy Press, 1983), pp. 40–41.

24. Thomas Hobbs, *Leviathan*, ed. C. B. Macpherson (London: Penguin Books, 1968), p. 100. There is a superb analysis of Hobbes's relation to contemporary arguments about the legitimization of political and social analysis in Anthony J. Cascardi, *The Subject of Modernity* (Cambridge: Cambridge University Press, 1992), pp. 179–227.

25. See Charles Altieri, *Act and Quality: A Theory of Literary Meaning and Humanistic Understanding* (Amherst: University of Massachusetts Press, 1981), pp. 308–31, for a powerful attempt at using Hegel's understanding of *Geist* to construct a model of literary value. It is indicative of the topsy-turvy politics of contemporary criticism that Altieri's heterodox position on literary meaning is frequently labeled elitist by poststructuralist orthodoxy. See, for example, Paul Bové's review of *Act and Quality* in *Contemporary Literature* 24 (1983): 379–86.

26. Sabina Lovibond, *Realism and Imagination in Ethics* (Minneapolis: University of Minnesota Press, 1983), p. 64.

27. Stanley Cavell, *The Claim of Reason* (New York: Oxford University Press, 1982), p. 383.

28. Cavell develops this idea in "Knowing and Acknowledging," in *Must We Mean What We Say?* (London: Cambridge University Press, 1976), pp. 238–66. For a similar analysis of how Cavell's analysis of skepticism might be applied to de Man, see Michael Fischer, *Stanley Cavell and Literary Skepticism* (Chicago: University of Chicago Press, 1989), pp. 80–102.

In the Name of Theory

Sharon Willis

Feminism has no interior. That is, it has no fixed, permanent, or clearly bounded inside. Fractured by struggles over its own meanings and its limits, this is a terrain continually transformed and reshaped by its compelling political and theoretical alliances. For many of us, feminism is permanent turbulence.[1] And recently, the most intense turbulence has arisen in response to the challenge of identity politics and, on the more narrowly academic plane where its formal theoretical production takes place, in the dialogue that connects feminist theory to cultural studies.

While the identity politics that has sustained the most powerful political critiques of dominant feminism explicitly raises the issue of a "feminist identity," the question of identity also emerges implicitly when we consider the work of a growing number of male critics in gay studies as well as cultural studies. Now, because a feminist *identity* could have no fixed content, could never be anything but strategic and provisional, we will do better to think in terms of a feminist *identification*, a process rather than a state. However, despite its imaginary nature, feminist identity seems to be more and more the subterranean stake of our ongoing debates about the status of both theory and experience, those large, amorphous categories that we often set up as antagonists struggling around a phantasmatic borderline within feminism.

Speaking in the name of a politics of experience, in her provocative *Feminism without Women* (Routledge, 1991), Tania Modleski has suggested that in its eagerness to liberate sexuality from the defiles of gender, to de-essentialize the subject of feminism, feminist theory is racing headlong into a postfeminism that bypasses the central organizing category of gender. And as feminist theory takes its distance from gender and real women's experience, Modleski argues, it entertains an increasing, and well-rewarded, fascination with masculinity—in both theory and popular culture—

as well as a tolerance for "men in feminism." According to Modleski, then, we may well be "presiding over our own marginalization" (p. 98) and actually abetting masculine appropriations of feminist political gains.

Modleski's contentious book is powerfully useful, since while it aims to provide an analytical account of the state of feminist theory, its underlying structures embody many of the contradictions of current feminist theoretical positions. *Feminism without Women* pointedly figures the political contests that structure current debates as conflicts around borderlines—internal boundaries between white, heterosexual, middle-class feminism and the feminisms of working-class women, lesbians, and women of color, and external boundaries between feminists and their male allies. And while they are frequently articulated in terms of "insides" and "outsides," these feminist conflicts also seem to be organized by figures that relate "being" to "having." So theory and experience are treated, perhaps unconsciously, as something that one *has* rather than something one *does*. At the same time, increasingly in recent debates, we link our identities as feminists to our positions on theory, and to the status we give to our experience.[2]

If *Feminism without Women* is exemplary for its documentation of theory-experience conflicts, in its struggle to confront and work through feminism's relation to identity politics, it invites us to scrutinize the means by which Euro-American feminists attempt to respond to the critical work of African-American theorists. In her provocative opening chapter, "Postmortem on Postfeminism," Modleski critically analyzes what she considers to be the irresponsible political use to which Sojourner Truth's famous question "Ain't I a woman?" is put by another feminist critic, Denise Riley. Modleski contends, quite properly, I think, that in her effort to make Truth a spokesperson for anti-essentialism, on the basis of her "double jeopardy" as a black woman, Riley engages in a dangerous dehistoricization and dematerialization.[3] On the other hand, Modleski's account itself has an unfortunate corollary effect: even as it criticizes Riley for ventriloquizing Truth, constructing Truth as a figure through whom she may speak, Modleski's critique ends up having to restage truth's reduction to a figure, albeit with a more progressive political aim in mind.[4]

As Deborah MacDowell has recently pointed out, this kind of effect is a common and symptomatic occurrence in recent Euro-American feminist theory.[5] All too often, as we are all too painfully aware, Euro-American feminism confronts racial difference in terms of embodiment—where theoretical accounts look to African-American women to embody racial difference or to account for the meanings of "race"—or in terms of borders, in theoretical accounts that hear African-American women's voices as coming from "outside" feminism, or as speaking across an internal division that the very speaking establishes.[6]

In this context, it seems, what we see more and more are debates that imagine a politics of identity confronting a politics of difference in a chiasmatic structure where advocates of identity politics very often get treated as the figures of difference within mainstream, white, heterosexual feminism. This is certainly not a deliberate and willful effect. And precisely because it is not, it is worth investigating the underlying structures that may help to facilitate repetitions rather than workings through within the context of feminist theory and practice as it concerns the politics of difference. Moreover, such repetitions only shore up the status of certain forms of feminism as the privileged interlocutor of the dominant cultural order, at the expense, direct and indirect, of other feminisms, oppositional feminisms, often constructed by that feminism, as by the dominant order, as "native informant" speakers who have authority only over a certain limited domain, a domain limited precisely by the speaker's experiential and embodied relationship to social realities. In this respect, heterosexual feminism's response to the challenges of lesbian identity politics resembles its response to African-American feminist criticisms.[7] And if these effects are largely symptomatic, then it is well worth interrogating the unconscious structures of identification that underlie our ideas about identity and may underpin our theoretical positions.

Psychoanalysis has been one site where the question of theorizing difference has become particularly heated. At the same time, in a variety of recent debates, psychoanalysis has figured as a border sentinel, alternately rigid, marking as it does a particularly visible site of feminist theorizing, and remiss, since it opens onto a terrain shared by a wide variety of theorists "beyond the borders of feminism."[8] I want to explore why it is that, from its "outside," psychoanalytically based feminist theory is considered unwilling and unable to study the interactions of sexual difference with differences of race, class, and sexuality. In fact, psychoanalysis is often figured as steadfastly antipolitical, or at least as steadfastly resistant to political action; in short, as a depoliticizing and dehistoricizing discourse. This view fascinates me, because it constructs psychoanalysis to look like the unconscious, which *does* offer resistance to politics. Consequently, it attributes to psychoanalysis itself the very features of its object of study.

On the other hand, I want to consider why it is that, from its "inside," psychoanalytic theory continues to claim that other differences are fully accessible to its analysis but to leave that work as a future horizon. No doubt, any examination of this problem needs to begin by asking how the inside and the outside have emerged here. But, further, we need to ask how psychoanalysis and the social have come to be constructed as such rigidly separated spheres, the one apparently organized around sexual difference, the other either a kind of catchall space, not to say a dumping ground, for all those other differences, the place where it is left to someone else to assess the "difference they make."

A common feminist criticism of psychoanalysis argues that its use of the term *sexual difference* is itself asocial and dehistoricizing. As Constance Penley has pointed out, the effort to replace *sexual difference* with the notion of gender, taking this latter as the more "social" expression, ignores the incommensurability of these two terms in the interests of finding a "new totalizing theory of difference." She contends that we may desire this kind of theory in order not to have to "shift levels of analysis in order to account for the entire range of differences: they are now all to be seen as historically determined social differences and therefore answerable to the methods of empiricism and behaviorism."[9]

As Penley suggests, this position effectively reduces sexual difference to a representation of the psychic and reduces gender to a representation of the social. Such reductions are part of a drive to produce a theory capable of respecting and accounting for all differences in the same register, and with the same tools—those of empiricism. At the same time, however, we need to acknowledge that differences other than the sexual one are equally unruly, equally psychically saturated, and therefore demand the kind of treatment we give to the complexities of sexual difference in both psychic and social representation.

From the beginning, sexual difference is inscribed within linguistic and family structures that are embedded in social differences. These are not simply mapped on later. Unless we maintain that sexual difference is always already social, we risk allowing the category of the psychic to obscure political and social conflict by enclosing it within a false "interior." In order to transform psychoanalytic feminist work on sexual difference in the direction of understanding its broadest social articulations, we need to redefine *priority*, to conceive these problems in terms of a different temporality, so that we do not mistake one sense of priority for another. That is, the historical priorness of sexual difference in subject formation cannot be taken to be a permanent priority. While sexual difference is always at work, it is not constructed once and for all; rather, it is continually reconstructed in a social world.

The tendency to make sexual difference the primary and privileged difference against which all others are measured and around which they are mapped often leads to the now familiar litany of feminist political correctness: "sexual difference" or "gender," and "race, class, ethnicity, sexuality, etc." A rhetorical structure that lines up differences in a series, seemingly open to infinity, renders all differences equal and interchangeable and forecloses any need to take account of their interaction. To imagine or arrange differences in this manner depends on the theoretical and political error of metaphorizing all of these registers, producing false analogies, in order to articulate them all together.

In certain contradictory yet significant ways, feminist discourses that grant priority to sexual difference abet the interests of the dominant cultural order which would prefer to confront the problem of difference at consolidated, punctual sites. This strategy can deal with the perceived demands of white, middle-class, heterosexual feminism at the expense of all other contesting and oppositional positions. By studying how the subject is formed in view of the difference between masculinity and femininity, such feminist theory also has made *that* difference the "truth" of sexuality—giving us a heterosexual couple, which forecloses consideration of the differences between homosexuality and heterosexuality and the ways they may inflect sexual difference itself. Constructed this way, "sexual difference" permits "sexuality" to stand for heterosexuality and sees race, class, and ethnicity as attributes that collide with or interfere with sexuality. But this does not allow for the intersections in which these registers of identity are reciprocally structuring, in which they are neither separable nor entirely coincident and noncontradictory. Thus, we need to get over the idea of an originary moment, not to deny it, but to place it back in relation with all our other moments.

However, the drive toward a general theory of difference also emerges out of very animated conflicts, both local and generally theoretical, that look like a search for the "key" difference that will organize all the others. This tendency testifies to an urge to keep categories pure and separate so that political priorities can be clear. But such categorical purity can only end up maintaining strict analogies through which one may substitute one category of difference for another, leaving little room for specificity, overdetermination, and antagonism. This seems to be the main difficulty attending extreme forms of identity politics, which often articulate a powerful underlying drive to keep other social differences separate from the sexual one, as if sexuality were a contamination that came from the "outside." Some of feminist psychoanalytic theory's insistence on sexuality, then, contests precisely this desire to erase or set aside the sexual as too complicated, as a sort of Trojan horse by which fantasy and the unconscious, those recalcitrant resistances, are "imported" in to cloud political clarity.

Perhaps part of the problem is in the topographies within which we imagine sexuality. We need to see it as a fully embedded structural component of cultural and material social order, not as only a channel or site that is somehow borrowed for politics. Until we are able to understand sexual difference in an overdetermined way, we will not effectively treat questions of class politics, race, ethnicity, or sexuality. Nor will we successfully explore the ways in which, roughly speaking, psychoanalysis is made to compete with politics. This is a crucial problem, since it is echoed in the way theory, in general, is often figured as competing with experience, and the way feminist theory is often constructed as competitive with minority discourses. Such structures reflect institutional situations that map and instrumentalize differences so that they are contained within competitive arenas.

Anyone working within the U.S. academy can see that the rhetoric that insists on simple and direct analogies between women's studies and African-American studies, for example, usually results in their being endlessly compared and asked to compete for space, visibility, and support. Moreover, such a structure asks the two disciplines to look the same and to treat each other as models and rivals in ways that replicate social conflicts and antagonisms and that successfully minimize the very different challenges each discipline poses to traditional institutional constructions of knowledge and culture.

Within women's studies, as well as within dominant academic feminist theories, the shape of our knowledge about sexual difference works structurally, I think, to thwart or at least to distort most attempts to study its relationship to other differences. Other differences are constructed and figured as either analogous or somehow serially added on. And this problem expresses itself in most white feminist cultural analysis of several crucial areas. In our considerations of masculinity, our failure to see race and sexuality as structurally fundamental to the construction of sexual difference leads to two common scenarios in relation to our own subject positions as well. One of these subsumes all men under a monolithic masculinity and inadvertently attributes to all of them the privilege of white heterosexuality. Instead, psychoanalytic theory should lead us to recognize the need for a specified and differentiated conception of masculinities, which do not have the same relation to social or symbolic power, and which operate through and upon divisions according to race, class, and sexuality. Thus, we should be producing an analysis of gender construction and its representations in view of the recognition that *no one* has the phallus, so all subjects have a troubled and failed relation to it, although these relations are different and specific and are always charged with social investments.

If one scenario writes men of color and gay men out of the picture in order to preserve a manageable and singular masculinity, another writes white feminists out of any racial location. We fail to take into account our own phantasmatic investments, most particularly our desire to see ourselves as outside white heterosexual male discourse. That is, our account of the dominant discourse and culture attributes to white heterosexual males alone the "bad" representations that we deconstruct. Such a position allows us to figure gay men and men of color as unproblematic allies, as situated "near us" in the power register, based on a phantasmatic identification that works to obscure our own white heterosexual privilege. At the same time, such analyses often entirely overlook women of color and lesbians, and certainly overlook their alliances with these men.

Indeed, both the "additive" and the "analogy" approaches to difference end up imagining social differences as though we could treat them materially and politically as we treat them rhetorically— like interchangeable attributes. When white heterosexual feminism analyzes other differences, it is frequently within a discourse that imagines itself to be expanding its boundaries. Yet the issue of race as a crucial structural determinant of U.S. culture, as well as a structural feature of our social political organization, is rarely addressed as a matter interior to feminism and to all feminist identities.

White heterosexual feminism all too often sees clearly that femininity is constructed but fails to see itself as also racially and ethnically constructed and instead treats race as an attribute of "others." In U.S. culture, nearly all representations assume whiteness as a given, as a curiously nonracially marked term. But this construction is intimately dependent on a complex social imaginary organized around the idea of race. This imaginary depends on a being/having dichotomy that allows the dominant culture to imagine race as quite differently constituted on either side of the racial divide. Such a construction imagines race as only contingent for white people, while projecting it as an essential aspect of all other identities. That is, people of color incarnate race and, in a strange displacement, racial difference, for the entire culture. Consequently, we have to begin to understand white identities as always functioning within this disavowal. That is, those of us raised to think that we are white need to begin interrogating what that means, to understand *that* it means, in resistance to hegemonic cultural representations that act as if whiteness means nothing at all, while marking blackness as bearer of a variety of meanings, all addressed to and read off by the dominant culture.

Despite the fact that cultural analyses frequently have absorbed all psychoanalytic tools into the study of sexuality, we need to begin considering their necessity in analyses of race as constructed identity. For the study of representations, we need particular attention to the precise ways in which the contemporary fetishization of difference in our culture may operate to transform only the figures and rhetoric of established racist discourse without changing its structural effects. This will entail careful study of the ways in which collective fantasies are based in and reproduce racism, along with other forms of cultural and material oppression.

To take such a step will clearly involve reconceiving and renegotiating questions of identification—in order to understand that in constructing gendered identifications, subjects are always more or less unconsciously engaging with racial identifications as well. What I want to propose are specific analyses of the reciprocal structuring of racial and sexual difference as articulated in cultural representations and the forms of address they construct, induce, or permit. And this interaction can be understood only in the context of power relations—racial difference in a racist and sexist context, sexual difference in a context of heterosexism and racism. Necessarily, then, any analysis will have a bearing on identity and identifications—which can only be considered as *relations* and can no longer be read in terms of a stable inside and outside. If we feminists have not found more splits in our identifications, this testifies to the success and pressure of white dominance in our cultural representations, where whiteness appears as seamlessly bonded to gender, and therefore to have no impact on it. This is what keeps us from examining constructions of sexuality as fully embedded in our culture's intimate dependence on a racial divide for its self-definitions.

Notes

1. This essay was originally written and presented as a twenty-minute contribution to a panel at "The Ends of Theory" symposium, Wayne State University, March 1991, and presented in a revised form at the International Association of Philosophy and Literature, University of California at Berkeley, May 1992. In both cases, I conceived it as an "occasional piece," aimed at a specific and limited context, broadly sketched as a forum for interdisciplinary exchange that might take stock of current histories and developments on the question of theory. To this I should add my own contemporary local context, that of a vital women's studies program whose internal exchanges continue to be marked by more and less productive tensions around the status of theory in relation to women's experience, ideological tensions that we more

and less accurately attribute to the disciplinary divisions among us, as a group of scholars from the humanities and social sciences. Equally important to stress, as I am writing about the turbulence within which the field of feminist inquiry and exchange continues to reshape itself, I can only grasp specific sites and at specific moments. Thus, this piece seems to me permanently in danger of outliving itself. At the same time, I am relatively confident that the primary problem I have chosen to investigate —the ways in which psychoanalytically based theory may, almost despite itself, produce or contribute to certain structural obstacles within feminist negotiations with identity politics—remains in need of substantial working through. In order to revivify it on this occasion, I use these notes as a framing device, where I hope to offer some specific and contemporary detail to support the more general and abstract claims that seemed appropriate to conference presentations and to the oral format. The notes also restore to the reader some of the massive body of debates and interventions that lie behind my apprehension of some of these issues.

2. For a rigorous and thorough interrogation of the status of "identity" and "experience" in debates around essentialism, see Diana Fuss, *Essentially Speaking: Feminism, Nature and Difference* (New York and London: Routledge, 1989).

3. Much recent theoretical work on the specific position of African-American women and of African-American feminism addressed this kind of "double jeopardy" in various ways that do not reduce it to an abstractly "privileged" site but also a "figure" for feminist theory. Rather, such theorists analyze the rigorous structural demands on such a position and suggest that serious dialogue around the social positions inhabited by subjects who are always attending to the competing demands of gender and racial politics might change the shape of identity politics altogether. Certainly, such work asks us to get beyond the strictures of the "essentialism" debates, especially as they figure "identity" and "experience" in ways that turn out to be too rigidly fixed to accommodate the current complexity of almost any position within contemporary U.S. culture, let alone within feminism. To cite just a few examples of this kind of work: bell hooks, *Black Looks: Race and Representation* (Boston: South End Press, 1992), *Talking Back: Thinking Feminist, Thinking Black* (Boston: South End Press, 1989), and *Yearning: Race, Gender, and Cultural Politics* (Boston: South End Press, 1990); Hazel Carby, *Reconstructing Womanhood: The Emergence of the Afro-American Woman Novelist* (New York: Oxford University Press, 1987); Hortense Spillers, "Mama's Baby, Papa's Maybe: An American Grammar Book," *Diacritics* 17:2; Cheryl Wall, ed. *Changing Our Own Words: Essays on Writing by Black Women* (New Brunswick, N.J.: Rutgers University Press, 1989); Hazel Carby, "The Multicultural Wars," and Michelle Wallace, "*Boyz N the Hood* and *Jungle Fever*," both in Gina Dent, ed., *Black Popular Culture* (Seattle: Bay Press, 1992). In Toni Morrison, ed., *Race-ing Justice, En-gendering Power* (New York: Pantheon, 1992), two essays focus on the relationship between the specific identity positions of African-American women and the facility with which the dominant culture constructed Anita Hill iconically. These are Kimberlé Crenshaw "Whose Story Is It, Anyway? Feminist and Antiracist Appropriations of Anita Hill" (pp. 402–40), and Wahneema Lubiano, "Black Ladies, Welfare Queens, and State Minstrels: Ideological War by Narrative Means" (pp. 323–63).

4. See *Feminism without Women*, pp. 20–22, for the full unfolding of this discussion.

5. MacDowell presented this analysis in a lecture delivered at the University of Rochester in fall 1991.

6. Perhaps the most rigorously critical analysis of the demands that white feminism in general addresses to black feminists is Christine Stansell's, in her essay "White Feminists and Black Realities: The Politics of Authenticity," in Morrison,

Race-ing Justice, Engendering Power, pp. 251–67. Stansell maintains that Euro-American feminism seems wishfully to imagine that "black women's political role [were] somehow to harmonize the interests of white feminism and the Afro-American community" in a curious "political division of labor whereby black feminists come to serve as go-betweens between their white counterparts and other black people," a division of labor that "also reproduces the old distinction between the politics of race and the politics of women" (p. 253).

7. For a historical analysis of the construction of lesbians as figures within and for heterosexual-dominated feminism, see Katie King, "The Situation of Lesbianism as Feminism's Magical Sign: Contests for Meaning and the U.S. Women's Movement, 1968–72," *Communication* 9, 1 (1986): 65–91. See also Judith Butler, *Gender Trouble: Feminism and the Subversion of Identity* (New York and London: Routledge, 1990), an analysis that entirely cuts the ground from under any such figurations, from any such constructions of identity.

8. For a rich analysis of the ways our theoretical positions may be related to unconscious identifications, as well as of the particularly compelling force of identification within feminist politics and theory, see Teresa Brennan's Introduction in Teresa Brennan, ed., *Between Feminism and Psychoanalysis* (London: Routledge, 1989), pp. 1–23.

9. Constance Penley, *The Future of an Illusion* (Minneapolis: University of Minnesota Press, 1989), p. xix.

Orientalism and the Ethnographer: Said, Herodotus, and the Discourse of Alterity

Catherine Gimelli Martin

The Foucauldian investigation of the complicity of knowledge and power has been extended by Edward Said to a critique of the ethnographic enterprise in general, an enterprise he finds not only epistemologically but practically and ethically corrupt from its inception to its most subtle and sympathetic modes. No longer able either to suppress or to transcribe alterity, the West has paid for its "failure to take the Other seriously" by an inevitable lapse into "contemplative irony,"[1] the inevitable result of a hypocritical discourse whose purpose is not to elucidate but to silence its Other(s), primitive or, at least, non-Western society. Because in anthropology, especially, "the imperial setting . . . after all *is* pervasive and unavoidable,"[2] the discursive conditions embedded in its territorial, political, and methodological enterprises undermine all possible communication between interlocutor and investigator. Along with the most blatantly "Orientalizing" practices, "the vogue for thick descriptions and blurred genres acts to shut and block out the clamor of voices on the outside asking for their claims about empire and domination to be considered. The native point of view, despite the way it has often been portrayed, is not an ethnographic fact only, is not a hermeneutical construct primarily or even principally; it is in large measure a continuing, protracted, and sustained adversarial resistance to the discipline and the praxis of anthropology (as representative of 'outside' power) itself, anthropology not as textuality but as an often direct agent of political dominance."[3] What is remarkable in this critique of anthropological praxis is not, of course, its fore-

Reprinted from *Criticism* 32, no. 4 (Fall 1990): 511–29.

grounding of the hermeneutic problems inherent in the enterprise but its rejection of these problems as grounded in those of textuality. The irreducible alterity of the native point of view is attributed to its insuperable resistance to Western power, and this power *specifically and directly* attributed to the agency of Western anthropology. Thus, it is not knowledge per se that Said condemns but some historically predetermined (if vaguely situated) conjunction of Occidental science with political hegemony, a conjunction that acts as a contamination. The source of this contamination can be traced to "the almost insuperable discrepancy between a political actuality based on force and a scientific and humane desire to understand the Other hermeneutically and sympathetically in modes not always circumscribed by force."[4]

Said's position in "Representing the Colonized: Anthropology's Interlocutors" on the one hand extends the point of view adopted in *Orientalism* and on the other departs from that of his early essays, especially those collected in *The World, the Text, and the Critic*. Nevertheless, there is ample suggestion of his later stance in the ambivalent, at times paradoxical, relationship to Foucault developed in these essays. Said's consideration of the relative validity of Derridean and Foucauldian methodologies, "Criticism between Culture and System," naturally enough praises the latter for displaying a greater awareness of "the impressive constitutive authority in textuality of . . . power as . . . a broadly based *cultural* discipline, in Foucault's sense of the word."[5] Yet this approval is only tentative; even this "broadly based" construction of textual authority ultimately rests upon too vague a sense of historical imperialism, an imperialism that is not merely passive and conditional but active and absolute, a "power virtually of life and death." Not only does Said find Foucault paying an "insufficiently developed attention to the problems of historical change," but he charges him with being "unaware of the extent to which the ideas of discourse and discipline are assertively European and how, along with the use of discipline to employ masses of detail (and human beings), discipline was used also to occupy, rule, and exploit—almost the whole of the non-European world."[6] However, Said's anti-Foucauldian admonitions are theoretically suspect for at least two reasons, the chief of which is that, at other times in the collection (and, we might assume, for other reasons), he comes to a diametrically opposite conclusion concerning Foucault's conception of history. Here he makes the surprising claim that Foucault puts "too great a premium on dramatic change" and proposes that we should instead view the text as "a dynamic field, rather than as a static block, of words."[7] Thus, his later about-face wherein Foucault's history is now too static and his text somehow too dynamic, too incapable of accommodating the absolute hegemony of European discourse, becomes suspect. In fact, his strategy merely collapses *both* forms of dynamism, textual and historical, by replacing a relatively mediated and diffuse notion of discursive power punctuated by change with a notion of power in which *plus ça change, plus c'est la même chose*. In what is essentially a prelude to *Orientalism*, Said comes to the somewhat startling conclusion that the proper "space" of criticism is not "merely the text, not even the great literary text," but the "pure" space of the signifier, one that by now has little to do with Foucault's: "what has counted in the continuity and transmission of knowledge has been the signifier, as an event that has left lasting traces upon the human subject. Once we take that view, then literature as an isolated paddock in the broad cultural field disappears, and with it too the harmless rhetoric of self-delighting humanism."[8] What ultimately disappears, however, is not merely "self-delighting humanism" but discourse itself. Taking Foucault's dictum that "Speech is no mere verbalization of conflicts and systems of domination . . . it is the very object of man's conflict,"[9] Said interprets the "object of conflict" as a "site of domination" rather than as a "ground or source of struggle," in the process detaching the double meaning of *pouvoir* from its dual function as noun and verb (as both "power" and "to enable, be able," from *potere*). The result is that the "signifier" now functions as the signified of power itself, a transposing of Foucault's terms so as to anticipate the definition of the Other-as-object, a result of a univocal determination on the part of the colonizing subject, and discourse as a similarly univocal determination, paradoxically *outside* a history of change that is ontologically hegemonic and European.

The distortions that arise from detaching *either* speech or writing from the broader context in which it provides the ground, site, conflictual locus, and irreducible dichotomy (Self/Other, presence/absence, etc.) of power will appear in what follows. Yet simply to dismiss as reductive Said's treatment of the role of textuality in the related hermeneutic enterprises of literature and anthropology is not without a potential reductivism of its own. Although history as we know it proceeds from the ontological separation of West and East, Self and Other, this history is for Said not without *its* Other, its silences or absences which *like* Foucault he attempts to recover. Further, although he feels that any transcription of the Other faces "almost insuperable" difficulties, he finds in some developments of Islamic linguistics[10] and in poets such as Frantz Fanon and Aimé Césaire a form of inclusive vision denied to Western anthropology. Since he suggests that this vision may become accessible to the science of the future, even though its past yields no parallels,[11] the positive as well as the negative aspects of his critique will bear some scrutiny—particularly as, with or without Said, recent anthropology is indeed implicated in a crisis of "contemplative irony." This crisis at least in part arises from circumstances noted by James Clifford: the ethnographic text, to be textualized at all, must have some authoritative focus, some subjective "I" behind it; anthropology consequently rewrites the discourse of its interlocutors and in so doing determines the conditions both of its "territory and of its power/ *pouvoir*.[12] To assess Said's critique fairly thus demands that we must decide whether his theory seriously distorts or merely exaggerates the power/knowledge dialectic.

In order to accomplish this admittedly difficult project, it will be necessary, first, to expand our definition of this dialectic and, second, to supplement the ontological and a priori view of history that is part of Said's inheritance from Foucault. Turning, then, to Pierre Bourdieu's work in *Outline of a Theory of Practice*, we find a suitably parallel, but at the same time broader, discussion of the inevitable silences surrounding anthropological discourse. For Bourdieu, this discourse is structured by corresponding *sets* of omissions rather than by a recurring *position* of exclusion. Both as hegemonic authority and as textual exchange, the power of the dominant discourse is simultaneously enabled and limited by inherent as well as external forms of lacunae: "If agents are possessed by their habitus more than they possess it, this is because it acts within them as the organizing principle of their actions, and because this *modus operandi* informing all thought and action (including thought of action) reveals itself only in the *opus operatum*. Invited by the anthropologist's questioning to effect a reflexive and quasi-theoretical return on to his own practice, the best-informed informant produces a *discourse which compounds two opposing systems of lacunae*." In this view, the silences of the native speakers are compounded by resistances informed not only by the necessity of translating practice into a discourse at once foreign to native discourse and its empirical schemas (thus implicitly disempowering them), but at the same time by the unexamined, hence *necessarily silent and unthinkable*, discourse that orients the native's relation to his own power structure: "Insofar as it is a *discourse of familiarity*, it leaves unsaid all that goes without saying: the informant's remarks—like the narratives of those who Hegel calls 'original historians' (Herodotus, Thucydides, Xenophon, or Caesar) who, living 'in the spirit of the event,' take for granted the presuppositions taken for granted by the historical agents—*are inevitably subject to the censorship inherent in their habitus*, a system of schemes of perception and thought which cannot give what it does give to be thought and perceived *without ipso facto producing an unthinkable and unnameable.*"[13] Bourdieu's discussion of the problem shared by the "original historian" and the ethnologist thus illuminates the broader historical situation of the discursive problem, one that must be traced not only to the irreducibly dual role of the native informants but also to that of the primary ethno-historians, of whom the first is Herodotus. Following him, nearly all early historians, like many modern ethnologists, wrote as either actual or virtual exiles *within their own as well as within the social discourse of the "Other."*[14] They thus share dual commitments which, as we shall see, position them both between and within each discourse, ultimately placing them between the *lacunae* of the dominant as well as of the alien discourse. Alternately filling the place of Insider/Outsider and Author/Other, they at once "take for granted" the presuppositions of the dominant discourses and, like native informants, ironically mimic or deflect it. In this sense, the original historian's situation always already conceals/exposes the textualizing strategies that establish both the boundaries and the power relations of discourse, inscribing at its source an instability reminiscent of Hegel's master/slave dialectic.

This is not to say, however, that the theoretical instability of representation rules out its overriding impulse: that of charting, informing, and hence dominating the physical and conceptual territories occupied by the alien discourse. This impulse, too, originates with Herodotus and, as Johannes Fabian notes, can be traced directly to a typically Western "philosophic" manipulation of ontology. All discourses derived from this foundation lend themselves to hierarchical constructions of space and time. As Fabian points out, theories of ontological priority tend to develop into scales of temporal advancement, and these into geographical charts of cultural progress or retardation.[15] In this way, as Said claims, the ideological project of Western discourse can no more be separated from its theoretical project than its absences or gaps can be turned into authentic presences. Yet if these two strategies are inevitably linked and in fact mutually "contaminated" by power relations, we must assume that the reverse is also true: that these false discursive presences cannot completely conceal their own absences or, as Derrida would have it, their supplementarity;[16] and that within the absent "space" of the supplement (that is, between and within the dual lacunae of discourse), some act not of full but of partial or mistranslation can occur. Yet this is not Said's position; his "solution" to the complicity of knowledge with power proposes no mediation between the two but an absolute separation of opposed forms of knowledge, a separation that ultimately looks very much like a collapse of science and theory into ideological absence on the one hand and on the other an affirmation of poetic expression and "openness" to the Other as authentic presence.

To examine Said's exensive critique of Western epistemology over the entire course of his writing on the subject is hardly possible within the scope of the present article. Instead, by focusing on Herodotus and particularly on the Orientalizing ethnology of this archetypal "father of history" and "father of lies," I hope to outline certain liabilities of Said's critique, particularly its tendency to reflect some of the more logocentric ambitions of that epistemology. Since I can give a thorough analysis neither of the entire nine books of *The Persian Wars* nor even of their ethnographic center (Books II through IV), I will concentrate on their foundational strategies, especially those of Book I, where, as David Konstan has pointed out, much of the ideological substrate is already being determined.[17] Here, many of the Orientalizing strategies Said associates with Western ethnology as a privileged mode of cross-cultural inquiry are in fact already in place. For Said, these strategies adopt a methodology that serves not to illuminate other cultures in their own terms but to objectify, displace, and alienate them from the superior standpoint of the Western observer. "Orientalism" is thus the species of epistemology of which ethnography is the genus; both set up a binary ontology of difference between Occident and Orient that privileges Self over Other and establishes a dominant discourse for describing, teaching, and ruling the Orient, finally of *producing* the Orient politically, socially, and imaginatively. Its creation of a surrogate and underground "Other/Self" thus enables and empowers Western authority by substituting "real" hermeneutic endeavor for theoretical conquest. As Said puts it, "the phenomenon of Orientalism . . . deals principally, not with a correspondence between Orientalism and the Orient, but with the internal consistency of Orientalism (the East as career) *despite* or beyond any correspondence or lack thereof with a 'real' Orient."[18]

What is strangely *not* at issue here, however (and we will return to this problem later), is the separation of authentic from real knowledge and of motives of power from methods of power; yet, for Said, neither distinction is problematic. He makes little attempt to distinguish between relatively interested and disinterested inquiry, because the theory of Orientalism implies Western hermeneutics are always the former *even though they could be the latter*. This very possibility (which Said nowhere denies) should lead him, like Bourdieu, to separate the *modus operandi* from the *opus operatum*, in theory, in practice, or, ideally, in both. Instead, Orientalism is described as a mode of false consciousness to essentially opposed nonideological knowledge, and to maintain this absolute distinction the two modes are, not surprisingly, often blurred.[19] Said maintains that regardless of its form, Orientalism *always* manipulates the category of the Other in the service of a political interest that is essentially coterminous with its objective mode of representation: "the essence of Orientalism is the ineradicable distinction between Western superiority and Oriental inferiority."[20] Thus, rather than a critique of Western epistemology, Said's East/West binaries repeat its own inherent dichotomies, which, according to Bourdieu, consist in the oscillation between an "objectivist reduction" of other cultures which "makes it impossible to understand how [social] . . . functions are fulfilled, because it brackets the agents' own representation of the world and of their practice"; and a "mystical participation" in which, even when the resulting interpretations "are asymptotic with scientific truth . . . are never more than the inversion of the false objectification performed by colonial anthropology."[21]

Yet since on the surface, at least, the reinstatement of these dichotomies is scarcely self-evident, Said's critique yields a convincing indictment at least of the "objectivist reduction" imposed by Occidental epistemology, even as it itself tilts toward "mystical participation." Considered from this point of view, Herodotus's discursive strategies ideally fit him to supply the figure of the prototypical Western Orientalist. Technically an outsider, he comes to his Orient—the barbarian or non-Greek world—as an "impartial" observer conspicuously armed with a formidable baggage of Hellenic concepts; for him, *barbarian* and *non-Greek* mean the same thing. Like many another Orientalist, our first historian consistently finds much that is admirable in the non-Greek world, including virtues he either polemically or nostalgically regards as typically Hellenic. In his chronological romance,[22] the Egyptians, not the Greeks, are the original human beings, the founders of religion, the primal authorities as well as ancestors. At the alternate pole of ascriptive value, he privileges the Scythians, whom he identifies as the newest of races and the first to successfully repulse the Great King, Darius. Thus, while the Egyptians are accorded spatiotemporal primacy because of their indefinite duration and their geographical hegemony within the nature/culture "machine" of the Nile, the nomadic Scythians are accorded a political primacy because of their (Greek-like) *lack* of this priority, one that makes them preeminently self-reliant. The Scythians desert their dwellings rather than pay tribute to the Persian king, as the Athenians themselves will desert their city during the course of the Persian wars. Obviously, this specifically relativistic valorizing of the non-Greek is far from value-neutral in fact, and actually serves to reinscribe Hellenic values in alien contexts.

The law governing this reinscription of value has been described by Francois Hartog in *The Mirror of Herodotus*. Here, the law of *le tiers exclu* or excluded middle produces binary oppositions not unlike those proposed by Said: fundamentally dual, their displacements and exchanges actually *produce* the stable category of Hellenic value. Consequently, the *Histories* reveal "what is other" by a procedure that is finally a rhythm as much as a rule, but always an opposition whose recurrences form "a beat which runs through the narrative. It appears that, in the end, in its effort to translate the 'other' the narrative proves unable to cope with more than two terms at a time."[23] Hartog then discusses at some length how at times the Persians, at times the Scythians, Amazons, etc., take on the position of Other in relation to the Greeks; the opposition of two markers is always constant, if not the terms that occupy their places. Again, this description is consistent with Said's classic exposition of Orientalism, which consistently produces sets of binary oppositions that identify and privilege the "same" over the "different."

A paradigmatic case of the Orientalizing practice initiated in Herodotus's Book I exemplifies the many permutations that can later be traced back to it. Herodotus tells the tale of the Lydian king Candaules who is overthrown by his vassal Gyges as a result of his own despotic and typically "Oriental" appetites. Obsessed by a peculiarly vicarious form of voyeurism, Candaules wants Gyges to see the "most beautiful woman in the world," his wife, naked. Gyges objects on the basis of long-established custom (*nomos*), which decrees that each male should view only his own wife. In asserting the priority of *nomos* or the rule of law over the free play of despotic whim and in upholding of the sanctity of the inner chambers, Gyges is behaving transparently and typically as a Greek. For, as Hartog and many others point out, a chief index of the Other or of barbarity in Herodotus is sexual excess, the extreme case being sexual or "bestial" intercourse in the open or public sphere, since the beasts, like tyrants, are without *nomos*. Candaules, in failing to feel either the shame or the reverence of the marriage chamber (the word *aidos* in the passage signifies both), thus defines himself both as a barbarian and as a despot whose power must necessarily be overthrown by the gods.

Hence this tale, represented as a historical and genealogical "explanation" of the fate of the Lydian empire (Candaules is the last of its first lineage, and Gyges' great-great-grandson Croesus will be the last of the second), actually exploits the Oriental Candaules in order to valorize the reflection of Greek values displayed in Gyges. Not surprisingly, Croesus later loses his empire when he in turn succumbs to an even more archetypal form of tyrannical hubris, that of simultaneously insulting the gods and their temporary stand-in, the Greek philosopher Solon. At this level, then, Said's description of the Orientalist is confirmed, in fact exemplified, by Herodotus. In this description, "Orientalism is premised upon exteriority, that is, on the fact that the Orientalist, poet or scholar, makes the Orient speak, describes the Orient, renders its mysteries plain for and to the West. He is never concerned with the Orient except as the first cause of what he says. What he says and writes, by virtue of the fact that it is said or written, is meant to indicate that the Orientalist is outside the Orient, both as an existential and as a moral fact."[24] Yet beyond this point the parallelism between Hartog's original ethnographer and Said's Orientalist diverges, illuminating gaps that suggest serious flaws in the latter's analysis of alterity. Although their premises and some of their methodology initially appear the same, Hartog's closer attention both to the semantics and the semiotics [of Orientalism] produces conclusions widely differing from Said's. These not only illuminate how the interrelation of symbolic, political, and ideological power allows for polysemy but also suggest the conditions under which polysemy is either maximized or minimized, and how at the latter or "Oriental" extreme a fully ideological discourse that detextualizes textuality and "fixes the referent" is produced.[25] Thus for Hartog, the ideological is one but by no means the only function fulfilled by the original ethnographer.

To see why this is so, we must first look more closely at Hartog's semiotic model. In it, the *Histories* are constructed by not one but two separate rhetorical codes, each of which employs binary oppositions along different axes. If we look at these codes as supplying a kind of mental graph, we then see that their axes intersect at right angles; and, inserted in the tensions between them, in their very intersection, is situated the problematic space of the Other. Hartog calls the first axis the code of space, the second the code of power. To describe the code of space, Hartog relies on G. E. R. Lloyd's *Polarity and Analogy*, which considers the force of these quasi-mathematical concepts in Greek thought. According to Lloyd, the opposition between polarity and analogy like the physical perceptions of symmetry and inversion upon which they depend, structure the conceptualization of space.[26] To conceptualize the code of power, Hartog opposes two different terms, the political binaries by now familiar from the tale of Candaules: imperial despotism and Hellenic freedom. Between these codes, a crucial difference overrides their similar use of polarities as well as their mapping functions: while the code of space uses polarity to establish *analogy*, polarity in the code of power is used to establish *difference*. This is not to say, however, that either rhetorical code is ever free from asserting power through transcribing alterity. Since Herodotus counts, measures, surveys, and charts the entire world of the Other in his travels, and since Greece is not rendered up in this fashion, it implicitly becomes the center of the numerically partitioned world. This strategy is not only part and parcel of Herodotus's Hellenic baggage, his inheritance from the pre-Socratics in general and Anaximander in particular,[27] but is also part of the prototypical stance adopted by Western ethnography: a rationalizing and moralizing stance that geometrically partitions native space and appropriates it (like other aspects of the "savage mind," including its temporal space) for its own purposes.[28]

Nevertheless, the fact that this spatial mapping and symmetrical imaging of the world is a *form* of power and not power itself creates an essential distinction in the evaluation of the code of space; collapsing it into the same lane as political and ideological power, on the other hand, distorts the multiple senses of both knowledge and power. Power in the sense of mapping cannot be meaningfully detached from the process of "making seen," and to chart the stars is not to conquer them in the same sense as to chart, rule, and hence conquer a neighboring or at least an accessible territory. Further, any process of "making seen" requires what Hartog playfully calls "the spectacles of Herodotus" or, alternatively, "the grid of the watercolorist." Without these conceptual spectacles, without this perspectivist grid, neither order nor form is at all possible. As Hartog notes, "The principle of inversion is thus a means of communicating otherness, by making it easy to apprehend that in the world in which things are recounted it is just the same except that it is the other way around. But it may also function as a heuristic principle: it thus becomes possible to understand, to explain, to make sense of an otherness which would otherwise remain altogether opaque. The inversion is a fiction which 'shows how it is' and makes it possible to understand: it is one of the figures of rhetoric which helps to elaborate a representation of the world."[29]

Taking up the code of power, one easily can identify an ideology of the *polis* inscribed within the Herodotian text, and here, if anywhere, Said's analysis should prove forceful. Hartog's parallel treatment appears equally incontrovertible here: "the question of power, barbarian—hence, royal—power, set in opposition to the world of the city runs right through the *Histories*, constituting an important element of its organization. Just as the watercolorist's grid cuts up and organizes the space of his painting, so the question of power provides the structure (at least in part) for the space of the

Histories.[30] . . . The text, then, valorizes the *polis*, the Greek Self as opposed to the barbarian Other, and this function corresponds to Said's analysis of Orientalism, particularly his central claim that "Orientalism responded more to the culture that produced it than to its putative object, which was also produced by the West."[31] Yet what can Said's work reveal about the *process* whereby this is achieved? Since he typically concerns himself more with semantics than with semiosis, and with ends rather than means, we learn chiefly that the Orientalist's object is *produced for* another culture, but in what sense and in what manner is this production achieved? Does an identical product result from every possible inquiry; does the receiver alone determine the message; is the sender (or object) always intrinsically mute? Finally, if the Western ethnographer inevitably acts as an agent for a nonnative audience, thus producing an object, the barbarians, so that the West may see its image or double in a self-validating mirror, is this mirror the director or indirect agent of power, and what kind of power does it wield? Are its reflections/representations hegemony itself or only its illusory double? These are the pertinent questions that Said's formulations would appear to raise but which he himself consistently evades: for him, the mirrors act only to affirm an idealized self, its distorted representations functioning only to "essentialize" (i.e., objectify, dehumanize) the Other. Western discourse has but one function, to suppress dialogue and usurp power, even though the very fact of its failure for Said necessarily implies its own Other—the lower-case *other* of dialogic equality, nonobjectification, and communicative "success"—and even though the exact terms of this success, like the terms of the original discursive failure, are never specified.

Hartog's mirror, on the other hand, is two- rather than one-dimensional. Since it exists both to see and to make seen, its mode is translation, and, like translation, it is dialogical in the limited sense that translation implies, that of approximation rather than correspondence. Polysemic and multivocal rather than monological or unidirectional in respect to signs, this translation model opens discursive possibilities ignored by Said's projection model (a model not only of mistranslation but actually of silence). Both agree insofar as hegemony remains a precondition upon which discourse is erected, and as every translation is a displacement of the language of the Other in favor of the language of the Self. There can be little doubt that the non-Greek world of Herodotus is mapped in terms of Greek science and conquered in terms of Greek political thought; the native populations he encounters are not allowed to "speak" for themselves, however often their customs are duly recorded and set down in their own vocabulary. The lacunae that inevitably distance

Herodotus from his informants are in fact repeated in the very stylistic lapses of the text itself, so that each of his famous digressions occurs precisely where an important Greek concept can be applied: continuity and the rule of order (the canals of Egypt); freedom and initiative (the Scythians); despotic whim (Persia/Lydia) versus the rule of *nomos* or *polis* (Hellenes/Scythians). Conceptually, the standards are always Greek, even while the value markers are radically unstable; the Greeks themselves do not consistently represent their own, but sometimes also despotic, values, as in the case of the Greek tyrants who refuse to aid the Scythians and remain loyal to Darius. Yet *even this* fairly superficial transference of symbolic markers is not thinkable in Said's terms, where the Other always remains Other, and the Self *itself*. In contrast, Hartog's model allows for a greatly expanded range of discursive possibilities, including the one most notoriously denied by Said, that is, the fact that only *some* of Herodotus's ethnographies represent privileged Others, while others are included randomly and without privilege, as independent textual effects.

This inclusion of random reality effects is, of course, neither random nor representative of the voice of "speaking natives." On the contrary, it serves two concrete purposes; by marking points of incomprehensibility, it guarantees the otherness of the Other, an opaqueness that serves to mark the truthfulness of the narrator along with his distance from the reader. Yet those lacunae also open the position of alterity to both the Other and the writer/narrator, Herodotus, and in this sense serve not simply to allow the inscription of a dominant discourse but also to permit the polysemic conditions of narrativity and language itself. While the chief function of language is to mark difference, difference implies both a positive and a negative potential, a capacity for generative as well as invidious distinctions, for both looking *upon* as well as looking *askance at* the Other (conditions already implicit in the Latin root of both *envy* and *invidiousness*—*videre*, "to look upon"). For Hartog as well as more widely known theoreticians of the role of discourse in the human sciences (Lacan, Derrida, de Man), the paradoxical duality of blindness and insight forms the very precondition of translation, as translation forms the recondition of all knowledge: "language is translatable . . . so [that] difference may be apprehended. Translation between the Old World and the New both maintains and reduces the distance represented by the ocean. It is thus simultaneously the ever-present mark of the severance between the two and also the constantly renewed sign of their stitching together. Severance and stitching together are two phases in a single moment at work within the text. The setting up of such a system of translation

presupposes the possibility of referring to a set of distinctions between being and appearance."[32] What is ultimately at stake, then, is
the possibility of distinguishing being from appearance, the condition that makes translation possible, and that paradoxically limits it.
To translate is at once irremediably destructive as well as affirma-
tive; it eliminates the possibility of a world of ultimate forms, of
Real Language, while at the same time it enables a Self/Other dialogue by putting the unknown idea in the form of the known concept, along with whatever distortions this may cause.

Said's analysis of Orientalism isolates an empowered Self
from a silent Other; Hartog's exploration of the mirror of Herodotus
reflects not one but two Others. The first and most obvious Other is
the barbarian or cultural Other; the second is the disguised narrative or textual Other, which produces a *hypocrite lecteur* effect. In
each case, one Self is privileged against another; what, then, in a
practical sense is changed by accepting Hartog's translation model?
Here, although several possibilities arise, we can speculate that if
Hartog is correct in insisting that the dual function of translation is
to "see" and "to make seen," then privilege itself, the intentionality
of discourse, must have two modes. "To see" would be to put the
spectacles or the watercolorist's grid in place, to activate a power
that is ultimately self-actualization and self-definition, a mode of
"being in the world," in Paul Ricoeur's Heideggerian terminology.
There can be no mode of "being in the world" without an appropriation of the Other; and it is this act that in Lacanian theory constitutes the Self, which at once models, determines, or limits it by situating it in language. Thus, this appropriation represents a mode of
power that is also a loss of power; the face in the mirror is also constituted by the mirror. In this form of "seeing," then, power is circular, dichotomous, intractable. But in its other mode, "to make seen,"
power operates as the privilege of defining Self and Other for the
Self, and thus, as Said suggests, controlling the Other. This control
can be fully effective, however, only if one translation is able to establish itself as "*the* translation," the locus of all linguistic power
and the occlusion of all dialogue. If, on the other hand, it must compete with other translations, it loses its complete efficacy as both a
mode of knowledge and a mode of power, becoming at most one
interpretation among innumerable possibilities, a potential rather
than an actual vehicle of coercion.

If these suggestions are correct, then it would seem to follow
that for a discourse to be fully empowering, fully ideological, and
hence Orientalizing, several constraints would have to be put upon
the profound duality of the Other: (1) the narrative Self would have
to control the reading Other in appearing to be voiceless, a not-

Other; and (2) the grid of interpretation would have to be univocal in both time and space, an originary and undisputed "reality," not a theoretical construct or translation. When these two conditions are met, then the Self would become completely ideological and empowered and, conversely, the Other fully disempowered, fully Orientalized. Even in this case, however, it would seem that the theoretical "map" of hegemony would not necessarily coincide with hegemony itself; as is well known, in many ways the Orient came to dominate the Greeks, not vice versa, beginning with the disasters of the Athenian empire and culminating with the death of Alexander. Maps of the stars have never yet succeeded in conquering them, but they have in the past and may yet continue to conquer us. Conversely, if the east "mapped" the West with its astrology, it was Islam, not Persia, whose physical incursions into Western territory proceeded farthest.

In returning to Said's work, it becomes obvious from these conclusions that he imposes on all knowledge the ideological and essentializing functions that operate only when the two poles of discourse collapse. For him, translations are silences and mirrors realities; the object of ethnography "is not inherently vulnerable to scrutiny; this object is a 'fact' which, if it develops, changes or otherwise transforms itself in the way that civilizations frequently do, nevertheless is fundamentally, even ontologically stable. To have such knowledge of such a thing is to dominate it, to have authority over it.[33] Knowledge for Said is thus, de facto, a form of oppression. Difference, from Saussure to Lacan and Derrida the precondition of both hearing and seeing is reduced to a form of raw suppression of the Other, hence a synonym for power itself. Even apart from Derrida's profound critique of Foucault's attempt to write the history of madness or silence, a history that, by renouncing "etiological demands," *has* an origin and yet *remains* "ontologically stable" outside a *logos* that "had no contrary,"[34] this conception of the function of both knowledge and difference cannot be sustained. For Derrida, the very function of language demands a process of "othering" as "the necessity from which no discourse can escape, from its earliest origin." Further, this necessity is *only* "violence itself, or rather the transcendental origin of an irreducible violence, *supposing . . . that it is somewhat meaningful to speak of preethical violence*: For this transcendental origin, as the irreducible violence of the relation to the other, is at the same time nonviolence, since it opens the relation to the other. It is an *economy*. And it is this economy which, by this opening, will permit access to the other to be determined, in ethical freedom, as moral violence or nonviolence."[35] As Derrida allies Foucault's inattention to "etiological demands" with his conflation of two kinds of madness, one popular, one scientific,[36] Said's more pronounced neglect of causality and change can be traced to his conflation of two kinds of violence, one preethical and one ethical, a conflation that collapses the economy as well as the origins of discourse. Within the boundaries of this economy, the speaker, like the text, is spoken by and speaks a discourse that is at once his own and an alien presence outside him. Its origins, insofar as they can be spoken at all, lie within the history of its fundamental metaphors (*logos*, being, reason, light), of which, with Derrida, we must ask, "Who will ever dominate it, who will ever pronounce its meaning without first being pronounced by it?"[37]

Lacking these distinctions, Said's discourse of the Other must resolve itself into intractable dichotomies that suppress rather than elucidate their own historical and ideological bases. History becomes the intolerable "presence" of Western hegemony which dictates the "absence" of the "real" Orient; conversely, only with the absence of this presence can the silenced Other begin to speak. As Derrida points out in the critique of Levinas cited above, this desire for absence, "'Face to face without intermediary' and without 'communion,'" will produce two predictable results: "Because they do not think the other, they do not have time. Without time, they do not have history. The absolute alterity of each instant, without which there would be no time, cannot be produced—constituted— within the identity of the subject or the existent. *It comes into time through the Other.*"[38] Said's history of pure alterity thus produces a similar if inverse omission, a narrative conspicuously lacking in temporal struggle or in any but a largely discursive violence: "Islam excepted, the Orient for Europe was until the nineteenth century a domain with a continuous history of unchallenged Western dominance."[39] By eliding China and conveniently "excepting Islam" (an Islam that retreated from its conquest of southern Europe as late as the siege of Vienna in 1580) from his history of domination, Said reveals that his commitment is less to explicating the foundations and development of Orientalizing discourse than to reifying it, a move that to him seems to promise its overthrow and reversal. That this promise is and can be only an illusory one is obvious from the fact that it rests upon a discursive impossibility, the elimination of difference itself; yet this, he states, "is the main intellectual issue raised by Orientalism. Can we divide human reality, as indeed human reality seems to be genuinely divided, into clearly different cultures, histories, traditions, societies, even races, and survive the consequence humanly? I mean to ask whether there is any way of avoiding the hostility expressed by the division, say, of men into 'us' (Westerners) and 'they' Orientals."[40] Despite its undeniable appeal to what is by now an almost wholly secularized Western mythology of prelapsarian community, on the basis of its own rhetorical model Said's question can be answered only in the negative. Since he consistently refuses to supply the means or even postulate the possibility of transcultural translation, his project is in its own terms doomed from the start. Positing the "fallenness" of difference as the source of world conflict is actually an attempt to turn Western thought back on itself, resuscitating a hope of regaining an originary "presence" best let alone, given the historical tendency of similar hopes to initiate violence and renewed repression rather than "authentic" liberation. Almost all human gains made on the basis of this *mythos* eventually reduplicate its mystifications, simply because polysemic discourse cannot be objectified as a "force" to be liberated any more than power can be reduced to a "thing" to be seized. Both involve processes, semicontradictory mediations that may be relatively accurate or inaccurate, mystified or deconstructed, or any of the infinite variations between.

Said's model of Oriental discourse thus can be viewed as participating in rather than overthrowing the malaise of postmodernism. Constructing not an escape from irony but only an anti-ironical inversion of an older ideology, Said's critique of Lyotard redounds upon himself: his is not an explanation but a symptom, a purported etiology which in fact "stands free of its own history."[41] While he advocates the possibility of seeing "Others not as ontologically given but as historically constituted,"[42] his own work is based on the ontological complicity of knowledge and power in a "Western" discourse which, by standing outside history, merely pretends to presuppose the conditions of all discourse. His formalism, like Foucault's but to a large extent exceeding it, presents a recirculating system of tensions of "control or of abandonment, of recollection and of forgetting, of force or of dependence, of exclusiveness or of sharing,"[43] a system that would appear better designed to recapitulate than to escape the ironic mode. The incapacity of this vision to transcend its own limitations stems from the fact that it is structured upon a reflection rather than a "reflexion" model of knowledge, the latter of which would depart from the discourse of false consciousness and acknowledge both difference and distance as conditions of apperception. This model, advocated even by those who, like Fabian, count themselves among Said's supporters, recognizes that "reflexivity . . . is always also self-reflexivity. Affirmation of distance is in this case but a way of underlining the importance of subjectivity in the process of knowledge."[44] All knowledge thus inevitably participates in an ongoing revision of present and past in which subject and object "share each other's past in order to be knowingly in each other's present"; only in this way can we recognize that "Hermeneutic distance is an act, not a fact." Distance between the observer and the observed, like the *coupure/suture* between the Old World and the New, is maintained through a constant severance and stitching together: not one-way reflection but two-way "reflexion."[45] For this to occur, interpretive "facts" must be represented as acts, partial recognitions that are never either fully translatable or fully incomprehensible. At the root of all knowledge remains the observation of difference and its translation from the unknown idea to the known concept, concepts that, like the knowledge they attempt to relate, can never be fully "real," fully "true." Herodotus, at the very beginning of narration, points toward this fundamental duality of the knowable; both in his own time and for all subsequent history, he has remained both the "father of history" and the "father of lies."

Notes

1. Edward W. Said, "Representing the Colonized: Anthropology's Interlocutors," *Critical Inquiry* 15 (1989): 223.

2. Ibid., p. 217.

3. Ibid., pp. 219–20.

4. Ibid., p. 217.

5. Edward Said, *The World, the Text, and the Critic* (Cambridge: Harvard University Press, 1983), p. 224.

6. Ibid., pp. 222, 223.

7. "Roads Taken and Not Taken," in ibid., pp. 152, 157.

8. "Criticism between Culture and System," in ibid., p. 225.

9. Said treats this quotation from *The Archaeology of Knowledge*, trans. A. M. Sheridan Smith (New York: Pantheon, 1972), p. 216, on p. 48 of *The World, the Text, and the Critic*.

10. See *The World, the Text, and the Critic*, pp. 36–39.

11. See "Representing the Colonized," pp. 224–25.

12. See James Clifford, "On Ethnographic Authority," *Representations* 1 (Spring 1983): 118–46.

13. Pierre Bourdieu, *Outline of a Theory of Practice*, trans. Richard Nice (Cambridge: Cambridge University Press, 1977), p. 18.

14. I am grateful to Normal O. Brown for focusing my attention on the relevance of this situation to Herodotian discourse.

15. Johannes Fabian, *Time and the Other: How Anthropology Makes Its Object* (New York: Columbia University Press, 1983), especially pp. 1–66.

16. See Derrida's well-known critique of Rousseau's linguistics in *Of Grammatology*, trans. Gayatri Spivak (Baltimore: Johns Hopkins University Press, 1974).

17. David Konstan, "The Stories of Herodotus' *Histories*, Book I," *Helios* 10 (1983): 1–22.

18. Edward Said, *Orientalism* (New York: Pantheon Books, 1978), p. 5.

19. See James Clifford, "Orientalism," *History and Theory* 6 (1980): 204–23.

20. Said, *Orientalism*, p. 42.

21. Bourdieu, pp. 114–15.

22. For the ethnographic perils of simple, sentimental, and more complex chronological forms of nostalgia, see ibid., pp. 115–18.

23. Francois Hartog, *The Mirror of Herodotus: The Representation of the Other in the Writing of History*, trans. Janet Lloyd (Berkeley: University of California Press, 1988), p. 258.

24. Said, *Orientalism*, pp. 20–21.

25. I borrow this very useful terminology from an unpublished article by Harry Berger, Jr., on textuality and detextualization.

26. See Bourdieu's related reflections on the "practical geometry" and "paradoxes of bilateral symmetry" (p. 119) as fundamental to what he calls the "practical space of practice," pp. 118 ff.

27. See Alan B. Lloyd, *Herodotus Book II* (Brill: E. J. Leiden, 1975).

28. One implication of this stance is, as Fabian observes, that it uses "naturalized-spatialized Time [to give] meaning . . . to the distribution of humanity in space. The history of our discipline reveals that such use of Time is almost invariably made for the purpose of distancing those who are observed from the Time of the observer" (p. 25).

29. Hartog, p. 214. As Hartog notes, this use of inversion corresponds to the mode of Greek thought that G. E. R. Lloyd calls "polarity": see Lloyd, *Polarity and Analogy* (Cambridge: Cambridge University Press, 1966).

30. Hartog, p. 322.

31. Said, *Orientalism*, p. 22.

32. Hartog, pp. 237–38.

33. Said, *Orientalism*, p. 32.

34. Jacques Derrida, "Cogito and the History of Madness," in *Writing and Difference*, trans. Alan Bass (Chicago: University of Chicago Press, 1978), especially pp. 38–44.

35. Derrida, "Violence and Metaphysics," in *Writing and Difference*, pp. 128–29. (Italics added.)

36. Derrida, "Cogito and the History of Madness," in *Writing and Difference*, p. 41.

37. Ibid., p. 92.

38. Ibid., p. 91.

39. Said, *Orientalism*, p. 73.

40. Ibid., p. 45.

41. Said, "Representing the Colonized," p. 222.

42. Ibid., p. 225.

43. Ibid., pp. 222–25.

44. Fabian, p. 90.

45. The term is coined by Fabian as a way of expressing the theories of C. F. von Weizsacker concerning "co-apperception of time." See Fabian, pp. 87–97; quoted, p. 92. Like Said, Fabian attempts to correct the commodification of ethnography but, unlike him, sketches a positive historical program.

From Ends of Theory to
Theories of the End

Wallace Martin

> "Let us hasten hence or I shall be tempted to make a theory, after which there is little hope of any man."
> "Come hither, then," answered he. "Here is one theory that swallows up and annihilates all others."
> —Hawthorne, "The Hall of Fantasy"

To put the "ends of theory" in question is to presuppose a unity (theory) and expose a duplicity: theory begins with an end in mind (for what purposes, in whose interests, will it be pursued?) and in the course of things comes to an end—perhaps interrupted by more practical concerns, completed, or simply discarded. The title of a collection of essays published in 1990, *The States of "Theory,"* calls attention to the unity and duplicity of theory in a different register. The quotation marks serve as forceps to extract the word *theory* from its use so that we can inspect and reflect on it, mobilizing our doctoral skills to distinguish its states of health and morbidity. Between its varied states and two ends, theory generates histories.

Heeding the advice of Rorty and Lyotard, who say that narratives are an appropriate medium for the grounding and transmission of knowledge in a post-philosophical era, I will tell a story about the ends of theory from the late 1960s to the early 1990s. The first half of the story has been told many times, notably in Frank Lentricchia's *After the New Criticism* and Art Berman's *From the New Criticism to Deconstruction*. Vincent Leitch tells almost the whole story in *American Literary Criticism from the '30s to the '80s*. My own version will be less a story than a plot analysis, emphasizing the moments Aristotle considered crucial: the beginning, the turning point, and the end. It's a story lacking in suspense because we all know how it turns out. I think we can agree that the epoch in which theory was the central enterprise of the discipline has ended, and other interests have taken its place.[1] There are, however, differences of opinion about the theme of the story, leading to alternative accounts of who the main actors were, what conflicts animated them, and how these have been resolved. Forestalling any suspense about my theme, I'll declare it in advance, in the form of a thesis: the decline of theory and its replacement by an interest in ideology and history have returned criticism to its relatively untheorized state prior to the 1960s. Theory has taken the place that formalism once occupied in criticism: it is a threat to the proper study of literature, which (according to the humanists and Marxists of the 1930s, the literary historians and old left of the 1950s, the new right and new left of today) should be grounded firmly in a social and ultimately an ethical (which is to say political) context.

My story begins in 1968, right in the middle of things, with a paper Derrida delivered that year: "The Ends of Man." Having been requested to provide a summary of recent philosophy in France, Derrida, in the second and third sections of his paper, showed how certain readings of Hegel, Husserl, and Heidegger had led not beyond or outside metaphysics but rather back to an occulted form of humanism. His argument uncovers the mutually conditioning ends of man in death and in the attainment of consciousness. Since World War II, Derrida argued, humanism or anthropologism had been "the common ground of Christian or atheist existentialisms . . . of personalisms of the right or the left, of Marxism in the classical style. And if one takes one's bearings from the terrain of political ideologies, anthropologism was the unperceived and uncontested common ground of Marxism and of Social-Democratic or Christian-Democratic discourse" ("Ends of Man," pp. 116–17).[2]

Given the endless recyclings of philosophy and politics, in which every declaration of a sublation or renewal can be interpreted as a return or repression, what hope could there be of escape? My own answer is that a displacement or sidestepping of philosophic dead ends sometimes can be achieved through theory.

There are nearly as many meanings of *theory* as there are people who talk about it. In literary contexts, the senses of the word inherited from classical philosophy (theory as contemplated truth or pure knowledge) were reanimated by Friedrich Schlegel but survive today only as traces of a negative theology. As Derrida says, our theory has nothing to do with its meanings for philosophers, mathematicians, or physicists. The opposition of *theory* to *practice* in ordinary usage seems adequate to account for the former's meaning in most critical contexts; within the realm of that vague distinction, I shall simply stipulate a working definition of the word.[3]

Theory, for present purposes, can be conceived as a temporal projection from any philosophy that looks to the past and attempts to subsume it in presence or the synchronic. Theory is a project for a future, one in which its purposes and conceptual structures will either be accepted or discarded by practice. In addition to this prospective end, theory has a second end in mind, one often forgotten by those who conceive theory as serving only a critical or negative function that can be equated with the constant vigilance of self-consciousness. The more ambitious end of theory is to disappear into the facts—to be so generally accepted that it is simply assumed to be part of the way things are, what we think *with* rather than what we think *about*. It is in this sense that the end of theory is genuinely the end of theory, the termination of theorizing. (In its disappearance, theory becomes ideology.) To simplify through revision of a schema proposed by Ricoeur: theory *prefigures*, practice *configures*, and history *refigures* as our futures move into the past.

Given its ends, theory elicits an interrogation different from that prompted by philosophy. Because it is prospective, theory must begin from possibilities, strategies, and conditions that require scrutiny. More fundamentally, the very ends that theory proposes, its own goals, and those of other practices that seem to work are exposed to questioning from the start. For what purposes, in whose interests, is a theoretical project undertaken?

The central sections of Derrida's essay concern the ends of philosophy. The beginning and end concern the ends of theory, as here conceived. The essay opens: "Every philosophical colloquium necessarily has a political significance." In his effort to identify the purposes and interests served by the colloquium for which his paper was written, Derrida raises nearly all the questions about ends that have by now become almost formulaic in the interrogation of theoretical and philosophical projects, including those of Derrida.

At the close of the paper, Derrida treats matters that I think of as pertaining to the other end of theory—questions of how projects are proceeding, what outcomes are likely from available strategies, and the like. The theoretical projects then under way in France afforded, in his view, the possibility of a rupture with humanism. One project was the purely formal "reduction of meaning," through attention "to system and structure, in its most original and strongest aspects." Another was the method characteristic of deconstruction, "repeating what is implicit in the founding concepts and the original problematic . . . using against the edifice the instruments or stones available in the house, that is, equally, in language." A third method, which he says "dominates France today," is "to decide to change terrain, in a discontinuous and irruptive fashion, by brutally placing oneself outside, and by affirming an absolute break and difference." Finally, there is a Nietzchean possibility. In each prospect, Derrida sees dangers—most significantly, the danger of falling right back into the ruts of prior philosophical and political practice ("Ends of Man," pp. 134–36).

This ends the beginning of my story. For me, it marks, though it did not initiate, the beginning of the epoch of theory. By way of summary, looking back to 1968 and all the possibilities it seemed to afford for theory and practice, I want to highlight three themes. First, Derrida's conjectures on the future of French thought now appear remarkably accurate. Deconstruction flourished. Among the "change of terrain" theorists, we can number Barthes, Foucault, Deleuze and Guattari, and Lyotard. Variations on the Nietzschean theme appear everywhere, especially in annunciations of postmodernism. Second, I would emphasize Derrida's assertion that the politics of *both* left and right were then grounded in anthropologism or humanism, with a view to posing the further question of whether any politics in the participatory sense, within a system, can be grounded on anything else. And, finally, I would import into Derrida's analysis of the ends of man a particular problematic that it seems to me has been misunderstood—namely, the relationship between the synchronic and the diachronic or, in more general terms, between theory and history.

Theory—especially those forms it took in the 1960s and 1970s —has been generally understood as privileging synchronic over diachronic analysis. Although it is obvious that theoretical explanations devote much more space to the treatment of structures than to sequences of events, this is a quantitative rather than an analytic observation. Far from trying to give synchronic analysis some sort of privilege, Derrida's efforts can be seen as an attempt to identify the *complicity of* the synchronic and diachronic in philosophy. Deferral and the trace insert a narrativity at the heart of any project that would sublate temporal difference, thus splitting the synchronic apart. On the other hand, traditional narratives, whether fictional or historical, lead toward a fusion of past and presence in their totalizing ends, which map conclusive themes on the chain of events. Among those who will later employ narrative as a tool to challenge the dominance of theory, one usually finds that the narratives or histories used for this purpose are totally subordinated to a synchronic structure that governs the end, as well as the development, of any story that will be told.

This leads me to the turning point of my story which, for purposes of symmetry, I place about a decade after Derrida's "Ends of Man." It had been a decade in which the possibilities outlined by

Derrida had been pursued, some critics dismantling traditional views of literature and literary history using quasi-deconstructive methods and others attempting to change the terrain of discussion entirely, either moving the assault into other disciplines or announcing apocalyptic postmodernist inversions of traditional hierarchies. For my purposes, amid the many signs that change was at hand in the expanding empire of critical theory, none was more significant than Jameson's writings—particularly Marxism and Historicism" (1979) and *The Political Unconscious* (1981).[4] Here one finds conclusive evidence that critics write their own kinds of history, but not just as they please; they do so under circumstances directly transmitted by prior critics.

By any standard, the problems that confronted Jameson at the end of the 1970s were monumental. In attempting to reinscribe history and politics in criticism, he would have to fight on at least two fronts. On the theoretical front were the poststructuralists, standing guard on the rubble that had been the edifice of humanism. On another front, Althusser had dismantled the Hegelian Marxism that Jameson had inherited from Sartre, Lukács, and the Frankfurt school. How, in these circumstances, could Jameson not only reinstate his version of the story but also make it prevail? Only through genius and circumstance.

As he indicated in the 1979 essay, poststructuralism had mounted what he called an "ideological" attack on three premises of traditional thought: historicism, representation, and the idea that there is only one valid interpretation. These three were, of course, foundational concepts in conservative as well as radical thought. In 1981, he identified another polemical target of poststructuralists: the concept of totality, which binds the other three categories together. His lines of defense against these challenges were as follows:

(1) The concept of hierarchy. Disputes about the course of history, representation, and interpretation are dialectical moments in an all-encompassing synchronic structure, the "master code" of Marxism.

(2) The methodological necessity to assume unity or totality. If we don't posit a relationship among all elements of human experience, "the unity of a single great collective history" (1981, p. 19), we can't make any sense of the past or the present.

(3) The human necessity to find ways of understanding experience. Even if there is no such thing as expressive causality or mediation, these "reflect a fundamental dimension of our collective thinking and our collective fantasies about history and reality." Rejection of such categories is a sign that we have repressed not

only our history but our "political unconscious" (1981, p. 34). Furthermore, such categories, like the concept of totality, are necessary as analytical devices, quite apart from their objective truth or falsity (1981, pp. 40, 52). Their use makes it possible to resurrect and reexperience the past, sometimes in a positive way, but more appropriately as an inescapable nightmare, that of "mindless alienated work and of the irremediable loss and waste of human energies" (1979, p. 162). For to imagine that there has ever been a redemptive moment of freedom is only to strengthen the grip of necessity. Hierarchy, totality, and a negative mode of recollective experience come together in history as necessity, and Necessity (his capital) means that history "must always tell the story of failure" (1979, p. 41).

Jameson's reinscription of humanism and historicism, based on the ways we usually think, or should think, or methodologically must think, deserves comparison with Schiller's inaugural lecture on universal history (delivered at Jena in 1789). From Schiller and Herder descend the discredited alternative versions of universal history (Whiggish progressivism, organic nationalism) that (with chiliastic Christian historiography) perforce serve as Jameson's dialectical opponents. The remarkably rich developments in the philosophy of history from the 1940s to the 1980s are not mentioned in these texts, apart from passing reference to Hayden White.[5]

Jameson's conclusions have in varied ways served as the basis of current critical polemics, within a revalorized horizon of humanism. Here I jump, precipitously, to the current situations of a historicism and humanism that can do without theory (theory being a provisional and falsifiable conjecture about proximate developments).

One consequence of Jameson's vision of history as Necessity is that history becomes a synchronic system—a conclusion that Jameson himself repeatedly asserts. Shifts from one mode of production to another require analysis, but within the epoch of capitalism, for example, nothing can really change. The *stages* of capitalism—as exemplified in the literary changes leading from Romanticism to modernism—give the appearance of an evolution, but it is dialectically marked out in advance. Capitalism, as Horkheimer and many subsequent writers conceive it, is "an epochal self-reproducing system of social relations," perhaps based on emergent cybernetic feedback mechanisms, through which administration and domination automatically shift to meet stresses.[6]

The paradoxical consequence of this synchronic vision of history as Necessity is that it is totally indeterminate. If everything had to happen as it did, there is no possibility of differentiating elements that may lead to one or another outcome. On a local level, one may inspect differences and point to a number of factors that might explain them. Different explanations can be subsumed in the concept of overdetermination. But as everyone outside the small circle of literary study and classical Freudianism agrees, overdetermination is another name for indetermination, especially when no alternatives are accessible.[7]

Another consequence of totalization under the reign of necessity is that prediction is imposible, in fact or in principle. Because there is no way to single out features that might lead to different outcomes, there is no way to determine how to bring something about—for example, a revolution.

Beginning from capitalism as a mode of production and historical epoch, within which all the changes identified by others are really just variations of the same, one tries to explain the stability of the system. This attempt is an inversion of scientific method. Rather than identifying causes of change, one seeks every cause of nonchange. These are in principle countless. It is not just hegemony, disciplinary practices, ideological mystification, and reification that cause nonchange. Every successful assault on the worst aspects of capitalism may have abetted its survival.

The total indeterminacy of this determinism is not just a logical consequence of Jameson's position; it is evident everywhere in today's polemics about history and criticism. One example is the difficulty that critics have encountered in deciding whether modernism is bad and postmodernism good, or vice versa. Especially crucial at present is the controversy about whether any shred of something called the aesthetic should be exempted from the gristmill of political history. Jameson cannily allowed for the possibility of utopian impulses in literature, wherein they can exist by being shifted into an imagined future. This was also a problem for Horkheimer and Adorno; the moments in which they try to exempt art from the inescapable domination of a comprehensively regulated society are among the finest in their writings.

Among the other issues that separate Marxists, cultural critics, and new historicists are disagreements about the relative importance of base and superstructure in effecting historical change, the question of what sites of resistance remain available in the face of hegemony, and the extent to which oppositional movements may prop up the system. I think that these disputes are superficial because each position taken by the participants can be generated from assumptions that they share. Their mode of thought has the uniquely productive capacity to lead, logically, to antithetical conclusions—and hence to interminable arguments.

The tenets of Stephen Greenblatt's new historicism seem to me essentially the same as those of his Hegelian Marxist opponents, despite differences of emphasis. In his essay "Resonance and Wonder," I find the following principles:[8]

(1) *Pandemic intentional causality.* Historically significant events are caused not just by intentional actions but by intentional inaction. "Every form of behavior, in this view, is a strategy: taking up arms or taking flight are significant social actions, but so is staying put, minding one's own business, turning one's face to the wall. Agency is virtually inescapable" (p. 74). Just as inaction can cause events, so action can cause nonevents (things remaining the same): "it takes labor to produce, sustain, reproduce, and transmit the way things are" (p. 76). Totalization results from the superimposition of a new way of describing actions. Each act and nonact has two meanings—one connecting it to its ostensible context and result (planting a crop, staying put, joining a union), the other connecting it to the totality (producing the way things are, sustaining or subverting the way things are, etc.). "The way things are" is a unified totality, not just the sum of its parts. Marxists would call the totality capitalism.

(2) *Pandemic intentional indeterminacy.* Often we fail to realize our intentions. But failure or success at the mundane level of intentionality (the crop didn't grow, the union achieved its aims) may be the opposite of its result in relation to totality. "Actions that are single" at the level of ordinary causality "are disclosed as multiple" when considered in relation to "the way things are": "a gesture of dissent may be an element in a larger legitimation process, while an attempt to stabilize the order of things may turn out to subvert it" (p. 75). As in Hegel (but without teleology), often we know not what we do. Some of Greenblatt's opponents would treat such events through analysis of the contradictions immanent in capitalism, but their assumptions and methods differ little from Greenblatt's.

(3) *The doubling of intentionality.* Implicit in the first two principles, this one requires separate treament. History is not quite as indeterminate as it appears if one understands that the word *intention* now has two meanings, the second having emerged from the totalizing causal analysis. In citing "minding one's own business" as an example of intentional historical action, Greenblatt cannot mean that the person so engaged would *deny* the intention of minding his or her own business. It is precisely that claim of intention (attending to my own affairs and hence not acting as an agent of history) that Greenblatt would challenge. His point is that, knowingly or unknowingly, the person "intends"—in another sense—to affect his-

tory (e.g., by reproducing the way things are). I don't see much difference between Greenblatt's argument and those that ascribe
similar causality to ideology, though he does raise the ethical stakes
by making every action morally culpable (because "intentional").

(4) *Totalizing explanation of untotalized historicism.* Action and
inaction, by agents with two kinds of intentions, lead to results they
may not intend. The cunning of the new historicist, standing in for
Hegel's cunning of reason, makes history intelligible. The founding
principle of this historicism, as of all others, is *post hoc, ergo propter
hoc.* But what the *hoc* causes is not, for Greenblatt and his opponents on the left, one of the many states of affairs we encounter
around us. Each event and nonevent in the past has caused the current totality, the singular "way" that many different things were and
"are." It is a nation, a monarchy, hegemony, a phase of capitalism, a
stage of the world spirit, issuing from all the forces that support and
oppose it. So long as it survives, dissent must have supported it;
when it falls, conservative forces will have contributed to its subversion. Those who engage in this mode of thought should not quibble
about whether things might have been different or whether necessity can be distinguished from indeterminacy. Their assumptions
make it impossible to answer such questions.

The charges and countercharges in the collection of essays *The
New Historicism* are proof, if any were needed, of the problems that
result from determinate indeterminacy.[9] The champions and opponents of the movement enter into a veritable competition to prove
that *they* find less emancipatory potential in literature than do their
opponents. Catherine Gallagher charges that their opponents want
to preserve literature as a site of potential resistance to the system,
rather than accepting the new historicist recognition that it offers no
such potential (p. 45). Frank Lentricchia charges that Greenblatt
wants to recover, from his totalizing account of power, a subjectivized sense of freedom in literature, not recognizing the spuriousness
of that consolation (pp. 241–42). What is at stake here is nothing
less than the litmus test of any current criticism: does it contribute
to the possibility of liberation, or is it "conservative of the dominant,
ethno-centric concerns" (p. 272)? The participants share the ethical
commitments and the vision of the past as a totality that should be
enough to mollify their disputes. The problem is that, given this
agreement, there is no way of knowing whether saying one thing or
another about literature will be conservative or emancipatory.

The ultimate proof of one's acceptance of the totality/indeter-
minacy thesis is to move beyond the relatively tame assertion that
literature cannot contribute to emancipation and argue that it props
up the system. It is not just that "poetry makes nothing happen," as

Auden said; it is the *cause* of nothing happening. Having occasionally surfaced in earlier phases of the dispute, this conclusion is now well on its way to becoming a consensus. It appears, for example, in Lennard J. Davis's *Resisting Novels* (1987), D. A. Miller's *The Novel and the Police* (1987), Vincent P. Pecora's *Self and Form in Modern Narrative* (1989), and Sacvan Bercovitch's "The Problem of Ideology in American Literary History" (which appeared in *Critical Inquiry*, 1986). Given that the mode of production has not changed, it logically follows that something caused it not to change and further (positing totality) that it was everything that caused it not to change. That these writers give different explanations of how literature prevents a change is not evidence that one or another may be more or less correct.

At this point, it may be helpful to restate my thesis in its logical form—if you will, as a theory. The end of theory is certainty. But we can't attain certainty until the end, knowing that nothing new will happen. That certainty comes at the end of history, as Hegel said. Since we can't wait for that, we develop a *theory* of the end of history, involving the totality and necessity of a mode of production. We take this as an absolute standpoint and use it to speak with certainty. Capitalism is the end of history (or prehistory). But certainty, as necessity, can create a crisis of indetermination concerning what caused the past to be as it was. At this point, different theories may sneak in through the back door, so to speak, to provide explanations. There is no way to choose among them.

That one cannot find a demonstrable basis for choosing among literary theories is hardly new. This was, in fact, the authorizing force that made the epoch of theory possible, each movement (beginning with the phenomenological "criticism of consciousness") giving rise to others in dizzying succession. Underlying that succession, however, was a negative dialectic not entirely without consequence. Even if not falsifiable, each theory proved faulty when tested in argument, and the tests it failed were as a rule of two sorts: either the theory isolated literature from its contexts (readers, other disciplinary domains, society), or it employed concepts that, on reflection, dissolved into more fundamental forms (philosophical, ideological, psychoanalytic, historical) in a continuous process of demystification. In both cases, critiques focused on the *means* of theory—assumptions, methods, contexts, boundaries.

Once we agree that emancipation is the only useful end of theory, the end dictates the means. How does one decide whether literature is (a) a reflection of social contradictions, (b) a site of resistance, (c) a subjectivized escape from reification, or (d) an occulted tool of state power? One chooses the view most likely to encourage emancipatory tendences, especially in students. There is no place, within this framework, for literary or critical theorizing.

I have tried to explain the development of criticism in the past quarter-century as a chronology governed by logic. By doing so, I run the risk of falling into the totalization trap, implying that no alternative course of development was possible. There were and indeed are alternatives, but they lie outside the limits of the tradition I have discussed. Furthermore, this tradition has a history as well as a logic—a history that warrants a few comments.

I have been struck repeatedly by the similarities between Jameson's assumptions and those of Horkheimer and Adorno. The adjustments Jameson makes to meet charges leveled against Hegelian Marxism by Althusser and others lead him to positions remarkably like those of the early Frankfurt school. Just as Horkheimer and Adorno reworked Lukács's concepts of totality and reification in order to explain why a bureaucratically dominated society might extend the control of capitalism without foreseeable limit, so Jameson had modified both Lukács and Althusser to arrive at a parallel position. The similarities extend down to matters of detail, such as the assimilation of modernism to fascism. Further examples include the Horkheimer and Adorno conclusion that critical values are to be sought in the "suffering emanating from existing capitalist society" and their use of "emancipatory aspirations" as the standpoint for critique (Grumley, pp. 163, 177). That standpoint corresponds to the utopian standpoint claimed by Jameson—not a "place of truth" but at least an atopia free from the partialities of those confined to a specific position in history (1979, p. 176). Quite apart from details, the pessimistic thrust of the negative dialectic mounted by Horkheimer and Adorno, the feature for which they are best known, is very similar to that of Jameson and other current critics.

I am led to infer that, far from evolving out of Marx and Lukács in conjunction with Althusser, Foucault, Gramsci, and poststructuralism, the current consensus about totality, necessity, and negativity on the left comes from Horkheimer, Adorno, and Marcuse, as they were assimilated by those who were undergraduates in the late 1960s and early 1970s. France and Germany had worked their ways through the consequences of Hegelian Marxism by 1968; we did not undertake that project until the 1980s.

This reflection leads to a final one on finality. As many have noted (here I cite Habermas's observation in the subject), "critical theory was initially developed in Horkheimer's circle to think through political disappointments at the absence of revolution in the West, the development of Stalinism . . . and the victory of fascism in Germany."[10] Having discovered the stabilization of state capitalism under the New Deal when they arrived in this country, the pattern, as they saw it, was complete. Their explanation of why revolution had not occurred was so powerful that, by a kind of theoretical overkill, it explained why none *could* occur. "Against this background," Habermas observes, "it becomes intelligible how the impression could indeed get established in the darkest years of World War II that the last sparks of reason were being extinguished from this reality and had left the ruins of a civilization in collapse without any hope" (pp. 116–17).

If the prospect from which they looked back warranted their despair, it was equal warrant for Benjamin's "Theses on the Philosophy of History," written, as his friend Gershom Scholem tells us, as a reply to the Hitler-Stalin pact.[11] Benjamin's ninth thesis, based on a painting by Klee entitled "Angelus Novus," presents Klee's figure as the angel of history, who faces the past, being blown into the future by a storm from Paradise. "Where we perceive a chain of events, he sees one single catastrophe that keeps piling wreckage on wreckage. . . . The angel would like to stay, awaken the dead, and make whole what has been smashed. . . . This storm irresistibly propels him into the future to which his back is turned, while the pile of debris before him grows skyward. This storm is what we call progress."[12]

Stripped of its mystical undertones, this passage serves as an apt emblem of some current modes of historiography. Benjamin not only allegorizes Klee's angel but at the same time rewrites Hegel's account of the relation between history and philosophy. In Hegel, "the owl of Minerva begins its flight only with the falling of dusk." Wisdom is then ready to take flight. The wings of Klee's angel, Benjamin says, are "spread," but the storm strikes them "with such violence that the angel can no longer close them." Neither the angel nor the philosopher of history can fly to wisdom; they will be driven blindly into an unknowable future.

These allegories do not alter the fact that the sun sets every day and that every generation, as Goethe and Emerson say, writes its own history. That being the case, one can wish that these histories might be different, that some would undertake the project of writing histories from some standpoint other than that of a utopia that forecloses the possibility of learning anything from the past, of seeing it differently, or of revising the story as time passes. One might hope that the historian could occasionally be surprised, or find expectations disconfirmed, rather than maintaining the unruffled, untestable, wingless certainty that everything is governed by Necessity.

If my suspicion is correct that current versions of leftist historiography are based on views of totalization that descend to us from attitudes appropriate to the late 1930s and 1940s, then I think they are best understood through the image not of Klee's angel or Minerva's owl but of Lot's wife. Frozen in time by a backward glance at the horrors of destruction, at a certain moment in history, the gaze of Benjamin, Horkheimer, and Adorno has become not moving testimony to a moment in which what they saw was true but an attitude that we must ritually reinvoke and experience, drinking the blood with Tiresias, as Jameson says, to reanimate the suffering of the past (1981, p. 19).

Having joined forces to decry theory during the past decade, the left and the right can return to politics as they knew it before the 1960s and, in the name of emancipation, pragmatism, solidarity, suffering, democracy, postmodernism, or traditional values, write progressive, regressive, or static histories. The epoch of theory is over, ended, and not likely to resume soon within the sphere of Anglo-American literary study. This end might be emblemized best by Stanley's sweatshirt. At the 1989 MLA convention, Stanley Fish wore a sweatshirt on which was printed: "It works in practice, but will it work in theory?" Exeunt theories, amid laughter and catcalls. But there are still a few who sometimes encounter acts and texts that make them feel curious, surprised, puzzled, or just plain stupid. How can that be? Remembering Kant's admonition that if it exists it must be possible, they theorize.

Notes

1. Some may disagree. I was astounded to be told that "theory reigned supreme" at the 1989 MLA convention. On asking for the source of this information, I was given a clipping from the *Chronicle of Higher Education*, Jan. 17, 1990, which asserted that "the meeting program was full of references to . . . deconstruction" (p. A6). That word does not appear in the 751 session titles or the 2,000-odd paper titles of the program. Other terminology generated during the epoch of theory appears frequently, but applying inherited concepts to new sets of texts is seldom a "theoretical" activity.

2. "The Ends of Man," in *Margins of Philosophy* (Chicago: University of Chicago Press, 1982).

3. Jacques Derrida, "Some Statements and Truisms about Neo-Logisms, Newisms, Postisms, Parasitisms, and Other Small Seismisms," *The States of "Theory,"* ed. David Carroll (New York: Columbia University Press, 1990), pp. 81–88. While accepting Derrida's contention that what is meant by *theory* in America has no counterpart in Continental literary study, I think our use of the term is less indigenous than one might infer. Although Richards's use of the phrase *practical criticism* was in part responsible for the conclusion that the field could be divided into the practical and the theoretical, the title of Wellek and Warren's *Theory of Literature* owes less to na-

tive sources than to the *teoriya* that Wellek inherited from Russian formalism. That same usage led Todorov to entitle a collection of translations from the formalists *Théorie de la littérature* (1965). Apart from proximate sources, the opposition of theory to practice in literary and critical contexts has been common since Kant and Goethe.

4. "Marxism and Historicism," in *The Ideologies of Theory: Essays 1971–1986*, Vol. 2 (Minneapolis: University of Minnesota Press, 1988); *The Political Unconscious: Narrative as a Socially Symbolic Act* (Ithaca: Cornell University Press, 1981).

5. Few twentieth-century historians have endorsed the "universal history" espoused by Jameson (the idea that the past constitutes a single, encompassing story). That single story is usually an ethnocentric one. "No doubt it was this dependence on the principle of the uniformity of human nature that accounts more than anything else for the decline of the idea of Universal History with the rise of modern sociological consciousness—that is, with the acceptance of cultural pluralism by modern common sense. . . . The history of mankind thus became dispersed into an encyclopedia of biographies, customs, ideas, local institutions, languages, peoples, and nations." Louis Mink, "Narrative as a Cognitive Instrument," *The Writing of History*, ed. Robert H. Canary and Henry Kozick (Madison: University of Wisconsin Press, 1978), p. 139. For reviews of the varied modes of historiography that have emerged since World War II, see Paul Ricoeur, *Time and Narrative*, Vol. 1 (Chicago: University of Chicago Press, 1984); Hayden White, "The Question of Narrative in Contemporary Historical Theory," in *The Content of the Form* (Baltimore: Johns Hopkins University Press, 1987); Phillipe Carrard, *Poetics of the New History: French Historical Discourse from Braudel to Chartier* (Baltimore: Johns Hopkins University Press, 1992).

6. John Grumley, *History and Totality: Radical Historicism from Hegel to Foucault* (London: Routledge, 1989), p. 159. For a critique of the Marxist functionalist explanation of how capitalism propagates itself, see Jon Elster, *Explaining Technical Change* (Cambridge: Cambridge University Press, 1983). In *How Institutions Think* (Syracuse: Syracuse University Press, 1986), Mary Douglas shows that the criteria Elster proposes for an adequate functional analysis sometimes can be met (pp. 32–43). It seems clear, however, that Marxist theories of functionalism based on the totality thesis cannot satisfy these criteria.

7. Of the many sources one might cite in support of this conclusion, the following is most useful for my purposes: "An overdetermined system, one with more hypotheses than are needed to explain the observable facts, is not in testable form since, if it succeeds its tests, it is impossible to determine which of the hypotheses has been vindicated and which might still be false." Murray Wolfson, *A Reappraisal of Marxian Economics* (Baltimore: Penguin, 1966), p. 15. This criticism also applies to Althusser's "structural causality," but the most useful aspects of that concept (best conceived in relation to Aristotle's "formal cause") might be defended through appeal to G. H. von Wright's analysis of necessary and sufficient conditions in *Explanation and Understanding* (London: Routledge, 1971).

8. Resonance and Wonder," in *Literary Theory Today*, ed. Peter Collier and Helga Geyer-Ryan (Ithaca: Cornell University Press, 1990), pp. 74–90.

9. *The New Historicism*, ed. H. Aram Veeser (London: Routledge, 1989).

10. *The Philosophical Discourse of Modernity* (Cambridge, Mass.: MIT Press, 1988), p. 116.

11. "Walter Benjamin and His Angel," in *On Walter Benjamin: Critical Essays and Recollections*, ed. Gary Smith (Cambridge, Mass.: MIT Press, 1988), p. 82.

12. *Illuminations*, ed. Hannah Arendt (New York: Schocken, 1969), 257–58.

Part II
Aims and Ends

With so many narratives in the air, I certainly
had better take myself off.
—Henry James

The (End of the) End of History

Christoph Cox

We "Last Men"

My title registers a network of texts and proper names. It invokes Hegel, of course. But it also calls upon a more recent, minor text, which has become quite well known—a text situated between Hegel, the *New York Times*, Alexandre Kojève, Allan Bloom, *Time* magazine, the RAND Corporation, and a number of other loci. I am referring to Francis Fukuyama's article "The End of History?" which first appeared in the summer 1989 issue of a small neoconservative quarterly, was soon syndicated in a number of American and European periodicals, and subsequently has been expanded into a book.[1] Under Bloom's mentorship and guided by Kojève's reading of Hegel, Fukuyama, a former RAND analyst and U.S. State Department policy director, argues that the "end of history" is realized in post-Cold War America, which represents the culmination of human ideological development.[2]

Fukuyama's article provides the impetus for my remarks here. But I will only briefly and indirectly analyze his argument and its philosophical, textual, and political claims. Having placed myself in this strange company, I want to insinuate another set of texts and figures, to retrace or reiterate—with Nietzsche, Heidegger, Derrida, and Deleuze—some grammatological[3] questions concerning time and history. In this way, I hope to make more tenuous the bonds that link Hegel and Fukuyama with our current historical situation.

I note in passing that Fukuyama's text is already marked in relation to my own. Regarding his confrontation with deconstruction and poststructuralism at Yale and in Paris, Fukuyama told *New York Times Magazine* editor James Atlas: "I was turned off by their nihilistic idea of what literature was all about. It had nothing to do with the world. I developed such an aversion to that whole overintellectual approach that I turned to nuclear weapons instead."[4] Clearly, the field of inquiry is made up not of simple elements but of terms that are complexly determined and overdetermined.

Fukuyama's text moves in a curious way between the philosophical and the political, the academy and the state, the esoteric and the exoteric. Yet I will not explicitly discuss the odd sociocultural phenomenon of this text and its "history." Though my topic is bound up with it, I will not even say much about this text's relation to a whole eschatological field that could be said to characterize our epoch, our "postmodernity": a field that stretches at least from Hegel's and Marx's "end of history," through Nietzsche's "death of God," Heidegger's "end of philosophy," Barthes's and Foucault's "death of the author," Foucault's and Derrida's "end of man," and all the endings announced by Baudrillard, to mark but a few indices. I mention only that Fukuyama's text situates us—Americans—as these latecomers, these "last men" (*letzten Menschen*),[5] a phrase Nietzsche used to parody not only the utilitarians but also the Hegelians, who, with remarkable hubris, claimed to stand at the zenith of human history, satisfied and all-knowing yet without the capacity to love, to desire, to long, or to be different.[6] With none of Nietzsche's irony and all of Hegel's arrogance, Fukuyama tells us that the world process ends here.

Of course, Fukuyama has been strongly criticized for this unabashed complacency.[7] Yet it is my contention that these critiques have been raised in the name of the same conception of history that motivates Fukuyama's project. I want to argue that only through a critique of this conception of history will we disturb its apocalyptic economy, which never ceases to recuperate the other and whose devastating movement may truly and imminently produce the End.

Deconstruction and the Critique of History

> Are we the latecomers we are? But are we also at the same time precursors of the dawn of an altogether different age which has already left our contemporary historiological [*historischen*] representations of history [*Geschichte*] behind?
>
> —Martin Heidegger, "The Anaximander Fragment"

Throughout Nietzsche's and Heidegger's texts, there runs an insistent call for a critique of metaphysical conceptions of time and history. But it is only with Derrida, I think, that this critique is made explicit, rigorous, and decisive. Derrida's project in its entirety may be said to be a deconstruction of both the history of metaphysics and the metaphysics of history. Following Heidegger's notion of *destruktion*, Derrida understands deconstruction not as a violent demolition but as a positive undertaking that stakes out and foregrounds the unarticulated, forgotten, subordinated, or repressed possibilities of the philosophical tradition. It seeks to unsettle or de-sediment our philosophical heritage so as to let appear a notion that has been all but foreclosed by that tradition.[8] Before sketching the theory of temporality and history that emerges from deconstruction, let me first rehearse its critique of the metaphysics of history.

For Derrida, our notions of time and history are fundamentally metaphysical insofar as they are founded upon, and operate according to, a privilege of presence. They "have been determined," he writes, "as detours *for the purpose* of the reappropriation of presence."[9] Time and history are said to organize an economy whose goal is the reduction of alterity and the recuperation of a lost unity, totality, and homogeneity. Hence, according to Derrida, history always has been conceived as circular, and becoming always has been a becoming what *is*.

Yet Derrida claims that this history is also linear and progressive. Its economy is speculative; it profits from its loss. Though it marks the space of an interval, that interval is not a dead zone or a useless passage but is transformative. All the binary oppositions that have structured metaphysics stand in as the alpha and the omega of this passage: nature/culture, necessity/freedom, actual/ideal, empirical/rational, content/form, time/eternity, becoming/being, and so on. Moreover, this passage is not only figured as a movement *between* presences; it cannot proceed but by marking presence *within* its movement. It marks not only an *arche* and a *telos* but a center: the now, the present, being as presence. ("*Istoria*," Plato notes in the *Cratylus*, designates "the stopping [*istanai*] of the stream.")[10] The time of history is conceived, from Plato and Aristotle on, as a sequence of nows, presents that—however corrupted by the flow of becoming—are the temporal representation of the eternal: Being itself. Thus, metaphysics conceives of time and history *sub specie aeternitatis:* the Eternal, which is the end and goal of history, is also its source and resource.[11]

The critique of history articulated by Nietzsche, Heidegger, and Derrida, then, is that it has only ever been a story of the identical, of the progressive leveling-off and recuperation of difference (what is not-this, not-here, and not-now). Becoming and difference have only ever been figured as indices of being and identity; and history has only ever been eschatological and ontotheological. In short, whether determined as circle, line, or point, time and history never have ceased to support a metaphysics of presence.

This critique is delivered not only against idealist history (whether in its Platonic, Judeo-Christian, or Hegelian forms) but against all notions of history including realist conceptions (whether materialist, empiricist, or positivist), insofar as history privileges being-presence not only at the extremes of its movement but within that movement as well. The very evidence and presence of the "real," the "fact," and the "event" that structure realist history are put into question by deconstruction, which criticizes the very notion of representation whereby a "sensible," "exterior" world is "represented" to the "subject," whose historical writing is then of a second order. To cite Nietzsche, "there are no 'facts-in-themselves,' for a sense must always be projected into them before there can be facts."[12] In Derridean terms, the "real" is always already "written," its presence deferred.[13]

Grammatology wants to ask: How are "events" produced and individuated? What does it mean that an "event" "occurs"? By what agency and within what structure can an "event" "occur"? And what does it mean that a moment or particular now "passes," producing a sequence of nows? How and by what necessity does a former or future now dislodge the present now from its position? The very notion of causality called upon to explain this movement—a mechanistic causality in which an effect is produced by virtue of a preceding material cause—is based on a temporal relationship that cannot, without circularity, be used to explain time itself. And the notion of agency involved in this mechanistic causality is based on a notion of time as an object-ive, ontic category: the now as a being-present, a full and substantial entity. Within this scheme, what could cause this plenitude to be overcome, or made "to pass"? And what other entity could it affect, since there is only one now (the present) admissible in this temporal scheme? If another now appears, this other somehow already must have dislodged the present now, making of it a former now.[14] Against this conception of time as an objective category, perhaps we should heed Nietzsche and guard against the attribution of linguistic conventions and logical or conceptual categories to the "nature" of "things."

Yet this is not to suggest that time and history are "subjective" categories, as they are thought from Aristotle through Kant; nor is it to make history merely a *historia rerum gestarum* rather than a *res gestae*. The givenness of the "subject" as well as the "object" is put into question, for the "I," Nietzsche writes, is a fiction projected behind the deed.[15] In Derridean terms, both subject and object are always already "written."

We find ourselves led back into the aporiae of temporality and historicity so remarkably formulated by the Eleatics, who found no way out but the reduction of time and history to being and the present. Following from this move, metaphysics has continued to figure time and history as either an idealist (spiritual, teleological, expressive) movement or a realist (materialist, archeological, mechanistic) movement—the former privileging being-presence as the goal of history, the latter privileging being-presence as its origin and center. In neither case, though, do these formulations escape what Heidegger called "onto-theology," the desire for presence that is a form of the desire for that supremely present eternal being: God.

Grammatology wants to write "history" otherwise. It wants to write history in the wake of "the death of God," which would certainly amount to writing something other than history, traditionally conceived. Yet it also wants to show that history has always been written so—indeed has always been *written*, in Derrida's generalized sense of the term—even if this difference has been ceaselessly recuperated into the restricted economy of a history of presence. Deconstruction consists in precisely this double writing: the articulation of history as an incessant closure and opening, the production of history, the historical, and the real as always already written and rewritten.

Contrary to a standard critique, deconstruction and poststructuralism in no way circumvent or fail to account for questions of temporality and history. They do not retain the structuralist bracketing of diachrony. To the contrary, I want to argue that they engage us in a profound reformulation of the problematic of temporality and historicity. It is not that they refer the notion of structure to some "real history" that is "determinant in the last instance"; rather, they indicate the manner in which a temporalizing destructuration is implicit in, and even the condition of possibility for, the very notion of structure. The time of this deconstructuration is marked in the notions of "play" and *différance*,[16] whose operations I will discuss. First, with the grammatological critique in hand, I want to return to Fukuyama and his Hegel so that we can begin to *write* that history and its "end," to set them into play and differ-defer their presence.

Fukuyama's Hegel, Derrida's Hegel

Following Hegel, Fukuyama's conception of history mobilizes all the hierarchical binary oppositions that have structured metaphysics. It narrates the production of essences from the contingent "flow of events," essences that give "coherence and order to the daily headlines."[17] Hegel's teleological conception of history is called upon to explain the movement from natural necessity to rational, technical freedom—a movement that reaches its completion in the "universal homogeneous state" and is thus spent, exhausted, and discarded. And, as with Hegel, this historical movement is said to have "return[ed] full circle," having realized the goal that was already implicit in its origin. For Fukuyama, history is the "history of thought about first principles";[18] and it is these first principles that are the origin, the present, and the end of historical movement. To cite Hegel: "the progression is a retrogression into the ground . . . the whole is a circular motion in itself, in which the first also becomes the last and the last also the first."[19]

Fukuyama's ethnocentrism, totalization, and leveling of difference are explicit and without nuance; they need not be further indicated here. Though lacking a Hegelian subtlety, Fukuyama's article and the discussions surrounding it manage to lay out all the logocentric operations of history I rehearsed above, the definitive expression of which one finds in Hegel. Derrida's critique of Hegel, then, can guide our critique of Fukuyama.

Derrida grants Fukuyama's and Hegel's point that the West has experienced a closure (which is not to say the "end") of history as the history of metaphysics. Derrida writes:

> We believe, quite simply and literally, in absolute knowledge as the *closure* if not the end of history. And we believe *that such a closure has taken place*. . . . The history of presence is closed, for "history" has never meant anything but the presentation of Being, the production and recollection of beings in presence, as knowledge and mastery.[20]

Hegel's system could be the most exemplary history of philosophy and philosophy of history precisely because it closed that history and that philosophy—as Hegel himself remarked, "the Owl of Minerva spreads its wings only with the falling of dusk."[21]

The Hegelian notion of determinate negation and the speculative concepts of *Aufhebung* and *Erinnerung* (sublation and interiorizing memory) are, Derrida writes, *the* concepts of history and teleology as the production of meaning and presence through the consumption of difference and the trace.[22] The notions of self-consciousness and absolute knowledge mark a stopping of the historical metonymy—the slipping of its signifiers—in the final unity and presence of the transcendental signified.

But, for Derrida, Hegel's closure (like any other) does not mark an end. Hegelianism and metaphysics continue indefinitely, as we witness all around us (for instance, with Fukuyama). The notion of closure marks a certain *relatively* circumscribed region, a certain *effect* of ending or delimitation. It marks the *desire* for an end, a desire to delimit inside and outside and the effects of this desire—the desire for an economy restricted by presence and meaning. But however rigorous its negations, exclusions, and interiorizations, that end never properly takes place. The end is always inscribed within a general economy that submits the proper (the interior and its limit) to an alterity that defounds it. The transcendental signified finds itself inscribed as another supplement in a trace structure that displaces it and submits it to a chain of infinite substitution. There is no outside of the general economy of this general text precisely because it is not rigorously delimited, because *différance* operates such that no limit ever could produce the structure of the trace as a presence, because the gathering up of traces never could produce a proper end.

Yet if, for Derrida, following a Heideggerian motif, the effects of this gathering are the most extreme in Hegel, they are also the most excessive, such that, for Derrida, Hegel is both "the last philosopher of the book and the first thinker of writing."[23] Again, this is not to say that with Hegel, or for that matter with Heidegger or Derrida, we find ourselves outside, somewhere other than metaphysics, having transgressed its end or limit. Rather, what Hegel's text lends itself to is a double writing that elicits the effects of meaning, the proper, the same, and the end, while at the same time giving them over to excess and alterity, a diremption without *Aufhebung*.

Derrida's Writing of Hegel: History as *Différance*

> That which is not subjected to the process of *différance* is present. The present is that from which we believe we are able to think time, effacing the inverse necessity: to think the present from time as *différance*.
>
> —Jacques Derrida, *Of Grammatology*

The grammatological strategy consists in such tactics as paleonymy, neologism, and transfiguration—the reinscription of metaphysical terms, the grafting of these terms onto other chains that transmute and pervert them. Grammatology submits all the crucial Hegelian figures to such a rewriting, which exceeds their restricted sense. We saw that, for Derrida, the basic operations of Hegelianism are also the basic operations of the most extreme notion of history—the speculative dialectic with its primary figures, *Aufhebung* and *Erinne-*

rung. Derrida sees these as the basic strategies for the production of the same and the recuperation of difference. As a counterstrategy, grammatology seeks to rewrite these notions as *différance*, the play of traces that writes history as a differing and deferral without end.

Hegel's speculative dialectic is constituted by the diremption of the one (an immediate unity) into the other (its negation), along with a subsequent return to the One produced through the *Aufhebung* (or sublation: negation plus sublimation) of the two prior moments. The resulting higher, mediated unity thus retains, as traces, its prior moments. Hegel writes in the *Phenomenology*:

> What used to be the important thing is now but a trace; its form is enveloped and becomes a simple shadow. This past runs through the individual whose substance is the more advanced Spirit just as one who takes up a higher science goes through the preparatory studies he has long since absorbed, in order to make their contents present: he interiorizes them in the memory, but has no lasting interest in them.[24]

Thus, for Hegel, as for Derrida, the movement of difference produces a trace structure that refers the present to an absent other. The present is but a synthesis of traces; or, rather, the present is a sign.

For Hegel, however, this signifieds of this sign are simply past presents, negated though retained in the interiorizing memory (*Erinnerung*). The past constitutes a proper ground, and the present a synthesis: a retention of former presents and protention of future presents. History is the movement of a present that refers at once to a former present that it comprehends and to a more vast future present that will comprehend it. The movement is continuous, successive, and cumulative, centered in the living present as in a traveler whose itinerary is decipherable through the tracks he has left, iconic signs of his former presence that simply point to the telos of his present being. This is what Deleuze calls the time of Chronos: temporality and historicity as an ever-widening, ever-consuming circle.[25]

For Derrida, as for Hegel, the present exists only in relation to the past as an absent other. But, for Derrida, that other never was, is, or will be properly present.[26] The past is not a sequence of former presents, and the present not their progressive comprehension. Rather, the past is the field of the trace—a nontotalizable, variegated, and shifting field of forces that are either dormant or active. It is a differential field of traces, nonpresences constituted only within a network of differences. Thus, the present does not spring from the past as from a proper ground but rather is articulated out of it and inscribed within it. The present does not re-present at a higher level a former present or presence. It is itself a trace, or rather a *retrait*: a graft or citation that differently repeats a prior inscription. The present is constituted through a double spacing: at once through its differences with the active traces that make up its relatively "present" context and yet also overdetermined by its dormant prior or possible inscriptions. Deleuze calls this the time of Aion: an errant, ever-retracing, labyrinthine temporality and historicity.[27]

The present, then, can neither interiorize nor sublate the past. History is at once constituted of and hollowed out by the past as a fabric of differences, as *différance*. And it is this overdetermination of the present by the past, this nonplenitude of the present as trace, that lends the present to substitution, producing its *relève*, to cite Derrida's transformative translation of Hegel's *Aufhebung* that inscribes in this figure not a sublation or memory but a loss and a forgetting. *Différance*—the incessant differing and deferral of the present, its articulation within a structure of differing and deferral—is the "cause" of the present's passing, its withdrawal or retreat (*retrait*). To cite Deleuze: "If it was not already past at the same time as present, the present would never pass on. The past does not follow the present that it is no longer, it coexists with the present it was. The present is the actual image, and *its* contemporaneous past is the virtual image, the image in the mirror."[28] This virtual past—what Deleuze, following Bergson, calls the "past-in-general"[29] and Derrida, following Levinas, calls the "absolute past"[30]—is to be distinguished from the past conceived as a series of former presents. Derrida's and Deleuze's virtual past is the past as a structure of traces, which is "the condition of the 'passage' of every particular present."[31] Of course, the terms *past* and *present* no longer have a proper meaning here. The past becomes the field of the other, the trace, and *différance*; while the present becomes a retrace articulated out of this field, a trace simulating presence.

Hence, the present is not merely a dialectical complication that retains the prior moment and protends the moment to come. Such a notion still adheres to the metaphysical conception of history as a sequence of nows that privileges the plenitude of the "living present" and Eternity, the center and *telos* of this succession. For grammatology, on the contrary, the traces that articulate the present are not those moments in closest proximity with the "present" moment. Again, the present is articulated only within a general field, a multiple overdetermination that produces delayed effects and activates what Heidegger calls "quiescent" (*ruhig*) forces, traces that surround the present at a distance like the spaced field of harmonic tones that sound in the note though they have not themselves been played.[32] The past surrounds the present and articulates it through many intervals.

According to their grammatological formulation, then, time and history are no longer closed sets made up of simple elements. Their movement is no longer the continuous, successive, cumulative, and teleological realization of an itinerary determined at the origin. Cast adrift from the anchor of the transcendental signified (whether as *arche, telos*, or the present-as-presence), the movement of history becomes, to cite Derrida, "'unmotivated' but not capricious": unmotivated because it lacks a metaphysical anchor, but not capricious because overdetermined and not free-floating.[33] Time and history become so many *Holzwege*, paths through the woods that, as Heidegger writes, are never paths of salvation and bring no new wisdom.[34] Time and history become labyrinthine, forming a "labyrinth which includes in itself its own exits."[35] No longer what Deleuze calls a set (*ensemble*), a succession of items enclosed by parentheses, history becomes a whole (*tout*),[36] a mobile network that remains open because every element is what it is only through its difference with and deference to others, making of history an incessantly destructuring structure that *plays*.

Or, rather, time and history *become*, and become what they have forever been: the excess of every being and every present, an excess that has rendered time ever problematic for metaphysics and has led constantly to the requirement of its reduction to being and presence. But if time and history *become*, we should not understand this as a primordial and continuous flux, the way perhaps Nietzsche, following Heraclitus, still understood it. Becoming should be understood not as a fluid unity that is only subsequently divided but as *différance*, the structured and structuring movement of division, an incessant differing and deferral, a play of presence and absence, memory and forgetting.

Fukuyama Retraced: The (End of the) End of History

In this sense, therefore, it is not only today—with postmodernism, at the so-called end of history—that history is available only as pastiche.[37] The movement of the *retrait* that lacks a "proper" context, history has never been other than a structure of pastiche or the different repetition of the trace. And if that trace is lifeless, it is not because its life is spent but because it must bear within it, as its condition of possibility, *différance*, which Derrida says is "another name for death,"[38] the trace of absence in the present.

Becoming, time, history, and life are what Heidegger calls a "being-toward-death," a "being-toward-the-end";[39] but death and the end no longer constitute an outside or absolute limit. This death and this end are folded into the present, the now, and thus produce its passing. *Différance* is the name of the present's relation to death, its relation to an absent other, the infinite or abyssal ground out of which it presences and withdraws. The present is a warp woven upon a woof that is not its own; and history is the name of this fabric of the trace, this interweaving of the present with its death or end.

Thus, with Nietzsche, Heidegger, Derrida, and Deleuze, we can affirm the end of history—not, surely, the end of difference in a static and fully available present, as Fukuyama and Hegel would have it; but, rather, the end of history-as-the-metaphysics-of-presence. Contrary to a historicism that affirms the present and construes all other moments as preparatory, the grammatological model outlined here affirms an "untimely" history. History conceived in this way is not a continuous and progressive incorporation of the past but an errant movement whose present is troubled by a retrace that it never articulates once and for all. With "the death of God" (the very paradigm of presence), we find ourselves not so much at the end of history as wandering in the middle, an infinity stretching before and behind us.[40]

The history of metaphysics and the metaphysics of history often have been told as culminating in a present that never turns out to be the end: for Hegel, it was Napoleon's victory at Jena; for Marx, the imminent triumph of communism; for Kojève, the American victory in World War II; and for Fukuyama, the fall of communism and thus the removal of any real challenge to American capitalist democracy. It is not that such "ends" turn out to have been miscalculations but rather that they turn out to have been so many instances of a dream: a millenial desire that there be an end of history and that that end be now. To question this conception of history is to disrupt a desire for presence that can only ever maintain itself by force, terror, the threat of the annihilation of difference, or annihilation *simpliciter*.[41] The questioning initiated by grammatology reconceives the present as a tenuous assemblage of differences that are not quelled once and for all in an incorporating present but incessantly disassembling and reassembling in different presents.[42] Such a conception of history and the present as a complex and uneven articulation of differences attempts to combat the ethnocentric and metaphysical notion that this difference merely indicates the lag time before all others are, as Fukuyama puts it, "brought up to the level of [human civilization's] most advanced outposts . . . in Europe and North America."[43] The grammatological conception of history I have pointed toward here seeks to exacerbate those differences so as to differ the Present and defer the End.

Notes

1. Francis Fukuyama, "The End of History?" *National Interest* 16 (Summer 1989): 3–18; and *The End of History and the Last Man* (New York: Free Press, 1992).

2. Fukuyama studied classics as an undergraduate and comparative literature as a graduate student at Yale. He became an analyst at RAND and then, during the Reagan administration, deputy director of the State Department's policy planning staff. His academic mentor was the late conservative classicist Allan Bloom, who edited and introduced the 1969 English translation of Kojève's *Introduction à la lecture de Hegel* and whose laudatory response to Fukuyama'a article immediately followed it in the same issue of the *National Interest*, along with responses from Gertrude Himmelfarb, Irving Kristol, and New York senator Daniel Patrick Moynihan. Shortly following the original publication of "The End of History?" full and partial reprints of the piece, follow-up explanations by, articles and editorials about, and interviews with Fukuyama appeared in the *New York Times*, the *Houston Chronicle*, *Time*, *Harper's*, *Esprit*, *London Review of Books*, the *Chronicle of Higher Education*, *Nature*, the *Economist*, *Professional Georgrapher*, *Current History*, and even *Opera News*. Fukuyama makes explicit that his reading of Hegel derives from that of Kojève, the "greatest" "modern French interpreter of Hegel" who tried "to save Hegel from his Marxist interpreters and to resurrect him as the philosopher who most correctly speaks to our time" ("End of History?" p. 4). Fukuyama acknowledges, however, that other readings of Kojève and of Hegel are possible, since Kojève's students included "Jean-Paul Sartre on the Left and Raymond Aron on the right" (p. 34). I add that one of Kojève's most dedicated students, Georges Bataille, insisted "that Alexandre Kojève's interpretation [of Hegel] does not deviate in any way from Marxism." *Theory of Religion*, trans. Robert Hurley (New York: Zone Books), p. 124.

3. I use the term *grammatology* to cover not only the work of Derrida, who coined the term, but a whole genealogy of figures ranging from Nietzsche and Heidegger through Derrida and Deleuze, all of whom undertake a critique of the metaphysical tradition by foregrounding and generalizing traits subordinated by that tradition, traits that Derrida groups under the general notion of "writing." In my usage, *grammatology* is readily interchangeable with *deconstruction*. The advantage of the former term is that it has not been submitted to the variety of (largely negative) uses that the latter term has and still retains a positive neologistic force.

4. James Atlas, "What Is Fukuyama Saying? And To Whom Is He Saying It?" *New York Times Magazine* 138, 38 (Oct. 22, 1989): 40.

5. Unlike the English phrase *the last men*, Nietzsche's German *die letzten Menschen* is not gender-exclusive and should perhaps be rendered *the last humans*. Nonetheless, I keep the former rendering not only because it has become the standard English translation of Nietzsche's phrase but also because it figures prominently in the title of Fukuyama's recent book.

6. See Nietzsche, *Thus Spoke Zarathustra*, "Zarathustra's Prologue" and passim, in *The Portable Nietzsche*, ed. and trans. Walter Kaufmann (New York: Viking, 1954); also "On the Uses and Disadvantages of History for Life," in *Untimely Meditations*, trans. R. J. Hollingdale (Cambridge: Cambridge University Press, 1983), §8.

7. See Paul Hirst, "Endism," *London Review of Books*, November 1989, pp. 14–15.

8. See Heidegger, *Being and Time*, trans. John Macquarrie and Edward Robinson (San Francisco: Harper and Row, 1962), §6; Heidegger, *What Is a Thing?* trans. W. B. Barton and Vera Deutsch (Chicago: Henry Regnery, 1967), p. 44; and Derrida, *Of Grammatology*, trans. Gayatri C. Spivak (Baltimore: Johns Hopkins University Press, 1976), pp. 10 ff.

9. Derida, *Grammatology*, p. 10.

10. Plato, *Cratylus*, 437b, in *The Collected Dialogues of Plato*, ed. Edith Hamilton and Huntington Cairns (Princeton: Princeton University Press, 1961), p. 471.

11. See M. A. Gillespie, *Hegel, Heidegger and the Ground of History* (Chicago: University of Chicago Press, 1984), p. 98.

12. Nietzsche, *The Will to Power*, ed. Walter Kaufmann, trans. R. J. Hollingdale and Walter Kaufmann (New York: Vintage Books, 1967), §556, emphasis in the original German, *Nietzsche Werke, Kritische Gesamtausgabe*, eds. Giorgio Colli and Mazzino Montinari (Berlin: Walter de Gruyter, 1967–78), VIII 2 [149].

13. Derrida, *Grammatology*, p. 9, 157, and passim. With the term *writing (écriture)*, Derrida designates a host of traits that have been traditionally subordinated by the metaphysics of presence: extension, physicality, plurality, ambiguity, difference, deferral, nonpresence, and so on. The deconstruction of the metaphysics of presence seeks to generalize *writing* in such a way as to subsume being-presence and thus reveal it as only ever an articulation within a differential system. This strategy has similarities to the move in Anglo-American philosophy undertaken by W. V. Quine, who provides an antifoundationalist, holistic critique of the "givenness" of both transcendental notions of logic and language and primitive, empirical "facts." See his "Two Dogmas of Empiricism," in *From a Logical Point of View*, 2nd ed. (Cambridge: Harvard University Press, 1961), pp. 20–46; and "Ontological Relativity," in *Ontological Relativity and Other Essays* (New York: Columbia University Press, 1969), pp. 26–68. For further comparisons between Quine and Derrida, see Samuel C. Wheeler III, "The Extension of Deconstruction," *Monist* 69, no. 1 (January 1986): 3–21; and "Indeterminacy of French Interpretation: Derrida and Davidson," in *Truth and Interpretation: Perspectives on the Philosophy of Donald Davidson*, ed. Ernest LePore (Oxford: Basil Blackwell, 1986), pp. 477–94; and Edith Wyschogrod, "Time and Non-Being in Derrida and Quine," *Journal of the British Society for Phenomenology* 14, no. 2 (May 1983): 112–26.

14. These difficulties are discussed by Gilles Deleuze in *Cinema 2: The Time-Image*, trans. Hugh Tomlinson and Robert Galeta (Minneapolis: University of Minnesota Press, 1989), pp. 78 ff.

15. See Nietzsche, *Will to Power*, §481, and *Twilight of the Idols*, "Reason in Philosophy," §5, "The Four Great Errors," §3, in *The Portable Nietzsche*.

16. See Derrida, "Structure, Sign, and Play in the Discourse of the Human Sciences," in *Writing and Difference*, trans. Alan Bass (Chicago: University of Chicago Press, 1978), pp. 278–93; and "Differance," in *Margins of Philosophy*, trans. Alan Bass (Chicago: University of Chicago Press, 1982), pp. 1–27. The characterization of deconstruction and poststructuralism as ahistorical seems rather misplaced given that, in "Structure, Sign, and Play"—one of the inaugural texts of deconstruction and poststructuralism—Derrida explicitly argues that structuralist synchrony will always give way to a temporalizing and historicizing destructuration. The charge of ahistoricism, then, seems to be symptomatic of an inability to conceive of time and history other than as the linear consecution or narration of "real," formerly present events.

17. Fukuyama, "End of History?" p. 3.

18. Fukuyama, "Next Question: What Follows the End of History?" *Houston Chronicle*, Dec. 17, 1989.

19. *Science of Logic*, cited in Gillespie, *Hegel, Heidegger and the Ground of History*, p. 98.

20. Derrida, *Speech and Phenomena*, trans. David B. Allison (Evanston: Northwestern University Press, 1973), p. 102.

21. *Hegel's Philosophy of Right*, trans. T. M. Knox (New York: Oxford University Press, 1967), p. 13.

22. Derrida, *Grammatology*, p. 25.

23. Ibid., pp. 24–26.

24. *Hegel's Phenomenology of Spirit*, trans. A. V. Miller (New York: Oxford University Press, 1977), p. 16; translation modified.

25. See Deleuze, *Logic of Sense*, trans. Mark Lester, ed. Constantine B. Boundas (New York: Columbia University Press, 1990), pp. 162–68.

26. See Derrida, *Grammatology*, p. 70, where, referring to Emmanuel Levinas, he calls upon "the alterity of a past that never was and never can be lived in the originary or modified form of presence." See also "Differance," p. 21; and *Positions*, trans. Alan Bass (Chicago: University of Chicago Press, 1981), pp. 91–96, where Derrida distinguishes *différance* from contradiction, clarifying that *the other*, in his sense, is not a *position* (*Setzung*) that could be held or occupied but the defounding of positions, what he calls "spacing."

27. See Deleuze, *Logic of Sense*, pp. 162–68.

28. Deleuze, *Cinema 2*, p. 79. This analysis of time runs throughout Deleuze's work. See also *Nietzsche and Philosopy*, trans. Hugh Tomlinson (New York: Columbia University Press, 1983), pp. 47–49; *Proust and Signs*, trans. Richard Howard (New York: George Braziller, 1972), pp. 54–64; *Bergsonism*, trans. Hugh Tomlinson and Barbara Habberjam (New York: Zone Books, 1988), chap. 3.

29. See Deleuze, *Prost and Signs*, pp. 54 ff; *Bergsonism*, chap. 3; and *Cinema 2*, chaps. 3–5.

30. See Derrida, *Grammatology*, pp. 66 ff; "Differance," p. 21. Also see Levinas, "The Trace of the Other," in *Deconstruction in Context*, ed. Mark C. Taylor (Chicago: University of Chicago Press, 1986), pp. 345–59. Both Levinas and Deleuze cite Bergson, a relatively neglected figure, as the main source of their rethinking of time. See Richard Kearney, "Dialogue with Emmanuel Levinas," in *Face to Face with Levinas*, ed. Richard Cohen (Albany: State University of New York Press, 1986), p. 21, where, in a remarkable passage, Levinas replies: "The relation with the other is *time*: it is an untotalizable diachrony in which one moment pursues another without ever being able to catch up with, or coincide with it. The nonsimultaneous and nonpresent are my primary rapport with the other in time. Time means that the other is forever beyond me, irreducible to the synchrony of the same. The temporality of the interhuman opens up the meaning of otherness and the otherness of meaning."

31. Deleuze, *Bergsonism*, p. 56.

32. Heidegger, *What Is a Thing?* p. 44. It is a pervasive theme in Heidegger's work that what is "near" is not at all what is closest at hand as a being-present. See, e.g., "Building Dwelling Thinking" and "The Thing," in *Poetry, Language, Thought*, trans. Albert Hofstadter (San Francisco: Harper and Row, 1971), pp. 143–86. For more on these delayed effects, see Derrida, "Freud and the Scene of Writing," in *Writing and Difference*, pp. 196–231, an analysis of Freud's concepts of *Nachträglichkeit* and *Verspätung*.

33. Derrida, *Grammatology*, p. 46.

34. Heidegger, "The Thing," p. 185.

35. Derrida, *Speech and Phenomena*, p. 104.

36. See Deleuze, *Cinema 1: The Movement-Image*, trans. Hugh Tomlinson and Barbara Habberjam (Minneapolis: University of Minnesota Press, 1986), chaps. 1–3.

37. So argues Fredric Jameson in "Postmodernism, or the Cultural Logic of Late Capitalism," *New Left Review* 146 (1984): 53–92.

38. Derrida, *Grammatology*, p. 71.

39. Heidegger, *Being and Time*, pp. 279 ff.

40. See Nietzsche, "On the Vision and the Riddle," *Thus Spoke Zarathustra*.

41. For more on the "terror" that threatens to eliminate every alterity, see Jean-François Lyotard, *The Postmodern Condition: A Report on Knowledge*, trans. Geoff Bennington and Brian Massumi (Minneapolis: University of Minnesota Press, 1984), especially the Introduction and §§11, 14.

42. See Derrida, "Differance," p. 3.

43. Fukuyama, "End of History?" p. 5. For a critique of this ethnocentrism and metaphysics, see Ernesto Laclau and Chantal Mouffe, *Hegemony and Socialist Strategy: Towards a Radical Democratic Politics* (London: Verson, 1985); and Samuel C. Wheeler III, "True Figures: Metaphor, Social Relations, and the Sorites," in *The Interpretive Turn: Philosophy, Science, Culture*, ed. David R. Hiley et. al. (Ithaca: Cornell University Press, 1991), pp. 197–217. Conservatives, too, have criticized Fukuyama's thesis on the basis of a similar diagnosis of our historical, cultural, and political situation. See Irving Kristol's "Response" to Fukuyama's article in the *National Interest* 16 (Summer 1989): 26–28. I would like to thank Molly Whalen, Elizabeth Grosz, and the anonymous readers for Wayne State University Press for helpful comments on earlier drafts of this paper.

The Textual Logic of Democracy: Theory and the Crisis of Representation

Steven Goldsmith

With peace breaking out all over the world, it should not surprise us to find apologists for democracy breaking out all over the Western media. In a now famous article published in the *National Interest*, Francis Fukuyama, a State Department policy advisor, brought the theme to its inevitably eschatological pitch: "What we may be witnessing is not just the end of the Cold War, or the passing of a particular period of postwar history, but the end of history as such; that is, the end point of mankind's ideological evolution and the universalization of Western liberal democracy as the final form of government."[1] One might expect such extraordinary events at the end of a millennium to occasion this sort of apocalyptic declaration, even on the part of a self-styled conservative. What one might not have anticipated is the recent tendency of left-leaning writers to take up the cause of democracy, to defend it as a political form by linking it to the assumptions of poststructuralism. In political philosophy, Claude Lefort has led the way with his assertion that "Democracy . . . proves to be the historical society *par excellence*, a society which, by its very form, welcomes and preserves indeterminacy."[2] Ernesto Laclau, coauthor of a book subtitled "Toward a Radical Democratic Politics," argues that because society can be defined as "the unstable order of a system of differences," it must be understood according to the model of discourse proposed by Derrida in "Structure, Sign, and Play."[3] And in a recent seminar at Berkeley, Derrida himself referred frequently, and somewhat mysteriously, to "the democracy

Adapted from Steven Goldsmith, *Unbuilding Jerusalem: Apocalypse and Romantic Representation*, pp. 165–90. Copyright © 1993 by Cornell University. Used by permission of the publisher, Cornell University Press.

yet to come." In the field of history, the kinship between theory and democracy has led to a reconsideration of the eighteenth-century democratic revolutions, with figures such as François Furet, Lynn Hunt, and Dick Howard all contesting the economics-centered analysis that sees "the rights of man" as merely the ideological legitimization of developing capitalist relations. The primary achievement of the revolutions, they contend, was to create a substantially new and powerful discourse, the discourse of politics.[4]

In this essay, I consider the symbiotic, mutually invigorating relationship between contemporary critical theory and democratic politics, a coupling that is perhaps a cause for caution. Critical theory and modern politics, I would suggest, emerge together in the context of the late-eighteenth-century revolutions, each focusing on a crisis of representation. By theory, I mean generally the modern discourse that rises from the realization that representations are indeterminate and therefore lacking in ontological authority. To point out a certain fit between this central concern of theory and democratic culture is not to disparage either term; I distinctly want to avoid evaluation here. By placing side by side a literary and a political passage from the 1790s, I merely hope to suggest that whatever we think of theory must be bound up with what we understand of the democratic societies in which theory is practiced. Any claims on the part of contemporary critical theory to contestation and even subversion find their limit in the participation of such theoretical practices within a specifically democratic context. In democratic societies, in other words, critical theory may very well serve more a stabilizing than a disruptive function.[5]

The two texts I want to juxtapose are a single proverb from William Blake's *The Marriage of Heaven and Hell* (1793) and a passage from Thomas Paine's *Age of Reason* (1794). Both texts address the problem of apocalypse, a problem more familiar to readers of Blake than to readers of Paine. And for both texts the problem of apocalypse concerns representation: how can one represent in merely human terms the *logos* that transcends both history and material form? Paul Mann states plainly the Derridean crux of Blake's dilemma: Blake's text "asks whether the very forms in which a visionary poet works are not ultimately futile, whether poetic apocalypse is not a contradiction in terms."[6] And yet, what is often perceived as an aesthetic or epistemological crisis in Blake—that representation undermines apocalypse—is also the first principle of a political strategy, one very much aligned with the primary demand of radicals such as Paine: the demand for expanded representation in government. The foregrounding of representation in Blake's work ensures that every pretense to apocalypse gets refocused as a representation of apocalypse. Apocalypse is global; at a stroke, it ends and displaces an entire world. By definition, representation is partial; it registers an act circumscribed by contingency, produced within a limited social horizon. The very fact of representation, then, disables the most dangerous feature of apocalypse, its claim of totalization, and returns any potentially authoritarian *logos* to the place of multiple voices where it is one preapocalyptic word among many. Blake subverts his own apocalypse in order to dramatize how one subverts the claims of power.

In 1793, while he was still enthusiastic about events in France, Blake included the following proverb in *The Marriage of Heaven and Hell*: "Truth can never be told so as to be understood, and not be believ'd" (10: 69).[7] Although the proverb does not at first appear to involve apocalypse, matters of truth are for Blake inevitably implicated in matters of apocalypse. In "A Vision of the Last Judgement," Blake contends that "whenever any Individual Rejects Error & Embraces Truth a Last Judgment passes upon that Individual" (562), and later in the same piece he associates the revelation of truth with the conventional imagery of apocalypse: "Error is Created and Truth is Eternal Error or Creation will be Burned Up & then & not till then Truth or Eternity will appear" (565). As Derrida has suggested, this tendency to perceive knowledge in terms of an apocalyptic narrative is a recurring feature of Western philosophy. "Truth itself is the end, the destination," he writes, "and that truth unveils itself is the advent of the end. . . . The structure of truth here would be apocalyptic."[8] This secular eschatology implies not only that apocalypse is a cognitive event but that it is ideological as well. Last Judgment involves restructuring the way one thinks one's world, and, to the extent its truth is widely internalized as knowledge or belief, it stabilizes a particular order or *logos*. The concise, epigrammatic form of the proverb suggests how quickly truth can be understood and believed, how quickly it can amount to a minor apocalypse. Aphorisms offer the opportunity of instant digestion; they subordinate the fact of their representation to a truth immediately and uncritically intuited, a truth which, as Wordsworth might say, is its own testimony, carried alive into the heart by passion.

Blake begins, then, with an ideologically dangerous form, dangerous because its truth seems to transcend the conditions of representation. The proverb, however, allows nothing of the sort. In the first place, its compact message would need no expression at all were it not implied that truth is often told, misunderstood, and disbelieved. Apparently, the transparency of communication cannot be taken for granted, leaving us no guarantee that this is a sentence we can understand, let alone believe. This initial possibility of doubt is then enhanced by the strange surface of the words, a rhetorical surface that is anything but transparent. Blake could have written, "Truth told and understood must be believed," but instead he compels the reader to negotiate a double negative that complicates meaning along with syntax. Blake goes out of his way, in other words, to ensure the possibility, even the probability, of being misunderstood. The sentence consists of a series of obstacles or negations that suddenly give way in the end to a positive and perhaps unearned reversal. The final clause arrives like the parousia; belief redeems truth, converting linguistic pessimism into plenitude, replacing Babel with *logos*. But do we believe it?

To write a narrative of the reading process entailed by this proverb is to witness the obstacles to revelation. The proverb unfolds in four stages:

Truth

Truth can never be told

Truth can never be told so as to be understood

Truth can never be told so as to be understood, and not be believ'd

The reader begins with a confident self-presence, the thing itself, but by the end of the first complete thought, truth has been severed altogether from verbal representation. The very sentence "truth can never be told" performs its own content; it is a paradox of the type "This sentence is a lie" and so denies the possibility of determinate meaning. By the time the reader reaches the proverb's caesura, the burden of indeterminacy expands to include reception as well as production, audience as well as author. If truth can be told, it cannot be communicated; there exists no ground to secure the transmission of ideas through the deflecting medium of language. The subjection of truth to debilitating linguistic contingencies signals a direct contradiction of the proverb's overall and sanguine meaning, a meaning that can be completed, appropriately enough, only through the introduction of yet another negative. First slowing the reader by a tricky syntax and then commenting internally on his own representational act, Blake undermines the proverb's teleology and thus the closure upon which its apocalypse depends. Indeed, the very proverb that anounces the simultaneity of truth and belief represents the distance between them, something Blake literalizes by placing the key terms at opposite ends of the sentence.

If representation thus marks an aesthetic or epistemological failing, it acts at the same time as a defense mechanism against any claims that apocalyptic truth might have on us. Blake's proverb opens the option of disbelief. Because truth must pass through language, and because that passage is made visible, it forfeits its grounds of authority and thus the aura that allows it to be bound to power. This particular strategy, this insistence on linguistic suspicion, characterizes Blake's writings throughout his career. His discourse is a primer in surveillance, a lesson in policing the movement of power within language, whether his own or that of others. One observes in Blake with particular clarity, I would argue, a phenomenon general to the emergence of democratic discourse—the demand for linguistic vigilance, a sensitivity to the work of representation in either the perpetuation or the critique of power. Like so many of his contemporaries, Blake saw power everywhere; and because language was the field in which power became visible and was contested, it took on unprecedented—and perhaps inflated—significance. One lasting success of the democratic revolutions was to make power seem inseparable from language, to make its appearance in discourse seem coterminous with its very existence. This assumption meant, for one thing, that power might be subverted by a linguistic act. It meant, for another, that power could be linguistically redistributed through a representational system of government that allows all qualified interests a say in its operations. The collapsing of power into language marked the invention of modern politics, something one sees everywhere: in Paine's demand for a written constitution, in Madison's idea that representation institutionalizes conflict and thus contains it, in John Stuart Mill's argument, half a century later, that Parliament should serve a "talking" function, debating policy without itself initiating or enacting it. In each of these cases, one can observe the characteristically democratic faith that power is emptied to the extent that it is made to pass through words, to the extent, in other words, that it is represented.

The opening gambit of Paine's *Age of Reason* is a case in point. In many respects, *Age of Reason* is nothing more than a popularization of eighteenth-century assaults upon the Bible as literal history. And yet, while all of his specific evidence is derivative, Paine's initial argument introduces a general principle of subversive reading unavailable before the emergence of democratic discourse but central ever since. After explaining that all official religions ground their authority in one sort of revelation or another, Paine begins, with his inimitable clarity, to define revelation and to outline its consequences.

> Revelation, when applied to religion, means something communicated immediately from
> God to man. No one will deny or dispute the power of the Almighty to make such a

communication if he pleases. But admitting, for the sake
of a case, that something has
been revealed to a certain person, and not revealed to
any other person, it is revelation
to that person only. When he tells it to a second person,
a second to a third, a third to a
fourth, and so on, it ceases to be a revelation to all those
persons. It is revelation to the
first person only, and hearsay to every other, and consequently they are not obliged to
believe it.
It is a contradiction in terms and ideas, to call anything a
revelation that comes to
us at second-hand, either verbally or in writing. Revelation is necessarily limited to the
first communication—after this, it is only an account of
something which that person
says was a revelation to him: and though he may find
himself obliged to believe it, it
cannot be incumbent on me to believe it in the same
manner; for it was not a revelation
made to me, and I have only his word that it was made
to him.[9]

In what is perhaps the central assumption of representative
democracy, words protect us from the imposition of authority; they
intervene in the form of discourse between us and the self-repre-
sentations of power. I write "discourse" here because language for
Paine is necessarily mediated by the contingencies that make it partial, limited, interested, and therefore variable according to speakers
and circumstances. If language were unmediated by cultural and
other factors, then revelation could retain a universal authority,
then John's claim in the Book of Revelation that he merely records
without loss the voice and visions of Christ would at least be plausible. By foregrounding the failings inherent in any verbal transmission, Paine circumscribes revelation so tightly that without ever denying the possibility of its existence, he renders it harmless. In a
way thoroughly compatible with Blake's art, he introduces the right
to suspicion, insisting that the "fallen" nature of human language
releases us from an obligation to believe and thus ensures our independence from power if we assert it. No one ever so relished the
obstacles to a determinate text: "The continually progressive change
to which the meaning of words is subject, the want of a universal
language which renders translation necessary, the errors to which
translations are subject, the mistakes of copyists and printers, to-

gether with the possibility of willful alteration, are themselves evidences that the human language, whether in speech or in print, cannot be the vehicle of the word of God" (p. 23). To put the matter simply, our contingencies set us free. The very fact that we have interests, that our thoughts and our language are inescapably informed by the local conditions of history and culture, makes the airtight communication of revelation impossible. Representation redeems us from the authority of a totalitarian *logos*.

By setting representation at odds with revelation, Paine brings into explicit theory a widespread democratic practice of the 1790s. In no way, however, does this explain the specific urgency of his text in 1794. Not simply a register of religious dissent, *Age of Reason* is also a thinly veiled challenge to Robespierre and the Terror. Paine himself was arrested by the Committee for Public Safety within hours of completing Part One of his book. Curiously, Paine's confrontation with the Jacobins had little to do with religion; both he and Robespierre were confirmed deists. Instead, their dispute involved the very nature of democracy, so that when Paine wrote about the intervention of representation in revealed religion, he also, covertly, with risk to his life, wrote about the necessity of representation in government. With his Anglo-American background, Paine meant "representative government" when he said "democracy." It was this very position, the one he had argued so forcefully in *Rights of Man*, that jeopardized his standing in France. Indeed, the Jacobins rolled into power in Paris *because of their opposition to representation*, because of their claim to embody immediately "the will of the people." The most radical assumption of the Terror, an assumption that far exceeded any such claims to popular power in America, was that the people could govern themselves directly without any mediation between them and power. Representation, according to this view, lay closer to the old system of government than to the new; it simply reorganized elite power without genuinely redistributing it. Legislators differed from kings in degree, not kind; they still ruled the people who still obeyed. The only entity that could legitimize power during the crisis of 1793 and 1794 was "the people," the idea of a unified, homogeneous populace acting its collective will directly, and the fierce political competitions that eventuated in the ascent of Robespierre involved the attempt by various parties not to represent the people but to establish themselves as popular agency itself.

Only in this context does the full force of Paine's critique of revelation, which is essentially a linguistic or hermeneutic critique, become clear. Jacobin democracy comes into being with a set of linguistic assumptions sharply different from those involved in American or representative democracy. Far from being tangential, language is precisely at issue here. According to Lynn Hunt, the French fixation on national unity reflected "the revolutionary belief in the possibility and even the desirability of 'transparency' between citizen and citizen, between citizens and their government, between the individual and the general will."[10] Based on this predominantly linguistic model, the Terror marked an attempt to govern without the mediating functions typically served by representation. Paine's suspicion of revelation in the opening pages of *Age of Reason* is precisely a suspicion of "transparency" as a misguided and dangerous political model: "Revelation is necessarily limited to the first communication—after this, it is only an account of something which that person says was a revelation made to him." Addressed covertly to the Jacobin Tribunal, this says, "You say you speak the will of the people, but neither I nor anyone else am obliged to believe your words." Paine could see that Robespierre had merely inverted the Book of Revelation, locating his unmediated inspiration not in God above but in "the people" below. In either case, apocalyptic authority was generated by insisting upon an absolute source of power and the undeviating coincidence between that power and the voice of its spokesman. By disallowing the possibility of transparency, representation served two functions for Paine: first, it collapsed Robespierre's authority back into the multiplicity of social voices, of party and individual interests, something the Jacobins claimed to have transcended; second, it denied the very existence of a unified national will that could authorize power. For Paine and the republicans, power was something to be negated perpetually, and this could be accomplished only by exploiting inherent social divisions, by making the very lack of a universal community and a universal language the basis of liberation. Paine's democracy is thoroughly pluralist; one cultural interest contradicts another, and all are partial representations with no claim on the communal whole. Representation thus becomes the means by which people simultaneously form a government and resist all attempts to reduce them to a single identity—"the people."

At the very moment Paine repudiates the Terror as an apocalyptic text, he demonstrates most clearly how democratic politics has become implicated in problems of linguistic form. Republican government, one could say, is structured like a text, or, taking a deeper risk of anachronism, one might say a poststructuralist text. In this sense, representation is an attempt to institutionalize, to give positive form to, the decentering of meaning in discourse on the one hand and the decentering of political power on the other. In both cases (government and language), this form of democracy is defined primarily by what it sets out to deny: the idea of a determinate and homogeneous social order purged of conflicting interests. Paradoxically, its institutions are the positive form of an essentially negative process, the emptying out of power into the play of minute social fragments that in turn has for its model the emptying out of the *logos* into the play of multiple and irreconcilable interpretations. The self-criticism implicit in the act of foregrounding representation that we saw in both Blake and Paine becomes a founding principle of political structure. Whether in text or in government, what matters is the way one undermines one's own ability to produce determinate meaning and thus one's own authority over others; what matters is the ability to affirm a negative relation to power. In this way, a common denominator of democratic practices is the production of forms that enact their own incapacities, their own debilitating contradictions, in deference to the freedom constituted by an untranscendable social and linguistic diversity. What has become a leading methodological principle in a variety of contemporary literary theories has been and continues to be a central feature of the governments under which such theories are generated.

I conclude with a familiar example. In a series of extraordinary documents commonly known as the Federalist Papers, James Madison articulates precisely these aesthetic principles as part of his proposal for the American Constitution. His chief innovation, the system of checks and balances, consists of a perpetually self-subverting mechanism, a way of "contriving the interior structure of government as that its several component parts may, by their mutual relations, be the means of keeping each other in their places."[11] Madison imagines his American government to be as dependent on the people as Robespierre would a few years later in France, but, for Madison, the people preserve their freedom because their very differences guarantee that the exercise of power will be dissipated with the variety and inevitability of conflict: "Whilst all authority in it [the federal republic of the United States] will be derived from and dependent upon the society, the society itself will be broken up into so many parts, interests and classes of citizens, that the rights of individuals, or of the minority, will be in little danger from interested combinations of the majority" (p. 88). Destabilization has become definitive of political structure. As Madison explains with characteristic wariness, the failings of human nature make it necessary that "ambition must be made to counteract ambition" (p. 86). Paine is considerably more optimistic. What Madison calls ambitions, he calls interests, meaning the distinctions in property that he believes arise from the uneven distribution of natural talents. Both Madison and Paine, however, endorse the creation of an arena wherein division and conflict are not merely foregrounded but made constitutive of society itself. That arena is called politics, or, more properly, government. "By ingrafting representation upon democracy," Paine states in *Rights of Man*, "we arrive at a system of government capable of embracing and confederating all the various interests and every extent of the territory and population."[12] Paine's arguments of 1791 often recapitulate those put forth in the *Federalist* only four years earlier and in this context might be schematized as follows: the social text is free to the extent that its differences and even its contradictions make the centralization of power impossible; the text of government mirrors and protects that freedom by making itself an empty center, a play of relational forces without any shared or determinate essence. Underlying both of these considerations is what I would call an intoxication with discourse, the exhilarating but often uncritical assumptions about language that enable Enlightenment radicalism. According to this intoxication, power, like anything else, takes shape only as it is represented; in turn, representation is socially contingent and therefore multiple, interested, and indeterminate—in other words, without firm ontological standing; power thus subverts itself the moment it *asserts* itself. Modern democracy emerges with the same wishfulness characteristic of much contemporary theory, the belief that emancipation from power corresponds to the capacity for perpetual subversion in and by language.

Notes

1. Francis Fukuyama, "The End of History?" *National Interest* 16 (Summer 1989): 4.
2. Claude Lefort, *Democracy and Political Theory*, trans. David Macey (Minneapolis: University of Minnesota Press, 1988), p. 16.
3. Ernesto Laclau, "Metaphor and Social Antagonisms," in *Marxism and the Interpretation of Culture*, ed. Cary Nelson and Lawrence Grossberg (Urbana: University of Illinois Press, 1988), pp. 249–54.
4. See François Furet, *Interpreting the French Revolution*, trans. Elborg Forster (Cambridge: Cambridge Univesity Press, 1981); Lynn Hunt, *Politics, Culture, and Class in the French Revolution* (Berkeley: University of California Press, 1984); Dick Howard, *Defining the Political* (Minneapolis: University of Minnesota Press, 1989).
5. This argument and the cases that follow are more fully elaborated in my chapter on Blake and Paine in *Unbuilding Jerusalem: Apocalypse and Romantic Representation* (Ithaca: Cornell University Press, 1993). See Chapter 3, "Apocalypse and Representation: Blake, Paine, and the Logic of Democracy," pp. 135–208.
6. Paul Mann, "*The Book of Urizen* and the Horizon of the Book," in *Unnam'd Forms: Blake and Textuality*, ed. Nelson Hilton and Thomas Vogler (Berkeley: University of California Press, 1986), p. 61.

7. All citations of Blake are to *The Complete Poetry and Prose of William Blake*, ed. David V. Erdman (Garden City: Anchor, 1982).

8. Jacques Derrida, "Of an Apocalyptic Tone Recently Adopted in Philosophy," *Oxford Literary Review* 6 (1984): 24.

9. Thomas Paine, *Age of Reason* (New York: Pantheon, 1984), pp. 9–10. Further references are to this edition.

10. Lynn Hunt, *Politics, Culture, and Class in the French Revolution* (Berkeley: University of California Press, 1984), p. 44.

11. James Madison, *Selections from "The Federalist,"* ed. Henry Steele Commager (New York: Appleton-Century-Crofts, 1949), p. 85.

12. Thomas Paine, *The Rights of Man* (New York: Penguin, 1969), p. 180.

Tossings and Turnings: On the Alleged Shift in the Humanities from Theory to History

Joshua Kates

That currents in literary criticism have shifted somewhat in the last ten years is undoubtedly true. To say in what this shift consists, what direction it has taken, continues to be a difficult task. Often, of late, this shift has been depicted as a switch from literary theory to something else, usually to something of a more straightforwardly political, historical, cultural, or even ethical nature. Not only has the famous *Against Theory*[1] manifesto been influential in this regard, but many books released in the last four or five years seem to encourage this trend. For example, in a collection of essays titled *The Future of Literary Theory*,[2] a number of prominent theorists tell us the future of theory is, has been, or will be relatively grim.

Given the sophistication of those on both sides of this divide, it is surprising, however, that the divide, and these lines, have been established so simply. *Against Theory*, of course, had a polemical intent, and it contained more than one misunderstanding and more than one subversive twist. But when a critic of J. Hillis Miller's rank believes he or she is seriously summing up the critical activity of the last ten years by asserting that "there has been a shift away from an interest in 'reading' which means a focus on language as such, its nature and its powers, to various forms of hermeneutic interpretation, which means a focus on the relation of language to something else, God, nature, society, history, the self, whatever," something is seriously wrong.[3] Not because what Miller says is incorrect—this may not be so—but because he fails to take into account what may make it impossible to decide whether one has judged correctly here or not.

This failure and this impossibility come to the foreground in an ambiguity built into Miller's own distinction. Given his definition as it now stands, "reading" versus "hermeneutics" equals "language" versus "language's relation to something else," all sorts of approaches—such as structuralism, Russian formalism, semiotics, and others—would fall under the category of "reading." All of them examine language, not something else, but all assume, though in different ways, that they already know what language is. None of them, then, exemplifies reading in the sense Miller has in mind, certainly not if reading in this sense is to characterize a phase of "theory" but recently turned against. Though "reading" in the context of recent theory may connote a certain interest in language, it also seems to connote a change in the status of reference. The referent of most theory's "reading" is *produced* by way of that reading. Reading, though not necessarily, or wholly, absolved from any species of knowledge—neither theoretical nor historical knowledge—seems secured in advance by neither of these.

This is a feature of "theory" that entails that theory itself be something other than simply theoretical. As such, it has proved an obstacle to understanding "theory" in the past, and it continues to do so now. Consequently, I would like to begin by making the productive aspect of theory's reading a bit clearer, not simply because this problem in its own right may be of interest to some but because it goes to the very heart of Miller's concern, which is not finally with language or with reading but with the future, the future of literary theory.

After all, let us recall one of the two most prominent definitions of reading that a certain brand of theory has offered us:

> The question is therefore not only of Rousseau's writing but also of our reading. We should begin by taking rigorous account of this being held within or this surprise: the writer writes in a language and in a logic whose proper system, laws, and life his discourse by definition cannot dominate absolutely. He uses them only by letting himself, after a fashion and up to a point, be governed by the system. And the reading must always aim at a certain relationship unperceived by the writer, between what he commands and what he does not command of the patterns of the language that he uses. This relationship is not a certain quantitative distribution of shadow and light, of weakness or of force, but a signifying structure that critical reading should produce.[4]

I cite this passage because it emphasizes this moment of reading as production, but not only for this reason. From the point of view of Miller's remarks on language, the entire passage seems highly paradoxical. In contrast to his commonsense distinction between language alone and in relation to something else, here we confront language itself as somehow implicated in another moment, this moment of production. Yet how can one capture the energy and sense of language, language as even Derrida seems to mean it here—as the already given, as that which one is already supposedly "within"—all the while claiming that this, the already given, is yet to be, and must be, produced?

Of course, it is not simply language but a certain unperceived relationship to it whose production Derrida mandates. Yet this, at least from Miller's point of view, is equally problematic. It is just as difficult to see how not language but indeed a moment of language, a certain exchange or relationship within language, is the subject not of reproduction but of production.

Reading here, however, is the matter of a production, and the production of something very much like a language precisely because what corresponds to Miller's language alone, these "patterns of language" Derrida refers to, by no means simply proceed without this unperceived relationship to them. Though these patterns of language, this system within language, will eventually come to designate the language and the logic of language's own hold—this "being held within," the "surprise" of language itself—nevertheless they follow from what Miller would call a hermeneutic: an examination of language's relation to another entity (in this instance, Rousseau). In a certain way, this is Derrida's "point": only through this moment, only through this unperceived relationship that is yet to be produced (language's relation to Rousseau), does the access to language's singular self-relation, the difference language makes, or the difference that makes language first become available. Only through a reading of Rousseau does the latter, which Derrida calls "supplement," first become legible.

No wonder, then, that Miller's distinction between hermeneutics and reading tends to break down, since what marks the hyperproductivity, the unique productivity of Derrida's reading is precisely the fact that the hermeneutic moment here makes possible the moment of language. Reading in this sense is singularly productive precisely because it produces not just any referent but something like a language, indeed the language of language: language's take on itself.

I emphasize these facts not to cast doubt on Derrida's statements—as readers of *Of Grammatology* know, it is precisely this, unlikely as it may seem, that Derrida does—but, as I said, in order to shed light on Miller's question concerning the future of literary theory. There was a time when debates over the aftermath of deconstruction abounded. And though these have for the most part receded, it is important to see what was then quite often over-looked: the success of this facet of Derrida's text, of this moment of reading as production, rendered the whole question of the future of deconstruction infinitely problematic, and this prior to and apart from any considerations of reception—whether this reception was correct, incorrect, rebellious, mistaken, ignorant, what have you.

For this peculiar interweaving of hermeneutics and production, language and language's relation to Rousseau did not only entail a certain deployment of history (it is on the basis of Rousseau's relation to the history of logocentrism that one provisionally puts to his texts the question of language's relation to him).[5] But, moreover, it entailed a deployment, indeed something like an exhaustion, of Derrida's own history, of the "future" of his own work. In this regard, let me just quote from a little later on in this same section, when Derrida himself remarks on the exorbitance of his own enterprise:

> I wished to reach the point of a certain exteriority in relation to the totality of the age of logocentrism. Starting from this point of exteriority, a certain deconstruction of that totality which is also a traced path, of that orb, which is also orbitary might be broached. The first gesture of this departure and this deconstruction, although subject to a certain historical necessity, cannot be given methodological or logical intra-orbitary assurances. . . . The *departure* is radically empiricist. . . . It is affected by non-knowledge as by its future and it ventures out deliberately.[6]

The first thing to notice is that Derrida here speaks not of his future but of his departure, of his beginning or past. Yet this past, this departure, he tells us, is affected by nonknowledge *as* by its future. Derrida's statement, then, though similar to a protestation of ignorance about the future of his work, and perhaps even implying this, is nevertheless a number of steps removed from any such claim. Not only does nonknowledge stand in for that future, but this nonknowledge, which replaces Derrida's future, already will have affected Derrida's enterprise, and affected it from the start. Indeed, Derrida here is so far from considering how another future, someone else's future, might receive his work that this is almost unimaginable under the circumstances he presents—in which nonknowledge in lieu of the future has operated at the outset of his own radical departure.

Of course, in turn, this statement does not proclaim some totalitarian moment of deconstruction. It is not Derrida's business to imagine the future of another. His relation to that is one not of nonknowledge but of no knowledge. Yet it does raise a technical point concerning deconstruction, concerning, that is, our treatment of Derrida's own future—one that alters, I believe, if not suspends, any attempt to bring his future in line with our own, precisely because it suspends any attempt to bring his future in line with his own.

Let us read carefully what Derrida says here, what he has written about his radical departure. What he wished to reach, he tells us at the beginning of this paragraph, was the point of a certain exteriority to the totality of the age of logocentrism. Yet he discovered, in a manner of speaking, that the only way to reach this point was already to be there. For *starting* from this point of exteriority, he continues, it was only then that he was to undertake a certain deconstruction. The first thing Derrida's departure departs from is departing. Departing from departing, and already, though not yet, having reached a certain exteriority, it will signal this, its exteriority, the radicality of its departure, by remaining, by producing where it already has been, where it already, though not yet, is—outside, elsewhere—through reproducing where it already is and is not— here, within. And this remaining within is, then, the most radical exteriority, this departure from departing the most radical leavetaking.

This is why Derrida calls his departure radical and radically empiricist (though at the end of this paragraph, in line with the figure we are describing here, it is precisely a certain concept of empiricism Derrida will declare nonviable). Because, as he specifies, though there is some historical necessity to his claims, there can be, as he puts it, no intraorbitary assurances. One begins, then, by departing from departing, by remaining where one already is and has never yet been, and by that token never simply will go—since this future he draws on here, this draft, the nonassurance of a certain nonknowledge, the radicality of this empiricism, what defies the intraorbitary, will lead ineluctably not to itself but to a past, another past, a past that could not be were it not for this future, the detour through which, however, through this past, nevertheless forever checking that future from being, or becoming, itself. The future here operates as nonknowledge, and nonknowledge of itself, because it is the disseminated seed of a production that passes through another production or reproduction—that of the greatest totality—on the way to finding or losing the moment of its own. Indeed, it has the form of what Derrida calls a trace: the effacement of which is not only a possible but even a necessary moment of its own inscription.

This should suffice, then, to suggest—of course, only suggest, since in one sense I am arguing that no proof is ultimately relevant here, though that is not all or primarily what I am arguing—that in Derrida's work there is something like a productivity of reading, but one that stymies any chance to ask after its future. And this result may well appear rather disconcerting in light of the question we started out from. For if Miller has told us that the future of literary theory is grim, that it may not have a future, then I seem to be claiming not that it is bright but that literary theory, at least this phase of it, never had a future at all.[7]

This statement, were it true, would not mean, however, that theory is from here on out irrelevant, impossible, dispensable. There remains perhaps some difference between not having and never having had a future. Rather, what this assertion recognizes is that these texts *in principle* mandate a different set of expectations about them, and different relationships to them, from almost all of the theoretical or critical texts we meet up with. What is most important in them does not submit itself to dialogue, or finally even to reading, except of the most tentative sort. They do not allow in principle for corrections or additions, disciples, doctrines, or schools. They do not broach the future in any form with which we are currently familiar.

Consequently, I will postpone further discussion of these results until the end of my essay, when we will have occasion to approach this work out of a future not its own. For the body of this paper, I intend to remain on the other side of Miller's divide, on the other side of the current scene, with not the whence but the whither of literary theory.

2

I maintain, to return to our opening point, that what Miller has taken for a general falling off of reading is not that but is rather something closer to its advent: the advent of a certain practice of reading, indeed of reading as production. Given the paradoxes involved here, it is perhaps no surprise that Miller might mistake the latter for the former. Nevertheless, and despite the fact that Derrida's work may lack all other real relation to contemporary criticism, the practice of reading that we find in that work is not all that different from certain current trends, even some to which deconstruction is often opposed.

Of course, by its very nature, because it thus involves a change in the status of reference, no two instances of this style of reading

will be identical. In fact, in a certain way, it is as much the differences as the similarities that will be of interest to us in what follows,
since the one set will turn out to be as *unexpected* as the other. Nevertheless in every case, we should be able to make out this same
general schema: a hermeneutic that is also a production, in the
sense of a reading of what already will have been though never yet
has been, and which, as such, as a singular production of reference,
outstripping both history and theory, necessarily will configure
each time differently these fields through which it takes its rise.

Even granting the possibility of variation, however, it remains
far from obvious that the latest critical excursions do, in fact, have
this much in common with their recent predecessors. In order to
show how this may be so, I take up the work of one contemporary
critic in particular, Naomi Schor. Specifically, I wish to focus on a
shift from the essays of her earlier work, *Breaking the Chain*,[8] to her
later writings in *Reading in Detail*.[9]

Of course, Schor may not be the first critic one thinks of in an
anti- or post-theoretical context. Certainly, she has never distanced
herself from "theory" in the manner of other recent writers. Nevertheless, I believe an understanding of Schor's work is critical for
these issues. Well grounded in the structuralism and poststructuralism of the 1960s and 1970s, Schor's concerns have always been explicitly political ones. Schor was one of the first to attempt to meld
"high theory" with a species of political questioning. An investigation of her writing and the changes her project undergoes holds les-
sons for both sides of today's putative divide. Her work makes evident both the somewhat unexpected resources of theory or reading
and the central questions and problems facing today's post-theoretical configuration.

That political concerns always have been central to Schor's
work, that she attempted early on to move beyond a certain construal of theory, is clear even in her first book's opening essay, "For
a Restricted Thematics: Writing, Speech, and Difference in *Madame
Bovary*."

At the very outset of her piece, Schor makes a connection between what she is calling thematic reading (criticism as it was practiced in the late 1970s) and tropes of the feminine. As we shall see,
the problem of the feminine that Schor articulates here holds significance for the entirety of her project. Throughout the shifts her
thought undergoes, Schor's preoccupation will be, as here, not simply with this or that aspect of feminist struggle but with how the
feminine may be said to exist at all.

Schor begins her essay by proclaiming a shift in critical trends
that seems to draw into question our current self-understanding. In

"For a Restricted Thematics," written more than ten years before Miller's piece, Schor already announces a return of what she calls "an interest in themes.":

> It is time to say out loud what has been whispered for some time: thematic criticism, which was given a first class funeral a few years ago, is not dead. Like a repressed desire that insists on returning to consciousness, like a guilty pleasure that resists all threat of castration, thematic criticism is coming out from the shadows. (*Breaking the Chain*, p. 3)

According to Schor, in 1978, a return to an interest in themes, an interest in "language's relation to something else," was already under way. In Schor's eyes, however, this return to the theme is by no means opposed to what Miller might call an interest in "language alone." Rather, it is its outgrowth. Schor refers this thematism to its structuralist predecessor. This return is to a thematism "passed through the filter of a structuralist criticism." Thus, what Schor is about to call neothematism is what is more generally known as poststructuralism.

> This new thematic criticism is not, however, a nostalgic textual practice, a "retro" criticism. . . . Just as hyperrealism in painting is a return to the figurative passed through a minimalist grid, neothematism is a thematism passed through the filter of a structuralist criticism. (p. 3)

This is not all. Not only does Schor understand poststructuralism as already a return to the theme (thus calling into question our current self-understanding), but she takes matters another step. For her, what is decisive is the relation between the tropes through which this neothematism has been articulated—"the synonymic chains of Barthes, the 'chain of supplements' of Derrida, . . . the 'series' of Deleuze" (p. 3)—and traditional figurations of the feminine. The opening of Schor's essay renders questionable our current historical schemas. It also immediately situates these (thematic versus formalist criticism, etc.) in an overtly political context:

> The metaphors that these authors weave again and again are extremely significant, since according to Freud the only contribution of women "to the discoveries and inventions in the history of civilization" is a "technique," "that of plaiting and weaving." The thread unravelled by Ariadne, woven by Penelope, is a peculiarly feminine attribute, a metonym for femininity. There is thus cause to speculate about the relations

(necessarily hypothetical at the current stage of our knowledge) between a thematic and a feminine reading, by which I certainly do not mean that reading practiced uniquely by women. If my hypothesis concerning the femininity of thematism were justified, this would explain its culpabilization on the one hand, and its masculine recuperation on the other. (p. 5)

The manner in which Schor deploys the feminine here is important for all of her work. The feminine, it becomes clear, is not one theme, one topic among others. Rather, the turn to the theme itself turns around its tropes. This turn or return of thematism turns out to be both a symptom of a certain "suppression" of the feminine (its culpabilization and masculine recuperation) and in some sense already its singular product or representative (the postulated "femininity of thematism"). On the other hand, however, though neothematism is already in a double sense a consequence of the feminine, a feminine reading would only follow upon this its wayward representative. It remains "at the present stage of our knowledge strictly hypothetical."

For Schor, then, the feminine as such continues to be held in reserve. Indeed, in one sense there is no feminine as such. Not one subject or topic of criticism among others, the feminine resides at the heart of the very possibility of contemporary criticism itself. Critical practice, as Schor saw it at that time, somehow depended on this moment still held in retreat.

Schor's construal of the feminine here calls into question any attempt to treat this subject by way of a present history, a history of presence, whose stakes and topics give themselves without remainder. This is not to say Schor is not interested in history. Indeed, this self-situation of Schor's own project (this hypothetical feminine reading) will carry over into her later avowedly more historical writings. There, its peculiar conditions, its singular thought, will lead her to what we have been calling a certain reading as production.

For, in turn, we also must be aware, if in this essay (and the others in *Breaking the Chain*) Schor assigns to the feminine a central though problematic role, still her own practice continues to lag behind her reflection on its possibility. Though an attention to language and a certain thematism already seem to amount to the same here, reading—in the sense of a radical production of reference— cannot in this instance be identified with either of them. By her own admission, Schor's reading, while reversing the traditional order (for here it is the workings of language that will set the clue for the themes, instead of the themes providing a clue or solution for the

problems of language), while shifting from a metaphoric to a meto-
nymic mode and making important contributions to the discussion
of *Bovary* and the questions of the gender of writing, reading, and
the book, nevertheless remains within the pregiven confines of language and literature and remains with what is still correspondingly
a question of "themes," no matter how new.

That is, Schor's work is not as yet radically productive, productive in the strongest sense, precisely because the moment of language itself is here never drawn into question. Schor continues to
assume we *know* what language and literature are—what a theme,
what a text, what a work may be. The deconstruction that we saw
Derrida's hermeneutic (his reading of Rosseau) perform, of the very
certainties of text and language, here finds no counterpart. Schor's
hermeneutics does not begin soon enough. It is not a "hermeneutic
of language." In it (as in Miller), language—its sense, its limits, its
vocation—precedes reading and not the other way around. Thus,
Schor's models of language and history, despite this relative breakthrough, both remain confined by what appear to be traditional formalist renderings of "language and literature" themselves.

These limitations are most clearly in evidence in the closing
paragraphs of Schor's essay. Schor speaks of "a final demarcation
separating the new thematic from the old: concerned with thematic
structure or, better still, structuring themes, new thematic criticism
must not go beyond the framework of the individual novel (poem,
drama)." Schor's formalism becomes evident. Schor upholds the
most traditional renderings of language and literature: the
"framework" of the work, of "the individual novel (poem, drama)."
Though she has one eye on a historical horizon and the other on the
very possibility of the confluence of history and literature (the feminine), Schor's lines of sight are still held within the most familiar
contours of the literary. This, after all, is the sense of Schor's title,
her stress on a *restricted* thematics: only by way of the work, only
by way of a notion of language and literature that precedes reading,
will her return to the theme be accomplished.

Reading in Detail envisages a new approach to both reading
and history, a new working methodology. No longer will Schor's
criticism be immanent in this sense. And though the feminine will
continue to elude a certain positivity, it will be open to a far greater
range of effects. In *Reading in Detail*, Schor takes a step back, drawing the actual paths of her reading into that "retreat of the feminine"
we began to recognize above.

One chapter in particular in *Reading in Detail* draws attention
to itself in this regard. In it, Schor violates most of the rules she sets
out here—certainly the limitation or restriction to a single work and

the traditional hermeneutic assumptions about the confines of the literary object. The chapter, entitled "Decadence," is composed of three distinct readings: of Francis Wey, a 19th-century grammarian who wrote on photography; Adolf Loos, the Viennese modernist; and George Lukács. (pp. 42–65).

The status of this chapter remains a bit uncertain, however. In her Introduction, Schor writes that in it "the method, if not the focus, changes," and that it is her "most archaeological chapter." Yet the entire first part of her book appears under this same heading, "Archaeology" (p. 5).

At the conclusion of "Decadence," we find Schor addressing this difference once more, this time from a standpoint that makes it appear more rather than less exemplary:

> What I have attempted to make visible in this chapter is what Foucault calls a discursive formation, which by definition violates disciplinary boundaries. By juxtaposing the discourses produced by an obscure nineteenth century French polymath, a high priest of Viennese modernism, and the major twentieth century exponent of Marxist aesthetics, I have wanted to show both the persistence of an aesthetic thematics and its contextual modulations. But that is not all: to approach the history of an idea from a genealogical perspective is to reject the linear model and instead to give full play to discontinuities, overlaps, the disordered ebb and flow of intellectual events. Thus instead of going from Lukács to Barthes, following strict chronology, in the following chapter we will go back once again to the nineteenth century. For even as the main tenets of Academic aesthetics continued to cast their baleful shadow over the detail, the domestic, and the feminine, an epistemological break was taking shape that would at last bring the detail into the epistemological and aesthetic spotlight. (p. 64)

Contrasted, then, with her discussion of neothematism, what comes to the fore here is Schor's stress on *discontinuity*. Having already rendered this theme—the theme of thematics itself—ambivalent, it is precisely its opposite that Schor valorizes at this moment of methodological hesitancy. Not only is the genealogical perspective said to reject the linear model, and to give full play to discontinuities, but Schor announces a certain epistemological break, whose description is one of the primary goals of this part of Schor's book.

Yet what is equally remarkable in this moment in Schor's text is the role that discontinuity actually plays. For, though, as her introduction informs us, this chapter signals a break in "method," in turn this break, the discontinuity that is to be given full play, and the epistemological break taking shape are yet to come. The writings of Wey, Loos, and Lukács, so far from signaling a break, rather constitute a sort of mini-history stretching into the present and establishing not the end but the perdurance of the classical ideal. As Schor puts it: "My concern here is the persistence of neo-classical aesthetics well into the twentieth century." In this chapter, then, Schor will have established a certain continuity, and that past the point one would otherwise expect it. The substance of her chapter will have shown "both the persistence of an aesthetic thematics and its contextual modulations" (pp. 5, 64).

And our question of reading as production, of Schor's own reading as production, comes to devolve on the very peculiar interplay of continuity and discontinuity we find here. Why when Schor takes up the notion of a discursive formation, and does so in the name of discontinuity, do we rather find a certain (excessive) continuity come into play? Why in a chapter whose method is anomalous does Schor bring into view the fundamental sight lines of her project? And what will be the status of this other "break," which she both announces and postpones here?

In order to follow up these questions, we must take into account another factor. In *Reading in Detail*, so-called methodological and political questions cannot be easily separated. What interests Schor in these passages is not simply the detail, or even modernity, but rather these in relation to a certain issue of gender. It is the question of gender, indeed the "doubly gendered," the feminine, that Schor wishes to put. Only in light of this issue can one begin to appreciate fully the interplay just brought forward between Schor's concepts and her narrative.

In respect to the question of the feminine, then, Schor's entire investigation of detail has assigned itself two tasks: to add something to any possible history or concept of the detail, and to mark a certain absence, a certain operative subtraction from this concept.

Under the sign of addition, the plus sign, in her Introduction, she writes:

> To focus on the detail, and more particularly on the detail as negativity, is to become aware as I discovered, of its participation in a large semantic network . . . to focus on the detail is to become aware that the normative aesthetics elaborated and disseminated by the academy is not sexually neutral; it is an axiology carrying into the field of representation the sexual hierarchies of the phallocentric cultural order. The detail does not occupy a conceptual space beyond the laws of sexual difference: the detail is gendered and doubly gendered as feminine. (p. 4)

It is a matter of adding from the first this charge, not only to the history of the detail but to its concept: that it is gendered and doubly gendered as feminine. Yet if this concept, Schor's leading concept, does not escape the field of a certain gendering (if it does not escape what is here called "the phallocentric cultural order"), then, in turn, it is also to some degree precisely the subtraction of this gendering that Schor also wishes to remark. And it is in the service of this loss of the sign that the epistemological break noted above, the second later break Schor there refers to, will be mapped out. Schor also wishes to ask whether the triumph of the detail, the becoming improper and major of this concept, the epistemological break she has just referred to, wherein "the detail marches into the aesthetic and epistemological spotlight," signals a triumph of the feminine as well:

> Does the triumph of the detail signify a triumph of the femi-
> nine to which it has so long been linked? Or has the detail
> achieved its new prestige by being taken over by the mascu-
> line, triumphing at the very moment when it ceases to be asso-
> ciated with the feminine? (p. 6)

Schor here, then, in effect repeats her earlier questioning of the "feminist" thematics of continuity on a historicotemporal axis. Starting from a notion of detail within classical aesthetics, one that is, as she says, not sexually neutral, Schor will come to track the loss of this gendering, as the detail comes to triumph, as it breaks out of the confines of the academy and ushers in something very like our present.

What is important to us in the question of reading as produc-
tion, and what the indeterminacy of Schor's third chapter depends on, is the status imposed on Schor's referent, the detail, by the highly singular nature of this double movement, by the need to track the detail through this production and eclipse of the feminine.

More specifically, on the one hand, in one movement Schor restores to the detail a sign of gender it is about to lose once more. In a certain way, this moment, the work of her first chapter, "Gender," harks back to Schor's earlier work. It concentrates on a single example, Reynolds's *Discourses*, and brings forward an essential overdeterminacy. Nevertheless, there is already here a signifi-
cant difference from her earlier work, attesting to a change in the status of her reading. Though focusing on what appears to be a single piece of writing, Reynolds's piece is here not taken as a work but as a text. Its reading will not be confined by the traditional structuralist imperatives.

Indeed, though Schor's point is the gendering of the concept of detail, she herself will point out that "Reynolds never explicitly links details and femininity." Instead, Schor's reading invokes something like the highly unstable figure of totality that we began to examine in our discussion of Derrida. "By taking over a metaphorics grounded in metaphysics . . . [Reynolds] implicitly reinscribes the sexual stereotypes of Western philosophy" (p. 16).

Only by way of the peculiar "prehistory" of this concept, a reading scandalous in Schor's former terms, can the original gendering of this concept be exposed. Much like the "unperceived relation" of Rousseau's text, the detail already within the field of classical aesthetics, already within Reynolds's text, turns out to be not simply a concept itself belonging to this field. It already will have its starting point not there but within that field, already elsewhere, in a totality in some sense yet to be produced.

This points to the decisive issue: here reading precedes "language," not the other way around. Rather than being straightforwardly given, text, concept, and language all turn out to be up for grabs—their contours evident only in the active process of reading. Reynolds's language turns out to be implicated in a totality, in such a manner that we no longer can tell (absent reading) what this totality—language or history—may be.

We have only begun to glimpse, however, the genuine radicality, the singularly productive aspect that Schor's reading brings to bear. For if, as in Derrida (from whom she claims to draw this possibility), the concept of detail will have never yet, yet already have born this sign of gender, if its status as concept can be known only by way of reading, then it is equally important to see that Schor herself does not correlate her own moment of production (*her* reading), as did Derrida, with a certain future reintroduced as past. Rather, Schor subverts our expectations otherwise. She arrives at her own particular mode of readerly productivity.

Though the detail as read in Reynolds's aesthetics belongs to a totality in some sense prior, to read the detail thus, to read Reynolds in detail as Schor does, is to begin from another concept of detail than the one simply presented by Reynolds himself. Indeed, Schor's reading otherwise the proper concept of detail in classical aesthetics, as a reading *in* detail, from the first bears the marks of a certain "post-present." Reading the detail in Reynolds, as Schor makes clear, is itself an effect of the advent of detail Schor is otherwise about to produce.

But it is precisely this disjunction, the passage through this other past and this other concept of detail, that marks the singularity of Schor's own production of the concept of detail. Indeed, where Schor's work's own specifically productive moment comes to the fore is that it is rather from the never-present gendered concept of detail (a concept Schor is about to produce)—a concept already though not yet in the history of classical aesthetics, already though never yet the modern concept of detail—that it will produce, as if for the first time, its own "modernity." Schor, that is, produces our modern moment from a concept of detail neither simply belonging to it nor belonging to its simple past: she produces it out of a moment farther past than the past and coming after the future—prior to Reynolds's account and posterior to, consequent on, our current modernity. Appealing to a certain unheard-of concept of detail, Schor engages the present moment in a movement of originary reproduction; one that produces the production of the modern concept of detail as a reproduction of another movement, which produces that other movement by way of the originary reproduction of the modern production of detail it already assumes.

Indeed, that this is the case and a matter of production in no uncertain sense of this term may be seen not only in the cross-currents of Schor's third chapter (wherein both the continuity of that prior past and the discontinuity of this posterior future come to the fore) but also in how Schor situates her inquiry in regard to its origins. In a gesture that appears quite similar to the one we saw her make above, Schor will introduce her book by noting: "We live in an age in which the detail enjoys a rare prominence. . . . Nowhere have these tendencies been more spectacularly in evidence than in the writings of some of the major figures of poststructuralist France" (p. 3). Schor goes on to list Foucault, Barthes, and Derrida as practitioners of the detail—just as she listed Derrida, Deleuze, and Barthes as practitioners of the chain, or the thread, of a certain practice of weaving or text. Yet the difference between these moments is as significant as the similarity. For the detail, unlike the chain, will be the subject of Schor's own inquiry. That is, while undoubtedly not without a certain role in today's writings, the detail, unlike the chain or the web, is Schor's own theme, the matter of her own production. By pointing out the prominence of detail in these authors, Schor does not submit to their chains but rather inscribes their work within "her difference."

Yet what is paramount is not this feature, which is finally ambivalent, but rather the fact that this present is not simply or straightforwardly hers. Producing a certain version of the present (for the first time and as detail), she is also (already) calling into question the present, that same present, which makes this version possible. Indeed, Schor's gesture begins to produce that present, to reproduce it, before one has ever properly arrived at it. For one needs the present concept of the detail in order to read in detail, in the past, this concept's "original gendering"; but this is also to re-produce this present again otherwise, to reproduce it as a moment in the history not of detail but of detail as gendered, as feminine. And the productivity of Schor's reading consists in this: if she draws on the present in order to produce this extra mark of gender, then she also draws the present into this marking.

In sum, to put it in terms of a distinction Schor herself em-ploys elsewhere, we might say that Schor, reading a certain mo-ment in the "history of the representation of women," already reads that moment within the "and" of the question of "women *and* repre-sentation." If, as a history of detail, her narrative bespeaks a certain continuity, then, as a history of the present, it brings to bear anoth-er, unheard-of discontinuity, the discontinuity of the doubly gen-dered, of what Schor thinks of under the heading of "the feminine."

3

By way of conclusion, I will explore this last stage of Schor's text a little further, and I will return to the assertion made above that we are in the midst today of something like an advent of reading. For, though Schor's work alone does not constitute a proof of the latter claim, it does begin to suggest some of the lines such a demonstra-tion might follow. Indeed, it allows us to identify two recent trends —not only feminism but also, as this post-present witnesses, a cer-tain postmodernism—whose possibility as criticism, if not always their actuality in fact, may well be taken to be conditioned by this moment.

Allowing us to conceive this resemblance among critical ap-proaches, however, Schor's work also begins to indicate that there may be more than one critical question for criticism today; that what sets off her work and at least certain strands of feminism and postmodernism may be not only a certain reading as production but another factor as well. For not only does Schor allow us to envisage further instances of this style of reading, but, granting this, she also begins to suggest that the critical question here may finally concern not the relation to reading or language but the relation to history; yet the question of the relation to history in an almost unheard-of sense, a sense that cuts across the usual lines dividing theory from nontheory, thematic from formalist criticism, current criticism from its predecessors.

Turn for a moment to another recent trend in criticism, the new historicism. Though I cannot here treat this approach in any detail, I can, on the basis of what is already established, set out a general characterization. To the degree that Schor's work by no means dispenses with history, to the degree that it does not return us to Miller's original divisions (since, in the broadest sense, Schor's "language" incorporates a certain hermeneutics, her "reading" a certain history), we are led, as it were, by contrast, to look for the distinguishing character of the new historicism in something other than history's simple inclusion. That is, because, as Schor's example, as well as Derrida's, shows, history was never excluded in the first place, this suggests that the trait particular to the new historicism does not lie in its mere inclusion.

I would maintain that what is peculiar to the new historicism is not a "return" to history, a revival of the theme, but far rather the identification of this possibility of reading as production with the field of history itself. That is, what makes the new historicism new is not history but reading—the fact that the very possibility of historical criticism and the very concept of history are now informed by the practice of productive readings.

Against Theory itself attests to this. What becomes clear, in the author's ongoing give and take with E. D. Hirsch, for example, is not, as Hirsch claims, that Knapp and Michaels would abandon historical criticism altogether. Rather, they conceive historical criticism as not the reproduction but the *production* of a certain historical intentionality: historical reading, radically hermeneutic reading, must now produce as if for the first time that history constitutive of subjects and selves, authors and agents—rather than, as in the traditional hermeneutics, reproduce that history they had produced, or even reproduce that history that produced them.[10] Indeed, this is not the theoretical, not even the practical, but rather the rhetorical force of *Against Theory*. And it is almost patent, for anyone familiar with new historicist texts, that if writing or the text do not there receive any significant privilege, this is because history in the first instance is itself understood to be a text, understood as what is to be read in a strong sense, as what is in the first instance to be produced, not reproduced, by way of reading.

From this perspective, the new historicism is distinguished not by history per se but by the attempt to fold back this productive, readerly aspect of theory onto the field of history. It differentiates itself from old historicism, as well as Schor's work, by the attempt to identify reading and history without reserve or remainder, without that excess that Schor's "feminine" here denotes. As such, it represents an attempt to "historicize," not eliminate a certain radical reading.

So, too, ironically enough, in this respect Miller and the new historicism turn out to be in agreement. For Miller's complaint that theory has fled the current scene (that theory has not had a future) and the new historicists' renewal of historical research by way of productive readings, though resulting from different object choices, both entail the identification of reading as production with the mundane historical field. Both identify the present of history with the present of reading. Both assume one can identify reading with *historical present or presence.*

This brings me to my point, that both against theory and for it the critical issue today lies not only with reading, or even perhaps with language, but with history. For, though Miller and *Against Theory* may not agree on the importance of history, they do agree in some self-evident sense on what history is, or that there *is* history.

By contrast, what Schor's work suggests, as well as certain strains of postmodernism and feminism—and this thought is common to such unlikely bedfellows as de Man and Foucault—is not that there is no history but that the politics of history is at least as important as the history of politics and that, consequently, one never can take for granted that there is one, or only one, history.

That is the paradox Schor's work finally presents: writing a history of the present, she calls into question the present as history. She situates and captures our contemporary interest in reading in detail, by way of a notion of detail that belongs neither to our past nor to our present. Hers is a present the more, then, that also turns out to be a present the less, since in rendering history actively discontinuous, she suggests that there may not be any single history in which these various presents meet. Deploying a difference that divides the present by producing it (not, as in Derrida, producing the present by dividing it), Schor suggests that history itself suffers an irreducible relation to a plurality of histories that are never finally present to one another or themselves, histories whose relation to one another remains a problem or a question.

This is not to settle for simple pluralism—since neither is there guarantee of common ground nor are these histories allowed to resolve themselves into sheer indifference. Schor's view also contests all totalizing views of history, precisely because she makes the production of the totality (of history, of language) a part of her project and one of her themes—precisely because she practices reading as production and refuses to take the greatest totality for granted.

Does this mean, after all, that theory, perhaps historicized theory like Schor's, continues today to have a future? This remains unclear. All one can say for sure is that despite what some might think, no straightforwardly historical account ever will provide the answer.[11]

Notes

1. Steven Knapp and Walter Benn Michaels, "Against Theory," in *Against Theory: Literary Studies and the New Pragmatism*, ed. W. J. T. Mitchell (Chicago: University of Chicago Press, 1985).

2. Ralph Cohen, ed., *The Future of Literary Theory* (New York: Routledge, 1989). See also Peter Collier and Helga Geyer-Ryan, eds., *Literary Theory Today* (Ithaca: Cornell University Press, 1990); and Jonathan Arac and Barbara Johnson, eds., *Consequences of Theory* (Baltimore: Johns Hopkins University Press, 1991). While all three collections have different critical orientations, they all attest to the shift, or the appearance of a shift, to which I refer.

3. J. Hillis Miller, "Theory at the Present Time," in *The Future of Literary Theory*, p. 102.

4. Jacques Derrida, *Of Grammatology*, trans. Gayatri Spivak (Baltimore: Johns Hopkins University Press, 1974), p. 158.

5. See, in particular, the "Introduction to the 'Age of Rousseau,'" where Derrida undertakes to justify his choice of examples: "Within this age of metaphysics, between Descartes and Hegel, Rousseau is undoubtedly the only one or the first one to make a theme or a system of the reduction of writing profoundly implied by the entire age." *Of Grammatology*, p. 98.

6. *Of Grammatology*, pp 161–62.

7. This would hold, though differently, for the other case suitable for treatment here, namely the works of Paul de Man. Indeed, in this instance, matters are even more difficult, for it is not, or is not only, the writer's future but the reader's future that de Man exhausts—himself as reader, certainly, but that of his own readers as well. Of course, by this I do not mean that some actual person's future is thus exhausted but rather that the moment of being read in de Man's work plays an analogous role to that of having written in Derrida's.

And while on this subject, I should mention that part of the reason for the gloomy outlook we find among leading theoreticians is, of course, that they, as well as myself, have had to approach this issue of theory's future from out of the shadow cast by the controversy concerning de Man's wartime journalism. In respect to this matter, I emphasize, as far as this essay is concerned, that the almost complete absence of explicit discussion of de Man's work signals neither an indifference to these problems nor some sort of intent to shun de Man's writings, to exclude him from the critical community. Rather, there are distinct problems with even beginning to say what de Man said, no less what he didn't say or what he may have thought, especially about things he never spoke about at all. And I happen to think it is this feature of the de Man question—not so much what he said in the first place, though this was, of course, totally unacceptable, but what he didn't say in the second place—that would need to be scrutinized.

Yet it is from a confrontation with these and related issues in de Man's own work (technical issues involving what can be said and cannot be said, often about saying itself), especially as they figured in that work in relation to the reading of both Heidegger and Derrida, that I have been led to the set of problems I articulate here. These problems, as it happens (though for different reasons), are also those that *in principle* must be addressed if one is to confront the issues now posed by the totality of de Man's own corpus. This fact, that de Man's own later inquiries in principle provide the grounds for evaluating his earlier work, has never received the appreciation it deserves.

8. Naomi Schor, *Breaking the Chain: Women, Theory, and French Realist Fiction* (New York: Columbia University Press, 1985).

9. Naomi Schor, *Reading in Detail: Aesthetics and the Feminine* (New York: Methuen, 1987).

10. The most telling moment in this regard probably comes in the authors' reply to Hirsch's rather perceptive response to their original critique. "The historical project," they write, "rests on a claim about evidence—namely that certain kinds of documents (letters, diaries, manuscripts, etc.) are particularly relevant to determining the meaning of literary texts. It might seem plausible to suppose that an identification of meaning with the author's intention provides theoretical support for the historian's sense of the value of such documents. While historical evidence of this kind may well be valuable, nothing in the claim that authorial intention is the necessary object of interpretation tells us that it is. In fact, nothing in the claim that authorial intention is the necessary object of interpretation tells us anything at all about what should count for determining the content of any particular intention. To think for example that only the poem and no other document should count as evidence of the poet's intention is just as consistent with the thesis that intention is necessary. . . . One could believe that all poetry in every language and every age was written by a universal muse and that therefore no information about any other person could be of any possible interpretive interest—and this too would not be incompatible with the necessity of intention." Steven Knapp and Walter Benn Michaels, "A Reply to Our Critics," in *Against Theory*, p. 101. The critical point is that for Knapp and Michaels, not only would the muse be the author, but, as becomes clear on the next page, being the author, she also would be the *historical* author, and this no matter what sorts of decisions about documents and the value of historical evidence one arrives at. That is, it becomes plain that what Knapp and Michaels aim at is not simply or solely the cessation of theory but the withdrawal of history, of the concept of history and the practice of historical criticism, from what the authors here deem the "historical project"— and this in favor of a moment very like what I have been calling reading as production.

11. This aspect, this option, in some sense "against history," is particularly evident at the end of Schor's archaeology. To the historically determined question "Is the detail feminine?" Schor responds, "there exists no reliable body of evidence to show that women's art is either more or less particularistic than men's." She goes on to suggest that "further investigation of this question may lead us to formulate a surprising hypothesis, that feminine specificity lies in the direction of a specifically feminine form of idealism" (p. 97). It is this conclusion of Schor's, this decision for a specifically feminine form of idealism, that my own reading has kept in the foreground, in a manner perhaps not always identical to Schor's own.

Gilles Deleuze: Postmodern Philosopher?

Ronald Bogue

The end of theory is the end of theory. That is, the goal of theory is the elimination of theory as an enterprise, and the perpetual failure of this project is itself a constitutive component of the activity of theorizing. Theories, if they are truly theories, are abstract, general, and invariant accounts that are unavoidably foundational in their formulation, even if they are antifoundational in propositional content. (Hence the paradox of relativism: all theory is relative, with the exception of this statement, which is universal, etc.) And the goal of any theory is the establishment of an invariant and universal truth, which, if established, would put an end to further discussion. Theory, then, seeks to eliminate itself. But if this is the goal of theory, clearly no theory has yet been successful. No matter how powerful a theory may be, the enterprise of theorizing continues apace, and indeed seems to thrive on its failures as much as its necessarily temporary successes. But this is precisely the function of theory—to fail in its project of self-elimination.

Recent debates about the concept of postmodernism clearly illustrate the paradoxical nature of theory, and one theorist—Gilles Deleuze—has provided in his concept of structure what I regard as an apt characterization of theory. The question I pose—is Deleuze a postmodern philosopher?—is a question about theory, an inquiry into the theoretical status of both the concept of postmodernism and the role one might occupy within philosopy, that most theoretical of disciplines, as a postmodern philosopher.

In *Logique du sens*, Gilles Deleuze's 1969 *"essai de roman logique et psychanalytique"*[1] devoted to Stoic incorporeals and the logic of *Alice in Wonderland*, Deleuze defines a "minimal structure" as two

Reprinted from *Criticism*, 32, no. 4 (Fall 1990): 401–418. Copyright © 1990 Wayne State University Press, Detroit, Michigan 48201.

the affective dimension of schizophrenia, and their argument is that the decoding of fluxes and flows that characterizes schizophrenia is also manifested in the fundamental processes of capitalism. Everywhere capitalism develops, it undermines traditional social codes— kinship systems, religious beliefs, class hierarchies, taboos, ritual trade relations—and releases uncoded fluxes of heterogeneous matter, ideas, affects, and fantasies; but, unlike schizophrenia, it constantly recodes fluxes and flows within new forms of social organization (such as the Oedipal family) in an effort to maintain a controlled and universal exchange of commodities. It would seem that we have here a properly historical account of what Jameson has labeled a postmodern phenomenon—the schizophrenic "breakdown of temporality" in which "the present of the world or material signifier comes before the subject with heightened intensity, bearing a mysterious charge of affect."[22] Yet the schizophrenic decoding of flows in Deleuze and Guattari, although most evident in advanced Western capitalism, represents the limit of every form of exchange, a latent possibility that haunts all social systems and threatens their dissolution.[23] Capitalism is simply the first social system to institutionalize such decoding on an unlimited scale, and the emergence of schizophrenic affectivity, temporality, and fragmentation in postmodern art merely partakes of the accelerating tendency toward decoding that informs multinational capitalism.

It would be a mistake to regard Deleuze's assertion of the universality of simulacra, intensities, and schizophrenic decoding as signs of essentialism in his thought, for such concepts are merely tools for mapping possible worlds, not irreducible constituents of ultimate reality. But it is evident that for Deleuze there is no decisive break with which postmodernity is ushered in and no peculiarly postmodern phenomena that characterize our culture. Deleuze articulates postmodern themes and exemplifies postmodern practices, in short, but he does not offer a historicized theoretical account of postmodernity. From Jameson's perspective, no doubt, Deleuze's thought is symptomatic of postmodernity but insufficiently self-critical to recognize its grounding in its own historical situation. Deleuze would counter, I believe, that he is simply incredulous of *all* historical narratives, including the one that might account for the shape of thought in our present, postmodern condition.

3

Andreas Huyssen has wisely cautioned us against assuming too quickly that poststructuralism is necessarily the philosophical counterpart of aesthetic postmodernism. French poststructuralists especially, he notes, are relatively silent about postmodernity, devoting most of their attention to the works of high modernism. He argues, in fact, that French poststructuralism "provides us primarily with an *archaeology of modernity*, a theory of modernism at the stage of its exhaustion."[24] Huyssen points out that critics such as Roland Barthes not only concentrate most often on modernist writers and the problem of modernity but also reinforce modernist aestheticism in certain theorizations of *écriture* and reinstate the modernist distinction between high culture and low culture in such schemas as the Barthesian opposition of *jouissance* and *plaisire*. Deleuze is a poststructural philosopher, and he resembles other French poststructuralists in his fondness for modernist art and his interest in the question of modernity, but I do not believe that Deleuze articulates "a theory of modernism at the stage of its exhaustion," for his sense of the modern, I would argue, is decidedly *postmodern*, a point that may be demonstrated through a brief consideration of Deleuze's books on Proust, Kafka, Francis Bacon, and the cinema.

Proust is one of Deleuze's favorite writers, frequently discussed throughout his works and treated at length in *Proust et les signes*, published in 1964 and augmented in subsequent editions in 1970, 1971, and 1976. Proust, of course, is one of the established luminaries of high modernism, but for Deleuze he is not the modernist aesthete of subjectivity, the self-reflexive recluse who recaptures the past and creates in his novel an autonomous verbal icon. Deleuze treats the *Recherche* as the account of Marcel's apprenticeship in the understanding of signs, which are enfolded, implicated differences that Marcel interprets as he unfolds and explicates them. Marcel discovers the differential nature of worldly signs through lies, of amorous signs through jealousy, of sensual signs through involuntary memory, and of artistic signs through the Vinteuil sonata. And what he learns finally through artistic signs is that difference is the generative force from which issue the multiple compossible worlds that make up the real. Marcel, far from functioning as the consciousness that holds the *Recherche* together, is dispersed across the multiple signs of the text. The work itself does not express deep meanings or feelings but operates as a machine. For, says Deleuze, "the modern work of art is a machine, and functions in that fashion. . . . With the modern work of art it is not a problem of meaning, but only a problem of usage."[25] The *Recherche* is filled with machines that produce fragments and partial objects and machines that set them in resonance, while itself being a machine that produces various effects (in the sense that one speaks of the Doppler effect): truth effects, reader effects, and unity effects of "a One and a Whole which [are] not principal, but on the contrary 'the effect' of the multiple and its disconnected parts" (p. 195). "In truth," says Deleuze, "the narrator is an enormous Body without Organs," a spider within the web of the *Recherche*, the web and the spider forming "a single and same machine" (p. 218).

Kafka is another of Deleuze's favorite writers, whose works he and Guattari examine at length in their 1975 book, *Kafka: pour une littérature mineure*. For Deleuze and Guattari, Kafka is not the modernist prophet of *Angst* and existential gloom or the advocate of tragic, negative theology, but instead a joyous, humorous writer whose works constitute a political experimentation on the real. Kafka's writings, they argue, are rhizome-like in their structure and machine-like in their function, and hence constituted of multiple fragments and pieces that form unified wholes only as secondary effects. Deleuze and Guattari's Kafka, in this sense, resembles Deleuze's Proust. But in Kafka, Deleuze and Guattari also find a theorist and practitioner of what they call "minor literature," an avantgarde form of political writing that undermines the high modernist distinction of elite and mass culture and its separation of life and art. In Kafka's language, Deleuze and Guattari discover a minor usage of German, a Prague Jew's deliberate impoverishment of a foreign culture's "paper language" (as Kafka called it) that induces unexpected mutations in the dominant, major tongue. And in such works as *The Trial* and *The Castle*, they see a political experimentation on the social forces of Kafka's day, a minor practice that functions as a means of "prolonging, of accelerating an entire movement that already traverses the social field: it operates in a virtual realm, already real without being actual (the diabolic powers of the future which, for the moment, are only knocking at the door)."[26] If one accepts Huyssen's characterization of postmodern art as informed by a critique of the imperialism of enlightened modernity and the domination of minorities and marginal cultures by cultural majorities,[27] then the Kafka that Deleuze and Guattari describe—Kafka, the exponent of minor literature—must be considered postmodern.

In his *Francis Bacon: logique de la sensation* (1981), Deleuze may not discuss one of the classic examples of high modernism, but he certainly treats a figure who is much more commonly associated with modernist than postmodernist trends in painting. Yet what Deleuze regards as the basic problem addressed in Bacon's paintings is essentially a postmodern concern—that of representation in a world of ubiquitous images—even if Deleuze labels it a "modern" dilemma. Modern painting, says Deleuze, "is invaded, besieged by photos and cliches which are already on the canvas even before the painter begins his work,"[28] and the great task faced by painters is that of escaping received codes of representation and figuration. In Deleuze's analysis, Bacon rejects the strategies of abstract formalism or abstract expression and instead tries to wrest the figure from the clichés of figuration, to paint a portrait of a human being, for example, but to allow a catastrophic zone of chaos to invade the representation as it takes form, to follow the line of mutation induced by a chance brush stroke or haphazard color and allow it to deform the figure, to introduce "a zone of Sahara into the head," to split "the head into two parts with an ocean" (p. 65) in between, to turn a torso into a piece of meat or a leg into a puddle of purple ink. The representations that emerge may resemble certain objects in the world, but they are simply instances of a resemblance that "surges forth as the brutal product of non-resembling means" (p. 75). What Bacon ultimately paints, in Deleuze's view, is the network of invisible forces that play through visible forms. Hence, in Bacon's portraits of screaming individuals, Deleuze finds not an expressionistic rendering of psychological anguish but a figural mutation that seeks to "put the visibility of the cry, the open mouth as shadowy abyss, in relation with the invisible forces which are still only those of the future" (p. 41). In this regard, the Francis Bacon that Deleuze describes is a practitioner of Lyotard's postmodern negative sublime, which "invokes the unpresentable within the presentation itself; which refuses the consolation of good forms and the consensus of a taste that would allow the common experience of a nostalgia for the impossible; which explores new presentations, not in order to enjoy them, but in order to convey better the existence of the unpresentable."[29]

In his recent books on film, *Cinéma 1: l'image-mouvement* (1983) and *Cinéma 2: l'image-temps* (1985), Deleuze raises the question of modernity once again, this time by distinguishing two broad movements in the history of film—the classic cinema of conventionally coded narratives and coherent spatiotemporal coordinates, and the modern cinema of undecidable narratives and irreconcilable disjunctions in space and time. Yet here, too, as in his analyses of Proust, Kafka, and Bacon, what Deleuze labels "modern" could easily be classified as postmodern. This is perhaps most evident in Deleuze's account of the relation between sound and image in classic and modern films. According to Deleuze, space and time in the classic cinema are regulated through a "sensorimotor schema," an organization of the world in terms of human goals, purposes, obstacles, actions, and reactions, and it is this sensorimotor schema that coherent narratives presuppose as their condition of possibility. Sound and image reinforce each other in the classic cinema, and together they map a coherent world. In the modern cinema (beginning with Italian neorealism), the sensorimotor schema breaks down, and the elements of film begin to be related to each other differentially rather than synthetically. The cut, for instance, no longer connects two shots that belong to a single space and time but functions instead as a gap or blank that asks the viewer to discover a relation between two heterogeneous images based on their differences from each other. Sound and image, also, develop in a differential manner, the audio and the visual in modern film functioning as autonomous strata that test the limits of what can be seen and what can be heard. In the films of Duras, Straub, Godard, and others, Deleuze finds separate levels of sounds and images, bound in "an incommensurable or 'irrational' relation which ties them to one another, without forming a whole, without proposing the slightest 'whole,'"[30] that relation being based on the differences between the two levels and the ways in which each of the levels approaches its limits. Clearly, each level tends toward the Lyotardian postmodern negative sublime. But more importantly, what Deleuze sees as the characteristic relation between sound and image in modern film is a perfect example of what Jameson identifies as "the postmodernist experience of form," in which the viewer or reader is expected "to rise somehow to a level at which the vivid perception of radical difference is in and of itself a new mode of grasping what used to be called relationship: something for which the word *collage* is still only a very feeble name."[31]

4

In many respects, Deleuze is a postmodern philosopher: he abandons, and occasionally challenges, the *grand récits* of the Enlightenment; he thinks the unthought, but with no nostalgia for a missing whole and no claims to possess a privileged methodology; and he gives philosophical articulation to a number of postmodern themes —simulacra, intensities, and schizophrenic decoding, among others. He does not, however, offer any theoretical accounts of postmodernity, and, like many of his French contemporaries, he shows much greater interest in the problems of modernity and the monuments of high modernism than in postmodernism and postmodern art. Yet his treatment of modernist literature, painting, and film differs from that of many French poststructuralists in that the aesthetic features Deleuze values and discovers in such artists as Proust, Kafka, and Bacon are distinctively postmodern rather than modern.

Should we conclude, then, that Deleuze merely subscribes to a new theory of modernism, one that treats the twentieth century as a single period with characteristics that we are now beginning to label postmodern? I think not, for it assumes in Deleuze a willingness to periodize that simply is not there. He often speaks of modernity and modern art, but little that he identifies as characteristic of such art is exclusively so. As any section of *Mille plateaux* makes readily apparent, the features that Deleuze finds in Proust, Kafka, Bacon, and modern film he also discovers in different guises in art works from various eras and diverse cultures. One cannot say that Deleuze is uninterested in history or historical distinctions, but it is evident that he has no desire to formulate a single global history or even a limited history whose demarcations are hard and fast. Unlike Fredric Jameson, who sees a need for "cognitive maps" as guides for future political action and who offers his account of postmodernism as a contribution to the cartography of our age, Deleuze attempts a cartography of desire that charts the fissures and rifts of metamorphoses and becoming wherever and whenever they appear. The maps Deleuze draws are less emplotments of our era than diagrams of force, which function as do *Mille plateaux*'s "maps of regimes of signs: we can turn them around, retain this or that coordinate, this or that dimension, and depending on the case we will have a social formation, a pathological delusion, a historical event, etc."[32] Such cognitive maps have historical coordinates, but they are tentative, hypothetical, and strategically drawn, for they are always constructed to induce a mutation, to discover a locus of difference that will generate unexpected transformations. The task of modern philosophy, says Deleuze, is "to overcome the alternatives temporal/ nontemporal, historical/eternal, particular/universal. Following Nietzsche, we discover the untimely as something that is more profound than time and eternity: philosophy [in this regard] is neither the philosophy of history, nor the philosophy of the eternal, but untimely, always and only untimely, that is, 'against this time, in favor, I hope, of a time to come'" (*Différence*, p. 3). It is perhaps in this sense that Deleuze is most thoroughly postmodern.

Notes

1. Gilles Deleuze, *Logique du sens* (Paris: Minuit, 1969), p. 7.
2. Ibid., p. 55.
3. On postmodern arcitecture, see Charles Jencks, *The Language of Post-Modern Architecture* (New York: Rizzoli, 1977); and *Post-Modern Classicism: The New Synthesis* (London: Academy Editions, 1980). On postmodernism in the arts, see Stanley Trachtenberg, ed., *The Postmodern Moment: A Handbook of Contemporary Innovation in the Arts* (Westport, Conn.: Greenwood, 1985). On postmodern philosophy, see Richard Rorty, *Philosophy and the Mirror of Nature* (Princeton: Princeton University

Press, 1979); Richard Bernstein, *Philosophical Profiles: Essays in a Pragmatic Mode* (Cambridge: Polity Press, 1985); and Hugh J. Silverman and Donn Welton, eds., *Postmodernism and Continental Philosophy* (Albany: State University of New York Press, 1988). On postmodern science, see David Griffin, ed., *The Reenactment of Science: Postmodern Proposals* (Albany: State University of New York Press, 1988). For concise accounts of the social theories of Jean-François Lyotard, Fredric Jameson, and Jean Baudrillard, see Lyotard, *La condition postmoderne* (Paris: Minuit, 1979), and *Le postmoderne expliqué aux enfants* (Paris: Galilée, 1986); Jameson, "Postmodernism, or the Cultural Logic of Late Capitalism," *New Left Review* 146 (1984): 53–92; and Baudrillard, "The Precession of Simulacra," trans. Paul Foss and Paul Patton, in *Art after Modernism: Rethinking Representation*, ed. Brian Wallis (New York: New Museum of Contemporary Art, 1984). Unless otherwise indicated, all translations of French sources are my own.

4. Linda Hutcheon, "A Postmodern Problematics," in *Ethics/Aesthetics: Post-Modern Positions*, ed. Robert Merrill (Washington, D.C.: Maissoneuve Press, 1988), p. 2.

5. Félix Guattari, with whom Deleuze collaborated on *L'Anti-Oedipe* and *Mille plateux*, has taken up the issue of postmodernism in his recent *Cartographies schizo-analytiques* (Paris: Galilée, 1989), pp. 53–61. Although he is critical of postmodernism, regarding it as a latent form of structuralism, his remarks do not entirely rule out some degree of rapprochement between schizoanalysis and postmodernism, since, as I hope to show, the Lyotardian sense of the concept, with which Guattari takes exception, is not the only one available.

6. David Couzens Hoy, who identifies periodization as "itself a modernist tool," makes precisely this point in regard to Foucault: "In contrast to Lyotard's stance, a Foucauldian postmodern would not need to be an advocate of postmodernism. I think that Foucault was a consistent postmodern in that he would never have called himself a postmodern." "Foucault: Modern or Postmodern?" in *After Foucault: Humanistic Knowledge, Postmodern Challenges*, ed. Jonathan Arac (New Brunswick, N.J.: Rutgers University Press, 1988), pp. 13, 38.

7. Lyotard, *La condition postmoderne*, p. 7.

8. Lyotard, *Le postmoderne expliqué aux enfants*, pp. 37–38.

9. Gilles Deleuze, "Entretien 1980," *L'arc* 49 (rev. ed. 1980), p. 99.

10. On the importance of *Nietzsche et la philosophie* as a break from the Hegelian orientation of earlier French phenomenological and existential philosophy, see Vincent Descombes, *Modern French Philosophy*, trans. L. Scott-Fox and J. M. Hardin (Cambridge: Cambridge University Press, 1980), pp. 156–7. Cornel West recently has also noted the historical importance of Deleuze's study of Nietzsche, characterizing it as "an originary text" since "Deleuze was the first to think through the notion of difference independent of Hegelian ideas of opposition, and that was the start of the radical anti-Hegelianism which has characterized French intellectual life in the last decades." "Interview" with Anders Stephanson, in *Universal Abandon? The Politics of Postmodernism*, ed. Andrew Ross (Minneapolis: University of Minnesota Press, 1988), pp. 274–75.

11. Deleuze, *Nietzsche et la philosophie* (Paris: PUF, 1962), p. 9.

12. Lyotard, "*Energumen Capitalism*," trans. James Leigh, *Semiotext(e)* 2, no. 3 (1977): 11.

13. Hoy, "Foucault: Modern or Postmodern?" pp. 12–41.

14. Despite the Kantian framework of this analysis, it should be clear that Deleuze adopts a playful stance toward Kant's theory of the faculties. Deleuze suggests that faculties should be determined experimentally, the number of facilities proliferating as various forms of difference are revealed in contradictory and paradoxical phenomena. See *Différence et répétition* (Paris: PUF, 1969), pp. 169–217.

15. For a concise statement of Foucault's views on power, see *The History of Sexuality: Volume One*, trans. Robert Hurley (New York: Pantheon, 1978), 92–102. I develop the parallels between Deleuze-Guattari's notion of desire and Foucauldian power in *Deleuze and Guattari* (London: Routledge, 1989), 105–6, 130–45. See also Deleuze's *Foucault* (Paris: Minuit, 1986), which presents a systematic review of Foucault's thought within the analytical framework developed in *Mille plateaux*.

16. Eugene W. Holland, "The Anti-Oedipus: Postmodernism in Theory; or the Post-Lacanian Historical Contextualization of Psychoanalysis," *boundary 2* 14, nos. 1, 2 (1985–1986): 291.

17. Baudrillard, "The Precession of Simulacra," p. 253.

18. Deleuze first addresses this point in his 1967 essay *"Renverser le platonisme,"* reprinted in *Logique du sens* (Paris: Minuit, 1968), pp. 292–307, and develops the concept more extensively in *Différence et répétition* and *Logique du sens*. Derrida, of course, touches on the same motif in Plato in his *"Pharmacie de Platon,"* in *La dissemination* (Paris: Seuil, 1972), pp. 69–197, which appeared shortly after Deleuze's *"Renverser le platonisme"* in 1968.

19. Deleuze, *Différence et répétition*, p. 375.

20. Jameson, "Postmodernism, or the Cultural Logic of Late Capitalism," p. 64.

21. Deleuze, *Différence et répétition*, p. 187.

22. Jameson, "Postmodernism, or the Cultural Logic of Late Capitalism," p. 73.

23. See *L'Anti-Oedipe*, p. 180.

24. Andreas Huyssen, *After the Great Divide: Modernism, Mass Culture, Postmodernism* (Bloomington: Indiana University Press, 1986), p. 209.

25. Deleuze, *Proust et les signes*, 4th ed. (Paris: PUF, 1976), pp. 175–76.

26. Deleuze and Guattari, *Kafka: Pour une littérature mineure* (Paris: Minit, 1975), pp. 88–89.

27. See Huyssens, *After the Great Divide*, pp. 219–20.

28. Deleuze, *Francis Bacon: Logique de la sensation* (Paris: Editions de la différence, 1981), p. 14. There is a certain similarity between Deleuze's valorization of modern art's rejection of the conventional codes of representation and Roland Barthes's praise of the writerly text's subversion of readerly codes of narration. Barthes, however, tends to align popular art with readerly texts and high art with writerly texts, whereas Deleuze makes no such distinction, allowing for the possibility that a popular work of art may just as well undermine as reinforce conventional codes of representation. In this sense, Barthes's stance is modern, Deleuze's postmodern.

29. Lyotard, *Le postmoderne expliqué aux enfants*, p. 32.

30. Deleuze, *Cinéma 2: l'image-temps* (Paris: Minuit, 1985), p. 334.

31. Jameson, "Postmodernism, or the Cultural Logic of Late Capitalism," p. 76.

32. Deleuze and Guattari, *Mille plateaux* (Paris: Minuit, 1980), pp. 149–50.

Part III
Aesthetics and Poetics

I'd rather be one-dimensional than have no dimensions at all.
—Jessica Hahn

The Art World Revisited: Comedies of Similarity

Arthur C. Danto

I'll teach you differences.
          —*King Lear*

By contrast with the massive reassessment in our understanding of Rembrandt entailed by the claim that *The Polish Rider* is not by him —let alone in our conception of whoever it was who may have painted that profound work instead of Rembrandt—the question of whether something is or is not a work of art may seem pallidly academic and distantly philosophical. But such is the social prestige adherent to the identity of something as art that, in fact, both issues of reassessment are almost parallel. To be a Rembrandt is to claim pride of place in the greatest collections and to command the close aesthetic attention of artistic pilgrims. To be a great Rembrandt, like *The Night Watch*, is legitimately to enjoy the prerequisites of an altarpiece in a museum construed, like the Rijksmuseum in Amsterdam, as a cathedral to national identy. Whereas to be merely by the Master of *The Polish Rider* gives the work claim only on experts in the minor artists of the seventeenth century in Holland and a place in the lesser galleries devoted to the school of Rembrandt. There is the further consequence of revaluation in the crassest meaning of the term: were *The Polish Rider* to come onto the market as being genuinely by Rembrandt, it might just break the hundred-million-dollar mark the art world has been waiting for. But the reclassification of a piece of furniture as a work of art would have similar institutional and financial repercussions for the object, no longer appreciated merely as an examplar of fine craft but as a vehicle of meaning, and its maker no longer admired merely as a craftsman, whose lesser counterpart would be the carpenter and the cabinet-maker, but as an artist who uses wood or glass as media the way

Rembrandt used pigment or Michelangelo used stone. And the work, now art, is in candidacy for interpretations comically inappropriate for mere beds and vessels.

These parities notwithstanding, it is worth pausing to consider the difference in methods of determining as between Rembrandt and non-Rembrandt, on the one hand, and between art and non-art on the other. The Netherlands-based research team that has dedicated itself to establishing the true Rembrandt corpus consists of scholars armed with the latest in scientific aids to authenticity—Xray, molecular resonance, and the like—together with command of the documentary materials available from the seventeenth century and the disciplines of connoisseurship through which one can identify Ferdinand Bol, Govert Flinck, Gerrit Dou, Samuel Hoogstratten as different from and similar to one another and to Rembrandt. Its procedures are forensic and empirical, so if in the face of the claim that the provenance of *The Polish Rider* is dubious one cares to insist that it is not, one has to come equipped with the same scientific armamentarium they command and counter evidence with evidence. Both parties in such disputes will agree to the kind of document that could settle the matter either way. But even if something that is a work of art at a certain historical moment could not have been one at an earlier historical moment, and molecular resonance can tell us to which historical moment an object belongs, no such instrumental is available for establishing or disestablishing the claim that something is a work of art when it is historically possible for it to be one. The controversy seems not even remotely scientific. So how does one proceed?

The case of Wendall Castle, the acknowledged dean of the so-called studio furniture movement in America, is instructive. At one point, Castle was particularly miffed by the invidious distinction between craft and art, and he sought some strategy for erasing the hateful line that kept him from enjoying the benefits of the more exalted category. Clearly, it would do him no good just to proclaim himself an artist and walk around in smock and beret, and he hit on a strategy sufficiently philosophical that philosophers have come up with nothing much better to arbitrate the distinction between human beings and what Alan Turing designated "computing machinery." Turing's celebrated test was that if we cannot tell the difference, there is no difference—if for all we can tell a certain output is that of a human being, then there can be no difference essentially between humans and machines, in case the output, in fact, was that of a machine instead of a human. Castle fashioned an object that, though a stool, in fact looked enough like an abstract piece of wooden sculpture that he could submit it to a juried show of sculpture, into which it was, in fact, accepted by the experts who composed the jury. His strategy was this: Everyone allows that sculpture is art. If a piece of furniture cannot be told apart from a piece of sculpture by a jury of experts, there can *be* no difference between a piece of furniture and an artwork. It goes without saying that what I shall call the Castle test could not have been performed in the 1850s as in the 1950s, when, in fact, it took place. Sculptures were easily identified as such in the mid-nineteenth century, since most sculptures were statues, and most statues were realistic. No stool looked realistic enough to be taken as a statue, say of Liberty or of Mercy or of Louis Napoleon. But in 1959, when Castle submitted what he subsequently titled *Stool Sculpture*, such a thing was possible, since there were now abstract sculptures and sculptural furniture, and since *Stool Sculpture* looks far more like a prototypical abstraction than a prototypical stool. In fact, you can sit on it, providing you are as agile and wiry as Castle himself and someone has pointed out where you are to place your legs. (Stools in any case are prototypically not comfortable.) The difficulty with the Castle test, as I see it, is that it works only if it is difficult to see that something is a piece of furniture—only if you can't tell the difference, even though you are an expert, between furniture and sculpture. The issue, however, is not greatly advanced this way; the trick would be to get something that was prototypically a piece of furniture accepted as art, without the mediating step of disguising it as sculpture. Still, other than by appeal to experts, how is the matter to be resolved? Castle, who displays philosophical acumen throughout his career, had touched what comes to be known as the Institutional Theory of Art, according to which what makes something art and something else not is something the Art World—the "experts"—prescribes. This leaves only the question of who belongs to the Art World.

I raise this question in connection with the kinds of examples concerning which the Institutional Theory of Art was originally evolved as a response, though it must be noted that these examples put considerable pressure on the Turing and Castle sorts of tests. Some may feel that even if we cannot tell the difference between outputs of machines and humans, there is a difference even so. Turing would regard this as willful, no doubt, but that only shows the extent to which his view of differences was dominated by a kind of verificationist—or pragmatist—theory of meaning: if there is no difference in the effects or consequences, if there are no discernible differences, then there are no differences, *period*. For there to be a difference, there must be an observable difference; otherwise, the claim that there is a difference borders on meaninglessness. But, of course, a critic of Turing's famous test still might insist that the machine is at best capable of simulating the output of a human being, and though we cannot tell the difference between simulation and simulated, there is a difference, and a deep one—as deep as the difference between waking experience and its simulation in a dream. And, in any case, the examples from the art world were such that it was insisted that though we cannot tell the difference, there is a difference between, for example, a real Brillo carton and a work of art called "*Brillo Box* by Andy Warhol." To be sure, the resemblances were hardly so perfect that discriminability was out of the question. *Brillo Box* was made of wood and stenciled; Brillo cartons are made of corrugated cardboard and printed. Still, these cannot be where the differences between works of art and what I have termed "mere real things" are lodged. A philosopher would sound foolish who said that being made of wood is what marks the work of art, especially when so many artworks are made of paper. And it easily could have been imagined that the reverse happened—*Brillo Box* could have been a cardboard simulacrum of the good solid plywood containers in which the Brillo people shipped their soap pads.

So it was to have been with reference to the Art World that the Institutional Theory sought to erect the difference: the Art World decreed that *Brillo Box*—but not the Brillo boxes—was a "candidate for appreciation," to use George Dickie's famous phrase. And this brings us back to the question of who is a member of the Art World. It is widely conceded that customs inspectors are not, and, indeed, to the literal eye of the *douainer*, the Castle test works as follows: since there is no discernible difference between *Brillo Box* and a Brillo box, there is no difference. Toronto art dealer Jerrold Morris sought to arrange a show in 1965 of the notorious "sculptures," but Canadian Customs insisted that Warhol's so-called sculpture was merchandise and subject to a duty from which "original sculpture," under the law of the land, would be exempt. Dr. Charles Comfort was director of the National Gallery of Canada at the time. He sided with the customs inspectors. Looking at photographs, he declared, "I could see that they were not sculpture." It is true that photographs of *Brillo Box* and of the Brillo boxes are much less distinguishable than the boxes themselves. But is Comfort a member of the Art World or not? The director of the Stable Gallery, Eleanor Ward, felt absolutely betrayed by *Brillo Box*. "She hated them," Emilio de Antonio wrote me (he had arranged the exhibition, Warhol's first in a serious gallery in New York): "She was livid at the opening. People laughed." An artist friend of mine wrote "SHIT" all across the guest book. *I* thought they were art, but I was in no sense part of the art world at that point. And, of course, Leo Castelli, who had accepted Warhol into his gallery at last, thought of them as art.

But the Art World is clearly not a body that acts as one. We certainly would not want to define it as all and only those who thought *Brillo Box* a work of art in 1964—that would bring me, a philosopher, into the Art World and exclude the director of the National Gallery of Canada, let alone the owner of the gallery that showed them, who felt she had been hoaxed. And it certainly excludes the artist who sullied the guest book, not to mention a lot of very tony critics. Moreover, pop art was in fact popular—a good many quite ordinary people loved the *Campbell's Soup Cans*, in part, perhaps, because the "experts" hated them. People loved the fact that Warhol made art out of the most common of common things and got people to pay good money for it (in fact, *Brillo Box* was a flop as far as making money went, and it is one of the minor sorrows of my life that I did not buy one at the time).

My own essay of 1964, which was an immediate philosophical response to *Brillo Box*, was explicitly titled "The Art World," but it was less concerned with the question of what made *Brillo Box* a work of art than with the somewhat Kantian question of how it was possible for it to be one. And I thought there had to be something in the historical moment that explained this possibility, inasmuch as an indiscernible object could not have been an artwork at any earlier moment. I wrote this way: "To see something as art requires something the eye cannot descry—an atmosphere of artistic theory, a knowledge of the history of art: an art world." I think Matisse meant something quite close to this when he disclosed to Teriade:

> Our senses have an age of development which does not come from the immediate surroundings, but from a moment in civilization. The arts have a development which comes not only from the individual, but also from an accumulated strength, the civilization which precedes us. A talented artist cannot do just as he likes. If he used only his talents, he would not exist. We are not the masters of what we produce. It is imposed on us.

I thought of the Art World as the historically ordered world of artworks, enfranchised by theories that themselves are historically ordered. As such, I suppose, mine was a kind of institutional theory, in that the art world is itself institutionalized. But it was not the Institutional Theory of Art, which was bred of a creative misunderstanding of my work by George Dickie, who was less concerned with what makes a work of art such as Warhol's possible than with what makes it actual. And his notion of the Art World was pretty much the body of experts who confer that status on something by fiat. In a way, Dickie's theory implies a kind of empowering elite and is a distant relative of the noncognitive theory of moral language. "That is art!" has the logical status of "That is good!" as the latter was interpreted in the salad days of high positivism, when the advanced moral philosophers of the age thought all moral language did was give vent to feelings. It is to Dickie's credit that he sociologized where they psychologized, but in terms of truth conditions, there is little to choose between: his was, or is, a noncognitivist theory of art. The crux of his theory is that something is art when it is declared to be art by the Art World. And this has been the vulnerable part of his position: "Who is the Art World?" is the standard question, along with "How does one get to be a member of it?" Richard Wollheim slyly asks, "Do the representatives, if they exist, pass in review all candidates for the status of art, and do they then, while conferring this status on some, deny it to others?" Who keeps records of these decisions? Are they announced in art magazines? Do art writers wait outside the judging chambers, desperate to phone their publications with the scoops? How literally can Dickie mean what he says?

These are merely mischievous difficulties. It is not surprising to find that Wollheim's best argument appropriates that which Socrates used against Euthyphro when the latter claimed to be an expert on the topic of piety, said by him to be what all the gods love. The question then was whether it is pious because they love it, or they love it because it is pious. If the latter, then there still must be something that characterizes piety that has not been made explicit, namely that *on the basis of which* the gods love it. Once we know that, we can become as expert as the gods. If the former, the gods indeed are experts on what they love, but their love is quite without ground or reason. "Do the representatives of the art world have to have, or do they not have to have, reasons for what they do if what they do is to stick?" Wollheim asks. If so, then "these reasons will turn out to be all that we need to know. They will provide us with a a total account of what it is for a painting to be a work of art. . . . what is the further need for there to be representatives of the art world?" Reference to an Art World, at least as used by Dickie, drops out of any definition of art once we recognize the reasons in virtue of which a member of it will justify a claim that something is a work of art. There has to be more to the matter than mere fiat, and once we know what more there is, fiat seems gratuitous.

But perhaps the component of fiat is less central to a noncognitivist theory of ethical discourse than proponents of that originally believed as well; there may indeed be an element of declaration in saying "That is art!" as there is in saying "That is good!" But how frequently in our moral discourses do we actually say, as if we belonged in a story by Ernest Hemingway, "That is good!"? About as infrequently as we might pronounce something a work of art. And the reference to reasons calls for rather more by way of analysis than Wollheim provides. A distinction has to be drawn between having reasons for believing something is a work of art and something being a work of art depending on the reasons for it being so. A customs inspector indeed may use the fact that the director of a national museum says something is art as a reason for believing it is, just because of where directors are placed in the structures of expertness. But the director's saying it is a work of art is not a reason for it being one. Nevertheless, something being a work of art is dependent on some set of reasons, and nothing really is a work of art outside the system of reasons that give it that status; works of art are not such by nature. A rose is a rose whatever its name, but a work of art is not. That is part of what makes the concept of art ontologically interesting. If works of art were natural objects, something like the Institutional Theory could not even get started, roughly for the same reasons that noncognitivism could hardly get started if values lay strewn about the landscape like rocks. There could not be a noncognitive theory of rocks!

Two things must be said about these status-conferring reasons. First, to be a member of the art world is to participate in what we might term the discourse of reasons. Second, art is historical because the reasons relate to one another historically. *Brillo Box* had a shot at being a work of art because so many features thought to be central to something's identity as art, in the years leading up to that, had been rejected as part of the essence of art, so that the definition itself had become rather attenuated—to the point where pretty much anything could be a work of art. A member of the art world would be one who was familiar with this history of attenuation. What was remarkable about *Brillo Box* was that it was drawn from a kind of underground of familiar imagery so seemingly distant from the aesthetic preoccupations of those nominally interested in art that it came as a shock to see it in the art gallery at the same time as it was clear that there was nothing in the prevailing conception of art to rule it out. The fiat was perhaps Warhol's, but enough people who participated in the history of relevant reasons were prepared to admit it into the canon of art that it was admitted. So it is true that when we know the reasons, we have all we need. What is overlooked is that the discourse of reasons is what confers the status of art on what would otherwise be mere things, and that the discourse of reasons is the Art World construed institutionally. Of course, different individuals stand in different positions in that discourse: the director of the National Gallery of Canada was clearly *rétardataire*, making Canada, in the terms of the chagrined gallery dealer, the laughingstock of the art world. But there were plenty of others who were arrested at earlier positions in it, including the dealer herself, who was, even so, sufficiently up to date to have accepted a painting by Warhol of her "lucky two-dollar bill" as a work of art, and in exchange for which she gave him his first main show when no other dealer was quite willing to do that. It was, on the other hand, *Brillo Box* that converted Castelli to Warhol's side; his reservations had been only that Warhol seemed until then merely to be doing the sorts of things Lichtenstein was doing. And now that Warhol had moved into what Castelli unhesitatingly considered sculpture, the grounds for his reservations dissolved.

The thesis that emerged from my book, *The Transfiguration of the Commonplace*, is that works of art are symbolic expressions, in that they embody their meanings. The task of criticism is to identify the meanings and explain the mode of their embodiment. So construed, criticism is the discourse of reasons, participation in which defines the Art World of the Institutional Theory of Art: to see something as art is to be ready to interpret it in terms of what and how it means. Sometimes the meanings will have been lost, and intricate exercises in archaeology of the sort at which Aby Warburg or Erwin Panofsky are masters are required to bring them to light and to reconstitute what would have been transparent to the original Art World for these places. Simply in the nature of their being symbols, there is a system of communication and an implied audience for the work, and we can identify that audience as the work's Art World in that members of it are conversant in the discourse of reasons that constitute that work as a work, and then as the work it is. What made pop art popular is that the meanings its works embodied belonged to the common culture of the time, so that it was as if the boundaries of the Art World and of the common culture coincided. Movie stars, the stars of the supermarket shelf, the stars of the sports world, the stars of the comic pages—even, in the case of Warhol himself, the stars of the art world—were instantly recognizable to whoever lived the life of the common culture. The art redeemed the signs that meant enormously much to everyone, as defining their daily lives. Warmth, nourishment, orderliness, and predictability are profound human values that the stacked cans of Campbell's soup exemplify. The Brillo pad emblemizes our struggle with dirt and the triumph of domestic order. The comic strip panel distills the fantasies of our childhoods and graphically embodies, in its flagged colors and sharp outlines, the visual pleasures of innocence. In some profound way, the art was conservative, reconciling those who lived the form of life embodied in those works to the form of life they lived. Warhol celebrated the world in which he grew up and which he lost, much in the way, a decade later, Cindy Sherman, in her *Untitled Film Stills*, celebrated a vanished form of life: by the late 1970s, when she produced them, the stills she appropriated to such great effect were all but obsolete and belonged to the archives of a fading film culture. The difference between a Sherman still and a "real" still parallels the distinction between art and craft that Castle sought to cross, philosophically complicated by the fact that her stills are so like real stills that, according to Peter Scjheldahl, it was not uncommon for people to say they knew the film to which her still belonged. Only as a beginning of interpretation must we say that hers are *about* the class of real stills that they resemble to the point of being easily seen as exemplars of their denotation; and they are further about the values and attitudes of the life to which the stills belong. That is why her images are so rich. When real stills no longer form part of the common culture of the viewers—when Sherman's stills look merely like photographs— then it will require the archaeological and expository talents of a Warburg or a Panofsky to make their meanings accessible.

The kind of interpretation to which I refer here is under the constraint of truth and falsity: to interpret a work is to be committed to a historical explanation of the work. The theory of Art Worlds to which I subscribe is that of a loose affiliation of individuals who have enough by way of theory and history that they are able to practice what art historian Michael Baxandall terms "inferential art criticism," which, in effect, is simply historical explanations of works of art. Interpretations are then false when the explanations are. There is another kind of interpretation, to be sure, much discussed these days—what Roland Barthes identifies as "writerly" as against "readerly" interpretation. I have been discussing readerly interpretation. Writerly reading is close in logical kind to the noncognitive discourse that consists in fiats and declarations; it is what the work means to the viewer, without concern about whether it is true or false. It is under this sense of interpretation that works are sometimes said to admit of infinite numbers of interpretations and in which interpretation is a play with signifiers. It may be and in a way has been argued, by Joseph Margolis among others, that *writerly* implies a *readerly* interpretation: it is first required that something be recognized as a work before the question arises about what it can then mean "to me." It also may be argued that part of what makes art important is that it *can* or even must give rise to writerly interpretations and come to mean specific things to specific viewers without meaning the same thing for every viewer. If I think of my family history in viewing *King Lear*, that has no explanatory value as far as *King Lear* is concerned. If I observe with pleasure that sometimes I can see my daughter's features in those of Manet's *Olympia*, that is not inferential art criticism. Readerly interpretation is fallible, just because it has the form of an explanatory hypothesis, but it is not infinite and it is not subjective. My sense of Derrida is that for him there is only the free play of the signifier, and hence only writerly reading. My sense of Kendall Walton's interesting theory of representation as what he terms "makebelieve" is that I cannot see how it can tolerate the distinction between the two sorts of interpretation.

It is instructive to observe how members of the Art World respond to works of a kind encountered for the first time, where the task is to lay down something like a piece of theory for the work, and then against this some appraisal of it, as critics, for example, are called upon to do with great frequency. Roberta Smith, a critic for the *New York Times*, once told me that this is the part of her job that she finds most appealing. Often, she will be the first one to write about a given artist, with no available history or theory to help her, since the artist is quite unknown. Here, those outside the Art World will have considerable difficulty, for aside from the acknowledgment that it "must be art" since it is in a gallery or even in a museum, there is very little they can say, for they lack access to the discourse of reasons that apply. At best, they can describe it in nonartistic ways—"It is made of plywood" or "It seems just to be a pile of broken glass." But even when one has access to the discourse, and hence really is part of the Art World, one is not infallible. One merely will have begun the discourse for the work in question, which will stand subject to revision. The Art World does not respond as one.

Consider *Metronomic Irregularity I* by Eva Hesse, perhaps as great a sculptural influence as there is today but so unfamiliar when this work was first shown in 1966 that even a seasoned art-worlder would encounter it as almost radically alien. The work is quite small. It consists of two painted wood panels, each twelve inches by six inches separated by a space of about the same dimension. The panels have been drilled at regular half-inch intervals, so they look like industrial pegboards, though "made by hand." They are connected by coated wire drawn loosely in and out of the holes, so that it looks like a tangle. The panels are mechanical and orderly and look as though the wire should itself be taut and orderly, instead of which it is disappointingly slack and snarled; it looks like it has been drawn through the holes by someone who would have had trouble lacing shoes. In a way, the wire looks like corset strings loosened to allow the constrained flesh to breathe. Nothing quite like it had been seen in 1966, not unless one frequented Hesse's studio, and even then it was somewhat novel. It was hung on the wall in the Marylyn Fishbach Gallery in an exhibition organized under the title "Eccentric Abstraction" by Lucy Lippard. It was there that Hilton Kramer, then the *Times* critic, gave it a crushing misreading. "Secondhand," he wrote. "It simply adapts the imagery of Jackson Pollock's drip paintings to a third-dimensional medium." If one looks at the tangle of wire from this perspective, it seems almost a critical discovery that the work looks like a three-dimensional translation of Pollock's skeined pigment. And one could reconstruct the artist's intentions this way. Wouldn't it be wonderful to make a sort of sculptural analog to the drip painting and get into sculpture the same urgency, energy, and spontaneity that Pollock got into his painting? Against the proposed motive, the actual work would be pathetic, secondhand but also second-rate. The marvelous tensions of Pollock's paint simply are not to be found in the droopy and almost inept wiring.

But this interpretation leaves quite out of account the meticulously drilled panels. Kramer, seeing them as supporting the tangle and making it physically possible, may have regarded them merely as support, a kind of base or framework, with the work consisting in the wire. But suppose instead they are part of the work? Then it stops being Pollock-like altogether. It was no part of the Pollockian vision to make repetitiously structured arrays that resemble pegboards. These belong to a different order of impulse, not possible in the world of abstract expressionism but quite possible in the world of minimalism, to which Hesse belonged, with its deliberate use of industrial materials such as pegboard. There is a history that connects minimalism with constructivism, which made ideological use of industrial materials. In any case, once we have decided that the perforated boards belong as part of the work, Kramer's account is at once incomplete and false. A more adequate account, which now eliminates the "secondhand" epithet, goes as follows: the work consists of two opposed sorts of elements, one mechanical and orderly, the other irregular and disorderly. One is classical, the other Romantic; one is male and the other female. The work is organized around the tensions between them. The hopeless wire strives to unite the separated fragments of its counterpart, but they remain divided as it runs in and out of the openings in pursuit of unity and harmony and visual peace. It is then a funny, perhaps a very funny work. In a final interview, four years afterward, and published in the month of her early death, Hesse talked about the comedic qualities of her work, its objective absurdity, even (her word) its "silliness." But this may have been invisible, to her and to others in 1966, whether part of the Hesse art world or hostile to it.

Even the title, *Metronymic Irregularity*, is funny enough to give us a hint about the work, the metronome being that paradigm of regularity that would make an irregularly tocking metronome almost a Dada joke. Kramer's is a failure in what I would call interpretive seeing, inasmuch as he was oblivious to half the work and so interpreting a fragment as the whole. I do not offer this as a criticism of him. It is, in fact, remarkable, given the demands of his job, that he even had time for this curious work in this offbeat show and was able to evolve an intelligent theory for it, if a wrong one. But there would have been no room in the art world in which Kramer developed his "good eye" for responding to pegboard in the required way. He almost had to see it as outside the work, and as a kind of coarse support for it. Throughout Hesse's work is the ambiguity between something being a base as against being part of the work which, in virtue of having absorbed the only natural candidate for the base, then *has* no base. Her celebrated and admired *Hang Up* consists of a very large frame, around which she has carefully and evenly wound rope, and then a large, irregular loop of metal tubing that comes shooting out of one corner, invades our space, and then slinks back into the frame at the opposite corner. A decision has to be made about whether the loop is the work, a wormy sort of sculpture, or whether the work is a kind of balletic interplay between two components in a work that has no base at all. Hesse's work forms, in fact, a fairly consistent corpus which consistently expresses a strong artistic vision. Certain metaphors are implied, certain questions raised about the nature of sculpture, perhaps about the nature of women, perhaps even about the meaning of love. All this, in my view, is internal to the corpus and is made explicit through the discourse of reasons that her work requires. It is in no sense mandated by an institutionalized art world. Hesse would have been Hesse, perhaps, whenever she lived, but her work as we know it would have been impossible in 1926 or in 1886, and quite possibly her personality would have been impossible at those earlier times as well, given the way it is expressed in the work.

One thing, however, is perfectly clear: no one who understands how Pollock's tangles of pigment arrived on their surfaces can imagine the slightest parallel with the way Hesse's tangles arrived in the spaces between her panels. It is possible that Pollock's was the defining personality of his era—macho, sullen, shamanistic, hyper-romantic, impulsive, aggressive, urgent, dangerous, boozy, and wild. Hesse's was the very opposite of this: her hero was Warhol—cool, witty, conceptual. If Warhol expressed his age the way

Pollock expressed his, there was more than an artistic change between them, there was a historical revolution. If there were to be a connection between Hesse's and Pollock's tangles, it would be referential and satirical. Hesse, in fact, had participated in an exhibition whose very title was a put-down of abstract expressionism: "Abstract Inflationism and Stuffed Expressionism." She was a product of Yale's art school and a participant in the discourse of minimalist reasons that would have been incomprehensible to Pollock. Kramer's was a very different discourse and one, moreover, that led him into the inadvertent comedy of similarities that disfigures so much of the Art World's way of talking about art: if it looks the same (or even similar), it is the same.

The Art World is the discourse of reasons institutionalized, and to be a member of the Art World is, accordingly, to have learned what it means to participate in the discourse of reasons for one's culture. In a sense, the discourse of reasons for a given culture is a sort of language game, governed by rules of play, and for reasons parallel to those that hold that only where there are games are there wins and losses and players, so only where there is an Art World is there art.

The rules of play in Western art have been very much involved with a form of criticism, which is why the shape of art history in the West has been able to see itself as progressive. To be an artist in this art world is, in effect, to take a position on the past, and inevitably on one's contemporaries whose position on the past differs from one's own. One's work is therefore tacitly a criticism of what went before and what comes after. And that means that to understand a work requires reconstruction of the historical and critical perception that motivated it. Beginning with the pre-Raphaelites, artists have distanced themselves from their histories in a more or less total way, which meant that they were implicitly involved in a semiphilosophical enterprise of saying what was and was not art. The definition of art accordingly has come to play an increasing role in the making of art in modern times, climaxing in recent years when the question of whether something was art became more and more frequently and more and more stridently expressed. Is furniture art? Is photography? These questions helped define the shape of the discourse of reasons the Institutional Theory of Art endeavored to capture. On the other hand, they would not necessarily have been questions for other cultures and other discourses. The Chinese tradition, for example, prized exact likeness not at all, whereas our tradition celebrates the prowess of the simulator. So the advent of photography in the nineteenth century provided no initial problem for the Chinese art world. When it did pose a challenge, however, the whole shape of art history in China changed in order to accommodate it.

In the West, the point at which a work appears in the evolving discourse of reasons is central to its identity. A red square of 1915 by Malevich is a very different work from a red square that might otherwise resemble it minutely by Ad Reinhardt done in 1962, and that in turn is very different from one done in 1981 by Marcia Hafif. To be sure, Malevich in a sense broke the ice. But I would be very cautious indeed in saying of Reinhardt or of Hafif that their red squares were secondhand, that it had all been said before. I have only sought to make the Institutional Theory of Art more sensitive to history than it has been so far.

Criticism as Dimension: The Idiot as Artist/The Idiot as Critic

Donald Kunze

The problem is not what the theory of critics says to artists, or what artists say to critics that would significantly affect their theory, but the fact that from the standpoint of each, the other appears by all means of reckoning to be idiotic (Sloterdijk, p. 12). An idiot is, by way of his etymology, a private person. In this case, "privacy" is something of an insult. Art, after all, is thought to be, in spite of its subjectivities, the most universal of languages. Criticism, because of its commitments to discursive statements, is by its very nature geared in the direction of the other. To assert that either artist or critic is a private person in thought, word, or deed is to accuse him or her of failure. Yet such name-calling is inevitable given the lack of middle ground between the intentions and means of art and the reasoned scholarship of the critic.

In this paper, I attempt to bring a new problem to bear on this twin idiocy, a problem based on a fundamental aspect of perception, which may be accused of being a psychologism. Wishing to avoid psychologisms, I ground my argument in an anecdotal method, in hopes that the poetic dimension of the problem will prevail. And, in hopes of avoiding the feeling of abstraction that often comes from anecdotes, I will secure the illustrative services of the dimension that exists between the viewer and the viewed, what has been called "the saggital dimension." The sections of this paper thus alternate between anecdotal evidence and the discursive connections between art and the sciences of neuropsychology, semiology, and philosophy.

In keeping with the theme of idiocy, I have not made any attempt to connect these two kinds of evidence except to juxtapose them. Norman O. Brown, a wise fool rather than an idiot, relied on the aphorism to invite the readers of *Love's Body* to think for themselves. With the same sort of hope, I would intend the lack of connection between the sections to encourage the reader to inscribe an essay of his or her own among the mingled bones of the artist and critic.

Velázquez I

In a well-known painting by the seventeenth-century Spanish master, *Las Meniñas*, a room and its occupants—royalty and retainers—are shown in exacting perspective. Careful checking by art historians has demonstrated that the metrics of the original room, destroyed by fire in the eighteenth century, are reproduced faithfully. Likewise the personages in the painting are accurately represented and can be named. The paintings hanging in the dark shadows in the rear of the room can be and have been identified and were most likely hanging on the wall at the time. Michel Foucault, in his famous description of this painting (*The Order of Things*, pp. 3–16), has noted that there are, however, important voids in this otherwise crystalline work: the subject matter of the canvas whose back is turned to us; the room beyond, alluringly indicated by the hand of the *aposentador* pulling aside the curtain in the rear; and the objects of the collective gaze of the *infanta* and her attendants, whose ghosts seem to be irradiated rather than reflected by the mirror on the back wall.

To the space of representation, so well calculated through the theory of linear perspective that dominated this age, we can assign all those matters of criticism having to do with conditions surrounding the construction and correct inspection of the work of art. The space they occupy is an extension of ours, separated by the device of the canvas, which aspires in this instance to work as a window doing nothing more than offering a physical ground on which the paint might be stabilized. To that "other space," however, we can assign nothing but the mystery of looking itself: the contentious question of what and how the mirror reflects, the role of the unseen side of the canvas, the ownership of that real estate where the present-day spectator stands, which must have been occupied at one time by Philip and his queen, Mariana, and by the painter himself. This "other space" disturbingly interrupts the first, perspectival space; first, by not quite allowing the mirror to reflect the space in which we now stand; second, by holding the painting's most enigmatic truths within its dimensionality. The coincidence of these disruptions constructs what amounts to a painting-within-a-painting.

Representational and Enactive Spatiality

In painting, there is a conflict between two kinds of meaning that is, for the most part and in the main, a conflict between two forms of spatiality. The first we might label representational, but the other cannot be characterized as nonrepresentational except in that it refuses us the normal pictorial conventions of providing recognizable signs of the visible world. The second form of dimensionality works along what is most appropriately called the saggital or line-of-sight dimension, the one perpendicular to the surface of the canvas that connects the viewer, the painting, and the subject matter hypothetically "lying beyond" the canvas. Its logic is to give something in the process of withholding it, just as the saggital dimension gives us a line but shows us only a point. It is visible only in an end-on view. It forms an alliance with the other hidden parts of the representational space, and it seems that it is often the artist's intention to group all hidden parts into a syncretic mystery story. Thus, while painting can be located solidly within the tradition of representations of its age, it also claims membership in the class club emblems where images traditionally pose as riddles. But unlike the rebuses familiar to us through the many emblem books of the fifteenth and sixteenth centuries, it is possible to make this latter form of spatiality a parasite of representational space. The gains made exploring the shadows, the reflections, and the spaces outside the painting are carefully calculated to equal the losses inflicted on the contiguity of representation. And this formula proves to be so exact that we might expect that the painter must be thinking of that kind of carpenter who leaves no scrap of wood, or even sawdust, behind at the completion of a work.

This sort of economy is primarily rhetorical. The figure that embodies it most directly is named *aposeopesis*, or the more pronounceable *praecisio*. The speaker breaks off suddenly, in mid-sentence, sometimes with a purposefully unsuccessful attempt to conceal emotion. Semiotics has jumped in to save us from Latin and Greek by designating this as a situation of "privative opposition," where conventional signification has been brought to a halt: the so-called zero degree. Barthes notes that one should not think of zero as total absence. It is the point from which spring all poetic meanings, the departure gate of what Umberto Eco has advertised as "open semiosis." Nothing is still something.

The Aerial Darts

In *Posthumous Papers of a Living Author* (pp. 136–38), Robert Musil tells a story about a soldier at the Italian front during World War I, who experienced an aerial attack of a singularly horrifying nature. For a limited time during that conflict, airplanes hurled antipersonnel devices known as aerial darts, short metal rods that could pierce through an entire body. A curious property of this weapon was that its melodious ringing sound could be heard only by the future victim who stood directly in the vertical line of its trajectory. Someone standing only a short distance away would be unaware of the noise, and the victims of the darts frequently mistook this lack of common recognition as an excuse to ignore the reality of their impending doom. Like Paul of Tarsus, they were the only ones affected.

This story conveys the radical nature of that aspect of perception that depends on the body's particular position in space. Only the person standing directly in the line of view can experience exactly this glimmer, that contour. The particularity isolates us, but it is also that which we feel to be most real. We must be in a certain here-and-now to experience it; and an appreciation of that experience cannot be had by projecting it "to the outside." We must stand in the same shoes. It is reminiscent of Heidegger's "being-towards-death," which is perhaps an extension of the saggital to the question of existence. To say that it "had qualities" would be absurd.

The Zero Degree and Loss of Contiguity

At the zero degree, we cannot call on the relative experience of others; we cannot compare, characterize, or project. Yet the zero degree, as a nexus of unlimited poetic meaning, is understandably plentiful in poetry and art. Dante's use of light in the *Commedia* might be used as a textbook on the subject. Theology has borrowed freely from its imagery, as in the case of the blinding of Paul of Tarsus and the ecstasy of Saint Theresa. What we might say of it in relation to the close economies existing between the two forms of spatiality offers a convenient bridge to architecture: that there must be something broken to begin with, and this something typically has a projective character about it. I think there are two reasons why this is so.

First, it is important to observe that perspective sets up a certain atmosphere that, having gone up, is permitted by the imagination to involve just as much fun coming down; and that there is a certain pride in building this space of representation that makes it a visual version of the first half of a tragedy, defined in Chaucer's terms as a skyward arch of a hero who, because of a divine mark on his character, deigns to wind his fate to the unwinding point. The beautiful assemblage of courtiers surrounding the *infanta* would, to a more primitive mentality, offer too easy a target for the vengeful gods intent on planing mankind down to a humble datum. To Mediterranean eyes, *Las Meniñas* is a candidate for the evil eye.

Second, perspectivally representational spaces are, like other truths of correspondence, dedicated to the logic of contiguity. Things must touch, and in touching they must measure. Representation is fundamentally an inventory, a means of narrating each and every detail with respect to a single calibrated container: space. The advantage in undoing such a construct as perspective is that, like undoing logic in a riddle, a certain payoff comes from the particularity with which each and every detail meets its end. Unlimited semiosis is not interested in isolated battles by chosen combatants. It likes to engage the whole. But it likes to do this very slowly, one brick at a time.

Two Companions, One Landscape

The painter Hans Richter wrote of an experience that has been retailed subsequently as the best illustration of the problem of perceptual intersubjectivity (Gombrich, pp. 64–65). German artists living in Rome in the 1800s set out toward Tivoli to undertake an experiment testing their abilities as draftsmen. Sitting as close together as possible on a hillside, they aimed their pens at the same prospect. After comparing sketchbooks at the end of the session, their Teutonic sense of order was confounded to find each sketch as different from the others as the temperament of its artist was from those of his companions. Maurice Merleau-Ponty borrowed this situation for his essay "The Primacy of Perception," adding the important observation that, while it is physically and existentially impossible for any companion of ours to see, in exact particularity, what we see from our unique vantage point, there arises in us nevertheless a certain *demand* that he should. This demand has nothing to do with the difference of temperament, or of physical location in space, but with an essential human obligation that is felt along with every perception, that it is not our subjective interests that determine what is perceived but a compelling quality of the world that engages us in a particular manner, at a particular here and a particular now.

Aphasia in Social Situations

When the human brain is afflicted with lesions, the location of damage can lead to the loss of specific functions that demonstrate a certain symmetry of thought existing between matters of semblance (recognition, pattern, imitation) and matters of contiguity (syntax, structure, abstraction). Lacan has noted that this, to some extent at least, demonstrates the nature of the classic semiologic formula S/s, or signifier over signified, where the former designates all those tangible signs that form "speech" as distinguished from "language," and where s designates the idea or concept (pp. 152–53). The individual aphasia victim suffering from a loss of semblance will rely on strategies of contiguity to compensate, according to the classical work of Gelb and Goldstein (Cassirer, vol. 2, pp. 205–77). But it is easy, if a little arch, to see that several individuals looking at the same scene, unable to get a common idea of what lies before them, suffer at the social level from semblance aphasia, and that any conversation or graphic device of theirs that aims at consensus attempts, like the semblance aphasiac, to use contiguity to compensate.

One means of accounting for different views of the same scene is a map that describes the position of the viewers and the objects viewed as if seen from above. One might make just such a map of *Las Meniñas*, including the space in front of the picture-plane-turned-canvas. Merleau-Ponty is quick to point out that, by describing both visible and invisible regions in equal terms, this map suffers a lack of that very element that makes perception compellingly real, our inner insistence on the validity of the view from our particular viewpoint.

The loss of s in the S/s formula is, presumably, the basis for making perspectival representations in the first place. It also may be regarded as a constituent motive in all our communications which, more or less, attempt to overcome our differences in individual viewpoints. But where we collective aphasiacs are normally content with the token of a possible common view as is had in a photograph or a map, the artist induces another and more serious kind of aphasia that makes us retread the dimension we had hoped would disappear within the successful representation. The eyes on the canvas follow us, and we can easily dismiss this side effect of portraiture. But the artist who reinstates the saggital dimension makes us (and us alone) the new destination of the zero degree. The disease of the signifier, the zero degree, collaborates with all that is hidden by likeness, brings it all up again, into a darkness that shines out of the light of representation.

Diana and Acteon

Diana is bathing with her attendants; Acteon, the hunter, is out with his dogs. Acteon stumbles upon, does not seek, that sacred bathing grove with its forbidden disclosures of godly nakedness. He turns away, too late. He runs but cannot outrun the curse of Diana, which changes him into the image of running, the stag. His dogs do not mistake their role and devour the master, as his gaze had devoured the goddess.

In the ancient Persian burial tradition, the dog, not the worm, was the animal assigned to hasten the mortification of the flesh. Dogs trained to devour corpses were kept by priests for the occasion. With the refinement of sensibilities, this gruesome task was no longer carried out in full. It was sufficient to bring the dog into the room of the deceased, for the dog to gaze on the body. The word of final absolution in this ceremony was *sägdid*, "the dog has seen" (Rank, p. 62).

In the troubadour days of southern France, Cathar sentiments reigned. Perfect love was not between wife and husband but between a noble lady and one of lower birth who scourged himself with song, fasting, and feats. The object of his amorous argument was not sexual union but a formal opportunity, satisfied even with the husband present, to view his beloved naked. The appearance of the nonappearing, the passage of the virgin to the bride, the exchange of representative art for the saggital zero degree—these, according to Octavio Paz, are the mythic ingredients of Duchamp's "The Bride Laid Bare by Her Bachelors, Even."

The Zero Degree of Criticism as Dimension

Beneath the title *New Science* (1744), a lady known as *la Donna Metafísica* ("Lady Above-Nature") is shown leaning on an altar or plinth engaved with the motto *ignota latebat* ("she, unrecognized, lay hidden"). The "she, unrecognized" who lay "hidden" is most certainly *la Donna Metafísica* herself (see Verene). Appearing in the more revealing iconic garb of the frontispiece, she perches rather than reclines on an altar, and is poised in the middle of a gaze that connects the eye of God and Homer, the first poet, who stands here for the poetic mentality of the first humans. In terms of our discussion, she is the saggital dimension seen as a joint or angle that reverses or inverts.

Wings on the temples sometimes signify the Kabbalistic idea
of death of the kiss, where the head and its celestial associations are
allied with the separation of the *Nessamah*, the uppermost soul,
from the lower *Nephes* (Gaselee, pp. 349–59). In terms that at first
seem brutal, a decapitation takes place that fragments the cone of
vision optically—a chipping-off of the apex. This is reflected in the
iconographical connections between wisdom, as in the emblems for
justice, and the disappearance of the head in the clouds. There is a
Swedish fairytale in which the fairies disappear by turning side-
ways.

In Vico's discussion of the "method" of his New Science, he
asserts that the external facts of history are reflected internally, in
the mental development of the individual. He has been credited
with a motto invented posthumously, *verum ipsum factum*, "We may
know what we have made." The *ipsum* is the key: "itself." The mind
is made by itself. How does such a process begin? This is the poetic
subject of the New Science.

The reader, who is outside the text in a literal and theoretical
sense, proves the truth of the New Science by an anatomical method, so to speak. He (metaphorically a bachelor) becomes the object
of the ideal eternal history, and his experience of reading—which
moves from the literal to the allegorical to the analogical meanings
—confirms this. The final moment of proof, however, is
"anagogical." The separation of past, present, and future—essential
to any idea of historical development—collapses into the mind of
the reader. The historian himself is contaminated by his subject in
the final acts of realization. The event is both awful—for how can
meanings be stabilized in such a moment?—and pleasurable: the
kiss of the bride. "The reader," Vico predicts, "will experience in his
mortal body a divine pleasure as he contemplates in the divine
ideas this world of nations in all the extent of its places, times, and
varieties." The reader becomes Vico, becomes history itself, in a final collapse of text, author, and reader.

Velázquez II

Las Meniñas has several "feet" figuring prominently at the foot of
the canvas. The first is social, for the royal pair occupies the "top,"
which is also the back of the room, the *infanta* and her attendants,
and anonymous courtiers in the middle. The front and bottom of
the canvas is given to a female dwarf suffering from achondropla-
sia, a male dwarf—also a famous jester of the day, Nicolaso Pertusato (a case of growth hormone deficiency)—and a dog. The foot is

a compressed limb. Its articulate parts—toes, arch, instep, and heel —are flattened to meet the ground in a plane. The dwarfed figures are themselves flattened by nature and flattened again by the painter to the point that they come closest to the picture plane. The dog, flattest of all, nearly touches it. The jester, to maintain his relative superiority in this inferior position, keeps *his* foot on the dog. The achondroplast attempts dignity through dress and expression. The *infanta*, next in line, is compressed temporarily by childhood. Unlike the jester, Pertusato, she will overcome this disability. She is attended, and her attendants mimic the transition in scale from her present stature, marked by kneeling and an adoring glance, to full stature represented by the maid on the right. Velázquez's stature is limited by the horizon and perspectival space. Closer, and he would be hidden by the edge of the working canvas; farther, and he would shrink beneath the level of the mirror. The *aposentador* in the rear rises through the artifice of the stair; his curtain terminates the universe of the painting but suggests a space beyond, behind the mirror, beyond the room.

The Fool

William Empson outlines the main silhouette of the fool as (1) a person who is stupid, simpleminded, or lacking common sense; (2) a mocked person; (3) someone who is brash, ready to talk; (4) an innocent; (5) someone childish; (6) a dupe; (7) a clown, professional or amateur; (8) a knave, an obstinately and viciously stupid person; (9) a weak-minded or idiotic person (p. 111). We are prepared to find in this recipe the royal means of escaping the poison of power: a cultivated relationship with representatives of folly in hopes that a little evil deters a greater and more dangerous portion. Children, fools, and dwarfs solicit our pity and care. Like the dog, they are our pets. Like the painter, they retain a privileged relationship to delirium. They are permitted to stand outside our world and, like the *aposentador*, violate its edges. They fiddle with the zero degree, represent us in their fool play and tricks. They rule the world of semblance, which we lack as collective in need of royal dominance. The king may represent; his attribute, *royal*, means "real." The fool enacts the counterlogic of the end-on saggital dimension. Foucault wrote:

> [T]he madman fulfills the function of *homosemanticism*: he groups all signs and leads them with a resemblance that never ceases to proliferate. The poet fulfills the opposite function: his

is the *allegorical* role; beneath the language of signs and beneath the interplay of their precisely delineated distinctions, he strains his ears to catch that "other language," the language, without words or discourse, of resemblance. The poet brings similitude to the signs that speak it, whereas the fool loads all signs with a resemblance that ultimately erases them. (*The Order of Things*, pp. 49–50)

Velazquez ain't no fool, nosiree. He collects his fee where blindness is given with truth.

> *(now the ears of my ears awake and*
> *now the eyes of my eyes are opened)*
>
> (e. e. cummings, *i thank You*
> *God for most this amazing*)

Coda

Disney's Uncle Remus wants to know, "How can there be a tale when there ain't no tail?"

Works Cited

Adcock, Craig E. *Marcel Duchamp's Notes from the* Large Glass. Ithaca: Cornell University Press, 1981.

Barthes, Roland. *Elements of Semiology*, trans. Annette Lavers and Colin Smith. London: Cape, 1967.

Brown, Norman O. *Love's Body*. New York: Random House, 1966.

Cassirer, Ernst. *The Philosophy of Symbolic Forms*, trans. Ralph Manheim, 3 vols. New Haven: Yale University Press, 1953–1957.

Cummings, e. e. *Complete Poems, 1910–1962*, ed. George James Firmage, rev., corrected, and expanded ed. London: Granada, 1981.

Eco, Umberto. *The Role of the Reader: Explorations in the Semiotics of Texts*. Advances in Semiotics, ed. Thomas A. Sebeok. Bloomington: Indiana University Press, 1984.

Empson, William. *The Structure of Complex Words*. New York: New Directions, 1951.

Foucault, Michel. *Madness and Civilization: A History of Insanity in the Age of Reason*, trans. Richard Howard. New York: Pantheon Books, 1965.

———. *The Order of Things: An Archaeology of the Human Sciences*, 1st American ed. New York: Pantheon Books, 1971.

Gaselee, Stephen. "The Soul in the Kiss." *The Criterion* 2, no. 7 (1924): 349–59.

Goldstein, Kurt. *Language and Language Disturbances*. New York: Grune and Stratton, 1948.

Gombrich, E. H. *Art and Illusion: A Study in the Psychology of Pictorial Representation*. New York: Pantheon Books, 1960.

Kunze, Donald. "The Interrupted Gaze: Art and Folly in Velázquez's *Las Meniñas.*" *Les Bonnes Feuilles* 7, nos. 1 and 2 (Spring 1978): 3–23.

———. "Sciagraphy and the Ipsum of Architecture." *Architecture and Shadow* 11 (1990): 62–75.

Lacan, Jacques. *Écrits: A Selection*, trans. Alan Sheridan. New York: W. W. Norton, 1977.

Merleau-Ponty, Maurice. *The Primacy of Perception*, trans. James M. Edie. Northwestern University Studies in Phenomenology and Existential Philosophy, ed. John Wild. Evanston, Ill.: Northwestern University Press, 1964, pp. 12–42.

Musil, Robert. *Posthumous Papers of a Living Author*, trans. Peter Wortsman. Hygiene, Colo.: Eridanos Press, 1987.

Paz, Octavio. *Marcel Duchamp, Appearance Stripped Bare*, trans. Rachel Phillips and Donald Gardner. New York: Seaver Books, 1978.

Rank, Otto. *The Don Juan Legend*, trans. and ed. David G. Winter. Princeton: Princeton University, 1975.

Sloterdijk, Peter. *Thinker On Stage: Nietzsche's Materialism*, trans. Jamie Owen Daniel. Theory and History of Literature 56, ed. Wlad Godzich and Jochen Schulte-Sasse. Minneapolis: University of Minnesota Press, 1989.

Verene, Donald Phillip. "Vico's 'Ignota Latebat.'" *New Vico Studies* 5 (1987): 79–98.

Vico, Giambattista. *The New Science of Giambattista Vico*, trans. Thomas Goddard Bergin and Max Harold Fisch. Ithaca: Cornell University Press, 1968.

Willeford, William. *The Fool and His Sceptre*. Evanston, Ill.: Northwestern University Press, 1969.

Nonnarrative and the Construction of History

Barrett Watten

Poetry is always a dying language but never a dead language.
—Robert Smithson[1]

You are afraid of your finitude; we are afraid of our infinitude.
—Arkadii Dragomoshchenko[2]

Nonnarrative Poetics

The way time is organized in a work of art is one of the defining characteristics of its mode of historical representation. Narrative is conventionally thought to be both the implicit goal and explicit norm of art's temporal organization.[3] Time in modernist and postmodernist art and writing, however, often is organized in ways not dependent on narrative as formal guarantee of meaning or as necessary horizon of understanding. Further, there have been particular historical frames for the development of nonnarrative aesthetic forms. Individual practitioners of nonnarrative, of course, have assured places in literary history, from Sterne and Blake to Walt Whitman, Lautréamont, and Gertrude Stein. In the 1920s there took place, for however brief a time and with whatever instability, a culturally productive moment of nonnarrative writing among a group of American expatriate writers that was represented as a "revolution of the word."[4]

This movement had notable descendants in the postwar period, particularly in the abstraction of the New York School (both poets and painters) and in the aleatorical methods of John Cage and Jackson Mac Low. About 1975, new conditions for the social reproduction of nonnarrative forms emerged—during a period of national crisis at about the time of the Fall of Saigon—for a number of writers. This literary phenomenon has been related to the crisis of historical narrative in postmodernism;[5] a rejection of narrative for other forms of temporal organization took place, and was culturally productive, at a given historical time.

If nonnarrative is at once a form of temporal organization and a form of historical self-consciousness, it will be necessary to say what nonnarrative is, both in works of art and as a kind of history. In a defining sentence written by a historian wanting to pose the nonnarrative against what he sees as a positive and stultifying narrative among historians, it is a moment of negative totality that cannot be told: "A culture is reactive when it continues to narrativize itself despite, at any moment, being six minutes away (by missile) from its own nonnarrative obliteration."[6] If narrative for Sande Cohen is a species of ideology, nonnarrative must be the real that can only undermine it. Such a negative notion of nonnarrative must have ideological investments of its own, as are evident in Cohen's fantasy of self-destruction in retribution for a denial encoding a fearful reactivity to historical events. Negative notions of nonnarrative owe their formulations as well to linguistic models, in which, for example, a paradigmatic break in syntagmatic progression yields an atemporal moment in a temporal sequence presumed to be narrative. The distinction between synchronic structure and diachronic development has, of course, many consequences, some of which have contributed to the sense that nonnarrative can only be imagined as an impossible, self-undoing moment of negative totality.[7]

In works of art, however, nonnarrative is not simply an undoing, interruption, or denial of narrative; it is a positive form of temporal organization. As narrative comprises a number of forms of discourse, from oral epic to *Swann's Way*, that can be seen as a "discursive mode" in Gerard Genette's sense, nonnarrative compromises a "discursive mode" but not a single form of discourse. While set apart from narrative by the prefix *non-*, nonnarrative includes a number of forms of discourse that are not simply negating of narrative. Nonnarratives are forms of discursive presentation in which both linear and contextual syntax exist but where univocal motivation, retrospective closure, and transcendent perspective are suspended, deferred, or do not exist.[8] Nonnarratives range from a pure formalism of temporal accretion to the complex immediacies of modes of expression that would not be possible within the confines of narrative form. Sequential lists such as a ticker tape or a grocery bill are, in minimally formal terms, nonnarrative, as is the voice announcing times of departure and arrival at a train station—even if stocks and prices rise and fall or trains traverse a beginning, middle, and end. More complex forms of nonnarrative involve "immediacies" of presentation whose force would be lost if subsumed within narrative. The temporal dilation of Abstract Expressionism is an affectively motivated form of nonnarration realized in the form of the temporal condensation of its "all-over" mode of presentation. A minimalist sculpture such as Richard Serra's *Tilted Arc* is likewise nonnarrative, even if it has been inserted into narrative debates about the politics of authority and community. Nonnarrative forms, in their affective immediacy, certainly engage, rescript, and displace narratives in this way, even as they may not be reducible to species of narrative. The fifty random numbers I used to begin my poem "The Word" are nonnarrative, even as they serve as a "disorienting" device in a poem that has many features of oral narrative. Experimental writers often, in the words of Carla Harryman, "prefer to distribute narrative rather than to deny it."[9] Nonnarratives may subtend, deform, or even enable narrative, while leaving open questions of motivation, transcendence, and closure.

While it is useful to imagine minimal paradigms for nonnarrative such as a work of sculpture or a list, and while there has been a wide range of aesthetic use of just such forms, much nonnarrative art poses questions of motivation, transcendence, and closure in more complex ways. A "family resemblance" between minimally formal and more expressive instances of nonnarrative still remains in the way both are organized in terms of a single temporal moment or an open sequence of events. Both aspects of temporal organization structure the affective complexity of the following poem by Lyn Hejinian:

Exit

Patience is laid out on my paper
is floodlit. Everything's simile.
The cadence is detected, the cipher is broken, "resolved
the sky bears the enjambments, heavy clouds
the measure of one with a number block
changes shade. The flow of thoughts—impossible!
with which we are so familiar. The river
its visuals are gainful and equably square
in an automatic writing. Self-consciousness
to reclaim imagination . . . to rise early
that is, logic exaggerates the visible
to oppose laziness." Unto itself, built of bricks
is a cumbersome moment on whom motion
is bent over, having sunk a fork into the ground.[10]

This poem is nonnarrative. The way its discursive form is organized in a temporal series is basic to its intended effects. These effects are created by the positive and negative (and neutral) valences of the poem's progression from one increment to the next. The poem argues a particular form of self-consciousness, an intensified and disjunct present that will "reclaim imagination" in recognizing the discontinuities of thought. A virtually embodied sense of what the Russian Formalists called *ostranenie* (defamiliarization) is distributed here between the poem's thematization of self-consciousness and its techniques of discontinuity; the question of whether the poem is arguing the priority of one or the other clearly has been left open. It would be impossible to decide whether the poem's thematicization of self-consciousness presents moments of linguistic discontinuity, or whether its discontinuity demands a specific kind of self-consciousness. While the dissociation of thematization and technique is clearly central to the poem's affective presentation, it is also evident that these effects depend, in a number of ways, on a representation of narrative. For example, there are thematically resonant but disjunct narrative framing devices at the beginning and end of the poem; "Patience is laid out on my paper" takes the place of an orienting moment of oral narrative, while "having sunk a fork into the ground" marks a moment of finality much like Walter Cronkite's "And that's the way it is."[11] But these narrative frames are skewed, as are many more that are engaged in the course of the poem; it would be futile to go through it to prove that a single organizing perspective motivates the unfolding of the verbal material, however constitutive of narrative Viktor Shklovsky thought such discontinuities to be. The poem alternates the ironization of narrative effects with a nonironic materiality of language in its claim to self-consciousness; lines such as "a measure of one with a number block" are not simply negative obstructions to a hidden narrative but moments where language presents itself in its mode of signification. Hejinian's nonnarrative insists that the affective consequences of such a materiality of language be taken into account as a form of self-consciousness.

There may be disagreement with the notion that thematization is possible in a nonnarrative form, and this would be one explanation for the "folk theory" of such work that its meaning is completed by the reader.[12] Clearly, the poem's engagement of a range of narrative frames creates a field of referents for its explicitly stated theme of self-consciousness, even if the poem's gaps and discontinuities, as well as its moments of linguistic materiality, are as important to achieving these effects. Hejinian moves between transcendental and immanent (as well as impossible!) self-consciousness in the poem, all three of which possibilities can be read in the poem's title. "Exit" may indicate a narrative closure by which the conflicting frames of the poem are resolved; it may be a resistant exit sign that is the locus of a deferred question about meaning; or it may be a solution to a dilemma unstated elsewhere that motivates the poem's ephemeral form. But while a narrative reading of the poem would see its negative moments as simply aesthetic interference setting up a desire for transcendent closure, a nonnarrative reading keeps the entire range of meanings in play—such an allowance for material, contingent effects being exactly what Hejinian wants as a redeemed imagination. While there is no denying narrative in the poem, or the possibility of framing a narrative reading, nonnarrative organizes the poem's narratives for a range of possible effects—which may change in time as different frames are brought to the poem for historical reasons.

A reading of the poem's moment of false closure shows how its total form tries to engage these effects. "Having sunk a fork into the ground" is a condition of finality for the poem's material "bricks," which could either precede (having sunk a fork, all this came about) or follow from (this happened, and then a fork was sunk) the moment when "motion/is bent over" the "cumbersome monument." Split grammatical predication makes it impossible to find a retrospective moment outside the poem from which the prospective fork being sunk into the ground always would have been determinate of its total form. Not possessing narrative closure, the poem provokes historical retrospection into a series of positions from which to draw out the implications of that fatal fork. As with this moment of finality, time throughout the poem—in narrative tags, shifts and dislocations, orders of tense, disjunct predication, and resolutely immanent language—is organized to engage historical rereadings, beginning with its point of production.

It may be responded that if there is a potential for thematization here, it resides solely in the narrative elements being deployed by nonnarrative forms. In that case, it is instructive to look at a poem that is even more "language-centered," less provocative of overlapping interpretive frames, than Hejinian's. Jackson Mac Low's work reaches a certain limit of material effects—paradoxically based in a linearity of technique quite different from Hejinian's ephermerality—that produce an even more radical temporality. For instance, Mac Low has composed poems based on computer selections of Basic English word lists. The following poem, however, engages its formal implications in a more than simply aleatorical way.

Wall Rev

A line is a crack
is an entrance furrow
distracting between thighs

Attracting between sighs
a parallel cataclysm
cannot tell its name

Active well of flame
tense entrance clues
obligate avoidance[13]

More reduced in its construction than Hejinian's poem, this poem also moves between thematization and technique as it creates an affect of generalized eros in the structured displacements of language. In its opening and closing lines, "A line is a crack" and "obligate avoidance," the materiality of language evokes sexual tension and denial; between them, a sequence of definitional moments creates a semantic field in which the play of positive and negative attractions becomes a condition of equivalence that "cannot tell its name." The movement from approach to avoidance is dispersed among equivalent lines in a parallel structure, while the semantic distance between lines is so rigidly measured as to be virtually syllogistic. The poem presents the condition of linguistic equivalence that Roman Jakobson described as characteristic of poetic language, but nonnarration goes further than Jakobson's poetic "message for its own sake" in structuring effects that both invoke and withhold provisional closure.[14] Presented as an immanent effect of language, the poem's material displacements evoke both attraction and repulsion in a sequence of ambivalent moments within a bounded temporality. The experience of language from line to line may demand closure, but no retrospective motivation can be inferred. Mac Low's poem links the materiality of language to the representation of desire, but it is not given to desire, it seems, to know how things are going to turn out.

Seeing Mac Low's poem as a temporal series of parallel oppositions may resolve thematic readings (such as the surplus eros that makes most sense of the poem) into a formal immanence. But the sexual reading shows exactly how the equivalences staged in the poem, in a high condensed manner, produce self-consciousness (one that may not yet be historical) in their form of "parallel cataclysm." The equivalences Jakobson found as the basis of the "poetic function," strictly observed in Mac Low's argument of parallel increments, finds another value here in the relation between representation and event. Equivalence constitutes parallelism for Jakobson; for Mac Low, it invokes cataclysm—the devolution of negative totality that Cohen fantasized as nonnarrative. But this cataclysm, in a reversal not unlike Hejinian's forked closure, splits into two registers. Language and event must be brought together *as event* in order that the "parallel cataclysm" of representation resolves, but it cannot within the temporal duration of Mac Low's poem—a parallel series predicated on the dissociation of "A line is a crack." This notion of an event presented as a "parallel cataclysm" that at the same time exceeds the language of representation will have consequences for the following accounts of works of art at once dissociated from but "parallel" to moments of historical crisis.

The Construction of History

A poetics of "parallel cataclysm" may seem literally "the end of history" if imagined as taking place in a history rather than in a poem. But the creation, in a nonnarrative text, of a formal distance between narration (*fabula*) and event (*syuzhet*)—the one presentable, the other not fully representable—has critical force when applied to the construction of history itself, whose narrative form has been discussed by philosophers of history from Arthur Danto to Louis O. Mink, Hayden White, and Sande Cohen. Such a rupture foregrounds temporal sequence in dissociating the transparency between narration and event, severing transcendental organization from the progression of subordinated events toward discursive closure. Nonnarratives call into question the transparency of history toward event.

Several recent discussions have taken up what I am calling the ethical dilemmas of historical transparency, but without being able to conceive an alternative to narrative form. A critically modified narrativity, for example, seems to resolve the question of historical transparency in Joel Fineman's claim that "the anecdote . . . as the narration of a singular event, is the literary form or genre that uniquely refers to the real."[15] Fineman's sense of the "real" splits here between a commonsense notion of "real events" and an exalted one of the "real" as inaccessible substrate to events that can be known only through their failed representations; one of these registers refers to local, containable events and the other to grand narratives that subordinate them. Uniting both, the anecdote then would be a form of historical monad that Fineman terms the "*historeme . . .* the smallest minimal unit of the historiographic fact" (p. 57). As history, the anecdote asserts a unified temporal frame that is distinctly lacking in the incremental sequences of the poems discussed above. Even so, as Fineman observes, the notion that it takes such a fore-grounded literary form to conjoin registers of narration and event "is not as trivial an observation as might at first appear" (p. 56). That the anecdote works as an *exemplary* form for the renewal of history argues, it seems, against discursive transparency—the theory that narrative fully captures the reality of an event, with the corollary that events can be represented only in narrative terms.

It is the exemplary position of the anecdote within larger, not so easily narrated history that leads to the undoing of its transparency. In a skeptical discussion of fully narrative history, Louis O. Mink proposes the following test: if a given narrative can be said to refer uniquely to an event, as with Fineman's anecdote, it should follow "that historical narratives can be *added* to others, as in the periodization of political history by reigns."[16] In order to do so, however, there would have to be an underlying substrate of nar-rated events that would make such accretions possible; such a sub-strate could on no account be considered exemplary. There are two levels of narrative at issue—*petits récits*, which "*should* aggregate," and the *grands récits* of Universal History, in which "past actuality is an untold story" (p. 142). But by virtue of the formal properties of narratives—minimally, that each has the beginning, middle, and end proper to narrative unity—such a subordination cannot occur; the best that can be said for the objective continuity of Universal History is that it organizes the *petits récits* contained within it in the form of a chronicle that is not fully narrative. As a result, "narrative histories should be aggregative, insofar as they are histories, but cannot be, insofar as they are narratives" (p. 143).

With this distinction in mind, the identity of narration and event in Fineman's anecdote and in the theory of narrative trans-parency may appear as overdetermined in their quests for history. That the anecdote is a literary form, for Fineman, means that it works to renew history by defamiliarizing an already automatized narration (such as the one he offers later to support a historiograph-ical progression from Thucydides to the Renaissance to his own crit-ical moment): "The anecdote produces the effect of the real, the oc-currence of contingency, by establishing an event as an event within and yet without the framing context of historical successivity" (p. 61). Fineman's solution to Mink's dilemma of nar-rative history is thus that the anecdote need not worry about its ag-gregation with other anecdotes but instead may open a unique and individual "hole" that dilates temporal succession precisely by means of its formal opposition to teleological history. This is a dis-tinctly antinarrative moment.

The opening anecdotes of New Historicist exposition, seen as formally analogous to the more general agency of the anecdote in Universal History, thus work to dissociate and thus renew history by creating a disjunct moment of transparency between narration and event (which would not be sustainable through an entire text).[17] This moment, which often takes the form of proposing an eruptive, miraculous, or horrific event narrated to determine a given historical date, is valued precisely for creating an "effect of the real," which it then transfers to the total argument. History by that act will be renewed in the determination of an event as formally distinct from its narrative. The contingency of this eruption (and vice versa), however, leads from Fineman's analogy between anecdote and historical period to Mink's skeptical question concerning the status of retrospective periodization—"Is the Renaissance an event?" (p. 145); if an anecdotal event is an exemplary narration, what are the limits of its form?—from the transcendental position invoked by these transparent effects. Perhaps such a summoning of narrative would be accomplished just as well by a nonnarrative moment of expository orientation, such as the fifty random numbers referred to earlier, to establish an indexical substrate as much determining of the total form of narrative history as the anecdotal date (fig. 1). So in the discursive openings of oral narrative, if the listener's attention is both grounded and perplexed—indexically defamiliarized—it has done its job.[18]

The notion of an exemplary anecdote that renews history by creating an "effect of the real" provides an analogy for the ways in which transparent narratives are organized in everyday forms of historical representation. Raymond Williams has described the discursive accretion of seemingly isolated, reified, and often anecdotal narratives in larger narrative structures as a basis for mass communication, understood as reproducing beliefs about events more generally.[19] We see this mechanism on the nightly news, where, for reasons of both ideology and economy, events are packaged into short narrative units that can be assembled at any future date into larger narratives. The upper limit of this discursive totality would be an accretive horizon of continuous dates, to which the media in its historicizing capacity often refers (at moments of crisis, identification of narrative units with historical dates is particularly marked, as in the Iran hostage crisis or during the Persian Gulf War). Such indexing of narrative to event demands a transparency whereby accretion is not only unproblematic but immanent in the structure of narrated events. But it is exactly the eruptive discrepancy of the anecdote that renews an overarching discursive field; thus, paradoxically, the commercials interrupting war footage segued between sound bites

THE WORD

38	63	50	6	34
40	41	68	89	53
9	15	85	76	16
30	57	14	69	97
54	8	83	72	28
90	52	18	84	66
7	25	10	93	44
86	91	20	75	1
43	59	51	80	60
31	4	56	47	35

Fig. 1. From Barrett Watten, "The Word," in *Conduit* (San Francisco, 1988), 39.

that Williams saw as giving the formal totality of mass communication create overdetermining effects whereby discontinuity just is the guarantee of narrative. Any history of the present will have to take this paradox of interrupted, overdetermined, and undermotivated narrative into account. That this assembly line of events is discontinuous with its larger historical narrative is, however, clear.

A reconsideration of processes of historical accretion and subordination, in Mink's sense, is the point of the distinctions between annal, chronicle, and history that Hayden White sees as revealing the gaps that separate events as such from their narrative organization.[20] Annals are simply events with dates organized on a time line; chronicles provide a necessity of sequence such as "and then, and then" but come to no retrospective conclusion about why these events had to occur in this sequence. The chronicle "is usually marked by a failure to achieve narrative closure. . . . It starts out to tell a story but breaks off *in medias res*, in the chronicler's own present" (p. 5). A realist might find that, in the end, an objective time line unifies—by analogy with material causation—these provisional historical forms with historical narrative per se, thus making chronicle a species of narrative. But for historians with other ontological commitments, it has fallen to history seen as continuous with narrative to organize these events in a unified frame. White quotes Hegel to motivate this elevation of historical event to narrative in desire, "in the same way as love and the religious emotions provoke imagination to give shape to previously formless impulse" (p. 12), and asks, "What wish is enacted, what desire is gratified, by the fantasy that real events are properly represented when they can be shown to display the formal coherence of a story?" (p. 6). History takes place as narrative equally because consequent events are narratable and because we desire them to be narrative. But is narrative the only form that desire takes, in organizing events, "to give shape to the previously formless impulse" that is the mere succession of events in time? Could other forms of temporal organization, analogous to the sequence of dates or chronicle in the schema proposed by White, also make history?[21]

History in this larger sense may be constructed by a wider range of formal relations between narrative and event than has been supposed. Mink's notion that narrative fails to accrete in a Universal History creates a kind of "open form," a semantic field in Umberto Eco's sense, where specific narratives compete in the determination of events.[22] Oppositely, Fineman's defense of Universal History through the antinarrative formal moment of the anecdote restricts the range of such a semantic field by overdetermining the value of contingent effects. But the performative value of such a strategy also may be seen in nonnarrative forms that, while leaving the larger historical horizon open, specify a historical date within a total form. For example, in San Francisco artist Seyed Alavi's 1991 installation *Blueprints of the Times* (fig. 2), blueprints of the front pages of major international newspapers are mounted in groups of three in stainless steel frames. The pages are all from the same date, 31 December 1989, but the only alteration of any of the blueprints from their originals is that the dates have been removed. This

Fig. 2. Seyed Alavi, *Blueprints of the Times*, detail of installation at Terrain Gallery, San Francisco, 1990. Blueprints, metal, and glass. Photo: artist.

barely perceptible deletion causes the time-valued materials displayed on each page—stories of many levels of implication held in a kind of referential suspension—to be read in entirely different ways than if they were fixed in time by their dates. This removal of the date, as a device, is the formal opposite of the establishment of the date in the anecdote, but its negativity equally creates a hole in presumed historical time (the redundant sequence of dates that makes "yesterday's papers" old news). What results is a situation in which the viewer may create new narratives from the stories and images to be seen in a field of meanings; but this reading is bounded at an upper limit precisely in its determination of the historical date that had been removed. The entire form of Alavi's installation is a nonnarrative that by means of a specific form of displacement and reintegration constructs, in both senses of the word, history. Desire begins with the removal of the date and ends in a bounded field.[23]

Alavi's *Blueprints* comprise a kind of annal that, in its total form, presents world events to self-consciousness in a form of historical nonnarration. For Fredric Jameson, however, it is clear that nonnarrative can be thought of only as a deformation, incompletion, or deferral of narrative. Narrative is "an all-informing process" that Jameson takes to be "the central function or *instance* of the human mind," while it is inescapably historical in its revealing "a single great collective *story* . . . the collective struggle to wrest a realm of Freedom from the realm of necessity."[24] One test of such a story is in its encounter with the nonnarratives of postmodernism; so in his notably disjunct reading of Bob Perelman's nonnarrative poem "China," Jameson finds its discontinuity to be an example of the postmodern dilemma in which "the subject has lost its capacity actively to extend its pro-tensions and re-tensions across the temporal manifold and to organize its past and future into coherent experience."[25] At the same time, the poem's oblique reference in its title to China is an appeal to grand narrative, in which "it does seem to capture something of the excitement of the immense, unfinished social experiment of the New China" (p. 29). The latter reading is centrally thematic for Jameson, if somewhat ancillary to Perelman, in Jameson's identification of the postmodern condition as coincident with the end of the era of "wars of national liberation" (pp. xx–xxi). Jameson assumes that the negativity of Perelman's poem (as species of the genus postmodernism) reinforces the narrative he imposes on it from the position of History (but which may, in fact, be called up as much as denied by the poem itself). What follows, as from the evidence of Perelman's poem, is that "the breakdown of narrativity in a culture, group, or social class is a symptom of its having entered into a state of crisis" (p. 149). But a paradox emerges when Jameson identifies History as being itself nonnarrative: "It is fundamentally nonnarrative and nonrepresentational," and it is on the foundation of this inaccessible nonnarrativity that History "can be approached only by way of a prior (re)textualization."[26] If "history is what hurts," Perelman's poem is historical precisely because, appearing in the form it does, it makes Jameson account for its nonnarrative. Even so, such a historical presentation must relate to narrative or else lapse into an inchoate ground, for which Jameson invokes a narrative of "necessity" as "the inexorable *form* of events; it is therefore a narrative category in the enlarged sense of some properly narrative political unconscious" (p. 102). Sande Cohen's fundamental criticism of narrative history, his sense that "historical thought is located, intellectually considered, near its suppression of the nonnarrated," is here demonstrated in the way that postmodernism (aligned with a political unconscious) makes History happen for Jameson.[27]

Nonnarrative exists—demonstrably in the work of contemporary artists and writers but also in temporal forms that construct history. A critical account of nonnarrativity, as well as aesthetic strategies for its use, thus may proceed not simply in terms of the negation of cultural narratives (as with Jameson's postmodernism) but in a discussion of the historical agency of its forms. Jerome McGann discusses nonnarrative in this sense as a construction of history, distinguishing "antinarratives" as "problematic, ironical, and fundamentally a satiric discursive procedure" from nonnarratives, which "do not issue calls for change and alterity [but] embody in themselves some form of cultural difference. [Their] antithesis to narrative is but one dimension of a more comprehensively imagined program based in the codes of an alternative set of solidarities." These senses allow for particular forms of organization as proper to nonnarrative per se; even so, both are read against narrative "as a form of continuity; as such, its deployment in discourse is a way of legitimating established forms of social order."[28]

The historical meaning of nonnarrative, however, will not only be given in its opposition to narrative. There is more history to nonnarrative than in McGann's view, as is evident in the development of the modern American epic poem, which in many ways qualified or even abandoned narrative as its primary vehicle after Ezra Pound's disjunct appropriations of Ovid, Browning, and contemporary history in *The Cantos*.[29] The self-canceling millennarianism of Pound's moral conclusion in the fascist state led, at least in the formal possibilities of epic, to the identification of events with the allegorized but open-ended subject as history in Charles Olson's *The Maximus Poems*, as well as to an often nonnarrative linguistic subjectivity in Louis Zukofsky's *"A."* Olson's maxim as an epic poet indicated just what kind of problem he faced in his identificatory poetics: "It is very difficult to be both a poet, and, a historian."[30] The poet's dilemma here is similar to the problem of narration faced by the transcendental historian in Cohen's sense: "If . . . narration is the core of historical autonomy . . . the cultural-intellectual organization of this 'doing' is linked to its cognitive severing, which has to preclude thinking from appearing in the same scene of space as the told."[31] Olson's solution to the problem of transcendental position, the dilemma of "where to stand" in his epic, was to see himself, like any poet, in two places at once—for example, both in his body and outside it ("Offshore/by islands in the blood")—even if this solution led to a gradual devolution of narrative that is at the same time the argument of his poem. Olson raised the possibility of a nonnarrative history in his refusal to transcend or close his epic, even if his ultimate horizon in a tragic self—which inevitably must disintegrate to prove the discursive truth of history—qualifies his poem's inclusion of events that are not only to be subjectively identified, events within a present social horizon, for example. As a kind of "parallel cataclysm," *The Maximus Poems* substituted its own undoing for an account of such incommensurate events.

An Era of Stagnation

I want to give two examples, which I think of as both historical and aesthetic, of epic nonnarratives. The first is a painting from 1975 by the Moscow painter Erik Bulatov, one of a group of Soviet artists working pictorially but influenced by conceptualism in the 1970s, who became internationally known in the 1980s. The second is a literary genre of extended prose poetry developed in America at about the same time, the mid-1970s, under the rubric of "the new sentence," a central preoccupation of the Language School of poetry. I am thinking of the former in relation to the historical organization of the annal as an index of dates, the latter in terms of the chronicle as a linked sequence of dates; both use nonnarrative forms similar if not identical to these analytic constructions in achieving historical self-consciousness with their presentations of historical event.[32]

If a self-canceling subjectivity is immediately evident to the viewer of Erik Bulatov's *I Am Going* (fig. 3), the work's historical motivation, especially when seen in the disjunct context of an exhibition of Soviet painting at the Institute for Contemporary Art in London in February 1989, is equally so.[33] While the instant history offered by such recontextualization of ex-Soviet art in western galleries and museums may be epiphenomenal, another way to read Bulatov's painting as historical would be to site its nonnarrativity at its point of production (insofar as that can known). In the absence of any conclusive account of the formal meanings of emergent Soviet art in the 1970s, a speculative construction may help elucidate the formal values of Bulatov's historical nonnarrativity. In that spirit, I would situate the production of Bulatov's art in a mid-1970s context in which its extreme formal opposite, a depersonalized state-interpreted history embodied in the widespread deployment of both hypernarrative and nonnarrative memorial icons and statues to the Great Patriotic War, had reached a terminal horizon of meaning. Such a grand narrative would *most* invalidate the aspirations and formal possibilities of emergent art, which could then be read in terms of their immanent displacements of superseded meaning. At the same time, the new work's forms are continuous with nonnarrative aspects of the monumental presentation of the events of the war, even if these forms presented difficulties, to say the least, to be solved in the emergent art. The presentation of epic events in memorials, by the very formal nature of memorials as much as by their redundant, overdetermined placement in social space, participated in the creation of simultaneous remembrance and amnesia whose overcoming would be an immediate necessity for a self-consciously historical work of art.

By formal nature, I mean that a memorial could be said to represent an event not only by referring to it but by displacing its memory in the fact of its own occurrence. The memorial is itself an

Fig. 3. Erik Bulatov, *I Am Going*, 90½ x 90½". From *Erik Bulatov*, Institute of Contemporary Art catalogue (London, 1989). Reproduced by permission of Phyllis Kind Gallery, New York.

event, not just a reference to one, and in Soviet social space there was an organized system of such temporal displacements that created an affect of totalized loss as a continuing argument of state power. As a paradigm for this temporal displacement, we can imagine a State 1, preceding the memorial, of a consciousness of something that needs to be remembered—for example, a series of dates for events surrounding the liberation of the Ukraine as well as the superimposed date of liberation at the end of the war that organizes them—and a State 2, in which the placement of memorials has displaced State 1—these dates have been embodied in a spatial array of memorials in and around Kiev whose emplacement itself is a series of dates (fig. 4).[34] (Prior to both States 1 and 2 is an irrecoverable State 0, the traumatic events of the war as they occurred in "real

Fig. 4. An example of a monument to the Great Patriotic War in the environs of Kiev, USSR, 1970s. Reproduced from Novosti Press Agency–produced slide set: monument to security men who fought for the Revolution.

time," only recoverable as the historical "real" in a different sense.) The loss that is to be remembered becomes an object continuing to mean and exist; this is the memorial's function in the process of mourning. But loss in the form of State 1 at the same time has itself been lost, an entropic moment in which the meaning of the event to be remembered is dispersed with the coming into being of the memorial in State 2.[35] As much as reading a memory of event narratively from the memorial itself, we can read a nonnarrative amnesia where the displacement of events becomes interpretable as a universal tragedy identified with the state—one that elides the "fact" of loss, as much as many particular facts, in these events. In this sense, it is not so much the specific forms of the monuments, narrative or nonnarrative, that determine their totalizing meaning as it is their systematic placement. These memorials range from very narrative (heroic figures, depictions of battle) to very nonnarrative (obelisks, mounds), but their narrativity is in an important sense canceled out by the recurrence of the form of the memorial in social space.

The stakes of such a process are high in a culture such as the Soviet Union, which invested great authority in a historical record —primarily of World War II but also of the Revolution—preserved in memorial iconography. One has only to picture the colossal

Fig. 5. Erik Bulatov, *Krassikov Street*, 1976. 59 x 79". From *Erik Bulatov*. Reproduced by permission of Phyllis Kind Gallery, New York.

statue of Mother Russia at Stalingrad to understand the sacrificial affect being mobilized as the desire motivating the state's narrative. Such icons and statues are to be found everywhere, in Leningrad the "hero city" to the defenders of the Siege; in countless statues of Mayakovsky, myriad busts of Lenin; in Akhmatova tea cups and Pushkin feather pens; in the war decorations of veterans worn every day on the street. There is a system of such icons, and a repetitive pattern of their recurrence, but what is important here, and what I suggest motivated Bulatov, is the way the authority of historical narrative they were meant to reinforce had turned, in the forty years since the war, around on its axis to create a vacuum of meaning, an absence of narrative continuity. The narrative itself evaporates even as the meaning of loss remains, with no palpable image to assign it to, the memorial icon itself having embodied and thus displaced the desire for such a materialization.[36]

Significantly, Bulatov produces few paintings a year, perhaps two or three according to an interview, and each is a study in a delimited vocabulary of conventional figures for time, loss, and social reality.[37] Some of the recurring elements of his paintings include a horizon line obscured by the social space of Moscow suburbs toward which figures, in a flattened allegory of progress, move but can never reach (fig. 5), or a postindustrial natural landscape in which both nature and the incursions of the social are bracketed as mutual displacements. Bulatov also uses a vocabulary of purely ideological icons such as slogans and emblems, superimposing, for example, the word *edinoglasno*, "unanimity," in red over a mural of Soviet deputies raising their hands in unison; the words *programma vremya*, "program time" (the Soviet six o'clock news), appearing on a TV screen being watched by an old woman whose upraised leg creates a diagonal of perspective ending in the flattened screen; or the opaque, transparent image of Leonid Brezhnev himself, emblem of the era in which Bulatov worked, haloed by flags of the Soviet republics.

While *I Am Going* lacks such immediate social referents, its combination of iconic affect of loss with linguistic index of present time can be read as precisely social and historical. The time of the painting is 1975, the midpoint, one may estimate, of the Brezhnev "period of stagnation" (which from all accounts was experienced as nonnarrative, that is, as possessing neither beginning, middle, nor end). The era itself was named as soon as it ended; according to one ex-Soviet source, *zastoi*, "a period in which time stands still," was "the first word given to us after *perestroika*" in the first days of Mikhail Gorbachev (*stagnatsiya* is also used, but as description *of* something more than as a place in which to stand, *zastoi* being derived from *stoit'*, "to stand").[38] In Boris Kagarlitsky's history of Soviet oppositional culture, *The Thinking Reed*, such a retrospective periodization fits quite well with an amended Marxist narrative, thus invoking a paradox: the "period of stagnation," seemingly of indefinite duration, only became so after it was over.[39] For an artist like Bulatov, this dilated present would have been experienced not as a retrospectively designated era but as a state comprised simultaneously of State 1 and State 2. The open-endedness of that state, its mimicry of an "end of history" by virtue of sheer inertia, would coincide with the artificiality of its narrative within official culture while at the same time it was unnameable in unofficial culture. This oppositional moment of coincidence may be understood in relation to the following description of a mid-1970s monumental site from a contemporary history of Soviet city planning:

> Of the new cities of the decade, we shall mention Brezhnev, a city which began to be built in 1973 on the Kama river, together with a large truck-manufacturing plant. . . . The structure of the city, with an expected population of 400 thousand, follows the principle of a parallel development of the functional zones, already utilized in the creation of the city of Togliatti. . . . The city centre is linear, stretching along the main axis of the residential area, and parallel to the bank of the

river; this puts the centre within walking distance for most of
the population and ensures its lively activity both during the
daytime and the evenings. . . . The city is registering a regular
and organized growth.[40]

Here a story of "400 thousand," motivated by a "truck-manufactur-
ing plant," is entirely subordinated to a narrative of "regular and organized growth." The problem for unofficial culture during this period would be, in the face of such monumental inertia, to create an
appropriate scale for its own work. Later one may have realized that
history was going nowhere, but how to measure it in the event? Bulatov speaks of a kind of incontrovertible self-evidence of the social
world in the "era of stagnation"; there was no possibility of changing what was, simply, an atemporal condition, without the possibility of development. This atemporal state, which I identify with the
affect of loss, could be seen as the product of the memorial culture
and authority that had been imposed on social reality and embodied in monuments and icons that had lost their claim to historical
reality simultaneously with their reference to it—in a way that prefigures how naming the new Soviet city Brezhnev would later fail
the test of history.

Bulatov's solution to this dilemma is to work in a radically disjunct aesthetic space of self-evident immediacy and imaginative displacement, which are figured in his work as iconomic transparency
and linguistic opacity, respectively. Bulatov says, "My works have
an 'entrance' and 'no entrance' simultaneously. . . . From the
perspective of the painting's artistic space, there *is* an entrance, one
you can't avoid. But from the perspective of daily life, there's *no* entrance. . . . Both are at work equally and simultaneously."[41] Bulatov's schema of "entrance" and "no entrance" participates inasmuch
as it opposes Soviet memorial culture. In both, representation, intended to be transparent to event, becomes instead opaque; by virtue of its displacement of prior history, the present, intended to be
opaque in the materiality of representation, becomes transparent.
This reciprocity of embodiment and loss subtends the meaning of
Soviet ideological signs in social circulation at much wider levels; it
would be necessary to account for it in any discussion of the system
of signification in Soviet social space (Bulatov is certainly aware of
this relationship in his use of kitsch iconography as the coinage of
an accumulated economy of loss.)[42] So a recent history of Soviet
popular culture describes the urban appearance of linguistically
opaque and socially antagonistic graffiti, only possible once the
dominant system of transparent signs in circulation, precisely those
that Bulatov organizes in his work, had lost their authority.[43] Bula-

tov's juxtaposition of icon and sign attempts to realize such a simultaneous immediacy and reduncancy, without appealing solely to the ironization of his given materials, in the context of the period in which he was working.

In Bulatov's pictorial strategies, nonnarrative is not primarily the ironization of narrative—and hence is not merely a deformation of it. *I Am Going* presents history as an atemporal moment figured as simultaneously transparent and opaque, an effect accomplished by the overlay of iconic and linguistic elements. The visual image of massive Russian clouds breaking up (or perhaps forming for rain or simply being blown across the sky—any number of temporal vectors may be conjoined here) against the background of a deep blue sky freezes an event—the dramatic change in the weather—an atemporal moment of recognition. The change or movement that is occurring thus may be figured as the formation of an iconic memorial where State 1 has just been embodied and displaced by State 2. This means two things: self-consciousness finds itself in the reduction of movement to image, as one "knows" who one is in time only in achieving a distance on a rapidly moving sequence of events, the comprehension of an instant (the effect of coming into consciousness on seeing clouds breaking up after rain, or clouds massing for oncoming rain); and such iconic stasis is the necessary condition for the comprehension of movement. (This counterpoint works particularly well as an index to the Brezhnev era: memorial culture is being reproduced in the comprehension of change in an icononic displacement, against which self-consciousness can only distance itself from event—nothing further can be added to history than one's awareness of it.)

It is possible also to describe Bulatov's clouds as connoting an overlay of Russian iconography—one that nostalgically refers back to baroque clouds of state absolutism (where moving clouds may frame the action of foreground figures in genre historical painting—agents that are, of course, absent here), but which is given a more immediate register in modern images of clouds set against the progress of the Soviet state in its formative period. In Alexander Dovzhenko's film *Aerograd* (1935), for example, puny biplanes ply their way to their historic mission in the new Soviet Far East, moving left to right in a framing sequence for a drama of Stalinist ethics in which the necessity of the state is manufactured out of the inevitability of human loss. The massing of clouds takes on a similarly foregrounded role in Dovzhenko's documentary film on the liberation of the Ukraine (1943–45), where they stand for, by representing the affect of, a universal loss (and they maintain a relation to machine culture embodied in the tanks and weapons being destroyed beneath them). Later, Andrei Tarkovsky's film *Solaris* (1970), produced like Bulatov's painting in the "era of stagnation," reverses this relation of historical agency to temporal inevitability in placing the state machine, now become the space station in which the principle action takes place, in an ideal position of observer over the masses of clouds that form and reform out of the ocean of Solaris. Such clouds are exactly the loss of self out of which the mysterious neutrino replicas of human presence materialize. Self-consciousness is both lost in the clouds and formed out of clouds, a register of agency opposed to that of the scientistic space station; this is not only fantasy but a judgment of the subject's place in history. Clouds, in other words, in a Soviet iconographical tradition that runs from Dovzhenko to Tarkovsky to Bulatov, are a historical index of self-consciousness set against the progression of state narrative—even if clouds precede narrative, especially the one I have just made of them.

The contrapuntal historical index in Bulatov's painting is created by his use of language, the Russian verb *yidu* dropped out from the clouds, giving in English the title *I Am Going*. The typographically neutral setting of the word (predating Barbara Kruger's use of Futura Bold) is mapped onto an artificial perspective that leads from a viewer's position that must be coincidental with the frame of the picture toward a central vanishing point. This diagonal movement into a center reverses the Soviet modernist convention of diagonals moving left to right out of a center. If in expanding outward from center to right they denote progress (fig. 6), in collapsing in from left to center they reorient progress as a devolution into the infinitesimal origins of a failed transcendence. Here is a little allegory to draw out more history from the clouds. It is not, however, simply ironic (as would be the case with superimpositions of more objectified language in Kruger's work)—the subject, whose self-consciousness is already engaged in the determination of present time out of the movement of the clouds, is spoken for as if destined toward a nonexistent endpoint at the center of self-consciousness. There indeed is an ironic reference here to the "end of history" in communism, but one that must have been experienced as already undermined by the memorial state—so that when Little Vera in the film of the same name is asked by her boyfriend what her goals are and she answers, "I am going to communism" (*ya yidu k komunismu*, a pun on *miy yid'om k komunismu*, "We are going to communism"), we know that she has decided that there is really no alternative to an unmediated present for her. Such an unmediated present exists in Russian in the aspect of verbs of motion, *yidt'i* meaning a kind of going in which one is, at that time of speaking, "on the way." In the

Fig. 6. Alexander Rodchenko, *Books*, 1925. From Selim O. Khan-Magome-dov, *Rodchenko: The Complete Work* (Cambridge, Mass., 1987), 156. Repro-duced by permission of MIT Press.

system of Russian aspect, *yidt'i* is distinguished from an act that might be understood as completable (such as when "I go" to the store to buy a loaf of bread). So the "I" that speaks in Bulatov's painting is "on the way" toward an inevitable vanishing point in history—one that is, nonironically, an index to present time. A completed narrative scenario is equally suggested as it is denied in the verb of motion's having no origin or destination but iconic frame and vanishing point.[44]

Subjectivity here is indeed linguistic, by virtue of the incom-plete aspect of the verb of motion substantiating only itself—self-consciousness is seen apart from dialogic communication and in terms of an immanent movement. This linguistic subjectivity could further be read as an interiorized response to signs in "objective," historical social space urging, for example, "Praise to the Commu-nist Party of the Soviet Union" or "Welcome the Revolution"—in-vocations to generalized action to be countered by a derealization that Bulatov has exploited in other work. Alternately—and there is no end when one is on one's way into the clouds—the derealization and loss in Bulatov's painting open onto a metaphysical prospect that can be read as a political allegory. As in Kagarlitsky's narrative account of the conflict between law and spirit in official Soviet culture, a simultaneous opacity and transparency can be read here in terms of modernist state and suppressed Orthodox Christianity. The word as "legal culture" would be on its way toward dissolution in the "spiritual" clouds of religiously inspired Russian nationalism in this reading, which at the time of this writing seems only too available.[45]

While such expanded readings of Bulatov's painting offer a kind of romantic irony in terms of larger historical frames, *I Am Going* is nonironic in an important way. It is presented positively as the moment of transition from State 1 to State 2, much as a memorial to the system it supersedes. Where State 1 for the painting would be that "loss of history" preceding the work, State 2 includes the concretion that occurs when that loss is represented in the painting. *I Am Going* thus takes place as if in an annal's creation of a series of memorial dates (in which the work as date is added to the preceding and superseded historical series). It is tempting to propose that later interpretations of the work itself are condensed in this series, much as historical narratives accrete on the formal basis of the chronicle.

The Fall of Saigon

Bulatov's formal imitation of the date as a way of making a present cotemporal with history is very different from the ironic historicism of comparable art in the West. If in the 1980s Barbara Kruger attempted similar kinds of juxtaposition of historical icon and ideological sign, both worked generally to empty out a space of negation against which the real time of the viewer is rhetorically invoked as present—but only through a hyperrealized displacement (fig. 7). The clouds in Kruger's photomontage are anything but an emblem of consciousness; its familiar death's head is the kind of cloud that *most* prohibits identification. The viewer is pushed out of the frame in reaction to his or her fatal attraction to the historical cloud. The recurrent *you* of Kruger's work is thus on every level ironic; the object of historical address in *Your Manias Become Science* (Whose mania caused the bomb?), being identified with internalized self-consciousness (Whose mania is caused by the bomb?), is a shifter rhetorically displaced outward from the constructed gap between image and text. Kruger's short-circuited identification forces the viewer to admit a social totality as only the space created by these (and many similar) negations; looking at her work from a distance of several feet in a gallery or museum becomes perhaps the only "place to stand."[46]

Fig. 7. Barbara Kruger, Untitled ("Your Manias Become Science"), 1981. Photograph, 37" x 50". From Kruger, *We Won't Play Nature to Your Culture*, Institute of Contemporary Art catalogue (London, 1983), 51. Reproduced courtesy of Mary Boone Gallery, New York.

There are different cultural meanings for what appear to be similar strategies of nonnarrative, in short. The kind of nonirony deployed in Bulatov's pictorial strategies may have less to do with Kruger's self-evident irony than with nonnarrative writing produced under the rubric of the New Sentence at about the same time as Bulatov's painting.[47] American writers, myself among them, were then experiencing something similar to Brezhnev's "era of stagnation"—in 1975, the year of Bulatov's painting, the Vietnam War had gone on far beyond anyone's consent for it; a prolonged stasis occurred in which agencies of both perpetrators of the war and objectors to it had become exhausted, a state of loss culminating in abrupt temporal devolution with the Fall of Saigon. About that time, I published a poem, more accurately a self-reflexive notation based on signs in social space, which in retrospect seems to record a response to this semiotic stasis in which the linguistic and iconic dissociate each other in a manner similar to that in *I Am*

Going. "Place Names" opens with a moment of loss recognized literally as the remains of some prior conflagration:

> What I saw at the fire site.
> BAKER
> The men knocking over drums.
> WESTERN CARLOADING
> Signs on walls. Philosophy informs.
> DO NOT HIT FENCE

This moment of derealization poses the mobility of signs against a resistant affect of cultural meltdown, figured in burned-out buildings and "men knocking over drums" as objects of fascination and horror. The poem continues its reading of cultural detritus until the signs themselves, liberated in a space of negation, produce a kind of temporal free fall that is identified with a memorial self-consciousness:

> Old wooden letters. Propeller blades.
> ALLIED DIVISION
> 50
> NATIONAL ICE
> COLD OF CALIFORNIA, INC.
> TO LEASE HEAVY
> What I have always thought & said.[48]

I began this essay with the desire to know what I was doing in 1975 —or how emergent writing of the period of Vietnam crisis would look compared with visual art refiguring the defunct narratives of Brezhnev stasis. A sequence of signs encountered in social space— in this case, the intersection of 8th, Townsend, and Division, San Francisco, what was once industrial brick now become galleria— argued back a self-consciousness similar to Bulatov's at the moment of loss. These signs in social space seemed always to have been there before, already in history and thus arguing a denial, even in confirming "what I have always thought & said." Their desired synchrony took the form in writing of a diachronic progression where the prior possibility of identifying social space with historical agents acting within it becomes in the poem "a discrete or continuous sequence of measurable events distributed in time" (what Charles Olson described as "the message" in his pre-epic poem "The Kingfishers"), with the agent in effect standing still only to read the signs. This displacement of the object identified with self-consciousness has been described above as ironic in the visual work of

Barbara Kruger, but here the temporality of the poem as opposed to the simultaneity of the picture adds a nonironic dimension to the poetics of loss. Such a displaced temporality can be seen as an analogy not to Brezhnev-era stasis but to Vietnam-era crisis, in which the historical subject's identification with nonevent on the scale of empire also would work to deny his or her agency.

Where Bulatov's painting imitates the historical date as organized in a disjunct annal, the formal model for this progressive time frame and exteriorized, deferred self-consciousness is clearly the chronology, as for example in a sequence of events during the Fall of Saigon, May 1975:

1. Banmethuot overrun March 10.
2. South Vietnamese flee Banmethuot.
3. Pleiku and Kontum evacuated.
4. Thieu orders defense of Hue.
5. North Vietnamese cut highway leading from Hue.
6. One million persons flee from Hue to Danang.
7. North Vietnamese attack Chulai and Quangnai.
8. Hue falls March 25.
9. Panic at Danang.
10. Danang falls on Easter Sunay.
11. North Vietnamese headquarters move south.
12. American ambassador asks for increased aid.
13. President Ford speaks of the Vietnam War in the past tense.
14. President Thieu leaves Vietnam for Taiwan April 21.
15. North Vietnamese engaged thirty-five miles from Saigon.
16. Americans and South Vietnamese begin evacuation.
17. Helicopter evacuation begins April 29.
18. April 30: Saigon deserted.
19. North Vietnamese enter Saigon April 30.
20. General Minh surrenders to Colonel Bi Tin May 1.[49]

In the long duration of the Vietnam War, the event of the fall of Saigon may be understood as an entropic moment that divides, in a manner imitated by the memorial icon, a State 1 (the situation immediately preceding the fall being a kind of stalemate in which minor North Vietnamese victories at the negotiating table were being countered by minor American successes in the effort to Vietnamize the war) collapsing in an incremental sequence of events (beginning with panic in military region 1 in the north, followed by masses of refugees moving south, bringing with them retreating armies, and ending in the autodestruction of political power and then the defense of the southern military regions) to State 2, the defeat of the

Thieu regime. I participated in this event as a spectator only, but in a certain sense it also happened to me, as it did for any historical subject for whom State 1 had meaning as an imposed but untenable stagnation. The fact that the Vietnam War ended not in victory but in defeat has, as others have commented, created problems for its subsequent representation; and in a number of key forms, from Hollywood cinema to the Vietnam Veterans Memorial in Washington, narrative has been undermined as a commemorative vehicle. It is no accident that the form of the memorial to the war, for example, is not a single iconic image but a temporally organized chronicle of the names of those who died.[50] Loss in Vietnam was experienced as a temporal sequence of defeats rather than as an overarching and stabilizing narrative of victory. "We lost" is not the same as "They won"—there is, as Marita Sturken points out, no reference to the Vietnamese in the memorial (a situation artist Chris Burden responded to with *The Other Vietnam Memorial*, which lists on large bronze sheets some 1.5 million alphabetized, computer-generated, hypothetical Vietnamese names; fig. 8).[51]

The nonnarrative of this event—an incremental sequence of losses rather than a narrative sense of an ending such as "The North Vietnamese won, thus ending the war"—is one that has had a major impact on historical self-consciousness since the war. A poetics of loss that is at the same time a coming into consciousness, similar to Bulatov's fixed image of clouds being addressed by a voice in *I Am Going*, was organized by the fall of Saigon on a time line, its lack of closure making by analogy a chronicle of loss out of any time line. This effect has been imitated in writing since the mid-1970s in a genre of poetic prose that Ron Silliman has called the New Sentence, in which series of discrete statements organized "at the level of the sentence" generate a poetic matrix without overarching narrative form. The form is significant not simply for its individual style but precisely in its collective aesthetics; the particular formal properties of the New Sentence place it, as in a Venn diagram, at the center of a number of related nonnarrative techniques —ranging in value from lyrical to aleatorical—common to a wide range of poets writing in the mid-1970s.[52] Its evidence here is both its use as a site for formal reflection on the part of some writers and its virtually instant comprehension and acceptance by many more. In both didactic form and social reception, it is thus comparable to surrealist automatism—even if automatism precisely lacks the New Sentence's play of identification.[53] Silliman's own New Sentence work precisely explores the constructive potential of a deformed chronicle, seeking to qualify the self-consciousness of historical narrative by means of multiple and conflicting perspectives. So in his early collaborative project *Legend*, we find such sequences as:

THAN · BAO TINH · NGUYEN VAN DO · XUAN TIAN · AU TRUNG · BUI VAN BUU · VINH CAO DUC · AU SON TIEU · HO TUEN TRONG · BAO VINH YEN ·
· DAN VAN VINH · LE DUC TO · TRAN LE PHUNG · VO DINH HOA · TRU DINH VAN · HO CHU GAP · BAO THAN TRI · PHAM DUAN · DO LUC TRANG · D.
ANG · HO PHO HING · VO NGUYEN TRUNG · NGUYEN VAN NGO · LE DAN · TRAN LE PHAN · VO NGUYEN LU · XUAN LONG · VU VAN BAY · NGUYEN I
N VAN DU · TRAN NGOC DAI · NGUYEN HUU WIN · NGO DINH GO · VO NGUYEN HUNG · HA VAN TIN · XUAN SO · VO DINH HOC · LE VAN NHA · HO Tl
DUC THAI · VU VAN MANH · VINH THAT · LA THANH TAP · DO TAN DE · TRAN QUOC CAM · BAO VINH SI · HO CHU HING · BAO THAN · HUYNH DUC A
HUAN · VO VAN CHIEU · VU VAN THO · BAO THAM · VINH MAT · VINH DUC ONG · TRAN CHINH · DO DINH HAO · LE VAN ANH · DO LUC LONG · TRU V
AN · BAO DINH AN · NGO TRONG PHAT · AU TRUONG NAI · VO VAN CHIEU · BAO KE · TRAN LON · AU TAY MAI · VO DINH THANG · LE VAN XU · LE TI
U VAN VINH · VO QUAT · HO DAI · TRAN VAN VINH · DUONG LUYEN · CAU DANG · TRAN VAN THAI · HOANG SANG · TRAN TRUNG DINH · VINH AI · V
NH DUC MINH · AU TRUONG LAM · NGUYEN VAN BAO · TRAN NGOC DUA · NGUYEN CAO · DAN VAN LOI · DUO NG HOANG · TRAN HINH · AU VAN TAP
TRAN QUE DINH · HUYNH DUC DINH · HUNYH TO GAP · BUI VAN DAO · VINH LUONG · NGO TRONG VIEN · VO VAN SUNG · PHAM DOC DANG · PHAM
NGUYEN BICH · NGUYEN VAN DU · BAO BOI · LE DUC QUANG · TRAN LE KHANG · HO TIEN SO · HO CHU ANH · NGUYEN NGOC VU · TRAN KUAN · T
· CAU VAN BINH · VU VAN THANG · TRU VAN NGU · HUYNH PRAN DIEN · AU LE OAN · HO NAM T AN · VU TAY · HUYEN HAO · TRU VINH LOC · HO TH
LI · LA THANH TUAN · TRAN TRUNG THAI · HAO CHU · PHAN BOI CHAU · LE DUC VAN · VU VAN CHIEU · CAU DANG · VO DI QUAY · HO DUONG · TRAI
· VINH VAN TONG · DUONG ANH · HUNYH TO THUC · HO TIEN VIEN · TRAN QUOC CHAT · BAO KE · AU VAN DU · TRAN CHAU · NGUYEN THIAM · TRA
I CHIEU · VO AN SO · TRAN DIEM · NGUYEN DI AI · NGUYEN CAO NHAT · PHAM HUE · TRAN QUOC HUE · NGUYEN HOAN · NGUYEN KIEU · HAO LON
O HUNG · VO DI TAN · NGUYEN TIEN · DO DINH CHANH · AU TAY PUU · TRAN LE SOC · TRAN LE LOAN · XUAN TRUU · TRU VINH THUC · HUYEN NHE
AN · LE DUC VIN · NGUYEN VAN DU · HUYNH PRAN DUONG · NGO DINH THI · TRAN LE DINH · TRAN NGOC BICH · VU VAN NAM · HUYNH DIEN · LE TL
NH TUY · XUAN LAM · NGUYEN DINH DO · NGO TRONG VIEN · VU VAN BO · TRAN QUE BAY · VU HOANG · BAO THAN THIEP · BAO THAN DAO · NGUY
QUOC · TRAN LE TUYEN · HO TIEN DIEM · VU VAN MANH · VU VAN NGOC · BAO THIN · NGO DINH CHIN · TRAN VAN TO · VO DI LAN · AU TRUONG · A
DONG · HAOANG DUC LE · TRAN LE VINH · LA THANH NGHE · NGUYEN HUU YAN · TRAN QUE DUAN · TRAN QUOC ANH · BAO VINH MANH · VU TONG
N THANH GIAN G · TRAN QUE PHU · HAOANG DUC TIEU · HO CHU TUAN · DAN VAN TUEN · TRAN CHEN · VU VAN XUAN · LE ONG · AU TRAN PHU · A
N DANG · LE VAN MAC · LA THANH NGUYET · LE VAN TRANG · HAOANG DUC YUET · BAO BOI · DO TAN DUC · VU VAN TRUONG · AU TRAN QUAT · AU
VIEN DUC LOAN · TRAN BAO · HAOANG DUC TIEN · TRU VINH THIEN · VO DINH CHINH · LE VAN KIET · BAO VINH QUYEN · HUYEN NINH · VU VAN THO
HUYEN DUY · VO NGUYEN DANG · HO HING DUEN · TON LE KY · BAO THAN NHU · HAO SUNG · NGUYEN HUU BE · DO DINH HAC · VO VAN QUAN · HO
G XUAN SAM · HUYNH VAN BUA · TRAN LE PHAN · CAU VAN CHAT · TRAN LE NGUYET · HO PHO QUANG · VO VAN TRUNG · HUYEN LUU · TRU VAN BA
· TRU VINH THICH · NGUYEN VAN BAO · TRAN VAN DINH · TRAN NGOC LAI · BAO THAN TAP · NGO DINH DIEM · NGUYEN BONG · DAN VAN PHUC · T
IC SO · TRAN QUOC HUE · VO NGUYEN LAM · TRAN NGOC BUA · VO NGUYEN DU · TRU DINH LOAN · VO LON · VINH AI · HA DUC BEN · TRAN NGOC HC
I TRONG THAI · HUY NH TRI · TRAN VAN DU · VU VAN TRAN · LE AP · TRAN DUY TO · DUONG VAN TRAC · HUYNH LE · VU VAN CHINH · TRAN HIEU · LA
N · PHAN BOI MAU · HUYNH TONG · NGUYEN DINH DIEU · NGUYEN DINH THAN · DAN VAN LAM · BAO MONG · VINH VAN QUANG · VU VAN NGOC · NGC
ING · HUYNH THINH · HO TUEN NGUYEN · LE THO · TRAN QUANG · CAU DO · HOANG DONG · HO THANH DI · CAU VAN VU · VU VAN H OA · TRU VAN B.
UOC NGHE · PHAM DOC THO · AU VAN BAO · HO TIEN DIEM · NGUYEN DINH GIA · VINH VAN THICH · TRAN LE TAY · VINH CAO THO · VU HUU · VO VAI
DUONG GIANG · DO LUC MY · HUYNH LAN · VO VAN TRI · VO DINH DUC · AU TRAN TIEN · VU VAN HOAN · HUYEN THAT · LE VAN TAT · HAOANG DUC L
N GIAP · TRAN QUO C DINH · BUI VAN VIEN · NGUYEN TAN · TRAN QUOC BICH · PHAM DOC TRAN · NGO DINH LUYEN · PHAN QUAN TO · VU VAN TRON
· DAN VAN CHU · HAOANG XUAN HO · HAO YUET · VU AN · AU LE TRAN · HUYNH VAN LON · BAO DIEM MAI · TRAN LINH · LE VAN MAC · NGUYEN NGOC
H DAO · VO AN SON AN H · VINH DUC LAI · TRAN QUE BIN · NGUYEN VAN DANG · LE ANG · TRAN TRUNG VINH · VO LON · TRAN QUOC KHEIM · HAO MAU ·
QUY · PHAM BANH · TRAN QUE PHU · VINH THIEN · VO NGUYEN ONG · DAN VAN LUONG · LA THANH QUEN · BAO SOC · VINH VAN THUAN · NGO TROI
· TRA N DIEM · HUYNH DUC TRAN · HUYNH PHU BANG · VO NGUYEN ONG · VO NGUYEN XUAN · VU VAN THIET · VO CAP · AU TRAN TU · VINH DUC KH/
NH NHU · HO THANH LUYEN · VU TAY · VO BINH · AU TRAN TRONG · LE XUAN · PHAM KHI · AU TRAN LAO · CAU VAN CO · TRU ONG · TRAN QUOC BINH
RAN BE · TRU LINH · VO VAN NHU · TRAN TRUNG NHON · NGUYEN VAN LOI · XUAN BO · VINH DUC BA · LE VAN NG · LA THANH THAI · TRU LONG · LE I
I DUAN · BUI VAN QUEN · VINH DUC CAN · BAO NINH MUNG · VO DINH LUU · HOANG CO CUONG · VO DONG · HO TIEN DINH · NGUYEN NGOC TRI · NGO
i · HUNYH TO BAC · VO NGUYEN DON · NGUYEN LEN · LE VAN CAP · BAO DIEM NAN · TRAN QUOC BAC · HO THANH TO · TRAN THI HUONG · NGUYEN I
IU · HUYEN TON · HUYNH GIAN · TRAN THI HUONG · VU VAN GIAP · BAO KHA · AU TRAN TIN · VINH CAO BAI · NGUYEN VAN TONG · LA THANH QUEN · L
) QUYNH · NGUYEN THUAN · TRAN LE DINH · VO NGUYEN H UONG · HAO PHU · TRAN QUOC DANH · HO PHO TRUONG · TRAN DAI · TRAN QUOC VINH · L
DON · TRAN LE CHU · AU VAN BAI · LE DO · TRAN QUOC NGO · VU VAN CAO · PHAM DOC SIEU · VO NGUYEN GAI · BAO THAN TUAN · HUYNH THICH · C
IUONG · TRU QUAT · BAO DINH BINH · HO THANH MAI · TRAN QUOC · DUONG BAO · HAO LUNG · HAO THO · DO DINH LAN · HO TIEN DUAN · VINH VAN F
LOC · HAOANG DU C VAN · HO HING NHAT · HO CAO · VO DINH DIEU · NGUYEN DUONG · TRU DINH LUC · TRAN VAN GIAP · HOANG TUAN LY · NGUYEN N
N DINH THAN · TRAN BUU KHI · TRAN NGOC TAC · VO VAN VU · NGUYEN NGOC HUYNH · HA VAN LOC · VINH CAO THAM · XUAN DO · BAO THAN KIEM · T
· VO NGUYEN THIEU · VINH THANG · VO NGUYEN BONG · AU VAN LOC · LE VAN VIEN · TRU LONG · VO DINH THRUOC · AU LE DON · TRAN VAN DIEM · /
CAN · DUONG VAN LAN · BAO THAN TAP · TRAN NGOC DUAN · BAO THAN DHUYEN · AU LE PHU · VO DAI · NGUYEN BICH · PHAN BOI CHAU · VO DINH CA
ON · VINH VAN QUANG · NGUYEN BE · VU MAI · TRAN NAI · PHAM TRUONG · LE VAN CAN · HUYNH VAN VIEN · VU VAN THAI · VO DINH TRI · TRAN PHAN
HOANG · AU TRAN CAM · VU VAN TRI · DAN VAN VINH · TRAN TRUNG DAI · AY TRAN LOAN · CAU DU · HOANG FUC · BA O DINH ONG · HAOANG DUC THO
I DING · LA THANH LONG · AU LE CON · VU VAN LOAN · LE THUY · XUAN AN · TRAN NGOC TAP · HAOANG DUC THI · DO DINH DI · BUI VAN DU · BAO QUY ·
VIEN · PHAM VAN ANH · HUYEN NGUYET · VU VAN DAN · XUAN AI · TRU QUANG · LE DUC VIN · TRU BE · VU VAN HO · NGUYEN CAO VO · BAO YEN · VINH
N PHAN · AU TRAN PHU · XUAN THE · TRU VAN PHU · DO DINH QUOC · VIEN DUC PHAN · NGUYEN VAN CHU · NGUYEN DINH NU · TON LE NGOC · VU VAN
PHAN DINH GO · HA DUC LOAN · VINH DUC THACH · TRU DINH LUC · LE AP · HUYNH PRAN DAN · TRAN NGOC CHAU · AU VAN SAN · DO DINH CA · XUAN

Fig. 8. Detail of Chris Burden, *The Other Vietnam Memorial*, 1991. Etched copper plates, steel. Collection of the Lannan Foundation, Los Angeles; photo: Ellen Page Wilson.

1805   Writes poem "on the growth of a poet's mind."
1781   (July) The sparrow-hawks continue their depradations.
1880   Lieutenant-governor.
1960   "Door to the river."
1844   First attempt to assassinate Polk.
1915   Death of Gaudier-Brzeska.
1347   First one-man exhibition.
1959   Early notebooks destroyed.[54]

What Gerard Genette terms *paralepsis* (the elision of some but not all terms in the syllogistic movement from Proposition A to Proposition B) occurs in a movement between annal and chronicle;[55] this yields effects as between "Death of Gaudier-Brzeska" and "First one-man exhibition"—Was this the first one-man exhibition in history, or the first of a particualr artist? Silliman has written of the deferral of "above-sentence integration" in the New Sentence: if "the sentences 'All women were once girls' and 'Some women are lawyers' logically leads to a third sentence or conclusion, a higher level of meaning: 'Some lawyers were once girls,'" the writing that interests him "proceeds by suppression, most often, of this third term, positing instead chains of the order of the first two."[56] The "I" of the poet, as much as the referential continuum, is thus left open in the presented sequence, although it reappears as an overtone sufficient to infer syllogistic construction in, for example, "Early notebooks destroyed," which is interpretable as self-referring and hence allows for a reading of the other dates as potentially but not necessarily referring to the nonnarrator as well. In *Tjanting* (1980), a large-scale proto-epic work, Silliman is clearly engaged in the constructive possibilities of such a play with sequence:

> Narrativity. Some of us just thrash around in our private lives, never solving anything. Some days shoes will never stay tied. Somehow, in mid-September in the subway, the strong Xmasy smell of a pine tree. A paragraph I cld write for the rest of my life. Even in Chinese the sarcastic banter of highschool kids is specific. Ripples in the image thru an old window. I play Eddie cantor on the jukebox. I'm content to eat a salad. We stand naked in the open doorway & watch the rain. A star on the shoe means it's Converse. This is not some story. The gray mouse tries to climb the pole to the nightingales & their seed. Today it remains morning until nightfall. Winter chaos in the wind-chimes. In this photo the ocean looks just like the desert. I spring into the milling flock of pigeons wch leap into flight. Underfunded. A touch of Tahini for Mother Cabrini. Flat light & sharp shadows on the objects of a tabletop (camera, tortilla, half a tomato, the poems of Alan Davies, the shine of cups) after the first light rain. One sees in the faces of sleepers all the strain of their lives. The water is boiling. I step into the cafe to write but am immediately besieged by old friend D., his act at long last having totally collapsd in on itself & nobody else to tell it to. Bad art of rich students got up as punk. Since when?[57]

As is obvious from the first and last sentences, Silliman continually comments on the problem of narrative unity—the organization offered being one not of subordination but of an inductive *metalepsis* (another term borrowed from Genette, meaning a reference to the discourse as a whole). The meaning of the form, however, is being created in the ongoing qualification of that metalepsis—this accounts for the movement of the writing, and its intrinsic interest—

accomplished by what Silliman has called the "syllogistic movement" of the New Sentence form. Rather than deforming reference to a continuity of event in real time (in which case, nonnarrativity would be understandable simply as deviant narrative), Silliman defers the transcendental self-consciousness of history by formal means and keeps the narrative moral outside the limits of the form. The text has unity precisely in its deferral of discursive closure by means of a continually reinforced present tense, one that metaleptically determines the whole in constructing a historical "now-in-the-present."[58] The experience of reading Silliman at length (and the short excerpt here cannot do his work justice) is to engage a series of higher-order interpretants that still are multiple and that continually break down to the immediacy of single assertions. As in White's notion of chronicle, partial narratives dead-end in the writer's present; the experience of Silliman's lengthy accretions may be a kind of nominalist aporia—in which there is no exterior, transcendent "place to stand" to guarantee meaning or perspective—but it is one that is worked consciously toward certain effects of "being-in-history" as a continuous present. In this sense, the chronicle creates a present immediacy in the deferral of closure formally analogous to the effect of the incrementally asserted names of casualties on the Vietnam memorial, a politics of loss that Silliman intends at the level of Jameson's "ideology of form," with its socially specific overdeterminations.[59]

Where the New Sentence form has worked to undermine narrative, thus intending a critical if even subversive force, it is important to note that such sequences of incremental dates have been organized to different effects in the administration of nonnarrative meaning in the political sphere more generally.[60] Consider, for example, the mass media's turning the tables on Jimmy Carter at the time of the Iran hostage crisis, where more than 365 successive days of Ted Koppel's *Nightline* chronology were a sufficient reinforcement of lost national identity that Carter did, in the event, lose. I am fascinated by the way the authority of a poetics of loss can, in this way, be transformed into the agency of a poetics of denial—the inevitability of loss becoming the basis for an acceptance in the subject that events are beyond his or her control. The state, it turns out, in this way manages to recuperate a victory even out of its losses, turning the "Vietnam syndrome" around on its axis even if the Persian Gulf War provided only a pseudo-victory to restage its prior defeat. We have been in the present of a nonnarrative chronicle ("and then, and then") which, as it produces an unstable narrative only to break down, calls us back to ourselves in a series of continual denials—and the rest, or so they would like us to believe, is history.

Conclusion

The relations between narrative and nonnarrative in artists such as Bulatov and Silliman invite speculation about how forms of historical self-consciousness are constructed more generally. The "parallel cataclysms" of their epic nonnarratives clearly do not aim to represent history in the manner of a narrative; rather, history is presented in a form that in turn demands a series of displacements originating in the work as an event. In Bulatov's case, a work seeming to embody the poetics of loss of the "era of stagnation" was produced at a moment when that period had not yet been, and could not have been, named. Silliman's formal imitation of the chronicle of events that ended the untenable stasis of the Vietnam War occurred in a period in which the historical impact of the war had yet to be resolved, as has been attempted with the era-defining "Vietnam syndrome." In moving from work of art to historical period, there are differences of scale initially accounted for by the fact that art is often determined to create a temporal continuity of its own, substituting the time of its own emergence and development for that of the culture at large. But even allowing for disjunctions of time and divergence of scale, the temporal forms of art participate in the social production of historical time. Both nonnarrative and narrative art provide occasions by which historical narratives are produced, distributed, and undone. Processes of defamiliarization, foregrounding, and sequencing make the history that occurs as real-time events and eras unfold.

A story in the *San Francisco Chronicle* of 16 July 1992 reveals a continuing drama of antagonistic but constitutive relations between narrative and nonnarrative.[61] In an attempt to catch up to youth-market prime-time competitors, ABC TV executives sent down an order to "program suppliers": "The network has mandated that each show begin with a 'substantial program open'—in other words, action and dialogue—before the main title. End credits on programs are to be superimposed over continuing action and dialogue." The reason for this stylistic imposition is, simply, that narrative closure is to be deferred at all costs so that the viewer is not tempted to switch channels by remote control; action should be sequenced in a kind of "continuous present." The network "will also reduce the number of its own network I.D.'s, on-air promotions, and public service announcements." Where historically the interruptions of narrative framing superinduced a higher-order need for narrative, here the nonnarrative viewing competence of an audience armed with remote control devices is countered by a blurring of narrative boundaries for an even more overdetermined effect. This strategy, of course, like any advertising campaign, probably will not last long, even if it permanently may force the viewer's competence in nonnarrative and narrative into as yet unrealized forms.

Notes

This essay has a history, one that is still in the process of being made. It was originally written for a presentation on "The Narrative Construction of History" organized by Laura Brun at the Southern Exposure Gallery in San Francisco, March 1990; it was given in revised versions at a conference on "The Ends of Theory," Wayne State University, Detroit, April 1990; at the Unit for Theory and Critical Interpretation, University of Illinois, Champaign-Urbana, October 1992; and at the University of California, San Diego, March 1993. Thanks to all those who commented on earlier versions, in particular Randolph Starn.

1. Robert Smithson, *The Writings of Robert Smithson*, ed. Nancy Holt (New York: New York University Press, 1979).

2. Quoted in Lyn Hejinian, Michael Davidson, Ron Silliman, and Barrett Watten, *Leningrad: American Writers in the Soviet Union* (San Francisco: Mercury House, 1991), p. 35. Then-Leningrad poet Arkadii Dragomoshchenko is a post-Soviet writer of intense "linguistic subjectivity" in an environment of defunct narratives; see his *Description*, trans. Lyn Hejinian and Elena Balashova (Los Angeles: Sun and Moon, 1990); and for other emerging post-Soviet poets, see *Mapping Codes: A Collection of New Writing from Moscow to San Francisco, Five Fingers Review* 8–9 (1990); and *Third Wave: The New Russian Poetry*, ed. Kent Johnson and Stephen M. Ashby (Ann Arbor: University of Michigan Press, 1992).

3. Paul Ricoeur's *Time and Narrative*, 3 vols. (Chicago, 1984–88), for example, forcefully argues the necessary reinforcements between the two.

4. See Jerome Rothenberg, *Revolution of the Word: A New Gathering of American Avant-Garde Poetry, 1914–1945* (New York: Seabury Press, 1974).

5. Jean-Francois Lyotard, *The Postmodern Condition: A Report on Knowledge* (Minneapolis: University of Minnesota Press, 1984); Fredric Jameson, *Postmodernism; or the Cultural Logic of Late Capitalism* (Durham, N.C.: Duke University Press, 1991); Fred Pfeil, *Another Tale to Tell: Politics and Narrative in Postmodern Culture* (London: Verso, 1990).

6. Sande Cohen, *Historical Culture: On the Recoding of an Academic Discipline* (Berkeley: University of California Press, 1986), p. 1.

7. Claude Levi-Strauss, in *The Savage Mind* (Chicago: University of Chicago Press, 1962), originates a series of positions in which "there is thus a sort of fundamental antipathy between history and systems of classification" seen as synchronic (p. 242); cf. Seymour Chatman, *Coming to Terms: The Rhetoric of Narrative in Fiction and Film* (Ithaca, N.Y.: Cornell University Press, 1990), p. 9: "Nonnarrative text-types do not have an internal time sequence, even though, obviously, they take time to read, view, or hear. Their underlying structures are static or atemporal—synchronic not diachronic."

8. In Hayden White's summary of the Lacanian view in "The Question of Narrative in Contemporary Historical Theory," *The Content of the Form* (Chicago: University of Chicago Press, 1987), p. 36: "What is 'imaginary' about any narrative representation is the illusion of a centered consciousness capable of looking out on the world, apprehending its structure and processes, and representing them to itself as having all the formal coherency of narrativity itself." Such imaginary coherence—be

it fictional, millennial, or simply transparent—constitutes and is constituted by the specific transcendental overview.

9. Barrett Watten, "The Word," in *Conduit* (San Francisco: Gaz Press, 1988), p. 39. Carla Harryman, "Toy Boats," in *Animal Instincts* (Berkeley: This Press, 1989), p. 107.

10. Lyn Hejinian, "Exit," *This* 12 (1982).

11. Mary Louise Pratt synthesizes the work of William Labov on oral narratives with the notion of the "cooperative principle" in Paul Grice's pragmatics in *Toward a Speech Act Theory of Literary Discourse* (Bloomington: Ind.: Indiana University Press, 1977).

12. Theories of open reading practices, as in Umberto Eco, Wolfgang Iser, and others, have been frequently assimilated to the reading of language-centered writing; see Linda Reinfeld, *Language Poetry: Writing as Rescue* (Baton Rouge: Louisiana State University Press, 1992).

13. Jackson Mac Low, "Wall Rev," *This* 12 (1982). See also Mac Low, *Representative Works, 1938–85* (New York: Rool Books, 1985).

14. Roman Jakobson, "Linguistics and Poetics," in *Language in Literature* (Cambridge, Mass.: MIT Press, 1987).

15. Joel Fineman, "The History of the Anecdote: Fiction and Fiction," in *The New Historicism*, ed. Aram Veeser (New York: Routledge, 1989), 49–76.

16. Louis O. Mink, "Narrative Form as Cognitive Instrument," in *The Writing of History: Literary Form and Historical Understanding*, ed. Robert H. Canary and Henry Kozicki (Madison, Wis.: University of Wisconsin Press, 1978), pp. 129–49, 140.

17. An example of a New Historicist anecdote that makes an argument out of the performative value of its disjunct date is to be found in Simon During, "The Strange Case of Monomania: Patriarchy in Literature, Murder in *Middlemarch*, Drowning in *Daniel Deronda*," *Representations* 23 (Summer 1988): 86–104.

18. Pratt, *Toward a Speech Act Theory*, pp. 45–46.

19. Raymond Williams, *Television: Technology and Cultural Form* (New York: Schocken Books, 1975), esp. pp. 96–108.

20. White, "The Value of Narrativity in the Representation of Reality," in *Content of the Form*.

21. Desire as a concept is here an admitted place holder for motivations of ideological effects, as indicated by Slavoj Zizek, *The Sublime Object of Ideology* (London: Verso, 1989): "What is missed by the . . . idea of an external causal chain of communication through which reference is transmitted is . . . the fact that naming itself retroactively constitutes its reference" (p. 95).

22. Umberto Eco, *The Open Work* (Cambridge, Mass.: Harvard University Press, 1989).

23. Barrett Watten, "Seyed Alavi," *Artweek*, 14 March 1991.

24. Fredric Jameson, *The Political Unconscious: Narrative as a Socially Symbolic Act* (Ithaca, N.Y.: Cornell University Press, 1981), pp. 13, 19–20.

25. Jameson, *Postmodernism*, p. 25. George Hartley sums up the presuppositions in Jameson's periodization of this and other instances of postmodern culture in "Jameson's Perelman," *Textual Politics and the Language Poets* (Bloomington: Indiana University Press, 1989), pp. 42–52; Perelman responds in "Exchangeable Frames," in *Non/Narrative, Poetics Journal* 5 (May 1985): 168–76.

26. Jameson, *Political Unconscious*, p. 82.

27. Cohen, *Historical Culture*, p. 69.

28. Jerome McGann, "Contemporary Poetry, Alternate Routes," in *Politics and Poetic Value*, ed. Robert von Hallberg (Chicago: University of Chicago Press, 1987), pp. 253–76; see also responses by Charles Altieri and Jed Rasula. For statements by a

number of contemporary writers on the question of narrative and nonnarrative in their work, see *Non/Narrative, Poetics Journal* 5.

29. Michael Andre Bernstein discusses the American epic tradition in *The Tale of the Tribe: Ezra Pound and the Modern Verse Epic* (Princeton, N.J.: Princeton University Press, 1980); Joseph Conte, *Unending Design: The Forms of Postmodern Poetry* (Ithaca, N.Y.: Cornell University Press, 1991), treats a range of "serial" forms that reject the epic vocation but insist on an experience of temporality.

30. Charles Olson, *Selected Writings*, ed. Robert Creeley (New York: New Directions, 1966); Olson, *The Maximus Poems*, ed. George F. Butterick (Berkeley: University of California Press, 1983); Butterick, *A Guide to the Maximus Poems of Charles Olson* (Berkeley: University of California Press, 1978); Barrett Watten, "Olson in Language: The Politics of Style," in *Total Syntax* (Carbondale, Ill.: Southern Illinois University Press, 1985), pp. 115–39.

31. Cohen, *Historical Culture*, p. 105.

32. These appear against the background of another form, the primary process Freud located in the unconscious with his analytic method of "evenly hovering attention," which has been imitated in language writing from Gertrude Stein to the present and which I am not exemplifying in this discussion as an instance of nonnarrative form. Jameson, of course, would see it as the primary instance of nonnarrative form.

33. *Erik Bulatov*, exhibition catalog (London: Institute of Contemporary Art, 1989). For other emerging then-Soviet visual artists, see Matthew Cullerne Brown, *Contemporary Russian Art* (New York: Philosophical Library, 1989); David A. Ross, ed., *Between Spring and Summer: Soviet Conceptual Art in the Era of Late Communism* (Cambridge, Mass.: MIT Press, 1990); Margarita Tupitsyn, *Margins of Soviet Art: Socialist Realism to the Present* (Milan: Giancarlo Politi Editions, 1989).

34. To illustrate Soviet memorial culture, I have presented this essay along with slides of a number of memorials to the liberation of the Ukraine in the vicinity of Kiev. On cultural memory and memorials, see Randolph Starn and Natalie Zemon Davis, eds., *Memory and Counter-Memory, Representations* 26 (Spring 1989), esp. James E. Young, "The Biography of a Memorial Icon: Nathan Rapoport's Warsaw Ghetto Monument," pp. 69–106.

35. Robert Smithson, "Entropy and the New Monuments," in *Writings*, presents a metaphor of "crystallization" in discussing contemporary minimalist sculpture that is related to this model of States 1 and 2.

36. After a visit to Leningrad in August 1989, I wrote about the social space of Soviet memorial culture at length in Davidson et al., *Leningrad*, pp. 72–73.

37. Erik Bulatov, interview in *Arts*, November 1989, p. 85.

38. Conversation with Moscow poet Alexei Parshchikov.

39. Boris Kagarlitsky, *The Thinking Reed: Intellectuals and the Soviet State from 1917 to the Present*, trans. Brian Pearce (London: Verso, 1988). Kagarlitsky's account itself is significant in terms of its negotiation of narrative; while not wanting to abandon Marxist-Leninist dialectic, particularly because of its explanatory force in the actual Soviet state, Kagarlitsky wishes to complicate matters by adding a Bakhtinian multiplicity to the historical process, by which he means to take account of "culture" as in a mutually constitutive but open-ended dialogue with the political. He writes: "We have to understand the culture of the past as a whole, as an independent system, and development not as a process of steady advance but as a more complex accumulation of historical experience through a dialogue of cultures" (p. 280). Such a "more complex accumulation" would account for the wildly divergent belief systems rationalized by the modern Soviet state, but it would probably not find the formal moment of Bulatov's *I Am Going* to be more significant than one cultural strand among many, including Marxism.

40. Andrei Ikonnikov, *Russian Architecture of the Soviet Period*, trans. Lev Lyapin (Moscow: Progress Publishers, 1988), pp. 387–88.

41. Claude Jolies and Viktor Misiano, "Interview with Erik Bulatov and Ilya Kabakov," in *Bulatov*, pp. 38–48.

42. A Moscow artist of the same period who deals with the *kitsch* side of memorial culture (an important component of Soviet pop culture) is Ilya Kabakov; see his *Ten Characters* (London: Institute of Contemporary Art, 1989), published in conjunction with the exhibition "Ilya Kabakov: The Untalented Artist and Other Characters," ICA (London), February 1989.

43. John Bushnell, *Moscow Graffiti: Language and Subculture* (Boston: Unwin Hyman, 1990).

44. See discussions of narrative envisionment in Paul Kay, "Three Properties of the Ideal Reader," unpublished paper; and of the cultural expectations to be educed in the metaphorical structure of the "journey" in George Lakoff, "The Public Aspect of the Language of Love," *Marginality: Public and Private Language, Poetics Journal* 6 (1986): 26–32.

45. Kagarlitsky, "Nationalist Currents," *Thinking Reed*, pp. 216–37. Central to this reading is his discussion of neo-Slavophile "spiritual freedom" in relation to modernist "legal culture": "The Russian people—and here Kozhanov refers to the Metropolitan Illarion—is the bearer not of 'law' but of 'grace.' Law, Kozhanov explains, means 'spiritual slavery,' whereas grace 'is the embodiment of spiritual freedom'" (pp. 224–25). Kagarlitsky would see this opposition united at many levels of Soviet culture, for instance in the figure of Stalin: "A similar contempt for law as something beneath consideration is characteristic also of Stalinism" (p. 225), the embodiment of the scientistic state, and this simultaneity of law and grace also could be read in Bulatov.

46. Barbara Kruger, *We Won't Play Nature to Your Culture* (London: Institute of Contemporary Art, 1983). A number of recent reviews of Kruger's work draw out the political horizons of her ironized narrativity; see Ken Johnson, "Theater of Dissent," *Art in America*, March 1991, p. 128; David Dietcher, "Barbara Kruger: Resisting Arrest," *Artforum*, February 1991, p. 84.

47. If there are different uses of nonnarrative between cultures, there are certainly different meanings for alternative or emergent cultures in them as well. The at times fluid boundary between oppositional and official cultures in the post-Stalin Soviet Union is suggested to be a way that "legal culture" organizes culture as a whole by Kagarlitsky; referring to a dissident writer, he says: "A certain kind of '*samizdat*' patriotism' is apparent here, for it turns out that for him only in the underground is creative thought alive among us. I beg to differ. . . . All the most important phenomena in *samizdat* . . . were engendered by processes that began in the *legal* culture" (p. 272). Kagarlitsky is referring to oppositional political theorists here, and this may not be quite as true for the avant-garde; however, after *glasnost* and the opening of barriers to publication and distribution, many avant-gardists complained of a loss of direction; see Davidson et al., *Leningrad*, for reports of such conversations. If Bulatov's intervention in the culture of memory and representation can be seen in the Brezhnev era as a kind of "social learning" developing from a dialogue of official and unofficial practices, its political horizons have greatly changed after Bulatov's emigration to the West. The alternative cultural practices of artists in the West, of course, are quite various: Kruger is a mainstream gallery and museum artist, and the scale of her work has recently become vast and socially comprehensive (see Dietcher, "Kruger," for recent architectural projects), while the collective practice of the New Sentence in the writers of the Language School developed through a network of alternative presses, distribution schemes, and art spaces.

48. Barrett Watten, *Opera—Works* (Bolinas, Calif.: Big Sky Books, 1975), pp. 49–50.

49. From Stanley Karnow, *Vietnam: A History* (Harmondsworth: Penguin Books, 1983).

50. The Vietnam memorial may be experienced as a narrative, but it is not structured as one—a central distinction of this essay. In fact, its capacity to engender more narrative approaches to it in historical time—unlike monuments to World War I casualties in many American town squares, which tend to restrict meanings and not develop them—is one of its great successes as a work.

51. Marita Sturken, "The Wall, the Screen, and the Image: The Vietnam Veterans Memorial," *Representations* 35 (Summer 1991): 118–42. Lyric and narrative possibilities for remembering Vietnam are discussed in David E. James, "Rock and Roll in Representations of the Invasion of Vietnam," *Representation* 29 (Winter 1990): 78–98. For Chris Burden's "other" Vietnam memorial, see Robert Storr, *Dislocations* (New York: Museum of Modern Art, 1991).

52. For the range of these practices, see two anthologies: Ron Silliman, ed., *In the American Tree: Language, Realism, Poetry* (Orono, Me.: National Poetry Foundation, 1986); and Douglas Messerli, ed., *"Language" Poetries: An Anthology* (New York: New Directions, 1987).

53. I discuss the relation between surrealist methods and those of the postwar American avant-garde in "The Politics of Poetry: Surrealism and $L=A=N=G=U=A=G=E$," in *Total Syntax*, pp. 31–64.

54. Ron Silliman et al., *Legend* (New York: Root Books, 1980), pp. 10–13.

55. Gerard Genette, *Narrative Discourse: An Essay in Method* (Ithaca, N.Y.: Cornell University Press, 1980).

56. Ron Silliman, *The New Sentence* (New York: Root Books, 1987).

57. Ron Silliman, *Tjanting* (Berkeley: The Figures, 1980), p. 125.

58. If Ann Banfield's "sentence of narration" is a "now in the past," the New Sentence is a "now in the present"; see Banfield, *Unspeakable Sentences: Narration and Representation in the Language of Fiction* (Boston: Routledge, 1982).

59. For more detailed discussion of Silliman's techniques, see McGann, "Contemporary Poetry"; and Watten, "Total Syntax: The Work in the World," in *Total Syntax*, pp. 65–114.

60. The poetics of denial in post-World War II American politics are discussed in Michael Rogin, "'Make My Day!': Spectacle as Amnesia in Imperial Politics," *Representations* 29 (Winter 1990): 99–123. I am pointing here to the temporal form that presents such negativity and by means of which specific ideological effects (not the least anxieties about "who is speaking" and a consequent desire for narrative) are created.

61. John Carman, "ABC Honcho Says He's Having Fun," *San Francisco Chronicle*, 17 July 1992.

Parataxis and Narrative: The New Sentence in Theory and Practice

Bob Perelman

Parataxis is the dominant mode of postindustrial experience. It is difficult to escape from atomized subject areas, projects, and errands into longer, connected stretches of subjectively meaningful narrative—not to mention life. As objects of the media, we are inundated by intense, continual bursts of narrative, twenty seconds of heart-jerk in a life insurance ad, blockbuster miniseries ten nights long, but these are tightly managed miniatures set paratactically against the conglomerate background that produces them. Some language writers have attempted to use parataxis oppositionally in the form of the *New Sentence*; but AT&T ads where fast cuts from all "walks of life" demonstrate the ubiquity and omniscience of AT&T are also examples of parataxis. Clearly, the nature of the units and the precise ways they are placed together need to be considered before useful political judgments can be made.

The *New Sentence* is a term coined by Ron Silliman to describe certain prose works by various language writers, including himself, in the late 1970s and early 1980s.[1] To simplify his wide-ranging discussion, a New Sentence is more or less ordinary itself but gains its effect by being placed next to another sentence to which it has tangential relevance: New Sentences are not subordinated to a larger narrative frame, nor are they thrown together at random. Parataxis is crucial: the internal, autonomous meaning of a New Sentence is heightened, questioned, and changed by the degree of separation or connection that the reader perceives with regard to the surrounding sentences.

This essay first appeared in *American Literature* 65, no. 2 (1993) and appears as a chapter in Bob Perelman, *Marginalization of Poetry: Language Writing and Literary History* (Princeton, NJ: Princeton University Press.)

As one of the marks of the postmodern, parataxis has become yoked together with a host of cultural-literary terms in a basic controversy between parts and whole. On one side, there is narrative, totality, the subject, presence, depth, affect; on the other, fragmentation, simulacra, schizophrenia, surface, pastiche, and, standing side by side with its allies (as it should, etymologically), parataxis. These literary, rhetorical, medical, philosophic, and topographic terms are not, as readers of critical theory know, merely descriptive. Fredric Jameson, in the course of his mini-discussion of language writing in "The Cultural Logic of Late Capitalism," not only identifies language writing with the New Sentence—a reductive move, as we will see—but with depthlessness, simulacra, Lacanian schizophrenia, and the end of personal identity. Jameson's style, with its long periodic sentences, the clauses packed with qualification, seems far removed from such phenomena, but in the overall organization of its materials, his essay is itself paratactic: Warhol, my poem "China," Michael Herr's *Dispatches*, the Bonaventura Hotel are among the units it considers. Jameson does not intend an easy moral denunciation of postmodern practices, but in discussing the parataxis in "China," his vocabulary registers significant alarm: when "the relationship [of signifiers to each other] breaks down, when the links of the signifying chain snap, then we have schizophrenia in the form of a rubble of distinct and unrelated signifiers."[2]

It will be useful to examine this rubble more closely before language writing is swept wholesale into the postmodern phalanx of Jameson's analysis. While it may suggest fragmentation and schizophrenia to Jameson and other critics, the New Sentence had an import in the development of language writing that was precisely the opposite of what Jameson would suggest. I'll be discussing "China" later; for now, let me cite the first few lines:

We live on the third world from the sun. Number three. Nobody tells us what to do.

The people who taught us to count were being very kind.

It's always time to leave.

If it rains, you either have your umbrella or you don't.[3]

What from one perspective may look like a sign of radical disconnection may from another be a gesture of continuity. For some, there may be utter gulfs between these sentences; others, however, may find narrative within any one of them. In the context out of which I was writing, each sentence of "China" seemed to me almost transgressively relaxed, long-winded, novelistic.

At the beginning of the language movement, the primary writing techniques or genres were (1) a high degree of syntactic and verbal fracturing, often treating the page as a structural frame; (2) use of found materials, cutting up borrowed texts; (3) a focus on rhythmic noun phrases, bop rather than incantatory, with semantics definitely soft-pedaled but not inaudible; (4) a hyperextension of syntactic possibilities, more Steinian than surreal; and (5) philosophic lyrics.

These techniques were irregularly accompanied by theories ranging from, on the one hand, conscious marxist critiques of commodity fetishism extended into aesthetics as attacks on narrative and referentiality to, on the other, more intuitional senses of the liberatory—or at least literary—potential of nonnormative language. In all cases, there was a political dimension: Jerome McGann is accurate when he writes that language writing developed in a climate where the hegemony of the American military and multinational capitalism was manifest.[4] But given the political urgency felt by marxists, lyricists, and syntactic guerrillas alike, the prevailing techniques and theories did not provide much possibility for direct political statement.

For some language writers, writing in sentences was one way to bring practice, politics, and daily life closer together. Writing in fragments might have kept one uncontaminated by the larger narratives of power, but to write in sentences was to use a publicly legible unit. Sentences per se were not the answer, however, as they were also being written by other writers who had quite different political and aesthetic aims:

> Today I am envying the glorious Mexicans,
> who are not afraid to sit by the highway
> in the late afternoons, sipping tequila
> and napping beneath their wide sombreros
> beside the unambitious cactus. Today
> I am envying the sweet *chaparita* who waits
> for her lover's banjo in the drunken moonlight
> and practices her fingers against the soft tortilla.
> Today I am envying the green whiskers of God. . . .[5]

The smug colonialism of this is particularly offensive. But one of its formal features is something that is common to much mainstream poetry: the poetry sentence, laden with adjectives ("glorious," "unambitious," "drunken"), verbal moods a sign of emotion ("I am envying . . . I am envying . . . I am envying"), nouns chosen for piquancy ("cactus," "*chaparita*," "banjo"). The results are rarely this egregious, but the incantatory lyricism of the poetry sentence, where writer finds voice and universe fitting together without struggle, is an ideal environment for aggrandized sensitivity and myopic or minimized social context.

The New Sentence, on the other hand, with its relative ordinariness and multiple shifts, encourages attention to the act of writing and to the writer's particular position within larger social frames. In the following small excerpt from Silliman's *Ketjak*, his first book written in New Sentences, the subjectivity of the writer is not absent, but neither is it the center of attention:

> Those curtains which I like above the kitchen sink. Imagined lives we posit in the bungalows, passing, counting, with another part of the mind, the phone poles. Stood there broke and rapidly becoming hungry, staring at the nickels and pennies in the bottom of the fountain. Dear Quine, sentences are not synonymous when they mean the same proposition. How the heel rises and ankle bends to carry the body from one stair to the next. This page is slower.[6]

Contrary to Jameson's analysis of the New Sentence, this writing seems to me self-critical, ambitiously contextualized, and narrative in a number of ways. Far from being fragments, these sentences derive from a coherent, wide-ranging political analysis, one that is quite similar to Jameson's; it is far less nuanced philosophically, but in that it factors in its own writing practice, it is in fact wider. Many sentences are themselves brief narratives, but more important is the overall frame Silliman shares with Jameson: the marxist master-narrative that sees reification not as stable reality but as a necessary stage of history. This master-narrative links these sentences: the domesticity of the kitchen with the spectacle of identical bungalows with the minute units of the pennies in the fountain with the small verbal differences between sentences that Quine ignores; the renter with the home owners with the homeless person; housing policies with positivism with writing practices. Silliman's sense of the broken integers produced by capitalism is inseparable from his commitment to the emergence of a transformed, materialist society.

New Sentences imply continuity and discontinuity simultaneously, an effect that becomes clearer when they are read over longer stretches than I can quote here. In the following juxtaposition— "Fountains of the financial district. She was a unit in a bum space, she was a damaged child" (3)—clearly we have switched subjects between the sentences: the child is not in the same physical location as the fountains. But in a larger sense, she is in the same social space. Throughout the book, Silliman insists on such connections as the one between the girl and the larger economic realities implied by the corporate fountains. The damage that has been done to the child has to be read in a larger economic context.

But we don't focus on the girl: she is one facet of a complex situation; she is not singled out for novelistic treatment. There's a dimension of tact involved: she's not a representative symbol of the wrongs done to children, but she's not given the brush-off, either.[7] The degree of attention Silliman accords here can be read as analogous to the way one recognizes individuals in a crowd (and perceptions in a crowded urban setting), giving each a finite but focused moment of attention. This can be compared favorably to the generalized responses of Eliot and Wordsworth to London: phobia in the case of Eliot—"I had not thought death had undone so many"[8]—and despairing scorn in the case of Wordsworth, for whom "the increasing accumulation of men in cities," "the uniformity of occupations," "the great national events which are daily taking place," and the "craving for extraordinary incident which the rapid communication of intelligence hourly gratifies" result in minds "reduced to an almost savage torpor."[9]

In his essay "The New Sentence," Silliman writes that the sentence represents the horizon between linguistic and social meaning. Parataxis keeps in check what he calls the "syllogistic movement" that would bind sentences into larger narrative, expository, and ideological unities;[10] One such unity would be the novel, a possibility that is only entertained in *Ketjak* a sentence at a time. In a novel —and here I'm trying to ventriloquize the sense of "the novel" that was in the air in the nonnovelist language writing circle—we might have two basic possibilities of resolution. If "She was a unit in a bum space, she was a damaged child" had to be turned into a novel, we might get a *Bildungsroman*: the girl overcomes difficulties, becomes an empowered adult. Or the resolution could be tragic in some degree: death, drugs, loveless marriage, anomie. Silliman's sentence is *narrative* (in an adjectival sense) but is not *a* fully formed narrative (noun).

By keeping free from fictitious totalization, each New Sentence represents an enclave of unalienated social work. Where Jameson sees signifying chains snapping, Silliman sees the cobwebs of the reified narratives of false consciousness being swept away. But alongside such denarrativization, I want to reemphasize that continual possibilities of renarrativization are offered. In *Ketjak*, the sentences are semiautonomous units, but they are not atomized into sameness: they are variously expressive, analytic, and narrative, especially if the reader is alert to the connections offered.

In fact, it is interesting to see Jameson, in another context, write that "new readers can be electrified by exposure to *Tarr*, a book in which, as in few others, the sentence is reinvented with all the force of origins, as sculptural gesture and fiat in the void. Such reinvention, however, demands new reading habits, for which we are less and less prepared."[11] While this sounds like praise for something close to the New Sentence (as well as a call for the new reading habits the New Sentence implies),[12] we should remember that the sum of Lewis's electrifying sentences is the novel *Tarr*, a narrative that Jameson reads as, among other things, a "national allegory," with Kreisler as Germany, Soltyk as Poland, Anastasya as Russia, all against the background of World War I. In other words, he sees in Lewis's sentences a thoroughgoing homology between part and whole—even though in the same study he writes that "every serious practicing critic knows a secret which is less often publicly discussed, namely, that there exists no ready-made corridor between the sealed chamber of stylistic investigation and that equally unventilated space in which the object of study is reconstituted as narrative structure."[13] By refusing to construct larger narrative wholes beyond the provisional connections made at the time of the reading (or, to put it another way, by making the reader renarrativize), Silliman allows air into the sealed chambers Jameson mentions.

However, there are often more bonds than this between the sentences Silliman writes. Even though his analysis of the new sentence doesn't mention it, one device that is crucial to his initial work with the New Sentence in *Ketjak* and his next book, *Tjanting*, is a highly developed structure of repetition. Both books are written in series of expanding paragraphs where the sentences of one paragraph are repeated in order in subsequent paragraphs with additional sentences inserted between them, recontextualizing them. Schematically, it looks like this, with each letter representing a sentence, and the uppercase letters a repeated one:

a.
A. b.
A. c. B. d.
A. e. C. f. B. g. D. h.[14]

This creates a strongly narrative effect of a peculiar kind as the sentences keep reappearing juxtaposed against different sentences. "Look at that room filled with fleshy babies. We ate them." A little later: "A tall glass of tawny port. We ate them." Later: "A slick gaggle of ambassadors. We ate them." Quite a bit later: "Astronauts hold hands, adrift in the sky. We ate them." The recontextualized sentences can seem almost like characters reappearing in a novel, but it would be more accurate to say that their meanings change with the changing contexts and that this process emblematizes Silliman's goal of materialist transformation.

In his more recent work, such as his book-length poem *What*, Silliman uses the New Sentence but without any repetition devices, thus embodying a more "pure" degree of parataxis. It seems to me that the results are significantly different over the course of the whole book.[15] It will be hard to demonstrate this because a short excerpt from the later book will seem similar to the previous excerpts:

> The cash register makes a deeper tone
> if the Universal Product Code isn't picked up
> by the sensor. One after another,
> cars bounce in the pothole. . . .
>   "No on F,"
> "Stop dirty politics," giving no clue whatsoever
> what the issues might entail. (92–93)

These three sentences deal with the same reified material as in *Ketjak* or *Tjanting*: decontextualized units—grocery store items, cars, slogans all passing through the grids of "the service economy." But where in the earlier work the repetition and recombination of sentences distanced, framed, questioned, and at times ironized their contents, here the sentences, appearing one time only, seem to insist on their truth and presence. With no chance for recontextualization, the act of writing each sentence repeatedly pits writer against world (and against the mass of prior sentences), building up pressure for validity and for a novelty that is at times hard to keep separate from the story of cultural reification against which the writing directs itself. In other words, can "One after another, cars bounce in the pothole" be read as a description of these New Sentences themselves?

To suggest this is seemingly to circle back to Jameson's vision of the anomie of postmodern schizophrenic production. But rather than homologize the cars and the sentences, the pothole and the perceptual vacuum created by multinational capitalism, as Jameson might, I want to emphasize the tension between the sentences and the reified world they confront and depict. This tension has the effect of foregrounding the personal, though not in the commodified sense of the mainstream voice poem—the narrative here is not of Silliman's life but of Silliman writing. Consider the following three New Sentences:

I have flight (half-light). The audience for poetry not being "the masses" can be quite specific—you choose the poem or it chooses you (years later possibly you meet the author at a party, a little, bald bespectacled fellow, talking not art or politics but baseball and gossip, the edges of everything general and rounded) and your life is altered irreparably by that decision, you change majors, jobs, become passionate suddenly in ways opaque to your lover, and frightening: you didn't know poetry could be like that but it's what you'd wanted all along, so deeply in fact that you think for a while it might be genetic or that you were "destined" as that poem seems also to have been destined for a particular life, and maybe you are and it was, if not in that sense in some other, the way it has for all the others been just likewise, each one choosing the poem, the poem choosing them, even the ones who seem to you (for who are you to judge?) completely muddied in what they do, in how they think, the ones who publish a single chapbook and get no response, no one coming to their readings and they going to fewer each year, writing less and one day they realize they haven't even thought of publishing in ages, the job is harder, the kids demand time, and yet almost as if at random copies of that chapbook dot the crowded shelves of small used bookstores, just waiting to be chosen and to choose, loaded as a minefield. I heard mindfield.[16]

The length of the second sentence strikes me as exemplary of the unresolved pressure for social narrative that Silliman's practice of the New Sentence creates. This excerpt is not purely paratactic, as these three sentences are somewhat anaphoric. "Mindfield" refers back to "minefield"; and the various anxieties over the success of writing careers, methods, and schools that stir so disturbingly through the elephantine second sentence can be detected, in germ, in the tiny pun of the first: "I have flight (half-light)." Is one, as a poet, really flying with Pegasus, or is one simply a dimwit? But these qualifications aside, the relatively complete commitment to parataxis in *What* also entails a commitment to Silliman's moral authority as a writer, since there is nothing else to motivate the appearance of the next New Sentence.

It is symptomatic that among *What*'s many sentences, the stories of Silliman's marriage and his grandmother's death occupy more than two—in other words, in some spots the book becomes autobiographical at the thematic level. Larger narrative frames, though theoretically repressed by parataxis, clearly return, even within the boundaries of a single sentence. The long sentence just quoted is anomalous; nevertheless, it demonstrates that the New

Sentence creates euphoria ("Your life is altered, you become passionate") by its freedom from social narratives, while at the same time producing pressure to get everything—include life narratives —said before the period.

I've been concerned here not to generalize; what I've written about Silliman does not necessarily apply as accurately to other language writers, not that many of whom actually use the New Sentence in the ways Silliman describes in his essay. To care for the reading I've tried to sketch here requires a commitment to unities that are provisionally autonomous: poetry, language writing, the work of an individual language writer. And then, such qualifications need to be set back into a more totalized context; it is of value, in other words, to set the New Sentence beside postmodern architecture and television, as Jameson does. But any specific work written using the New Sentence cannot be read in a focused way without attention to the original context.

Discontinuity or continuity in writing results from complex conditions of reading. The parataxis of Whitman's catalogs that seemed bizarre and discontinuous to most of his contemporary readers is much more likely to denote, for this century's readers, connection and a totalizing embrace of society. (One can see a *doppelganger* of this embrace in the economically calculated shots in the ads alluded to above: the airline pilot, the old couple, the stockbroker, the construction worker, the waitress, and so on. And there's often a patriotic subplot in these ads that also recalls Whitman.) Novels, on the other hand, which would seemingly be connected narrative by definition, can register as paratactic in a number of ways. Camus's use of the *passé composé* in *The Stranger* is commonly pointed out to students of French as a mark of discontinuity: "What does [Mersault's] habit of not relating events to one another tell us about his character?" asks *Cliff's Notes*.[17] And the sentence-by-sentence writing in *Bouvard and Pecuchet*—as well as the plot as a whole—is comic precisely because there is no contact between items that are supposedly in immediate connection with one another. Bouvard and Pecuchet's pedantic steps toward understanding the world lead nowhere.

First what is beauty?
For Schelling, it is the infinite expressing itself in the finite; for Reid, an occult quality; for Jouffroy, a fact incapable of analysis; for De Maistre, that which is pleasing to virtue; for Father André, that which gratifies reason.
And there exist several kinds of beauty: a beauty of science, geometry is beautiful; a beauty of behavior, it cannot be

denied that the death of Socrates was beautiful. A beauty of the animal kingdom: the beauty of the dog consists in its sense of smell. A pig could not be beautiful on account of its filthy habits; nor a snake, because it awakes in us ideas of baseness.

Flowers, butterflies, birds may be beautiful. In fact the first condition of beauty is unity in variety; that is the root of the matter.

"Yet," said Bouvard, "two cross-eyes are more varied than two ordinary ones and produce a less good effect, as a rule."

They entered upon the question of the sublime.[18]

Each sentence or phrase here is something of a "New Sentence," though for a purpose very different from that in Silliman's case. The elementary completeness of each little pronouncement here is the result of authoritarian abbreviation. The ironic gaps that Flaubert wants us to read between each assertion reveal the lunatic abyss underlying the pedagogical narrative of organized knowledge.

I should remark here that the rhetorical tone of "China"—to my mind one of the basic features of the poem—is the opposite of Flaubert's irony in *Bouvard and Pecuchet*: the poem touches on the matter-of-fact utopian feelings that early education can evoke.[19] The opening line—"We live on the third world from the sun. Number three. Nobody tells us what to do"—combines rudimentary astronomy with an assertion of complete independence, as if learning about the solar system in second grade marks a liberation from older narratives of fate. But despite the ingenuous tone of the poem, irony does appear in the assertions of collectivity. Nobody (from other planets or from heaven) tells us what to do: but "we" tell each other what to do. The same tension appears in a line such as "everyone enjoyed the explosions." It means one thing if "everyone" refers to a rural village celebrating the new year with firecrackers; there is solidarity, camaraderie. But if the context is the Vietnam War, the meaning changes: the explosions now are deadly, and "everyone" loses its utopic-communal character, becoming a designation that embodies colonialist repression.

Let me conclude by reiterating that Jameson and Silliman both make wide theoretical claims; both are trying to fight reified parataxis—commodification—with a more committed, oppositional parataxis—the finding of hidden categorical similarities. Denarrativization is a necessary part of construction in these wider paratactic arguments. But in both cases, this process needs to be seen for the combined reading and writing practice that it is: renarrativization is also necessary. If we try to separate out the results of these practices, we are left with fictions, metaphorical condensations, reifications, the purely autonomous New Sentence on the one hand and the rubble of snapped signifying chains on the other.

Notes

1. See "The New Sentence" in the book of the same name (New York: Roof, 1987), pp. 63–93.

2. Fredric Jameson, *Postmodernism, or the Cultural Logic of Late Capitalism* (Durham: Duke University Press, 1991), p. 26.

3. Bob Perelman, *The First World* (Berkeley: This, 1981), p. 60.

4. Jerome McGann, "Contemporary Poetry, Alternate Routes," in *Politics and Poetic Value*, ed. Robert von Hallberg (Chicago: University of Chicago Press, 1987), pp. 253–76.

5. Michael Blumenthal, "Today I Am Envying the Glorious Mexicans," in *The Morrow Anthology of Younger American Poets*, ed. Dave Smith and David Bottoms (New York: Quill, 1985), p. 95.

6. Ron Silliman, *Ketjak* (San Francisco: This, 1978), p. 17.

7. Especially in subsequent expanded versions of the sentence: "She was a unit in a bum space, she was a damaged child, sitting in her rocker by the window" (6, 7, 11, 18, etc.). I discuss these repetitions in a moment.

8. T. S. Eliot, "The Waste Land," in *The Complete Poems and Plays* (San Diego: Harcourt Brace Jovanovich, 1971), p. 39.

9. "Preface to the Second Edition of *Lyrical Ballads*," in *William Wordsworth Selected Poetry*, ed. Mark Van Doren (New York: Random House, 1950), p. 679. Also see the description of London in Book Seven of *The Prelude*.

10. "The New Sentence," pp. 90–91.

11. *Fables of Aggression: Wyndham Lewis, the Modernist as Fascist* (Berkeley: University of California Press, 1979), p. 3. The Jamesonian "we" is an odd construction; he is exempting himself from the "we."

12. Jameson concludes "The Cultural Logic of Late Capitalism" with a similar gesture: "the new political art . . . will have to hold to the truth of postmodernism . . . the world space of multinational capitalism—at the same time at which it achieves a breakthrough to some as yet unimaginable new mode of representing this last" (p. 54).

13. *Fables*, p. 7.

14. The opening pages of *Ketjak* don't conform perfectly to this system; most of the book does, though. The system of repeats in *Tjanting* is more complex, involving Fibonacci numbers.

15. In "The New Sentence," Silliman claims that New Sentences are a phenomenon occurring only in prose. But his later practice does not bear this out.

16. *What* (Great Barrington: The Figures, 1988), pp. 94–95.

17. Quoted in Alice Kaplan, "The American Stranger," *South Atlantic Quarterly* (Winter 1992): 91.

18. Gustave Flaubert, *Bouvard and Pecuchet*, trans. T. W. Earp and G. W. Stoner (Westport: Greenwood Press, 1954), pp. 166–67.

19. In fact, I wrote the poem after looking, not at a book of photographs as Jameson writes, but at some sort of a Chinese primer containing simple four-color pictures of "the world": family, kitchen, school, rivers, airports, etc.

their production" (*Revolution in Poetic Language*, p. 103). If theory is accommodated, it must be as a provisional stability to be passed through and finally jettisoned. Kristeva, then, demands for the readerly domain the replacement of a theoretic with a heuristic agenda to solve theory's metalinguistic dilemma. The attempt to stabilize discursively (by hypothesis, explication, or description) a radically unstable practice is abandoned, and the negativity previously "swallowed" into theory is released into instinctual play (p. 96).

Kristeva's textual practice will stand in healthy contrast to Murray Krieger's critical assimilation:

> This poem before me—as an alien "other," outside me and my consciousness—imposes upon me to make it no longer "other." (*Theory of Criticism*, p. 203)

And his unification of textual heterogeneity by appeal to the aesthetic paradigm:

> The poem unifies itself aesthetically around its metaphoric and its counter-metaphoric tendencies, even as its oppositions remain thematically unresolved. It is, then, self-demystifying, but as such it does not fall outside the symbolist aesthetics so much as it fulfills what the aesthetic, at its most critically aware, its most self-conscious, is able to demand: nothing less than a waking dream. ("'A Waking Dream,'" p. 22)

Though a significant improvement on Krieger's aestheticism, Kristeva's formulation is not entirely satisfactory. Textual practice delimits and inaugurates an elite vanguard of writing predestined to a cultural marginality. It does not permit a radical "readerly practice" to be envisioned. One that would involve a split subject-in-process, of the same status as the writer, who could effect more radical encounters with meaning and its loss than the tracing of a prior textual practice. Kristeva's prelinguistic concerns commit her to supporting the presence of certain psychic essences, while her notion of the textual relation as intrasubjective does not permit a critical approach to writing and reading as differing logics of action.[5]

We will turn to Michel de Certeau to find two such logics precisely delineated in the strategy and the tactic:

> I call a "strategy" the calculus of force-relationships which become possible when a subject of will and power (a proprietor, an enterprise, a city, a scientific institution) can be isolated from an "environment." A strategy assumes a place that can be circumscribed as *proper* and thus serve as the basis for generat-

ing relations with an exterior distinct from it (competitors, adversaries, "clienteles," "targets," or "objects" of research). (*The Practice of Everyday Life*, p. xix)

A tactic, on the other hand, is "a calculus which cannot count on a 'proper' (a spatial or institutional localization) nor thus on a borderline distinguishing the other as a visible totality" (p. xix). Deprived of the spatial advantage of a base, tactics take the form of temporal, nomadic, and necessarily provisional actions: "a tactic depends on time—it is always on the watch for opportunities that must be seized 'on the wing.' Whatever it wins, it does not keep. It must constantly manipulate events in order to turn them into 'opportunities'" (p. xix). Tactics require "a logic articulated on situations and the will of others" (p. xx) and must "produce without capitalizing, that is, without taking control over time" (p. xx).

Certeau recognizes theory to be an operational partition carrying a discrete practice of discourse (i.e., a regulated specialization) whose main effect is the maintenance of social *reason*. The strategic nature of theoretical practice can be inferred readily from Certeau's words above. Enjoying the spatial advantage of a base in the "proper" (being both an institution and an enterprise), theory generates relations with its numerous target fields, intervening in the everyday drift of reading to recover it from temporal erosion and forgetfulness. However, the deployment of reading *as a tactic* results in something quite different, closer to a loss or slippage of the text in hand and which Certeau likens to poaching as a practice of insinuation and mutation:

> a silent production: the drift across the page, the metamorphosis of the text effected by the wandering eyes of the reader, the improvisation and expectation of meanings inferred from a few words, leaps over written spaces in an ephemeral dance. . . . He insinuates into another person's text the ruses of pleasure and appropriation: he poaches on it, is transported into it, pluralizes himself in it like the internal rumblings of one's body . . . the viewer reads the landscape of his childhood in the evening news. The thin film of writing becomes a movement of strata, a play of spaces. A different world (the reader's) slips into the author's place. (p. xxi)

Rather than retracing the instinctual drives and gestures inscribed within an initial production, Certeau's reader enters a textual space to enjoy an indeterminate production of detours, personal accretions, and mutant assimilations, but as a "consumer practice" that *fails to generate a discursive configuration*. Between the production of poems and their annexation by theory lies the nondiscursive practice of reading whose range might be fixed as a passive voyeurism at one end and an unfettered, idiosyncratic usage at the other.

> What is called "popularization" or "degradation" of a culture is from this point of view a partial and caricatural aspect of the revenge that utilizing tactics take on the power that dominates production. In any case, the consumer cannot be identified or qualified by the newspapers or commercial products he assimilates: between the person (who uses them) and these products (indexes of the "order" which is imposed on him), there is a gap of varying proportions opened up by the use that he makes of them. (p. 32)

There is an ideal generality in Certeau's judgment that nonetheless inscribes accurately a repressed algorithm of power. Refusing to capitalize and invest its experiences in a discursive production, readership maintains a tactical relation to its reading as an incommensurable manipulation of "situations and the will of others." Such tactics bear comparison to Foucault's "happy wreck," itself a drifting through knowledge claims as provisionalities. Resisting the stability of social prediction, tactics remain intractable to theory. Umberto Eco argues a similar freedom of state for the empirical reader:

> we must keep in mind a principle, characteristic of any examination of mass communication media (of which the popular novel is one of the most spectacular examples): the message which has been evolved by an educated elite (in a cultural group or a kind of communications headquarters, which takes its lead from the political or economic group in power) is expressed at the outset in terms of a fixed code, but it is caught by diverse groups of receivers and deciphered on the basis of other codes. The sense of the message often undergoes a kind of filtration or distortion in the process, which completely alters its "pragmatic" function. (*The Role of the Reader*, p. 141)[6]

Whereas Kristeva reformulates reading along the lines of a fixed agenda, an action of "retracing" the route of semiotic production, both Certeau and Eco endorse a freer, less predictable model. The everyday practice of reading takes the form of an improvisation upon constraints, the insinuation of errant itineraries that produce innovative redirections and perversions of the original text to incalculable degrees.

We reach the insufficiency of theory when we approach writing and reading not through Kristeva's interesting contestation but through the model of the quotidian and the mass as a *tactical* operation. It is no coincidence that much in contemporary American writing adopts the tactic as its specific calculus of action and not Kristeva's textual practice. *Bricolage*, the found poem, the treated text—all utilize procedures akin to those of "contemporary consumption . . . a subtle art of 'renters' who know how to insinuate their countless differences into the dominant text" (Certeau, p. xxii). They help revision writing without appeal to a psychic model of heterogeneous orders. Neither the conscious nor the unconscious need be petitioned for tactic's insinuation and manipulation of an imposed system, its unsettling of textual stability by way of a reading that invades to play among its signs according to the laws of a different power.

Out of a multiplicity of contemporary works whose form and mode of production are resistant to theory, I will limit discussion to two: Ronald Johnson's *Radi os* (1977) and Lucette Finas's *La Crue* (1972). Johnson's poem consists of a tactical intervention into the normative system of Milton's epic poem *Paradise Lost*. Through a process of selected deletions and excavations Johnson arrives at a text within a text. *Radi os* exploits its source poem as a lexical supply, the precise mode of production being conveniently illustrated on the inside covers of the book:

> OF MAN'S ~~first disobedience, and the fruit~~
> ~~Of that forbidden~~ tree ~~whose mortal taste~~
> ~~Brought death~~ into the World, ~~and all our woe,~~
> ~~With loss of Eden, till one greater Man~~
> ~~Restore us, and regain the blissful seat,~~
> ~~Sing, Heavenly Muse, that, on the secret top~~
> ~~Of Oreb, or of Sinai, didst inspire~~
> ~~That shepherd who first taught~~ the chosen ~~seed~~
> ~~In the beginning how the heavens and earth~~
> Rose out of Chaos: ~~or, if Sion hill~~
> ~~Delight thee more, and Siloa's brook that flowed~~
> ~~Fast by the oracle of God, I thence~~
> ~~Invoke thy aid to my adventurous~~ song,
> ~~That with no middle flight intends to soar~~
> ~~Above the Aonian mount, while it pursues~~
> ~~Things unattempted yet in prose or rhyme.~~

Johnson does not argue for a prescriptive poetic for text generation but, like the everyday practices enumerated by Certeau, insinuates a prior writing "opportunistically" to improvise upon the words at hand. Less a writing, *Radi os* transcribes the results of a tactical reading, a type of production within consumption that subjects the object "consumed" to a nondiscursive operation. Johnson's method in the poem bears a canny parallel to Certeau's description of the housewife shopping in the supermarket:

> (thus, in the supermarket, the housewife confronts heterogeneous and mobile data—what she has in the referigerator, the tastes, appetites, and moods of her guests, the best buys and their possible combinations with what she already has on hand at home, etc.); *the intellectual synthesis of these given elements takes the form, however, not of a discourse, but of the decision itself, the act and manner in which the opportunity is "seized."* (p. xix; italics added)

Johnson's poem does not relate to *Paradise Lost* parodically by setting up a parallel space but rather induces spaces within a space through a selective deployment of reading. This "poached" text is exemplary, too, of Eco's empirical reader as incommensurate utilizer, infiltrating and changing a prior message and radically altering the historic, "pragmatic" function of the given words.

Whereas *Radi os* might be seen to circumscribe itself within a tactical sovereignty to call theoretical appropriation into doubt, Lucette Finas situates her work within the metalinguistic presuppositions of strategic discourse from where theory can be subverted and unsettled. *La Crue* is purportedly a complex textual analysis of Georges Bataille's short novel *Madame Edwarda*. In effect, however, it tests the limits of critical method in a kind of defecational parody. The project *La Crue* embodies calls for a reader conceived as "a state of forces" through which pass, as ingested displacements and eventual excretions, a potentially infinite variety of anagrammatic extractions. The analysis is thus singular in its irrational pursuit of the letter sound embedded in stable semantic patterns. In place of a critical metalanguage, Finas provides a porous ingestion and expulsion of lettristic turbulence. She describes her method in the following manner:

> I wished to push my reading to a point of indecency, to a wild, excremental depth, as if the heterogeneous, rising "between the imperative and the subversive form of agitation" might be literally taken by attack and attraction, by the letters' strangeness and embrace of one another. As if the letters were fomenting . . . (*La Crue*, p. 106)

It is precisely because Finas does *not* incorporate her *dechétism* into the taxonomic closure of a semiotics of drive (as does Kristeva) that its provocations are maintained and held close to a seduction model of meaning.[7] Such a model has been outlined by Baudrillard, who, via a dilated epiphany, announces seduction as "the world's elementary dynamic" *The Ecstasy of Communication*, (p. 59). Seduction creates an alinguistic condition for the sign. Such signs, according to Baudrillard, are "without a subject of enunciation . . . they are pure signs in that they are neither discursive nor generate any exchange" (pp. 59–60). Seduction is a surface operation carried out among appearances, precipitating detours, deflections, reversals, and cancellations, which force meaning to manifest as intensely provisional apparitions. Most significantly, Finas's reading opens up theoretical appropriation to self-expenditure by remodeling the critical project as a wild, parodic gesture of the sign's own errancy. It is important, too, in its attempt to break down the polemological fixation of theoretic power upon its Other. Treating the letter sound as both sensuous and wandering, Finas shifts concentration away from formal interpretation or analysis onto a liberation and mapping of shifting transphenomenalities.

The implications of *La Crue* open up to one of writing's most resistant materialities: its irreducible paragrammatic disposition, which guarantees the ultimate insufficiency of attempts at absolute theoretical mastery. The paragram (which as a rhetorical figure would include acrostics and anagrams) is a fundamental disposition in all combinatory systems of writing and contributes to phoneticism its partly transphenomenal character. Paragrams are what Nicholas Abraham terms *figures of antisemantics*; they are that aspect of language that *escapes* all discourse and commits writing to a vast, nonintentional reserve. A text may be described as paragrammatic, according to Leon Roudiez, "in the sense that its organization of words (and their denotations), grammar, and syntax is challenged by the infinite possibilities provided by letters or phonemes combining to form networks of significance not accessible through conventional reading habits" (Kristeva, p. 256). The paragram thus provokes a crisis within any closed semantic economy, for while engendering meaning eruptively and fortuitously, it also turns unitary meaning against itself. Paragrams open a text to infinite combinant possibilities that refuse a higher symbolic integration. If form, as Denis Hollier proposes, is "the temptation of discourse to arrest itself, to fix on itself, to finish itself off by producing and appropriating its own end" (p. 24), then the paragram is form's heterological object, structured upon nonlogical difference and, as such, impossible to be claimed as an object of knowledge. As an expenditure from meaning's ideal structures, a nonutilitarian scattering of materiality through vertiginous configurations, the paragram returns negativity to the field of the semantic.

Though neither Bataille nor Benjamin speaks of the paragram, its disposition attunes entirely with their respective notions of *heterology* and *constellational materialism*, both of which constitute critiques of that type of materialism that sentences its facts and data to an abstract and conceptual recovery by theory. We might recall here Bataille's own definition of substance as "just a provisional equilibrium between the spending (loss) and the accumulation of force. *Stability* can never exceed this short-lived, relative equilibrium; to my mind, it's not and can't ever be static" (*Guilty*, p. 15). The stability of substance in any poetical economy would announce itself as a provisional equilibrium between the lineal, grammatical accumulation of words that integrate into higher units, and the simultaneous expenditure of the letter components into potentially infinite indicial configurations.

We can see now that Johnson's *Radi os* exists latently as an unrecognized configuration within Milton's "different" *Paradise Lost*. Not emerging as a poem until released at the time of Johnson's written reading, it stands as the subphenomenal aspect of the Miltonic epic that both contains and represses it. Johnson's tactical production bears comparison with the status of poetic genius demanded by Bataille:

> Poetic genius is not verbal talent . . . it is the divining of ruins secretly expected, in order that so many immutable things become undone, lose themselves, communicate.
> (*Inner Experience*, p. 149)

> The term poetry, applied to the least degraded and least intellectualized forms of the expression of a state of loss, can be considered synonymous with expenditure; it in fact signifies, in the most precise way, creation by means of loss.
> (*Visions of Excess*, p. 120)

The common thread in both Johnson's and Finas's texts is a semantic obscenity obtained through the coupling of meaningfulness to a shifting materiality of language. Both *Radi os* and *La Crue* link to theory as practices upon another's writing. Yet from that unit of similarity, both texts explode to circumscribe theory's blind spot. The tactical use of seduction, the paragram, and the local improvisation within constraint all register as theory's unassimilable others. However, these also allow writing a number of alternative relations with itself. The negativity of the tactical can be recovered to production by allowing paragrammatic play to push the system containing it to new levels of complexity. It is such recovery that grants *Radi os* an intrinsic schedule in reading Milton's epic and authenticates *La Crue* as the complicating double of *Madame Edwarda*. Alternatively, this negativity may be reaffirmed and meaning equated with the experience of a loss of signification. Within theory itself, the paragram and the tactical reader might be acknowledged as the elusive and repressed elements inside its own discursive laws. Theory might then incorporate this affirmation as a motivation to subsequent agency and possibly disprove the ominous pronouncement of poet Basil Bunting that "the theoretician will follow the artist and fail to explain him."

Notes

1. This is, of course, an intentionally ungenerous description of theory's range and constitution. It would be utterly false to claim that theory relates to its object field solely by way of a unilateral empowerment. A cross-pollenation is always possible, and a poetic procedure can equally appropriate a theoretical field. We might even argue for a sort of poetic Darwinism and urge that theory and literary criticism are less an appropriation than the poem's own method of ensuring its reproduction via discursive proliferation. The intention of this paper is to maneuver into contention with appropriation as a sufficient, if not necessary, condition of the theoretical, and it *does* suppose itself to address a sedimentary aspect common to all theoretical practice. A more detailed study also should take into account the important distinction (claimed by Althusser) between theoretical *forces* and theoretical *relations*. The latter would include the social and ideological contexts in which theory finds itself realized (academic papers, scholarly journals, university seminars) and its incorporation into individual and collective careerisms, party interests, and the incommensurable range of wills to power. Deliberately, this paper concentrates on the *forces* of the theoretical alone. Similarly, while arguing that poetic economies are essentially nondiscursive, acknowledgment is made of a highly discursive context that frames, and to a certain extent governs, their appearance. This discourse is the institution of literature along with its cadre of procedures and implements: canonicity, the tradition, generic frame, master texts, and so on. Ultimately, it is impossible to separate either poem or theory from these complex networks of historical, economic, and institutional forces that govern and partake of their mutual production.

2. The suppressed connection between structuralist method and Duc's architectural terms was shown first by Hubert Damisch. If only the *Dictionnaire* of le-Duc were read, contends Damisch, "with attention to the dialectic of the whole to its parts and the parts to the whole which is the avowed motivation for this 'descriptive' dictionary, it will inevitably seem to be the manifesto, or at least the oddly precocious, definite outline of the method and ideology of the sort of structural thought that is famous today in linguistics and anthropology." Introduction to *L'Architecture raisonnée*, extracts from the *Dictionnaire de l'architecture française* of Viollet-le-Duc (Paris: Hermann, 1964), p. 14; quoted in Hollier, *Against Architecture*, p. 177. Angenet's valuable essay analyzes the syncretic nature of French structuralism with special scrutiny of the institutional appropriation of Saussure. Through the 1960s, argues Angenet, Saussure's terminology functioned as a "phraseological cement" binding

together basically heterogeneous and even conflicting interests. Saussure's comparatively late entry into French intellectual circles is also remarked: "Saussure's paradigm took forty years to travel from Geneva to Paris. French linguistics at the time, under the hegemonic influence of Antoine Meillet, opposed [sic] insuperable obstacles to Saussure's acceptance and discussion. That is why Saussure migrated *eastward*, as it were, and found a first institutional landing point in Russia during the first world war. . . . Saussure came to be polemically criticized and rejected in the late twenties (but at least understood in a pertinent light) by the major literary scholar of our century, Mikhail M. Bakhtin" (Angenet, "Structuralism as Syncretism," p. 153). "By the time it becomes de rigueur to read and draw inspiration from Saussure in France, it is clear that this Saussure is bound to be read through his cosmopolitan tribulations and through layers of superimposed mediations" (p.154). A similar fate seems to have befallen Derrida with the forced migration of his thinking out of its historically specific and momentous force within the history of metaphysics into a kind of terminological adhesive for miscellaneous theories. This applied and mediated "Derridanity" (if not Derrida himself) pushes literary theory perilously close to a one-dimensional phraseological consensus.

3. "What we shall call a *genotext* will include semiotic processes but also the advent of the symbolic. The former includes drives, their disposition, and their division of the body, plus the ecological and social system surrounding the body, such as object and pre-Oedipal relations with parents . . . even though it can be seen in language, the genotext is not linguistic (in the sense understood by structural or generative linguistics). It is, rather, a *process*, which tends to articulate structures that are ephemeral (unstable, threatened by drive charges) . . . the genotext can thus be seen as language's underlying foundation" (Kristeva, p. 86) The genotext is distinguished from the *phenotext*, which Kristeva uses to denote "language that serves to communicate, which linguistics describes in terms of 'competence' and 'performance.'" The phenotext "is a structure" and "obeys roles of communication and presupposes a subject of enunciation and an addressee. The genotext, on the other hand, is a process; it moves through zones that have relative and transitory borders and constitutes a *path* that is not restricted to the two poles of univocal information between two full-fledged subjects" (p. 87).

4. Georges Bataille, equally alert to the threat of appropriation and the implications of transgression, provides a curious solution to the problem of critical annexation. In his book *Sur Nietzsche*, Bataille demonstrates the proposition that to *not* betray an author, one must *not respect him*. "I could only write the projected book on Nietzsche *with my life*" (*Oeuvres complètes*, 6:17). Accordingly, Bataille writes an autobiography and thereby avoids reducing Nietzsche to an object of knowledge. Transgression of this kind exploits a practical, not theoretical, modality and thus claims the rank of a *tactic*.

5. In her complex theory of the unconscious, its drives, and their relation to language, Kristeva cites "modalities" and "articulations" that seem to mask an essential foundation. The most problematic concept is that of the *chora* which Kristeva borrows from Plato's *Timaeus* and describes as a "nonexpressive totality formed by the drives and their stases in a motility that is as full of movement as it is regulated" (p. 25). The *chora* purportedly precedes "evidence, verisimilitude, spatiality and temporality," is subject to both "vocal and gestural organization," underlies all figuration, and ranks as "a preverbal functional state" (pp. 26–27). The concept of the *chora* has been criticized by Derrida. In a footnote in *Positions*, Derrida states: "Beside the reading of Benveniste's analyses that I cited in 'La double séance,' the works and teachings of H. Wismann and J. Bollack also have guided me on this terrain. In the course of a seminar at the École Normale, I attempted to investigate the text of the *Timaeus* from this point of view, especially the very problematical notion of the *chora*" (p. 106).

6. Eco provides as an example of the political potential of a tactical, everyday reading *Les Mystères de Paris* by Eugène Sue. Sue's novel was generally considered a fashionable bourgeois consolatory fiction and was ridiculed by both E. A. Poe and Karl Marx. The novel, however, gained an unexpected popularity to such an extent that the book had a direct influence on the popular uprising of 1848. Details of this curious trajectory are contained in Louis Bory, "Presentation," in Eugène Sue, *Les Mystères de Paris* (Paris: Pauvert, 1963).

7. In full fairness to Kristeva, mention should be made of a less culpable theorization. In "Psychoanalysis and the Polis," Kristeva outlines a posthermeneutic enterprise. "The modern interpreter avoids the presentness of subjects to themselves and to things. . . . Breaking out of the enclosure of the presentness of meaning, the *new* 'interpreter' no longer interprets: he speaks, he 'associates,' because there is no longer an object to interpret; there is, instead, the setting-off of semantic, logical, phantasmatic and indeterminable sequences. As a result, a fiction, an uncentred discourse, a subjective polytopia comes about, cancelling the metalinguistic status of the discourses currently governing the post-analytic fate of interpretation." What Kristeva envisions is the intervention of desire into interpretive procedure with the resultant addition of a *transforming* to an *interpreting* power. "I would suggest that the wise interpreter give way to delirium so that, out of his desire, the imaginary may join interpretive closure, thus producing a perpetual interpretive creative force." Underlying her theory is the Freudian concept of the *Spaltung*, the basal breach in subjectivity, which holds configuratively and unpredictably a subject of desire and a subject of knowledge. It would seem then that the "new interpreter" provides the readerly counterpart to the writerly subject-in-process of Kristevan textual practice. It further renders my initial assessment, if not facile, then certainly deficient. Indeed, it is now possible to cite Finas's *La Crue* as an exemplary text of Kristeva's postanalytic theory. For a full presentation, see "Psychoanalysis and the Polis," in *The Kristeva Reader*, ed. Toril Moi (Oxford: Basil Blackwell, 1986), pp. 301–20, from which the above quotations are taken.

Works Cited

Angenet, Marc. "Structuralism as Syncretism: Institutional Distortions of Saussure." *The Structural Allegory*, ed. John Fekete. Minneapolis: University of Minnesota Press, 1984.

Bataille, Georges. *Guilty*, trans. Bruce Boone. Venice: Lapis Press, 1988.

———. *Inner Experience*, Trans. Leslie Anne Boldt. Albany: State University of New York, 1988.

———. *Oeuvres Complètes*. Paris: Gallimard, 1970–.

———. *Visions of Excess: Selected Writings, 1927–1939*, trans. Allan Stoekl, with C. R. Lovitt and D. M. Leslie, Jr. Minneapolis: University of Minnesota Press, 1985.

Baudrillard, Jean. *The Ecstasy of Communication*, trans. Bernard and Caroline Schutze. New York: Semiotext(e) Foreign Agent Series, 1988.

Certeau, Michel de. *The Practice of Everyday Life*, trans. Steven Rendall. Berkeley: University of California Press, 1984.

Derrida, Jacques. *Positions*, trans. Alan Bass. Chicago: University of Chicago Press, 1981.

Eco, Umberto. *The Role of the Reader*. Bloomington: Indiana University Press, 1979.

Finas, Lucette. *La Crue*. Paris: Gallimard, 1972. Quoted in Peter B. Kussel, "From the Anus to the Mouth to the Eye." *Semiotext(e)* II, no. 2 (1976).

Foucault, Michel. "The Discourse on Language." *The Archaeology of Knowledge,* trans. A. M. Sheridan Smith. New York: Harper, 1976.

Hollier, Denis. *Against Architecture,* trans. Betsy Wing. Cambridge: MIT Press, 1989.

Johnson, Ronald. *Radi os.* Berkeley: Sand Dollar, 1977.

Krieger, Murray. *Theory of Criticism.* Baltimore: Johns Hopkins University Press, 1976.

―――. "'A Waking Dream': The Symbolic Alternative to Allegory." *Allegory, Myth, and Symbol,* ed. Morton W. Bloomfield. Cambridge: Harvard University Press, 1981.

Kristeva, Julia. *Revolution in Poetic Language,* trans. Margaret Waller. New York: Columbia University Press, 1984.

Lyotard, Jean-François. *The Differend: Phrases in Dispute,* trans. Georges Van Den Abbeele. Minneapolis: University of Minnesota Press, 1988.

Plato. "Socrates' Defense (Apology)," trans. Hugh Tredennick. *The Collected Dialogues,* ed. Edith Hamilton and Huntington Cairns. New York: Bollingen Foundation, 1961.

Afterwords

Ross J. Pudaloff

Is not "The Ends of Theory" a strange title? Read as the conventions of English would seem to demand, the title would seem to suggest a multiplicity of meanings for *ends* but a singularity, thus an agreement, about *theory*—that is, some agreement about its identity with itself and/or for a community of interpretation. Or at least some agreement about what theory might do, even if what remains unclear or disputed. As I head down this path, a voice in my head says, as it may for readers, "We know what we mean by theory." A voice that might ask, echoing Archie Bunker and Paul de Man, "What's the difference?" A voice, that is, that might restrict interrogating the grammar of the title in order to get on with thinking about the various significations of *ends*—as the sermon title has it, "Whither are we going?"

That question, however, echoes oddly even if we shift defining theory from being to doing. After all, whatever theory is/was, it seldom ever claimed what theory ordinarily claims in intellectual discourse, namely to predict and to be evaluated in terms of the accuracy of predictions. That end of theory seems not only excluded but even irrelevant to whatever has been going on in the human sciences. On the contrary—poststructuralism's capacity to describe "whither" is itself ruled out on intellectual as well as practical grounds, even granting there is such as thing as poststructuralism.

So then, theories. Yet unity is asserted even as multiplicity is omnipresent. As an indicator of unity, if not exactly empirical evidence, consider the two popular anthologies edited by Hazard Adams, *Critical Theory since Plato* and *Critical Theory since 1965*. Both are clearly designed to meet the end of the transmission of knowledge; both suggest that theory is necessary for a literary education; both, in using the singular as this book does, imply that theory is one distinct and definable category, stable enough to be labeled, separated, and studied. On the other hand, as books of comparable size, covering almost ludicrously different time periods, the two texts whisper to the reader (as Twain puts it in his novel of identity and difference, *Pudd'nhead Wilson*) of discontinuities in the very center of identity (and, of course, the other way around). And at least one of these discontinuities is how much more theory we have to know and transmit to students post-1965, certainly provoking the questions of whether all this new theory (as it must, or why such a book as *Critical Theory since 1965*) hangs together and what differentiates it from everything from Plato on up.

So then, theory. Easier to imagine its end or ends if it is an it. Its singularity can, as has been pointed out elsewhere, be understood as a provisional "American" construction of what did not appear at all unified in European contexts. And with the evidence of *Critical Theory since Plato* and *Critical Theory since 1965* available either way, perhaps one should shift the question. Ask not whether theory is itself but rather what has theory, since 1965, done and why we can proclaim it has an End and or is at an end. If the first question can be answered, is not the second one also? One answer offered here is that theory (pre- and post-1965 alike) can be understood usefully as offering varying answers to a single question, that of the production of meaning(s), whether we take a word, a sentence, a traditional literary text, a film, a television program, a discourse, a society, a culture, etc., as the object of inquiry. Hence the break ascribed to 1965 is the appearance of arguments over the stability, indeed the existence, of meaning. This is a ruthless oversimplification and, as such, ought be regarded with skepticism and evaluated by its usefulness in this argument, as this argument needs to be evaluated in its place within the afterword, the afterword in terms of the volume, the volume in terms of the particular academic discourse in which it appears, and so on.

Every system of production, and every product therein produced, cannot be understood, however, except insofar as we consider both the value of the cultural capital it produces and, as importantly, its necessary complement of consumption. I recognize how that statement is itself informed by a taking for granted of "late" capitalism. If I only note here that theory has functioned as a source of wealth whose possession signified membership in an elite, I do so because the case seems obvious. Hence, the cynic might suggest that the dissemination of theory to the masses has caused its downfall. As Edith Wharton noted, "your real collector values a thing for its rarity" (*The House of Mirth*, p. 13). It was not the ideas, after all, but rather their scarcity—in which case, as I discuss below, the value of theory was consonant with the traditional mission of the academy.

As for consumption, that traces a more devious path, one that leads to (among other places) the rise of Cultural Studies. One might risk the broad generalization that theorizing since 1965 has simultaneously foregrounded and elided consumption because it admitted differences and *différance* to our discussions. Certainly, literary criticism, like capitalism (and, of course, like language itself according to theory), works by constructing endless differences and somehow investing them as desirable. But how? A focus on production of texts, discourses, language, subjects, the Subject—commodities all—and a reading of these categories as themselves systems of production raise a begged question: What does anyone do as consumer? Having always already been whispered to, what is the reader up to, what will that famously slippery figure, who is in many of these arguments, produced in reading that is also writing, make of this, do with this—this including language, text, theory, another grammatical evasion.

In attempting to see what keeping theory singular might lead to, I seem to have included in it both psychologically inflected models (e.g., reader response) and historically situated ones (e.g., Reception Theory). Many, including myself, might object to this as a stretching of a category past the point of usefulness. And others, again including myself, might object to it as performing other exclusions, most notably of race and gender, of postcoloniality, of politics, of morality, which were and are the omissions that may end and/or have damned theory before and after 1965. Twain's whisper, after all, marks the boundary of a literary text that signifies about race and gender—a text that until recently was marginalized because it "failed" both formally and morally. If the latter consideration can be smuggled into the tent or if it seems to mark the limit of theory, then it would seem we have reached an end to the usefulness of theory, whether a singular category or not. One could impose some (Hegelian, I suppose) dialectic to bring all this together, but would that not also involve a teleology that an awful lot of people who claimed to be doing theory took as an object of their critique? Perhaps even to imagine theory as congruent with a metahistorical task is the best evident that theory is at its end.

Or, to put the problem in terms already given: the dispute over determinate meaning and essential identities opened, even as it remained mostly unexplored, the issue of consumption in some large part because meaning and identity were reconceived as contingent effects rather than as necessary givens. From this perspective, much of the "New Historicism," like the old historicism and much else including Reception Theory and Reader Response, would seem to be as theorized, all right, but under the pre-1965 dispensation that continued through what followed (not then so different after all). Insofar as these are methods for determining meaning, for redefining the terms of production, we get new meanings—and often more useful ones—but we remain on the same path. The door that "theory" opened remains so, but who can or will go through it?

My argument, then, is not that (post-1975) theory was too much formalism and too little moralism (to borrow loosely de Man's formulation of the alternatives)—an argument with which I have never had much sympathy but which pervades the call for Cultural Studies and multiculturalism as the necessary correctives to the formalism of theory. Rather, it is that too much of theory and now Cultural Studies was the always already of lit-crit's search for meaning. If it has ended in failure, its failure was the not taking seriously (i.e., playfully) enough the possibilities for dispersion. Theory suggested every reader is a writer and every writer is a reader. It did not do much with the corollary that every reader is a reader. Which is not to advocate psychologizing texts or the world but rather to wonder if the professionals are willing to or could be forced to give up some of the control over interpretation now that we're at the ends of theory.

Easier, however, to call for the academy to give up its claims to determine meaning, which is not at all the same thing as agreeing, as theory suggested, on indeterminacy. Precisely because the gesture of such a call evokes categories we all assent to—openness, community, democracy—it is time to be suspicious and practice a rigorous skepticism about this end of theory. Asking what readers might be up to is not solely a historical question; it is also a political one. And in politics as in morality, a Ph.D. or any other indication of aesthetic or intellectual expertise does not and should not guarantee authority. Trying to understand what readers do with texts, then, involves admitting at least the possibility that they are as right in their interpretations and responses as we in the academy. The problem, of course, is that most members of the academy are less than happy with much of what our society does in its interpretive practices. "Universal Man and Universal Reason" are easy enough to disprove and mock when one is rereading the eighteenth century, but some basis for moral judgment begins to look mighty attractive to the professor when he or she sees what people are consuming. I understand the temptation but urge that we look to theory to resist it.

Theory focuses attention on signifiers as opposed to signifieds, to the sign as "empty and promiscuous," and to discourse and/or language as material and productive. If so, what might be called the representational anxiety of contemporary society is the suitably ironic triumph of theory, albeit one that ignores the variety of things that the reader might be up to. I mean by that phrase the power contemporary society now ascribes to signs and/or representations to affect individuals and groups, the apparent return of the *tabula rasa* as the definition of human nature and thus our apparent vulnerability to the sign. Theory is (was) not only a sign of the times; it also participates in the time of the signs.

Examples of representational anxiety are so numerous that any person might come up with several recent instances. Two come to mind. First, the Walt Disney Studio cut a scene from the film *The Program* in which characters lie down in the middle of a road to prove their manhood. When teenagers emulated this scene and at least one was killed, Disney pulled all the prints, cut the scene, and accepted responsibility. Second, MTV moved its cartoon "Beavis and Butt-head" to a late airtime (10 P.M. rather than 7 P.M.) because a five-year-old child set a fire after having seen the two protagonists do the same. In both cases, at best a provisional acceptance of the notion that signs motivate us to a degree heretofore unthought animated the decision. In a third instance, a rock band by the name of Bare Naked Ladies was removed from a public concert in Toronto in late 1991 because its name was perceived to be sexist and assaultive. This last is particularly ironic because, like such bands as Pearl Jam and Nirvana, Bare Naked Ladies is "politically correct" to a fault. Nonetheless, the name was enough—the sign wielded a power independent of intention or, for that matter, reception by most—or, indeed, independent of listening to the lyrics, hitherto the minimum standard for such interpretive practices.

How many examples are enough? Perhaps it is enough to cite the effort of Attorney General Janet Reno in seeking to limit television violence because it causes real violence. According to one poll, 80 percent of the American public assented to this proposition. Nor are these concerns confined to the United States. More than one person has argued that the decline of the American empire is nowhere more evident than in the fact that the rest of the world only wants the products of our entertainment industry. For things, the world goes elsewhere; but the United States is preeminent in the production and dissemination of signs. American television shows and movies pervade the world, raising nationalist anxieties everywhere and being blamed for the collapse of "traditional" cultures in Nepal, New Guinea, and, of course, the former Soviet Union. Setting aside any debate over the merits of such claims—and, indeed, setting aside whether Americans produce the best representations and the worst products—should make it clear that these debates and debaters all assume that signs have power, that in Baudrillard's postmodern world, he or she who makes the best simulacra wins. We are experiencing, as Fredric Jameson has pointed out, a transition from "the waning of affect" to its replacement by "intensities" ("Postmodernism," pp. 61, 64).

My mother used to say, "If your friend jumped in the lake, would you?" when she objected to some piece of idiocy on my part. At the time, I found her logic impeccable, even if I disagreed with its application in any particular instance. She did not imagine—nor did I in that more innocent age—that I might be more likely to jump in the lake if I saw it on television or in a movie. Yet such is now the case, if one can trust the media's representation of its effect on the rest of us.

What is going on, then, in the academy, in the United States, and in the rest of the world differs from the recurrent bouts of censorship that mark our history. We are not (just) witnessing what is conventionally (and incorrectly) described as the effect of our Puritan heritage, the usual explanation proffered and accepted in these cases. While anxiety over the power of representations—an anxiety that more or less dates from the beginning of print and the consequent dissemination of information and images to an audience in some sense beyond the control of cultural elites—has marked modernity, the ascription of power to signs has increased mightily, largely, one guesses, because of the explosion of technology and the coming of the information age. And, with it, anxiety. That is, a crucial shift has occurred from behavior to sign as the locus of power simply because we are better at producing and distributing signs. The "aura" has moved from the unique work of art and from an elite audience to (potentially) any sign and all of us. As Walter Benjamin wrote, "a plurality of copies" is substituted "for a unique existence" ("The Work of Art," p. 221).

Both theoreticians and practitioners of Cultural Studies have sought to make of this replacement a professional opportunity. The movement away from literature and the arts to reading an ever-increasing number of signs, media, and signifying practices, finally the culture itself—a movement spurred by theory's apparent capacity to decode—seemed to extend the authority of the academy into and over the world. Now it seems clear that the academy's understanding of its mission, based as that was on an economy of scarcity, has been transformed, and with it has come the prospect of a loss of professorial authority. As Benjamin also noted, "it is inherent in the technique of the film . . . that everybody who witnesses its accomplishments is somewhat of an expert" (p. 231). Cultural Studies, then, as theory's successor, might best be viewed as a tactic to recapture authority for a professional elite not simply through more fully extending the range of analysis but crucially through the (rhe-torical) call for political intervention to (re)claim what never was—the vanguard role for the intellectual. Hence, as was the case with theory, and now with Cultural Studies, the only constant has been the complaint by their practitioners about the ills of domestication, a discursive practice so congenial that we have perhaps not said the obvious: that being, of course, that domestication implies its extra- or precivilized other, the golden age that remains just within living memory of the academic who will evaluate students on the basis of their memories of and resemblance to the golden past. Is it neces-sary to remind ourselves that this is the always already of the acad-emy, its (perhaps necessary) conservatism at work? In any case, complaints about domestication of theory imply the possession of "the real thing" by a small group.

The illusion of those within the academy that controlling in-terpretation in the classroom necessarily will determine the world outside the university is operative only in an economy of scarcity. Perhaps such was the case when I. A. Richards was training a small number of young men to run the empire through close reading of a relatively few texts. It is unlikely to be the case now. A university education, especially one in the liberal arts, prepares one for unem-ployment in part because there are too many English majors for our economy to absorb and in part because Americans don't believe a literary education fits one to rule. Of course, the latter is exactly what the professors believe insofar as we believed our professors.

Moreover, especially given the lack of rewards, it's doubtful that our students are so easily written over in assenting to our theo-ries and methods. One would think the delusion would fall of its own weight. Since it hasn't, as the stridency of what are not quite (in any classical sense) arguments about the contents of the canon and speech codes on campus makes clear, one shouldn't be sur-prised that the move at the end of theory to Cultural Studies is a form of colonization, an attempt to bring under our benign gaze that which was allegedly devalued and marginalized. (Is it neces-sary to write the banality that a diversity of texts, minds, experi-ences, etc., are to be welcomed?) The proper answer to this piece of foolishness is a question: Devalued by whom? The arrogance in as-suming that the transvaluation of values somehow rests in the hands of the academics, that gays, women, Asians, persons of color, immigrants, et al., despised their experience until we said it was good is breathtaking—and nauseating.

What becomes clear, then, at the end of theory is the transfor-mation of how academics understand the mission of the academy. Once (maybe), when there were a few students, a few professors (all WASPS, all males in my personal mythology), the control of interpretation might have been correlated with access to power outside the institution. Thinking and writing about the "other" and "intervening," in themselves admirable, are no more likely to restore an age better off dead than they are to lead to a transformed social order.

Theory and Cultural Studies undoubtedly are better understood as a symptom than a cause of this condition and these anxieties; that is, inside and part of this phenomenon rather than safely outside and explanatory. The end of theory, its apparent replacement in the academy by approaches that stress history and politics, is thus not just the usual swing between formalism and historicism and certainly not the progressive triumph of better interpretive models supplanting their predecessors. Rather, theory's passing from the scene may be understood as the corollary of the ascription of power to signs, namely that signs and wonders, deriving their power from themselves rather than from reference or representation, have a very short shelf life. History occurs first as commodity, then as sign. Theory's triumph is its end. But, like any sign, it might be that recirculated Simulacra, like radio waves, never go away completely and never return as they were.

Works Cited

Adams, Hazard, ed. *Critical Theory since 1965*. Tallahassee: Florida State University Press, 1986.

———. *Critical Theory since Plato*. New York: Harcourt Brace Jovanovich, 1971.

Benjamin, Walter. "The Work of Art in the Age of Mechanical Reproduction." *Illuminations*, ed. Hannah Arendt. New York: Schocken Books, 1969.

De Man, Paul. "Semiology and Rhetoric." *Allegories of Reading: Figural Language in Rousseau, Nietzsche, Rilke, and Proust*. New Haven: Yale University Press, 1979.

Jameson, Fredric. "Postmodernism, or the Cultural Logic of Late Capitalism." *New Left Review* 146 (July–August 1984): 33–92.

Twain, Mark. *Pudd'nhead Wilson* (1894). Oxford and New York: Oxford University Press, 1992.

Wharton, Edith. *The House of Mirth* (1905). New York: New American Library, 1964.

Dorothy Huson

When (in the Book of Numbers) Balak, king of the Moabites, recognizes that the advancing Israelites are too great in number for him, he hires Balaam, a soothsayer, to "put a curse on" the Israelites so that he will be able "to give battle and drive them away." Balak's action is based on his knowledge of Balaam's reputation. "I know," he says, "that those whom you bless are blessed, and those whom you curse are cursed." Balaam wants to do what Balak asks, but he cannot. He explains to Balak: "I have come, as you see. But now that I am here, what power have I of myself to say anything? It is only whatever word God puts into my mouth that I can speak."[1]

Balak, hoping nonetheless that Balaam can do as he has asked, positions him on a mountain where he can see all the Israelites and provides him with animal sacrifices whose entrails he may read, but the words given to Balaam (and the oracle he speaks) are a blessing for Israel. So Balak takes him to another mountain, where he still has a view of the Israelites but "not the full extent of them" (Numbers 23:13); the words of the oracle are still a blessing. Then Balak takes him to a third place, saying, "Perhaps God will be pleased to let you curse them for me there" (Numbers 23:27). But Balaam, accepting Yahweh's decision, does not "resort to divination as before" (Numbers 24:1) but looks only at the Israelites and utters a final oracular blessing.

This narrative illustrates both the value placed on the *logos* in Greek and Judeo-Christian cultures and the frustration of those who would like to control the power ascribed to the text. Balaam desires the wealth and position promised to him as payment for producing the required curse and so risks his life by defying Yahweh's will. But as Balak moves him from one position to another, sacrificing new animals at each site to provide additional text, Balaam reads only—and, consequently, can speak only—blessings for the Israelites. No matter which text he reads, the "truth" is the same. Yahweh's speech and actions will create a univocal text in which speaking and acting are both present. So Balak turns out to have chosen a curse maker unwisely. He has correctly assessed the power of Balaam's words; those whom Balaam curses are indeed cursed (including the doomed Moabites). But he has failed to realize that the authority, truth, and power of Balaam's words derive from the fact that he is not the site of their origin. To be useful to the Moabites, Balaam needs to construct a text according to Balak's desire that Yahweh will stand behind. But Balaam is revealed to be a reader, not a writer; thus, he can know Yahweh's will but cannot control it.

It is this model of reading and writing that contemporary literary theories are often said to question. By insisting that texts are constructed within cultures—that they respond to the same pressures as other structures within cultures—poststructuralism denies the power of texts to reveal truths other than self-reflexive insights. By insisting on the insufficiency of linguistic systems ultimately to control or to determine meaning, deconstruction turns attention from the single author toward multiple readers and their multiplicity of interpretations. Thus, whereas Balaam reads the same message in all the different entrails, deconstruction would claim an endless proliferation of interpretations of the same entrails. Whereas Balaam reads the same truth on all three mountains, poststructural theory would deny the availability of any such privileged position and, further, would claim that since Balaam's oracles are spoken in a language constructed by his culture and in a discourse constructed by the traditions of divinatory practices, no unmediated, unique revelation would be possible.

But while such arguments question the power of texts to perform in certain ways, they also serve to illustrate the power of texts to engage us, to provide a space (or a time) for the discursive practices in which we find various pleasures. They also suggest that while we delight in challenging particular assumptions or interpretations, we are careful not to suggest that there is no point in interrogating the text.

Therefore, despite the claimed opposition between poststructuralism and hermeneutics, poststructural critics have not produced a large number of texts that refuse to interpret, nor have they encouraged a kind of interpretation that consists of only a group of competing texts. Although structuralist (including semiotic) critics have proposed ahistorical, nonevaluative models for production of texts, structuralism has not opened a space in the academy in which critical texts themselves can be read in a dehistoricized, nonevaluative way. Although structuralism and poststructuralism have questioned the concept of plagiarism, the assumption that a writer can own a text and can in some sense define the boundaries of a text continues to operate within the academy and elsewhere. We have seen that a critic may argue against the possibility of arriving at "the one/right" interpretation without being willing to value all interpretations to the same degree. Arguing that a text is constructed of various texts rather than "created" has not devalued the agent or the writing process (though it may seem so to a reader who valorizes "creation"); in fact, the difficulty of many texts produced in the practice of "literary theory" has operated, along with arguments that question the distinction between "primary" and "secondary" texts, to bring increased attention to critical writing and to specific theorists.

But that is not to say that literary theory has not made a difference. Rather, I would argue that much of the attraction of theory has been its ability to encourage critical discourse (to keep the game going) by opening up bases of difference largely overlooked by critics of the preceding few decades. I am not suggesting here that literary theories have discovered something previously unseen; I mean only that reading always involves overlooking and that a "new" reading involves overlooking something different from the "other" reading. For some critics, contact with theory has produced a sort of updated postlapsarian angst. But the reading that occasions their despair opens a space for John Caputo's "radical" hermeneutics, which he defines as "a sustained attempt to write from below, without celestial, transcendental justifications."[2] In fact, poststructuralism has encouraged a resurgence of biblical study among scholars of both literature and theology. Examples include Terry Eagleton's interrogation of the book of Jonah as a commentary on political action in "J. L. Austin and the Book of Jonah";[3] Mieke Bal's various considerations of gender issues in biblical texts;[4] and Meir Sternberg's studies of biblical narrative.[5] Stephen Moore, surveying the influence of literary theory on biblical studies, says: "Convinced now of the necessity of an iconoclastic moment in biblical studies . . .—a revision, though not a rejection, of foundational concepts such as Bible and exegesis—I feel a spring-like quickening of my intellectual and spiritual sap such as I have not felt since historical criticism's first rude accostation mated my quest for Reality . . . with a questioning."[6]

It is this kind of awakening interest that we hope for when we read, just as it is those moments in which the text falls inexplicably silent that we most dread. Whether we believe in the possibility of a privileged position or not, whether we look at reading as divination or diversion, what seems to matter most is that the text should not fall silent. So at a moment when historical (biblical) criticism and structuralism seemed intent on bringing textual interpretation into line with scientific methodologies, strategies that opened additional texts for many readers but closed off other areas of inquiry and metadiscourses, Derrida posed his "two interpretations of interpretation": "The one seeks to decipher, dreams of deciphering, a truth or an origin which is free from freeplay and from the order of the sign, and lives like an exile the necessity of interpretation. The other, which is no longer turned toward the origin, affirms freeplay and tries to pass beyond man and humanism."[7] Here and elsewhere, Derrida points toward the narrow band of human experiences in a gesture that may be read as both humbling and liberating. Our interpretations are, he says, bounded by the limits of our discursive practices so that the site of the text and the site of the interpretation are indistinguishable. We cannot "know"; we can only discern relations—unstable relations that shift as signifiers and signifieds float free of our control. Thus, the lack of referentiality between the word and the world, the impossibility of recovering or representing "reality," offers infinite uncertainty along with infinite discursive potential.

But, again, Derridean discourse does not speak to or encourage other texts to speak to everyone, nor am I arguing that any poststructuralist theory is "true" or verifiable in the "real world." I only want to suggest that those theories are not usefully (or correctly) placed in opposition to hermeneutics but, rather, that they interrogate parts of texts that are silent in response to some kinds of "truth-seeking" questions and describe conditions of reading and writing that derive from or coexist with (rather than contradict) the practice of hermeneutics. Hermeneutics is usually described as assuming a stable relationship between signifier and signified, a condition that would depend on (or result in) a perceptible ordering of reality. Biblical hermeneutics in particular is often defined as a project that intends to reconcile apparent contradictions or pluralities in biblical texts by appealing to the "high" spiritual truth or "deep" structure that makes scripture a closed system, sufficient in itself. But although the closings of the biblical canons were posited on the assumption that at particular historical moments what had been written was sufficient, there is evidence that both Jewish and Christian compilers included some biblical material as interpretive of other earlier biblical material, an act that questions the sufficiency of even the most sacred text. Further, even the most ancient biblical texts indicate that neither laws and covenants nor narratives are sufficient to reveal Yahweh's will or to order human behavior. There are moments in which the law and Yahweh are silent.

Standing inside and outside the laws—included among the minute details of prescribed ritual—are alternative ways to knowledge and determiners of action that fall under the general category of divination. Despite Yahweh's proscription against foretelling the future or practicing sorcery, divination of various kinds seems to have been practiced by kings, patriarchs, and priests; and the "casting of lots" is commanded by Yahweh himself as a means of dividing the promised land[8] and distributing priestly duties.[9] At those moments, the text acknowledges that the concrete specific moment is not accounted for—not perceptible—in the general rule, and so provides an alternative discourse that is discontinuous with but not opposed to "the law." Thus, in 1 Samuel 14, when Saul has fallen from favor with Yahweh and stands outside the law, casting lots offers him access to information that the law cannot supply and that Yahweh otherwise withholds. Having defeated the Philistines in the day's battle and having erected his first altar, Saul determines to attack the Philistines again that night, but on the advice of the priest he consults God: "Saul enquired of God, 'Shall I pursue the Philistines? Will you put them into Israel's power?' But this time he received no answer" (37). The problem is that Jonathan, not having

heard Saul's interdict against eating before the Philistines are defeated, has refreshed himself with honey. Thus, Saul knows the law
(having pronounced it himself) but does not know what Jonathan
has done; and Jonathan knows what he has done but does not
know it is against the law; and the law itself can define guilt but
cannot identify it. So when Yahweh refuses to speak, Saul has recourse only to the binary code of casting lots: "Saul said to the Lord
the God of Israel, 'Why have you not answered your servant today?
Lord God of Israel, if this guilt lies in me or in my son Jonathan, let
the lot be Urim; if it lies in your people Israel, let it be Thummim.'
Jonathan and Saul were taken, and the people were cleared. Then
Saul said, 'Cast lots between me and my son Jonathan'; and Jonathan was taken" (41–42). In this way, the law is recognized as insuf-
ficient and is supplemented but is not rejected. Yahweh is silent, revealing his disapproval, but Saul is not denied an answer.

Another instance—one that points in a different way to the insufficiency of the law—is the choosing of the goat "for Azazel"
(sometimes incorrectly translated "scapegoat"). After Aaron's sons
have died for offering "illicit fire," Yahweh tells Moses what Aaron
must do for expiation: "Then he must take the two he-goats and set
them before the Lord at the entrance to the Tent of Meeting. He
must cast lots over the two goats, one to be for the Lord and the
other for Azazel. He must present the goat on which the lot for the
Lord has fallen and deal with it as a purification offering; but the
goat on which the lot for Azazel has fallen is to be made to stand
alive before the Lord, for expiation to be made over it, before it is
driven away into the wilderness to Azazel" (Leviticus 16). In this
narrative, the law explains the guilt of Aaron's house and provides
a means of purification, but it does not identify which goat is to live
and which is to die. The goats provide a locus for the enacting of the
law, but they themselves are outside the law; their guilt or innocence is not a cause of their being selected but a result. They are arbitrarily (though ritually) chosen/signified and, once caught in the
system of signification, can be defined according to moral law and
exchanged for guilty humans, thereby signifying the fulfillment of
the law.

Thus, biblical texts repeatedly make the "both/and" gesture of
refusing to invalidate the law while acknowledging its insufficiency.
This is, I would argue, the main rhetorical gesture of the New Testa-
ment: to claim that the law has been fulfilled rather than erased,
that it operates toward the past to validate the Messiah but is un-
necessary for the future. Accepting the new covenant at once vali-
dates the old covenant and renders it inoperative. This point is
made most clearly in John (often called the most philosophical of

the gospels). Pilate, caught in a difficult position constructed by his impression that Jesus is innocent, the claims of the priests that Jesus has broken their religious law, and the threat that his defense of Jesus will be interpreted as sedition, questions Jesus himself, who answers him with questions and evasions: " 'So you are the king of the Jews,' he said. Jesus replied, 'Is that your own question, or have others suggested it to you?' 'Am I a Jew?' said Pilate. . . . 'You are a king then?' said Pilate. Jesus answered, 'King is your word. My task is to bear witness to the truth.' . . . Pilate said, 'What is truth?' " (John 18:33–38).

In the next chapter, Pilate, not having figured out the "truth," hears the law instead: "The Jews answered, 'We have a law; and according to that law he ought to die, because he has claimed to be God's Son.' When Pilate heard that, he was more afraid than ever, and going back into his headquarters he asked Jesus, 'Where have you come from?' But Jesus gave him no answer. 'Do you refuse to speak to me?' said Pilate. 'Surely you know that I have authority to release you, and authority to crucify you?' 'You would have no authority at all over me if it had not been granted to you from above; and therefore the deeper guilt lies with the one who handed me over to you'" (John 19:7–11).

Thus, Jesus becomes the means by which the guilty satisfy the law by rejecting the truth. As an innocent one justly put to death by the law, Jesus will "bear witness to the truth." As is the case with Jonathan's sin, the law explains the basis for guilt but does not identify the guilty. As with other sin offerings, Jesus must stand outside the law and then must be brought under the law so that guilt may be transferred to the guiltless. The rupture between law and truth, between guilt and punishment, between signifier and signified appears again when Pilate, who has received no satisfaction from the competing religious and civil laws, becomes a writer himself and commands that an inscription be affixed to the cross, reading "Jesus of Nazareth, King of the Jews." When the priests complain that he should have written, "He claimed to be king of the Jews," Pilate turns the implacability of the already-written back on the upholders of the law, saying, "What I have written, I have written" (John 19:19–22). Thus, the man who has "no authority" is made to write "the truth." Significantly, then, the text continues: "When the soldiers had crucified Jesus they took his clothes and, leaving aside the tunic, divided them into four parts, one for each soldier. The tunic was seamless, woven in one piece throughout; so they said one to another, 'We must not tear this; let us toss for it.' Thus the text of the scripture came true: 'They cast lots for my clothing'" (Psalms

22:18). Here again, as in choosing the goat for Azazel, the law requires an appeal to random occurrence and is satisfied and validated in arbitrary choice.

This, I would argue, is one inescapable position of the reader. Whether one "dreams of deciphering" or "affirms play," the reader's or writer's next move is to some extent determined by the prior move—the text that is already written/read—and is to some extent arbitrary. Further, we cannot know at any point which kind of interpretation we are engaged in. How can we even differentiate between casting lots for the promised land and throwing the dice to put a hotel on Boardwalk?

As I said earlier, this kind of reading has in the past decade allowed some critics to keep writing, whether in pleasure or in outrage (and I do not mean to imply that these are contradictory positions). In the final paragraph of *The Genesis of Secrecy*, Frank Kermode says:

> World and book, it may be, are hopelessly plural, endlessly disappointing; we stand alone before them, aware of their arbitrariness and impenetrability, knowing that they may be narratives only because of our impudent intervention, and susceptible of interpretation only by our hermetic tricks. Hot for secrets, our only conversation may be with guardians who know less and see less than we can; and our sole hope and pleasure is in the perception of a momentary radiance, before the door of disappointment is finally shut on us.[10]

But that was in 1979. Poststructural readings no longer arouse either the pleasure or the outrage that they once were capable of, so it is time to move on to different metaphors that construct a different set of relationships among textual elements. What those relationships will be is a matter of intense interest to those who conceive literary criticism as their work, but writers (like Pilate, Balaam, and Balak) are continually reminded that they are not in charge of the discourse. Their function is to articulate what was, in some sense, already there and to destabilize it if possible, to open a different and differing space for another round of play. Important questions, then, for those who want to predict the next fashion in criticism would be, "What obvious textual aspects has poststructuralism overlooked in order to make its case?" and "Which mountain do we need to stand on in order to articulate what we are overlooking?"

Notes

1. Numbers 22, *The Oxford Study Bible* (New York: Oxford University Press, 1992).

2. John D. Caputo, *Radical Hermeneutics: Repetition, Deconstruction, and the Hermeneutic Project* (Bloomington: Indiana University Press, 1987), p. 272.

3. Printed in *The Book and the Text*, ed. Regina M. Schwartz (Cambridge, Mass.: Basil Blackwell, 1990), pp. 231–36.

4. *Murder and Difference: Gender, Genre and Scholarship on Sisera's Death* (1983); *Death and Dissymmetry: The Politics of Coherence in Judges* (1988); and *Lethal Love: Literary Feminist Readings of Biblical Love Stories* (1987).

5. Meir Sternberg, *The Poetics of Biblical Narrative: Ideological Literature and the Drama of Reading* (Bloomington: Indiana University Press, 1985).

6. Stephen D. Moore, *Literary Criticism and the Gospels: The Theoretical Challenge* (New Haven and London: Yale University Press, 1989), pp. 176–77.

7. "Structure, Sign, and Play in the Discourse of the Human Sciences," in *The Critical Tradition: Classic Texts and Critical Trends*, ed. David H. Richter (New York: St. Martin's Press, 1989), p. 970.

8. Joshua 18.

9. Chronicles 24:3, 19; and Luke 1:9.

10. Frank Kermode, *The Genesis of Secrecy* (Cambridge, Mass.: Harvard University Press, 1979), p. 145.

Robert Strozier

Theory as a term is itself subject to a certain dispersion: from its traditional sense as the formal structure necessary to practice, it came to signify on the one hand the disciplined assumption of a questionable metaphysics which was then used to regulate thought, and on the other, especially in the United States, a transdisciplinary questioning of precisely those strategic relations of metaphysics and discourse. The organizers of "The Ends of Theory" conference and the authors of this collection of essays certainly have had the latter signification in mind, however often they may have found themselves compromised by the former. That, of course, was one of the original ends of theory: to point out how we continually compromised ourselves.

However, the idea of poststructural theory itself, as commentators have made clear, is an American phenomenon, the result of a certain kind of focus against the self-assuredness of Enlightenment rationality present in all the academic disciplines; this movement only began to gain quantifiable force when "it"—although poststructuralism as such never existed in France—was in decline in its country of "origin," at the end of the 1970s. In the 1980s, French intellectuals were issuing warnings about the political dangers of pursuing the idea of a "subject of discourse," and even Foucault, as it is widely reported, fell back in 1984 in his dying works onto the doctrine of a self-creating subject (Miller, Poster, etc.). And the poststructuralists of the 1960s and 1970s in Paris seem not to have been a group united by the questioning of metaphysics and hegemony but—so they have been described—as gargantuan egos vying for Sartre's mantle as the leading French intellectual (Miller, Poster). In the light of Derrida's critique of speech (set in a phenomenologist-subjective framework), Foucault's genealogy as a history without subjects and in general the critique of the autonomous subject, this "reality" is delightfully ironic. It raises a question of closure that will reappear presently.

In the United States, poststructuralism has had a unifying effect. Our own transformation of disparate (from a Parisian point of view) intellectual activity spearheaded the assault on traditional academic thought and replaced it with a continuous questioning of literally every assumption and metaphysic (or so it seemed). But the era of theory is familiar. What comes after? What has ended and what begun? There is a certain return, a certain fragmentation—although poststructuralism was rarely more than a vocal minority in the United States.

Poststructuralism, of course, has been perceived by both the extreme right and the left as politically dangerous, if not utterly useless, and often in the same terms as in France: the dangers of individual irresponsibility (the case of de Man, e.g.); the dangers inherent in the failure of totalization, which could lead to cultural incoherence (or already has) or to the lack of the unity necessary for revolution or change; the loss of an objective standard such as reason, or the absolute politicization of knowledge, by means of which the very idea of "politics" becomes amorphous and useless as an instrument of change.

The subject is a case in point. From the structuralist notion of the "death of the subject" in Barthes and others to the poststructuralist version of the individual subjected to and produced by discourses/practices, the one simply to elide the questioning of subjectivity and the other to take seriously and to work through those poststructural problematics of the subject—on the one side the inheritance of the autonomous subject present in the tradition since Descartes and Kant, and on the other the need to restore a sense of agency post-poststructurally.

The first route tends to characterize the poststructural questioning as excess, as in the following quotation taken from a cultural historian writing on the Victorian period:

Foucault and other poststructuralists have called into question the authority of the subject as a free, autonomous author of a text [we know what essay of Foucault she read]. Yet the fact that subjects are culturally determined does not mean that "human agency in a changing world is for the most part illusory." That individuals do not fully author their texts does not falsify Marx's insight that men (and women) make their own history, albeit under circumstances they do not produce or fully control. (Walkowitz, p. 9)

This statement shows no interest in the problematics of subjectivity at all; Walkowitz employs a strategy of splitting the difference so that she may no longer be deterred from the task of history, where subjectivity remains unproblematic. On the other hand, it is possible, as some critics have argued, to work through these issues on the road to a new problematic. Interestingly enough, not a few of these critics attempt to reinvent the Frankfurt School by such means (Dews, Poster). Another related instance: the attempt to reestablish a sense of individual agency by working through the generally poststructural sense of the subject constituted by discourse, but in particular the insertion of the individual into the discontinuous discourses of the symbolic—the Lacanian process by which subjectification occurs, but in which agency can be seen to produce itself in the gaps and discontinuities between constitutive discourses (e.g., Smith).

Poststructuralism's critique of reason and objective knowledge, when it came into contact in the United States with the earlier social movements of the 1960s, civil rights, minority rights, and ethnic consciousness, fostered an interest in the margins that was critical of centralized and hegemonic reason (as it was then seen). Feminism, which developed out of the movements of the 1960s, has become probably the strongest such force in the academy in the United States. Given the dangers inherent in representation—the traditional intellectual who "spoke for" the oppressed or included the other gender—there was a necessity for both the demise of the universal intellectual and the appearance of a new, specific intellectual (Foucault); that is, in terms of the problematic of subjectivity in poststructuralism, a tendency both to make use of a notion of the subject and to establish a new orientation while maintaining a general sense of the disappearance of autonomous subjectivity. This new kind of subject was to speak from the margins, to speak of its victimage and, by speaking, to manifest an always occulted power.

Given the problematics of essentialism in feminism, the repetition at the margins of the subjectivity and power of the center, there can be little doubt that a notion of the autonomous subject has returned to our discourses—a subject constituted by structures into which it is inserted but also able to gain some perspective on that structure and its own "having been structured." What else do we have here but a repetition of the self-reflexive subject of the Enlightenment? Yet Foucault says that self-reflexivity characterizes the modern and postmodern age.

If the thematic of the subject of discourse leads to a return, so does the poststructuralist notion of the politics of knowledge. This has led to a new constitution of knowledge—a notion of a regime of truth. But like the notion of the subject constituted by discourse, this notion has proved too open-ended and has led to a return. It has led in the post-post-age to the pushing of political agendas, to the kind of moral closure that is often noticed in cultural studies—an agenda to empower the margins—less reprehensible than liable to a forgetting and thus a return in those who persist in "speaking for" the margins. We seem in short to have come to a new age that must have some sort of closure: the return of the subject as a modified autonomous agent (often of social change), the closure of moral action (which never actually occurs in the academy), the closure of cultural materiality, everyday life, or information for its own sake. And so on.

The age of theory is over. And over and over.

A book by Mark Poster, *The Mode of Information*, argues that as oral cultures were replaced by print cultures, the latter has now been replaced by the mode of electronic information. This puts poststructural theory in a peculiar position. Deconstruction is a mode of analysis applied to books, although it transgresses the representational modes characteristic of print culture, "bringing to reading the vertiginous multivocality of the TV ad" (p. 65) and ungrounding the primary referent, the a priori or Enlightenment subject. Poststructuralism seems thus to stand in the middle, a mode of analysis of the book that is somehow appropriate to the age of electronic media—of nonlinear, nonidentical and nonrepresentational information.

The relation between the binary or digital and *différance* has been noted often but has rarely been exploited; instead, in the end of poststructuralism, what we seem to have is the reproduction of its mode of analysis in the context of the binary. Lest things seem too progressive at this point—the move to the mode of electronic information—it could as well be argued that *différance* demonstrated that there is no difference between the age of reading and of TV viewing, that language, whether print, electronic, or even oral, is always already (cliché) binary, and that also the claim for a referential reality is equally based on the presence/absence that is a production of difference. But poststructuralism now—with all the calls for the necessity of working through its problematics in order to arrive beyond it, in a new critical era—in the electronic era, becomes instrumental, as reason became in the Enlightenment. Baudrillard's hyperreality is an enclosure or screen within which the subject is constituted (however difficult it may be to represent this from inside). A new and virtual reality, one detached from representation, is constituted by the association of information bytes, and this in turn constitutes the subject as consumer (e.g., of a TV ad) or in general as a subject of this newly constituted but momentary language.

To speak about a TV ad is to assume an external control of electronic language, a selectivity that is functional and persuasive, even coercive, and productive—two levels of subjects, the producing and the produced. But suppose we reverse the demise of poststructuralism—information has always been binary, and there has always been the struggle to control the right to make the connections that constitute history, the political, the economic, and so on. We are not in a new age but in an age that has realized that truth is always a regime—an economics or a politics—that reality, including books, is always virtual—constructed from the archive of information bytes—and that the realization of the archive/data base has a possibly utopian and liberatory potential for anarchic play.

Subjectivity is momentary, fluid, the production of the archive. It produces and is produced by the hypertext, the electronic binary archive that can be accessed/produced electronically from "virtually" any perspective or subject position ("delete all definite articles")—thus, the end of logics of identity and linearity. Privacy comes to an end in the archive: more and more transactions are entered there, bulletin boards, E-mail; this gives rise to public play, which is a series of steps of hyperreality-become-virtual-reality, a series of relations enacted from within the archive and which are both fluid and discontinuous, a network stretching across the body without organs.

This is too much freedom, autonomy, and choice, the latter of which must always be the basis of virtual reality that is interactive. We face a return to the Enlightenment on the one hand, the control over nature now become the control over images, which are no longer representations; or, on the other, subjected to and by the virtual reality discourse constructed by higher-level subjects in order to produce political and economic ends. Only *tuché* mediates between choice and determinism.

The Enlightenment claimed that each (rational) subject had the power to control and (re)constitute the archive (which was, at that time, nature)—it claimed the circulation of power through a generic, rational human nature and at the same time sequestered that power through capitalism (ownership of means) and democratic/representational government. The electronic age reinvokes the Enlightenment in its demands for the free circulation of information/access to the archive, in the sequestration of the archive, and in the privilege of certain hypertextual configurations.

Is, then, theory or poststructuralism at an end of its usefulness? Are we not back where we began?

Computer writing. "The Greeks called him a 'poet.' . . . It cometh of this word *poiein*, which is, to make . . . we Englishmen have met with the Greeks in calling him a maker . . ." (Sidney). Today the deposed poet or once creative subject is more likely to *compose* than to make: what was the instrumental labor of the compositor in the book/print era becomes the "essential" work of producing the text, even in its diminished materiality. It is as if electronic media have made apparent what Saussure and the structuralist argue: that *langue* contains the limits of *parole*; that as computer writers we operate within a complex of binary oppositions of terms, not things. Freedom at the console is freedom from referentiality, and it is the possibility of constituting new "codes" (Baudrillard) by abstracting the synchronic from the diachronic and from the paradigmatic—in the latter, we are beyond Saussure and into the poststructural. The text is a schizophrenic, chaotic, overdetermined set of juxtapositions and relations of signs, totally experimental, misrepresentational (we don't even have a language to say anything other than "different from . . ."), drawn from the binary archive by random search or movement within this hypertext.

Electronic media make apparent the shift from the New Critical notion of the text as object, reified by ontology, or, what is the same thing in twentieth-century thought, a material object—the book—the shift from the reification of the text to the text as an ephemeral texture of binary traces drawn from the archive.

Electronic media make apparent the immanent spatiality of the archive, the overlaying of multiple screens to create a nonreferential "depth" of virtual reality within the monitor—in other words, hypertextual recursivity or overdetermination. Collaborative writing is the "verbal" approximation of this implicating spatiality; the layering of commentary text on commentary text without an original or Ur-text: Barthes's onion.

Structuralism and poststructuralism have brought us to, have paralleled, have made us aware of the implications of electronic reading and writing. Theory is not here an instrument of understanding; it is that understanding. The notion of the disappearance of the autonomous subject is not to be superseded by the political claim for the need of a (marginal) agential subject of (and for the rectification of) culture. We are not beyond theory. Theory is us: it constitutes our virtual reality, from which we have or cannot escape into the "real," the "real" being simply another version.

Works Cited

Dews, Peter. *Logics of Disintegration: Post-structuralist Thought and the Claims of Critical Theory.* London: Verso, 1987.

Miller, James. *The Passion of Michel Foucault.* New York: Simon and Schuster, 1993.

Poster, Mark. *Critical Theory and Poststructuralism: In Search of a Context.* Ithaca, N.Y.: Cornell University Press, 1989.

———. *The Mode of Information: Poststructuralism and Social Context.* Cambridge: Polity Press, 1990.

Sidney, Philip. *An Apology for Poetry,* ed. Forrest Robinson. Indianapolis: Bobbs-Merrill, 1970.

Smith, Paul. *Discerning the Subject.* Minneapolis: University of Minnesota Press, 1988.

Walkowitz, Judith R. *City of Dreadful Delights: Narratives of Sexual Danger in Late-Victorian London.* Chicago: University of Chicago Press, 1992.

Jerry Herron

"It's the same old place," my cousin Bruce advised when I saw him last, after twenty years, on a visit to the dry West Texas town where we'd both grown up as boys. "Except these days the crooks running it are all our age." Likewise for the academy, now that the middle-aged sons and daughters of the 1960s are in charge. It's the same old place, give or take a few of those mythical dead, white, European male authors, who used to poison the lives of kids of the sort that we used to be. After all that's been said and done—after the American mind closed and cultural literacy went bust, after the deconstructed leftie profs scammed their way to the top, after the tenured radicals seized control and forced their illiberal education on the unsuspecting progeny of middle America—after all that killing of the spirit was accomplished, nothing much seems to have changed. Not really. As John Searle has pointed out, "Given the history of . . . crisis rhetoric, one's natural response to the current cries of desperation might reasonably be one of boredom" (p. 86). The only difference currently is that we teach fewer students, proportionately, than in the generation midlife professors belong to; and the ones we teach are less well prepared, along with their teachers.

Less well prepared in the sense that all of us seem, now, even less sure what the nonessential elements of academic training are good for—the things left over when the "Johnny can't" debates about practical skills have run their dreary and predictable course. Except for a wish to solve at the level of representations problems that are probably not solvable at universities in the first place—problems denominated by the secular trinity of race, class, and gender—the "culture wars," as they are frequently called, have produced little in the way of belief, or believability. (Will social justice be achieved once we get enough women, gays, Indians, people of color, and other "Others" inducted into that formerly all-male club of the *Norton Anthology*? It's anybody's guess.) "With dim lights and tangled circumstance they tried to shape their thought and deed in noble agreement," "George Eliot" lamented in the Prelude to *Middlemarch*, her classic examination of ardor run amok. "But after all," Marian Evans speculated, under cover of her white male incognito, "to common eyes their struggles seemed mere inconsistency and formlessness; for these later-born [Saint] Theresas were helped by no coherent social faith and order which could perform the function of knowledge for the ardently willing soul." As for still later-born pretenders to messianic virtue, they are even further from the social faith (and the common idiom) that could translate to a justifiable relevance the inconsistency and formlessness that define academic culture.

Which is not to deny that academic literacy can change people, for both good and ill. For every Allan Bloom, there's a W. E. B. Du Bois or a Cornel West; or vice versa, depending on one's point of view. The problem is that nobody knows precisely why or how literary "culture" does what it does, so that the effects are impossible to predict or control, despite the protestations of institutional discourse. What little evidence exists is purely anecdotal and haphazard: the frequently inconsistent and formless memories of people who look back fondly on poems or novels or movies, or perhaps on the teacher who suggested them. What we would like to prove—just like advertising executives would like to prove ahead of time that a particular campaign will make the sponsor's hemorrhoid ointment seem desirable—is that people will quit being racists or sexists or homophobes or, conversely, that they will become righteous political conservatives if only they are exposed to the proper combination of texts. But nobody can demonstrate such effects. Nevertheless, the argument over canonical literary and/or its theoretical demise goes forward as if this *were* demonstrably the case. Hence the rhetorical *crucialization* of academic disputes and the giddy presumption of literary theory to a level of televangelical urgency. Both are expressive of an urge to compensate apocalyptically something missing in real life: a practical reason to exist.

Thus, too, the fellow-traveling of radical culture and political conservatism. Each has found in the other (as Other) a practical excuse, and an opportune cover for an otherwise vexing interdependency. This ideological marriage of convenience begins in 1968, with the election of Richard Nixon (an event presaged by the French publication, one year earlier, of Jacques Derrida's deconstructive *Of Grammatology*), and continues for almost a quarter-century until 1992, when the election of Bill Clinton marks an endpoint both for theory and for the political running-dogs of economic trickle-down. (The peanut years of 1976–1980 remain a sideshow excrescence rather than a return of repressed, historical subjects.) Radical theory, like political conservatism, has been concerned with the generational reassignment of resources and with a dissolving of old notions of an appropriate subject, whether the subject of Great Society entitlements or of critical practice. What junk bonds and S&Ls did for capital, deconstruction did for the academy: it introduced a whole new structure of profit taking based not on the creation of wealth but on the dismantling of "presences" already there. And both, more or less simultaneously, came to shame. At the end of Reaganomics are Charles Keating and Michael Milken; at the end of theory, Paul de Man and Michel Foucault, the one a Nazi collaborationist, the other an anguished figure who appears knowingly to have thrown away his own life and perhaps the lives of others through AIDS.

It would be wrong to propose a cause-and-effect relation between deconstruction and Nazi collaboration, or between a radical critique of the subject and irresponsible behavior, just as it would be simpleminded to conclude that the truth of an idea can be measured by the actions of the person who espouses it. What seems indisputable, however, is that we've ended up—in the 1990s—with both an academy and an economy in which culture went south. The question now is what, if any, difference this will make. As for what follows, politically, after the end of Reagan, even Bill Clinton seems unsure. The situation academically appears less difficult to develop, with the acceptance of cultural free trade verging on the status of a new, politically "correct" orthodoxy.

In the introduction to a volume the title of which reproduces the hot-button topic of 1990s academia—*Cultural Studies*—the editors approvingly quote one contributor's utopian gush to the effect that this enterprise might define "a location where the new politics of difference—racial, sexual, cultural, transnational—can combine and be articulated in all their dazzling plurality" (p. 1). This academic equivalent of the NAFTA treaty (now expanded to a global scale) makes Jesse Jackson's rainbow dreaming seem absolutely quaint in its parochial small-mindedness. Perhaps at the trickle-down end of theory there will be just such a cultural open market. Hyperbole notwithstanding, the same question arises here, however, as with the other free trade pact. What will happen to jobs? Is this really good news for the people who work in the academic culture industry (both teachers and students), or is it just an excuse a bunch of new crooks have devised to cover the fact that it's still the same old place as before, except that they're the ones who want to run it now?

At least at the level of language, there seems little difference, with jargon and obfuscation still being the order of the day, just as they were under the regime of theory. Which led Patricia Nelson Limerick in the *New York Times* to the following much-discussed observation, based on something she once heard a classics professor propose. "'We must remember,' he said, 'that professors are the ones nobody wanted to dance with in high school.'" "What one sees in professors repeatedly," Limerick concludes, "is exactly the manner that anyone would adopt after a couple of sad evenings side-lined under the crepe-paper streamers in the gym, sitting on a folding chair while everyone else danced" (p. 3). We professors disdain the sociable commonplace of intelligibility as a self-defensive reaction; we claim not to want, or value, what most people do because they seem not to value us.

Of course, not all the wallflowers are so wimpy as Limerick imagines. Nerds we may be, but it is possible to take a certain pride in our exclusion. As Fredric Jameson argued, way back in 1971, in defense of "Germanic" style (just as the Committee to Reelect the President was promulgating its own brand of obfuscations), "[T]he bristling mass of abstractions and cross-references is precisely intended to be read in situation, against the cheap facility of what surrounds it, as a warning to the reader of the price he has to pay for genuine thinking" (p. xiii). Who wants to go to their stupid old dance anyhow, with all its "cheap facility"? Better the imperial neologisms of the Big Think club. Jameson has played no small part in the popularization—if it can be called that—of theory (both German and French) as well as theoretical high style, which one dons magisterially, like commencement robes, "as a warning to the reader of the price he has to pay for genuine thinking." Thus, the nerds will not be denied their revenge. Which might all be well and good, except that, as George Eliot anticipated, to "common eyes" our state-supported obfuscations seem "mere inconsistency and formlessness." And more's the pity since those common eyes are set

in the heads of taxpayers on whose good will our continued liveli-
hoods depend.

So, if theory is what estranged academic culture from common
understanding, it's little wonder that (quoting the title of a recent article in the *Chronicle of Higher Education*) "Scholars Mark the Beginning of the Age of 'Post-Theory.'" Perhaps it's high time, as the
subtitle suggests, that "'isms' that have shaped literary study for 30
years have fallen off their pedestal" (Winkler, p. A9). In varying degrees, a panel of assembled experts agree—Jacques Derrida, Stephen Greenblatt, Jane Gallop, and Stanley Fish among them—some
more given to the rhetorical nerd's revenge than others: Yes, we've
reached the end of theory. So what then? What comes *after* the end
of theory?

If hyper-abstraction was the problem, then maybe primary
content is the solution, which is where cultural studies enters the
picture, at least its present vogue in America. Increasingly, "CS"
seems to be what lies at the end of theory, as both alternative and as
natural outcome: the end toward which theory all along was working. Cultural studies, as the editors of the anthology bearing that
name propose in their introduction, "is an interdisciplinary, transdisciplinary, and sometimes counter-disciplinary field that operates
in the tension between its tendencies to embrace both a broad, anthropological and a more narrowly humanistic conception of culture. . . . Cultural studies is thus committed to the study of the entire
range of a society's arts, beliefs, institutions, and communicative
practices" (p. 4). From seeming to be about nothing, academic practice now seems to be about everything: "the entire range of a society's arts, beliefs, institutions, and communicative practices."

If theory rose and fell in America, concomitant with the conservative political turn that began with Richard Nixon's election in
1968, then it might be possible to establish a similar association between the rise of Anglo-American cultural studies and the proliferation of TV talk shows, each of which aspires to the epiphanic trans-
port summed up in the Oprah hug. Oprah Winfrey's arrival is
concurrent with the first intimations that theory might be over; her
translation from local market phenomenon to national celebrity
takes place simultaneously with the bellwether publication, by the
University of Chicago Press in 1985, of *Against Theory: Literary
Studies and the New Pragmatism*. Oprah brought to TV something
that remained beyond the patriarchal, if scrupulously sensitive,
reach of Phil Donahue, just as cultural studies offered to academic
wallflowers a post-theoretical escape in the "pragmatic" embrace of
otherness.

Writing at the same time as Oprah went national, Frank Lentricchia looked forward to a moment when the theoretical culture of professors might get down to some real-life hugging. Imagining the therapeutics of self-discovery, in terms that Oprah (and cultural studies) would soon turn to mass-market advantage, Lentricchia says of the "radical literary intellectual":

> in some significant sense his struggle must be against himself, against his own training and history as an intellectual. . . . So except in a few rare instances, the radical literary intellectual in American universities will emerge out of and be indebted to his former traditional self. Against that very generalization, and on behalf of the rare instance, I would say that the intellectual of working class background, or more broadly of a background outside the social, racial, ethnic, economic, gender-biased, and homophobic mainstream, will in effect have to retrieve his outsider's experience, bring it to bear in critical dialogue with the traditional confirmation he has been given. (pp. 7–8)

Thus begins the self-othering, therapeutic culture that achieves epiphanic consummation in the Oprah hug: when we, through her simulacral presence, own up to difference by embracing him/her/it.

It might be more accurate, then, to think not in terms of cultural studies so much as culture-in-recovery studies. Like Oprah's producers, who must cast an ever wider net in order to supply audiences with a fresh supply of tearful reconciliations, culture-in-recovery studies issues a similar casting call. Gloria Watkins, writing as "bell hooks," makes this clear, or at least she makes clear the crucial role of others in the redemptive practice of "radical" academe: "Calling for a shift in locations in 'the intervention interview' published with the collection *The Post-Colonial Critic* (1990) Gayatri Spivak clarifies the radical possibilities that surface when positionality is problematized, explaining that 'what we are asking for is that the hegemonic discourses, the holders of hegemonic discourse should de-hegemonize their position and themselves learn how to occupy the subject position of the other'" (p. 346). In order to achieve this utopian end—the end of "hegemonic" discriminatory practice—it becomes necessary for academic culture to engage authentic others, to retrieve the "outsider's experience," as Lentricchia suggested, particularly when that experience comes from "outside the social, racial, ethnic, economic, gender-biased, and homophobic mainstream."

It seems fair to ask, however, whether the Oprah hug of academic culture-in-recovery studies is as good as the real thing. Is the othering of the canon likely to conjure anybody, teachers or students, into a sympathetic hegemonic deconstruction, or are the crooks merely upgrading their postcolonial wardrobes with a few native baubles? The language of the "bell hooks" citation offers a possible clue. Her "positionality" may be anti-hegemonic, but her style is surely not; she—like her distinguished subject, Gayatri Spivak—participates unabashedly in the "cult of obscurity" that Limerick identifies as "the trouble with academic prose," which is meant, as Jameson suggested, to remind the reader perpetually "of the price he has to pay for genuine thinking." What is perhaps most notable about high-priced prose, aside from sheer ugliness, is its "bogus religiosity," to borrow a phrase that John Berger coined twenty years ago in a somewhat different context: "The bogus religiosity which now surrounds original works of art, and which is ultimately dependent upon their market value, has become the substitute for what paintings lost when the camera made them reproducible" (p. 23). What I am suggesting is that cultural studies is to canonical literacy what Berger's "bogus religiosity" is to painting: a commercial solution, at the level of market "price" (to use Jameson's telling word), for a problem that is really about authority. "It is the final empty claim," Berger goes on to say, "for the continuing values of an oligarchic, undemocratic culture" (p. 23). The same old corruption, in other words, except that the crooks are all our age now.

Or to put this another way, there has been a displacing of traditional canons, and the presumptive authority of the white males (both living and dead) empowered by them, which is probably to the good; but there has been no displacing of canonicity, jargon, and all the esoterica of power, which is not so good. What we are left with, then, is an academic "culture of complaint," to borrow Robert Hughes's telling phrase: a culture predicated on the Oprah-driven assumption that one is entitled to a self only insofar as that self can be dramatized, publicly, in a state of post-hegemonic recovery. For those still in denial, a new canon of tough-loving Others is invoked to aid in the hard work of rehabilitation, or else to shout down any protestations to the contrary. Americans are invited to put our faith in a surrogate recovery, just like on Oprah, whereby a bunch of academics, by virtue of their orgiastic spectacle of humiliations, will summon the rest of creation to a state of social grace. As Hughes remarked of PC jargon, which is the *lingua franca* of cultural studies, "we want to create a sort of linguistic Lourdes, where evil and misfortune are dispelled by a dip in the waters of euphemism" (p. 18). But what are these euphemistic "solutions" worth? The answer, of course, is obvious: *nothing*.

Where is the putatively hegemonic culture of academe ever truly hegemonic except inside the academy? Consequently, how could the symbology of academic solutions be expected to have effect except there? The practitioners of evil and hate in this world, or even those who do harm through mere stupidity and greed, draw their inspiration, consistently, from other-than-academic sources, so that to presume we have faced down the devil when we have only changed a syllabus is the worst kind of self-indulgence and pandering. Of course, there is some "real work" being done here, as Lentricchia might have it—real, at least, to academics. One academic class is seeking, at the end of theory, to displace another. And this is being done not on theoretical grounds, which might prove ineffectual, since many of the old crooks have proved no less adept at theory than the academic new class. The confrontation now is quite literally other. A new canon of Others is being instituted in a particularly shrewd—if frequently dishonest, self-serving, and racist—fashion. The new canon of culture-in-recovery studies is everything Matthew Arnold hoped for; it is replete with foreign languages, esoteric references, and all the necessary trappings of Berger's "bogus religiosity." And what is perhaps best of all, from the standpoint of the postcolonial will to power, ignorance of the cultural studies canon constitutes *prima facie* evidence of hegemonic degeneracy, which is a far more serious (and therefore strategically opportune) accusation, obviously, than proof of a simple failure of knowledge.

Consequently, it is to promulgate an atmosphere of recrimination and dread that much of cultural studies work is undertaken. The point is not to know things so much as it is to demonstrate strategically what others, whose power one envies and wishes to displace academically, don't know. For that purpose, the agents of the new hegemony must be forever colonizing that which is distant, excluded, "queer." Which is not to say that there aren't more things in heaven and earth than are dreamt of in traditional, academic philosophy; or that people don't benefit by having the channels of communication opened, as Raymond Williams advocated so eloquently and often. The problem is that Others are being appropriated dishonestly and for reasons that apparently have little to do with the much invoked causes of human liberation and social justice (to which the middle-class university bears an equivocal and highly mediated relationship at best). In our newly canonized pantheon of the oppressed, it is not, in most cases, the oppressed themselves who are invited to speak; instead, it is their ventriloquial handlers who do all the talking. And for good—or at least unsurprising—reasons, because it is the handlers whose status is truly at stake.

More often than not, the "radical" practitioner of culture-in-recovery studies finds himself or herself (regardless of how consciously) in a state of what Charles Dickens—in a wonderful phrase —referred to as "telescopic philanthropy." In *Bleak House*, Dickens creates a wickedly prescient send-up of the whole enterprise in the persons of his two self-advertising mavens of appropriation, Mrs. Jellyby and Mrs. Pardiggle: the former with her haranguing on behalf of "Borrioboola-Gha," the latter with her maternalizing of the "Tockahoopo Indians," among many other poor unfortunates. For all their high-tech stratagems (and jargon), present-day avatars of the Other seem not to have got very far beyond the hucksterism and blindness pilloried by Dickens—or beyond the unconscious limitations inherent in his own point of view. Along with his good intentions come all the racist and classist biases of his presumptive, imperial insights, as suggested by such jokey, cartoon-like versions of others as Borrioboola-Gha and the Tockahoopo.

Culture-in-recovery studies, in its blind rush to embrace the Other, is guilty of the same colonialist pandering and the same opportune neglect of local subjects implicit in Dickens's satirization of a philanthropy that is only "telescopic." For example, the question is rarely, if ever, asked: What good is to be gained by Oprah-hugging the Other? What is it, precisely, that academic baby-boomers wish to accomplish—some of them, at least—with the imposition of a new multicultural canon? Is the point really to change things in Borrioboola-Gha, or is it something else? Fabienne Worth makes an interesting suggestion with respect to the pedagogy of political correctness, which is fundamental to the project of cultural studies. Referring to the twin pitfalls of "guilt and me too-ism," she concludes that "students [must] constantly put their identities on trial and . . . teachers [must] renounce all authority" (p. 7). At least teachers must *appear* to do this, and herein lies the attraction. The putative speechlessness of subaltern subjects (whether students or postcolonial Others) invites the precise ventriloquism that makes possible a new articulation of power on behalf of mid-career academics. But crucially it is not for themselves that they speak (the "authority" of the hegemonic old Adam having been long since deconstructed); it is as the virtual—and unchallenged—representatives of those Others that one's personal recovery proceeds. Even when representation appears direct, as in the case of "minority" faculty, it is not minority experience as such being represented. (For that purpose, popular culture is a much richer and more reliable source.) What is at stake is the represented competency of certain Others to matriculate the culture (and preferment) of academic institutions. It is submission—likeness—in other words, rather than difference, which is being sponsored, regardless of claims to the contrary.

Virtuous or not, the ventriloquial project goes forward, with the unassailable authority of a Pardiggle or Jellyby and with all the sublimated, paternal arrogance of their creator, which is the point of a cautionary "envoi" that Gayatri Spivak appends to her essay on "Subaltern Studies":

> In these pages, I have repeatedly emphasized the complicity between subject and object of investigation. . . . Situated within the current academic theatre of cultural imperialism, with a certain *carte d'entrée* into the elite theoretical *ateliers* in France, I bring news of power-lines within the palace. Nothing can function without us, yet the part is at least historically ironic. What of the poststructuralist suggestion that *all* work is parasitical, slightly to the side of that which one wishes adequately to cover, that critic (historian) and text (subaltern) are always "beside themselves"? (p. 221)

"Nothing can function without us." Nothing? But, in fact, almost everything does, with the virtual representations of academia being at best a (still) elite minority achievement (something for the *atelier*) and at worst an expensive irrelevance to the majority of citizens, who will never go to college, read an academic essay, or mince reputations at the MLA. And for those who do attend, one wonders how "the conflicts," to use Gerald Graff's term, will be remembered, except as professorial confusion.

Which returns things to what has been the real subject all along, and that is the displacing of a previous generation from power while preserving intact the structure that they inhabit: getting rid of the crooks, in other words, but saving the system that made their crookedness profitable. Writing fifteen years ago in the Introduction to *Orientalism*, his study of colonial ideology, Edward Said cautioned that "Perhaps the most important task of all would be to undertake studies in contemporary alternatives to Orientalism, to ask how one can study other cultures and peoples from a libertarian, or a nonrepressive and nonmanipulative, perspective. But then one would have to rethink the whole complex problem of knowledge and power. These are all tasks left embarrassingly incomplete in this study" (p. 24). Most academics, and surely those embarked on the enterprise of cultural studies, have preferred not to "rethink the whole complex problem of knowledge and power"— at least not insofar as it relates to the realities of state-supported employment—because to do so would threaten the structure of entitlement that most of us aspire to, a structure now being effectively colonized by the ventriloquial agents of cultural studies. And this colonial mission bears no incidental relation to the self-protective drive toward obfuscation. "[W]henever clarity threatens to break out," as Gerald Graff has suggested, ". . . the very organization of academic life works against it" (p. vii).

Cultural studies is succeeding, then, just as theory did before it, and with the same apparently paradoxical results. In order to disperse the supposed tyranny of canonical literacy, it became necessary for deconstruction first to reconstruct classic texts, great numbers of which had simply gone out of print, as a sign of their general irrelevance, culturally speaking. The aim was not to get over George Eliot, for example (many of whose works were unavailable prior to the Watergate break-in and Gayatri Spivak's English-language translation of Derrida's *Grammatology*), but to appropriate her resurrected authority to a more timely cause, for which purpose a new standard edition, together with a great number of critical books and articles, was called for.

And now it is the Other's turn, as cultural studies undertakes a simulacral theme-parking of difference. But not all differences are equally of interest. The fascination here is not simply with poverty and powerlessness, abuse or disease; or with alternative languages, music, and myths. (If that were the case, we would all recognize America's inner cities as the most pressing of postcolonial subjects because they are so clearly and desperately the result of "our" cultural practices.) Just as deconstruction became a neoconservative reflex of canonical literacy, cultural studies often undertakes a "telescopic" reenactment of the same hegemonic apparatus it purports to criticize: the academic equivalent of a Merchant-Ivory film. Its subjects of choice—in Africa and the Caribbean, the Middle East, the Indian subcontinent—are at once exotically distant and conveniently near (not to mention English-educated). Here is all the *frisson* of post-hegemonic cross-dressing, as one appropriates the old colonial habiliments only to disdain their origins. That's way headier stuff than merely going native.

If culture-in-recovery studies is what has come at the end of theory, then one begins to hope for something better—something about which theory will have little or nothing to say (given what has already been said and done). Which is possibly what Stanley Fish had in mind when he advised a reporter from the *Chronicle of Higher Education* to "look for more discussions about a new aestheticism," now that theory is over (Winkler, p. A17). But this new aestheticism, which Fish does not elaborate, still has about it rather too much the whiff of the lamp, as Henry James remarked of

George Eliot's historical novel *Romola*, which he found more an act of pedantry than of imagination. It's the same complaint that Susan Sontag made in 1964, at the very outset of the binge for theory: "Today is . . . a time, when the project of interpretation is largely reactionary, stifling. Like the fumes of the automobile and of heavy industry which befoul the urban atmosphere, the effusion of interpretations of art today poisons our sensibilities. In a culture whose already classical dilemma is the hypertrophy of the intellect at the expense of energy and sensual capability, interpretation is the revenge of the intellect upon art" (p. 17).

It is arguable whether such theoretical projects as deconstruction, feminism, poststructuralism, Marxism, and semiotics (of which Sontag herself became a considerable fan) were extensions of a larger cultural "stifling" or interrruptions of it. In any event, the atmosphere is perhaps less "befouled" now than when she wrote, for the simple reason that interpretation—especially academic interpretation—is far less important than it was then. Price, as Jameson suggested, has supplanted the bogus religious "aura" that once surrounded art and defined its value.

But, if anything, Sontag's conclusion seems even more pressing now than it did thirty years ago. "Our task is not to find the maximum amount of content in a work of art," she insisted, ending with her famous injunction: "In place of a hermeneutics we need an erotics of art" (p. 23). Now that cultural studies (like theory before it) has followed heavy industry offshore, metaphorically speaking, it seems even less likely that any sane person would link interpretation with erotic experience, at least not as it is practiced academically. *Reactionary* is the term more likely to denominate the project of cultural studies, which in good colonial fashion seeks to extract the "maximum amount of content" from its "Other" sources, and then to translate that content to high-end consumer goods for the domestic, institutional market. This is nowhere more obvious, and obviously wrongheaded, than with the various forms of popular pleasure, that cultural studies latches onto with a combination of envy and self-loathing. Apropos the academic fascination with pornography, for example, Andrew Ross raises the altogether relevant question, "What if the popularity of such cultural forms as pornography, for men, and romance, for women, speaks to desires that cannot be described according to the articulate terms and categories of an intellectual's conception of 'politics'" (p. 193)? What happens then is that the presumptive "politics" of academic debate become purely that—academic. In other words, the "articulate terms and categories" of cultural studies—whether in its self-othering or its pop-slumming mode—are no less anachronistic, and repressive, than the phallocentric empire it helplessly sublimates.

Which is only to say that academics have stupidly missed out on a real growth opportunity: a project based not on interpretation but on a technologically appropriate erotics. Consider, for example, the Merchant-Ivory phenomenon. That filmmaking team (along with Ruth Prawer Jhabvala) has appropriated a bunch of antiquated "classics" and turned them into mass-market successes. And they have done this by plying the same simulacral trade as cultural studies: by bringing the Empire back, in all its lush detail. What makes them different is that their nostalgia, unlike the nostalgia that motivates cultural studies, does not go unrequited; on the contrary, they inhabit their hegemonic fantasies with an extravagance that borders on obsession. One finds here—visually translated—all the opulence of an Oprah hug but with no hint of the "toxic shame" (to use John Bradshaw's phrase), which is the price exacted by cultural studies for indulging such guilty pleasures. And for good or ill, these are the pleasures that sell, so that E. M. Forster and Edith Wharton are once more important authors because they give rise so appealingly to movies. And now their successes will be followed by Jane Austen (with Emma Thompson working on a script for *Sense and Sensibility*) and Henry James (whose *Portrait of a Lady* is being filmed by Jane Campion, director of *The Piano*). But pleasure—as Patricia Limerick's strictures about dancing suggest—is something that academics have never been very good at, perhaps because pleasure (erotic or otherwise) has proved so indifferent to academic overtures, like the good-looking partner at the dance, who by definition would disdain to dance with us.

Instead, the academy has vengefully—one might even say perversely—identified itself with certain skills and habits of culture wholly irrelevant to contemporary Americans, whose experience is defined by an increasingly sophisticated informational apparatus, with the primary means of delivery being visual and screen-based. Academic work stands in relation to that kind of experience (and its pleasures) as an antiquarian curiosity: a dictionary for a dead language; a ticket to a dance that was canceled. So, following the Horatian maxim, we might do one of two things, at the end of theory. We might get involved in information that is *useful*: VCR programming, info highway trafficking, video production. Or we might try for things that are *beautiful*: the cultivation of the five senses, the pursuit of beauty for beauty's sake, as Walter Pater suggested to his Victorian undergraduates. (In a world where the body is perhaps the most colonized subject of all, the pursuit of sensuous pleasure might be the ultimately subversive act.) The problem is that academics probably know less about the former than an average teenager, and they have a positive dread of the latter. Perhaps, then, the best response at the end of theory is silence. The crooks may all be our age, in other words, but that's nothing to boast about.

But crooks being what they are—present company not excepted—silence is hardly an option. In other words, everybody knows what will happen at the end of theory, after cultural studies has run its histrionic course. What will follow is the same thing that has come before: writing. Not writing of the sort that writers do, obviously. Academics have never been any better at that than they have been at dancing, which was the point of Limerick's complaint in the first place. It's no less painful to watch a bunch of a-rhythmic Ph.D.s trip the light fantastic than it is to read their ungainly "works." This is particularly true of the "new," autobiographical criticism, wherein the academic subject submits to a self-administered Oprah hug, discovering in the process of auto-recovery a whole new "I" to explicate. But as far as writing goes, that doesn't change a thing; the practice only adds to the burgeoning (and boring) memoirs of Narcissus, of which there is already too ample a supply.

As Oscar Wilde pointed out, "We can forgive a man for making a useful thing as long as he does not admire it. The only excuse for making a useless thing is that one admires it intensely" (p. 6). So what if the crooks went straight? What if we admitted the sublime uselessness of academic work, but instead of despising the world (and ourselves) for our own superfluity, what if we embraced the sublimity of our acknowledged position? Maybe with the admission would come the courage to invite admiration for ourselves as *real* writers, whose only stock in trade is pleasure. Rather than courting a nerd's stylistic disdain, we might act—both writing and talking—in critical sympathy with the impulses that motivate the production and popular consumption of culture. What holds us back is not merely the ignorance of a few good moves; something far more blameworthy is afoot. At this dance, the nerds have taken charge of the CD player so that the only songs getting played are ones nobody can dance to, with the result that the longer our institutional party lasts, the greater the hostility on both sides. It's not so much patriarchy we need to get over, then, or homophobia or sexism or classism or racism, or an -ism of some other sort. The failure we can't seem to escape is a failure of forgiveness: we can't seem to forgive ourselves for being as wonderfully useless as the texts our careers are based on. It'll take more than Oprah to hug us out of that sad spot.

Works Cited

Berger, John. *Ways of Seeing*. Harmondsworth: Penguin, 1972.

Cultural Studies, ed. Lawrence Grossberg, Cary Nelson, Paula Treichler. New York: Routledge, 1992.

Graff, Gerald. *Beyond the Culture Wars: How Teaching the Conflicts Can Revitalize American Education*. New York: Norton, 1992.

hooks, bell. "Representing Whiteness in the Black Imagination," *Cultural Studies*, ed. Lawrence Grossberg, *et al*. New York: Routledge, 1992, pp. 338–46.

Hughes, Robert. *Culture of Complaint: The Fraying of America*. New York: Oxford University Press, 1993.

Jameson, Fredric. *Marxism and Form: Twentieth-Century Dialectical Theories of Literature*. Princeton: Princeton University Press, 1971.

Lentricchia, Frank. *Criticism and Social Change*. Chicago: University of Chicago Press, 1984.

Limerick, Patricia Nelson. "Dancing with Professors: The Trouble with Academic Prose." *New York Times Book Review*, Oct. 31, 1993, p. 3.

Ross, Andrew. *No Respect: Intellectuals & Popular Culture*. New York: Routledge, 1989.

Said, Edward W. *Orientalism*. New York: Vintage, 1974.

Searle, John. "The Storm over the University." *Debating P.C.: The Controversy over Political Correctness on College Campuses*, ed. Paul Berman. New York: Laurel, 1992, pp. 85–123.

Sontag, Susan. *Against Interpretation*. New York: Dell, 1961.

Spivak, Gayatri Chakravorty. *In Other Worlds: Essays in Cultural Politics*. New York: Routledge, 1988.

Wilde, Oscar. *The Picture of Dorian Gray*. New York: Dell, 1968.

Winkler, Karen J. "Scholars Mark the Beginning of the Age of 'Post-Theory.'" *Chronicle of Higher Education*, Oct. 13, 1993, p. A9.

Worth, Fabienne. "Postmodern Pedagogy in the Multicultural Classroom: For Inappropriate Teachers and Imperfect Spectators." *Cultural Critique* 25 (Fall 1993): 5–32.

Index